GALLERIES, PALACES & TEA

AN ILLUSTRATED GUIDE TO LONDON

CURLL PRESS

GALLERIES, PALACES & TEA: AN ILLUSTRATED GUIDE TO LONDON

Second Edition. First published 2014

Illustrations, maps, cover design, text, and text structure
© David Backhouse 2014

Cover design by Matt Swann: mattie.swann@gmail.com
Printed and bound by,
CPI Group (UK) Ltd, Croydon, CR0 4YY

British Library Cataloguing in the Publication Data

ISBN: 978-1-909542-04-4

CURLL PRESS is a trading identity for
DAVID BACKHOUSE
P.O.Box 63129, Blythe Road, London, W14 0PE
londonguidebook@gmail.com

Disclaimer
It is intended that this work should in no way malign anyone living. The author would appreciate that any provable error of fact should be brought to his attention.

INTRODUCTION

The principal reason why *GALLERIES, PALACES & TEA: AN ILLUS-TRATED GUIDE TO LONDON* came into being was its author's curiosity. Initially, he wished to understand both why London had grown and how the character of its districts had altered over time. The city's inhabitants and visitors are fortunate in being able to consult *THE LONDON ENCY-CLOPAEDIA*, a doorstopper of a book. The first edition of it was wrought into being by its editors Ben Weinreb and Christopher Hibbert. They created a work of substance and authority. However, the volume prompts questions as well as answering them. It came to be appreciated that there was scope for creating a complementary work that, through possessing a more cross-referenced structure and an open character, might be able to furnish for some people a means of extending their understanding of the metropolis. The process that was set in motion resulted in the 2010 publication of *LONDON: A SUBJECTIVE GUIDE* (ISBN 978-0-9562833-0-6), a reference book the idiosyncrasies of which were - in part - a reflection of the city that it addressed.

One of the great advantages about completing something is that you can then realise what you could have done differently. It was appreciated that *LONDON: A SUBJECTIVE GUIDE* could have been both longer and more concise. *GALLERIES, PALACES & TEA* is the fruit of the latter insight. It is a work that has been formed by filleting the touristy portions of its parent and adding both maps and illustrations. That it was not a book that was written *de novo* but rather one that evolved from a larger primary source has imparted it with a nature that many readers may find provides them with a richer experience than is customary for city guidebooks to furnish. For some people, reading it will prove to be a self-contained activity, while for others an inquisitiveness may be engendered that will lead them on to its sister volumes and then out into the literature of London of which *THE LONDON ENCYCLOPAEDIA* is the keystone.

There is a tendency for guidebooks to treat their subjects as possessing neatly self-contained units for consumers to experience. That is not how to appreciate London. As Europe's Global City, she sits upon a matrix that spans both history and the contemporary world. For some people the complexity and the size of this cultural reality can be daunting. However, it has an underlying structure. The texts of *GALLERIES, PALACES & TEA* and its sister books have been organised so that readers can gain some insight into the interconnectedness of the metropolis's diverse aspects - to one another, to the past, and to the world.

Expression of your views about *GALLERIES, PALACES & TEA* and *LONDON: A SUBJECTIVE GUIDE*, and indeed the city herself, would be appreciated. They can be communicated either by means of **londonguidebook@gmail.com** or *via* P.O. Box 63129, Blythe Road, London, W14 0PE.

You may also enjoy *LONDON STORIES, LONDON LIVES* and *BEANS, BEARS & PIRACY*.

ARCADES

See Also: DEPARTMENT STORES; SHOPPING

The Burlington Arcade

Oysters were a fast food of early 19thC London. It is reputed that people who were passing by Burlington House, the townhouse of the 1st Earl of Burlington, were given to throwing their empty oyster shells into his lordship's garden. In response to this phenomenon, the peer commissioned the architect Samuel Ware to design The Burlington Arcade (1819). This both shielded the peer's property and furnished him with a rental income from the shops that it contained.

A number of activities are banned within the Arcade. These include whistling and merriment. The former was used by pickpockets as a signalling system, while the latter was a euphemism for drunkenness.

In the mid-1950s the 11th Duke of Devonshire, a great-grandson of the earl, sold the passageway.

Location: Burlington House, No. 51 Piccadilly, W1J 0PW. On the northern side, to the west of The Royal Academy of Arts.

See Also: FISH & CHIPS, *ETC*. Oysters

Website: www.burlington-arcade.co.uk

The Royal Opera Arcade

The Royal Opera Arcade (1816) was London's first shopping arcade. The passageway took its name from Her Majesty's Theatre, which is located on its eastern side. The playhouse used to act as an opera house for part of the year.

Location: Pall Mall, SW1Y 4UY. On the northern side of eastern end.

See Also: THEATRES Her Majesty's Theatre

ARCHES

See Also: COLUMNS; HERITAGE Lost London and The Euston Arch; MEMORIALS; PARKS St James's Park, Birdcage Walk; ROYAL STATUES

Admiralty Arch

Admiralty Arch[1] (1910) was created as a memorial to Queen Victoria during the remodelling of The Mall.

The government put the Arch up for sale in 1996. A number of former senior naval officers voiced their disquiet at this development. As a result, the Conservative Prime Minister John Major made it known that the building would remain in public ownership. In 2012 a lease of it was offered for sale. No uproar was triggered.

Location: The Mall, SW1A 2BN. At the eastern end.

See Also: MEMORIALS The Queen Victoria Memorial

Constitution Arch

Constitution Arch (1828) was designed by Decimus Burton as part of King George IV's efforts to beautify London. The structure was erected opposite the main entrance to Hyde Park. Its gated central passage is reserved for the use of the royal family. In the mid-19thC this was something that Londoners would have been very aware of. Queen Victoria and her husband Prince Albert were given to displaying themselves to her subjects by going for afternoon carriage rides.

The Arch, in its original position, was topped by a statue of the 1st Duke of Wellington, the victor of the Battle of Waterloo (1815). (His grace's London townhouse, Apsley House, is to the north of the roundabout.) In 1883 the structure was moved to its present site and the duke's statue was posted to the Army town of Aldershot in Hampshire. Hyde Park Corner was restored to the commander's supervision five years later when a ground-level equestrian statue of him was erected.

In 1912 the statue of *Peace in Her Chariot*, cast in some sinister-looking metal, was placed upon top of the Arch.[2]

---

[1]   Admiralty Arch can reasonably be mistaken for a very short viaduct.

[2]   Ms Peace's bearing is such that she could give deportment lessons to the four horsemen of Apocalypse.

Location: Hyde Park Corner, W1J 7NT.
See Also: ROYALTY

Hyde Park Corner Screen: The be-arched Hyde Park Corner Screen (1825) was also designed by Burton. The structure's original relationship to Constitution Arch was destroyed by the shifting of the latter in 1883.

Location: Hyde Park Corner, W1J 7NT. To the north of Hyde Park Corner.

Marble Arch

Like Constitution Arch, Marble Arch (1827) owes its existence to King George IV's wish that London should be more attractive than it was. Originally, the John Nash-designed structure was erected in front of Buckingham Palace. There is a story that it had not been designed on a sufficiently monumental scale to allow for the easy passage of carriages through it. Whether or not this was the case, in 1851 the Arch was re-

erected as an entrance to Hyde Park. In 1908 a roadway was cut to the south and west of it, thereby marooning it upon a traffic island.

Only the King's Troop Royal Horse Artillery and senior members of the royal family may officially pass through the Arch.

Location: Marble Arch, W1H 7AP. On the north-eastern corner of Hyde Park.

See Also: MEMORIALS The Queen Victoria Memorial; MILITARY CUSTOMS Royal Salutes; PALACES Buckingham Palace; ROYAL STATUES King George IV Trafalgar Square; ROYALTY

THE BANK OF ENGLAND

King William III needed money with which he could finance the fighting of what was to prove to be the Nine Years' War. In 1692 he raised £1m through a life annuity scheme that had been devised by Lorenzo Tonti, an Italian banker. The subscribers bought the right to receive interest payments from the original sum. This entitlement was non-transferable and it expired with the death of the contributor. The money that was freed thereby raised the level of the payments that the other, living subscribers received. The money to finance the repayments was secured against Parliamentary-sanctioned duties that had been placed upon beer and spirits. The last contributor did not die until 1769. At the time, he was being paid £70,000 *p.a.*.

In 1693 the combatant monarch raised £1m at 10% interest over sixteen years. This was secured by a duty on salt that the legislature had passed. This loan incorporated a lottery element that added a further 4% interest to the cost of servicing it.

Neither arrangement proved to be financially satisfactory. Therefore, William and Parliament were open to fiscal experimentation. The king and his government needed money and the legislature wanted this to be obtained with a minimum expense being incurred. Thus, in 1694 £1.2m was raised at a rate of 8%. In return, the lenders formed a corporate body that was named the Bank of England. This entity received a monopoly of joint stock banking in England and Wales and the right to issue such bank notes as could be secured against the deposits that it held.

The idea for the Bank had been mooted by William Paterson, who was a Scot. The inaugural Governor was Sir John Houblon.[1] Initially, the body's place of business was Mercers' Hall in Ironmonger Lane. However, it soon moved to Grocers' Hall, where it stayed until 1734.

The Bank started to act as a central bank within the United Kingdom's economy during the mid-18thC.

In 1797 Britain was yet again at war with France. The conflict placed the national financial system under strain. The Treasury suspended the convertibility of banknotes into gold. The shortage of silver and gold coins was compensated for by the Bank issuing small denomi-

---

[1]   Part of the Bank of England site incorporates the land upon which Sir John's own home stood.

nation notes. This prompted James Gilray to draw a cartoon in which the company was represented as being an old lady, whose dress was made of them. She was being accosted by the then Prime Minister, William Pitt the Younger. The image gave the enterprise its nickname - the Little Old Lady of Threadneadle Street.

The country returned to the gold standard in 1821. Five years later the Bank of England's charter was renewed by an Act of Parliament. The measure extended the business's area of banking operations. A dozen years later the Bank's notes were made legal tender. In 1844 an Act of Parliament restricted other banks' right to issue banknotes. The overall soundness of the currency was thus improved.

The Bank was nationalised in 1945. Few Britons are aware that up until then the company had been a private business. It has remained in state ownership.

Location: Threadneedle Street, EC2R 8AR.
Website: www.bankofengland.co.uk

The Bank of England Building

The architecturally admired Sir John Soane-designed edifice (1788) had one major shortcoming - it was only a single storey tall. As a result, it was not viewed as being impressive enough for the keystone of international finance. During the 1920s and 1930s the Sir Herbert Baker-designed building superseded the company's previous home. The old Bank's windowless, outer wall was left intact.

The Money Trees: The Mongol invasion of China had a traumatic impact upon the country. The Ming dynasty succeeded to the imperial throne in 1368. They and their advisers appreciated that both the Chinese state and Chinese society needed to be reformed. The changes that they made included issuing the world's first paper currency. The banknotes were printed on paper that had been made from mulberry pulp.

The Ming proved to be greedy. They allowed their officials to print too many bills. Within fifteen years the notes were worth only a quarter of their original value. Therefore, in 1425, it was resolved that in future silver bullion would act as the basis for the Middle Kingdom's economy. Use of the paper money was ended.

Within the Bank building there are light wells that are open to the air. At the bottom of these are courtyards. In the 1920s a small grove of mulberry trees was planted in one of them. This was done to acknowledge the Mings' experiment with banknotes.

The Bank of England Picket

In 1780 the Gordon Riots occurred. The London mob dominated the city for several days. The Bank was one of the rioters' principal targets. Following the restoration of law and order, the practice was instituted that each night a detachment from the Brigade of Guards was deployed to protect the building. The arrangement was continued until 1973.

See Also: THE POLICE The City of London Police; THEATRES The Theatre Royal Drury Lane

THE BEATLES

MPL Music Publishing

Sir Paul McCartney owns MPL Music Publishing, a music publishing business. The company holds the rights to his solo material and the copyrights that he has acquired. However, the knight does not control the 259-song Beatles catalogue, which was part-owned by Michael Jackson, who bought his holding from Robert Holmes à Court in 1985. The American singer and a rival submitted bids that were of an equal amount. The entertainer swung the deal in his favour by flying to Australia and giving a private performance for the vendor.

Locations: No. 1 Soho Square, W1D 3BQ. MPL.

No. 30 Golden Square, W1F 9LD. Sony ATV Music Publishing controls The Beatles catalogue.

Websites: www.mplcommunications.com www.sonyatv.com

Location: No. 3 Savile Row, W1S 3PB. The former offices of Apple Corp.

GALLERIES, PALACES & TEA

BELLS

See Also: CHURCH OF ENGLAND CHURCHES

Big Ben

The bell that was intended for the Palace of Westminster's St Stephen's Tower (now the Elizabeth Tower) was cast near Stockton-on-Tees and then transported to London. The instrument was tested in New Scotland Yard. It cracked during this trial. Its metal was used by the Whitechapel Bell Foundry to cast a smaller bell that became known as Big Ben. This was rung for the first time in 1859.

The derivation of Big Ben's name is uncertain. There are two leading contenders for having inspired its coining. The first is Sir Benjamin Hall, a notably stout official, who supervised the bell's installation. (Hall's wife, Lady Augusta, wrote *The First Principles of Good Cooking* (1867), a noted cookbook of the era. Her culinary expertise may have contributed to her husband's 'bigness'.) The other is Benjamin Caunt, a popular boxer of the day, whose nickname was Big Ben.

Whenever Parliament is sitting the Tower's belfry is lit after dark.

See Also: PARLIAMENT The Palace of Westminster, Pugin and Barry

Website: www.parliament.uk/bigben

The Speed of Light: Big Ben's ringing tones can be used to demonstrate that radio waves travel at the speed of light. Radio 4's *Six O'Clock News* starts with the bell's chimes. If a person takes a radio to Parliament Square and listens to the radio station at the appropriate time, s/he will hear the bongs on the wireless a third of a second before s/he hears the sound travelling directly down from Elizabeth Tower. This is because the BBC's equipment within the structure will have already picked up the ring and relayed it into its transmission system, in which the noise is relayed in the form of light, and then broadcast.

Location: Parliament Square, SW1P 3AD.

Bow Bells

Cockneys are said to be 'born within the sound of Bow Bells'. These are the bells of St Mary-le-Bow.

Location: St Mary-le-Bow, Cheapside, EC4M 9DQ.

See Also: CHURCH OF ENGLAND CHURCHES St Mary-le-Bow
Website: www.stmarylebow.co.uk

Windblown Cockneys: *The Daily Telegraph* newspaper published a story in 1994 that Malcolm Hough of the Met Office had devised the Larkhill Ray Invariant (Larri) model. This enabled the identification of Cockneys to be placed upon a scientific footing. It was stated that the researcher had investigated London's wind and weather conditions for the period April 1991-April 1992 in order to ascertain the distances at which the sound of the bells of St Mary-le-Bow might be heard in a variety of meteorological conditions. The factors that he had taken into consideration had included the impact of traffic noise. During night-time, when there had been less interruption from other sound sources, the peels had been able to travel further. His analysis was stated to have revealed that a prevailing wind could cause there to be a concentration of Cockney births in suburbs at several miles' distance from the church in salubrious middle-class districts such as Dulwich that were not associated with traditional Cockney culture.[1]

See Also: STREET MARKETS Pearly Kings; WEATHER Wind

Saved By The Bell

In the pre-Modern era the sounds of London's principal bells were known individually by people who lived in the countryside around the metropolis. By 1700 Sir Christopher Wren's construction of St Paul's Cathedral had progressed sufficiently far that it became possible for a bell to be hung in the building's north-western tower. Its ring became known beyond the city's walls.

John Hadfield was a soldier who had been assigned a stint of night-time guard duty at Windsor Castle. His superiors claimed that he had fallen asleep while he had been at his station. The man denied the charge. He stated that he had heard the cathedral's bell ring thirteen times, when he would have expected it to sound out only a dozen chimes. Because of the distance involved, his assertion was ignored. His court-martial went ahead. He was found guilty and was sentenced to death. However, he remained insistent that he had been awake and that he had heard the bell peal an extra time. Before he could be executed reports reached the military authorities that in London other people had also noticed the oddity. A formal investigation into the matter was then mounted. The soldier was found to have spoken the truth. He was granted a royal pardon.

---

[1]   Roger Highfield 1 April 1994 edition of *The Daily Telegraph* p3.

Hadfield was a man who was born to live. When he died in 1770 he had reached the age of 102.

Locations: Glasshouse Yard, EC1A 4(JN). Hadfield's final home.
St Paul's Cathedral, St Paul's Churchyard, EC4M 8AD.
See Also: ST PAUL'S CATHEDRAL

The Whitechapel Bell Foundry

Trades that were viewed as being either dangerous or obnoxious tended to be pursued outside of the walls of the City of London. This accounts for why Whitechapel is home to the Whitechapel Bell Foundry. The prevailing westerlies meant that the district was downwind from the City for most of the year.

The Foundry was established at Houndsditch in 1420. In 1583 it moved to Whitechapel. In 1738 it relocated to its present premises on the Whitechapel Road.

The bells that have been cast there by its workers have included Big Ben, Bow Bells, and Philadelphia's Liberty Bell.

Location: Nos. 32-34 Whitechapel Road, E1 1DY
See Also: WEATHER Wind
Website: www.whitechapelbellfoundry.co.uk

BRIDGES

See Also: CITY OF LONDON; THE THAMES

The Albert Bridge

The Albert Bridge (1872) was designed by the engineer Rowland Ordish. He used the Franz Josef Bridge in Prague as his model.[1]

The structure is known as the *Trembling Lady*. She has a sign on her that states that troops must break step whenever they are crossing her in a body. This is because, if they did not and continued to march in unison, there would be a real danger that she might collapse from the vibrations that would be caused by their boots striking the span's road surface.

In 1959 the poet and architectural writer John Betjeman led a campaign that opposed an official plan that included the structure's demolition. The effort succeeded.

In 2006 it was reported that the Albert Bridge was suffering from structural damage. In large part, this was caused by the fact that about a third of the vehicles that were crossing her each day weighed over two tonnes.[2]

Location: Albert Bridge, SW3 5(HN) and SW11 4(NZ).

See Also: HERITAGE Lost London, The Euston Arch

Blackfriars Bridge

None of London's bridges are named after a monarch or a prime minister. This is unusual for a capital city. (The phenomenon is paralleled by the way in which very few of the metropolis's major roads are named after an individual.)

The building of the first Blackfriars Bridge (1769) was paid for by the Bridge House Estates. Initially, the structure was officially called the William Pitt Bridge. However, people took to referring to it as Blackfriars Bridge. The crossing's name was soon altered to reflect this reality.

Location: Blackfriars Bridge, EC4P 4(BQ) and SE1 8(NY).

Blow Up Bridge

Macclesfield Bridge carries the south-eastwards continuation of Avenue

---

[1]   Ordish went on to help William Barlow build St Pancras Railway Station.

[2]   4x4 road vehicles are known as 'Chelsea tractors'.

Road across the Regent's Canal into Regent's Park. The structure's nickname derives from an incident that occurred at 3 *a.m.* on 2 October 1874. A canal boat called the *Tilbury* was travelling along the waterway. She was carrying a cargo of gunpowder that was intended for a quarry in the Midlands. The vessel blew up. Three people were killed.

The bridge was damaged by the explosion. Subsequently, the structure was rebuilt. The new version incorporated its predecessor's vertical metal pillars. These had grooves that had been worn into them by the friction of their being rubbed against by the ropes that were secured to horses to enable them to tow barges. When the supports were re-erected they were turned around by 180°. As a result, new furrows soon came to bookend the old.

Location: Avenue Road, NW8 7PT.

Bow Bridge

Queen Matilda was the first wife of King Henry I. In 1110 she set out to visit Barking Abbey in Essex. While trying to ford the River Lea, she was almost drowned. This prompted the monarch to order the building of a three-arched bridge. The structure's shape led to it soon becoming known as Bow Bridge. The district in which it had been erected came to be reffered to as Bow.

The City Bridge Trust

The City of London owns Blackfriars, London, Southwark, and Tower bridges. The City Bridge Trust is controlled by the settlement's Corporation. The income that the body generates is intended primarily to pay for the maintenance of the crossings.

The Trust's progenitor was established by King John at the start of the 13[th]C.[1] This entity amassed a property estate during the Middle Ages from bequests that were left to it. King Edward I allowed the rent of what became the Stocks Market to be assigned to London Bridge's maintenance.

The Bridge House Estates Committee of the Corporation was set up in 1592. The body is the oldest of the Corporation's standing committees. Its chairman is the Chief Commoner, who is the leader of the City's Common Council.

The Council agreed in 1995 that the Bridge House Estate Fund's financial surplus could furnish income for a trust that would issue grants to greater London organisations and charities that have worthwhile

---

[1]   'Bad' King John, the younger brother of King Richard the Lionheart.

objectives. In 2007 the Fund was renamed The City Bridge Trust.
Website: www.citybridgetrust.org.uk

The Freeing of The West

In the 19[th]C private companies built several bridges across the Thames to the west of the City of London. Some of the enterprises proved to be financially troubled. This precariousness called into doubt the businesses' ability to maintain their structures in a safe condition. The necessity for action was underscored by the fact that when vehicles paid their tolls to be allowed to cross the river they stopped. This delay frequently had a knock-on effect that caused traffic to become gridlocked in the districts that abutted the bridges' ends.

The Metropolitan Toll Bridges Act was passed into law in 1877. Two years later Sir Joseph Bazalgette persuaded the Metropolitan Board of Works to use the measure's provisions to buy control of the bridges from Waterloo Bridge to Hammersmith Bridge. The authority made them toll-free. The engineer oversaw a number of improvements to their structures and replaced three of them: Battersea (1890), Hammersmith (1887), and Putney (1886).

See Also: THE THAMES The Embankment and Sir Joseph Bazalgette

London Bridge

Prior to the embankment of the Thames, the river was both broader and shallower. Therefore, depending upon the tides, at certain points it could be forded - a place just to the east of the present London Bridge was one of these. (Other sites upriver of it included Chelsea, Fulham, and Brentford.)

The Romans availed themselves of the easternmost ford's shallowness to build the first London Bridge. This wooden structure was kept in a state of repair until the late 12[th]C. It was then replaced by a stone crossing that had nineteen arches.

The moving force in the building of the new bridge was Peter de

Colechurch, a priest. The structure's 30-year-long erection and subsequent maintenance were overseen by the Fraternity of the Brethren of London Bridge, a church-based organisation. In 1282 this body was granted a royal warrant.

Shops were put up on the bridge in order that the rental income that they generated could be used to help to defray the cost of the structure's maintenance. The crossing developed a community that resided upon it continuously.[1]

In 1581 Pieter Morice attached a waterwheel to London Bridge. This was powered by the rush of the river through one of the structure's narrow arches. Sufficient energy was generated that water drawn from the watercourse could be pumped as far as Cornhill.

For many years there was a practice of displaying the heads of executed traitors upon the southern end of the crossing. These were heavily salted in order to discourage birds from devouring the flesh on them.

In 1756 an Act of Parliament sanctioned the demolition of all of the buildings that had been constructed upon London Bridge. Six years later Moorgate, one of the City's gateways, was demolished. Its stones were used to mitigate the deleterious effect that the tide had been having upon the crossing.

During some winters the numerous small arches of the medieval bridge enabled the Thames to freeze upriver of the structure. If the ice then proved to be thick enough for people to stand upon safely a frost fair was sometimes held on it. The last of these took place during the winter of 1813-4. A new crossing was designed by John Rennie the elder, who used Cornish granite. He died in 1821. The five-arch structure was completed in 1831 by his son Sir John Rennie the younger. With fewer obstruction's the river's current was able to flow faster. It became harder for the watercourse to freeze over. The waterwheel was not incorporated into the new bridge.

Three of the old crossing's alcoves survive. One is now in Guy's Hospital, while the other two are to be found at the eastern end of Victoria Park in East London.

The 19thC bridge was replaced by a new one in 1972.

Location: SE1 9RA. The Pool of London. Upriver (to the east) of Tower Bridge.

See Also: COLUMNS The Monument; FOOD MARKETS Borough Market; ROMAN REMAINS; THE THAMES The Pool of London

---

[1]   The only bridge in Britain that still has people living on it is Pulteney Bridge in Bath.

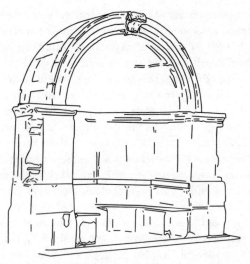

Website: www.cityoflondon.gov.uk/walks-tours-and
-architecture/bridges/Pages/default.aspx

Pasties In The Desert: Robert P. McCulloch was an American. His family wealth had been acquired through building electricity power stations. As a youth, he developed an interest in engines. He made his own fortune by manufacturing them first for lawnmowers and then for chainsaws. He diversified into the oil business while continuing to manufacture engine-driven outdoors products. A wish to acquire a larger share of the market for outboard motors prompted him to look for a site where powered boats could be tested. He opted for Lake Havasu in Arizona. This body of water had been created by the construction of the Parker Dam (1934-8) across the Colorado River.

In 1963 McCulloch concluded that there was potential for developing a residential city and holiday resort next to the lake. Therefore, he purchased a large waterside property on which to build it. To help him with the project he employed C.V. Wood, who had been one of the principal planners of the original Disneyland theme park (as well as being a champion chilli chef).

The City of London appreciated that London Bridge's weight was causing the structure to sink into the riverbed at the rate of an eighth-of-an-inch *p.a.*. The pulling down of the Euston Arch a few years before had triggered the emergence of a conservation movement that was seeking to preserve the finer examples of London's built heritage. Members of it were waging a campaign that was seeking to prevent British Rail from razing the St Pancras Station Hotel. The local authority appreciated that in such a climate a decision to demolish the crossing was not politically practicable. In 1967 the Corporation put the structure up for sale. Wood persuaded McCulloch that the span would furnish Lake Havasu City with both a focus and a sign that its developers were committed to it in the long-term. The industrialist purchased the crossing. According to an urban myth, he assumed that he was buying Tower Bridge and did not appreciate his error until it was too late for him to pull out of the deal. This was not the case.

What was erected in Arizona was a hollow concrete frame onto which the bridge's cladding was secured. The structure was built over dry land. When its assembly had been completed the area below its arches was flooded. The opening ceremony was held in 1971. This involved the then Lord Mayor of London attending in his ceremonial dress, a summit of Pearly Kings, and an Apache tribal dance. The food that was served included guacamole and Cornish pasties. The latter was an acknowledgement of the county in which the bridge's stones had been quarried.

One of the 19thC bridge's arches is still in place on the Southwark bank.

Reading: Travis Elborough *London Bridge In America: The Tall Story of A Transatlantic Crossing* Jonathan Cape (2013).

Websites: www.havasumuseum.com   www.golakehavasu.com

London's Shape

On the outer sections of the Thames's bends the water is deeper than it is at the opposite banks. It was easier to berth ships at such places. Therefore, at these points along the river's course a series of townships grew up.

Initial north-south growth was hampered by the limited number of river crossings. In part, this accounts for why London is longer east-to-west than it is north-to-south.

The Millennium Bridge

The Millennium Bridge (2000) is a pedestrian bridge that spans the Thames. It links St Paul's Cathedral to the Tate Britain at Bankside. The idea for the crossing was devised by architect Theo Crosby and his wife the polymath 'Polly' Hope. At the time, the couple were deeply involved in the creation of Shakespeare's Globe. In 1991 they proposed the scheme at a meeting of the theatre's development council. At the time, the project was at its nadir. Therefore, Crosby was challenged about this extension of the project at a time when it had effectively ground to a halt.

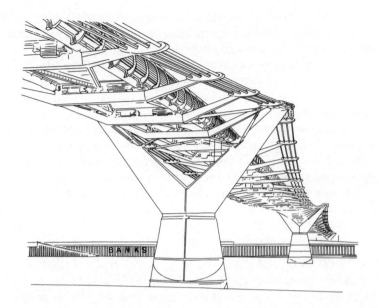

He replied 'My dear chap, we can't get bogged down by the petty present. We have to look to the future.'

The structure's principal designers were the architect Sir Norman Foster and the sculptor Sir Anthony Caro. When the crossing opened it was discovered to be possessed of a pronounced 'wobble'. It was promptly dubbed the *Wobbly Bridge*. The lateral oscillations were induced whenever a large number of pedestrians were walking across the structure at the same time. The phenomenon was countered by a technique that involved unobtrusive passive dampers being added to it.

Upon occasion strong winds prompt the Metropolitan Police to temporarily close the crossing.

Location: South of St Paul's Cathedral, EC4V 4E, and north of Tate Modern, SE1 9TG.

Tower Bridge

The idea of a bridge that would provide some relief for London Bridge was mooted in 1876. The crossing was designed by the City of London architect Sir Horace Jones and the engineer Sir John Wolfe Barry. Its construction was started in 1886. The exteriors of its two towers were intended to complement the Tower of London.

At the time of its completion Tower Bridge (1894) was disliked by many people. There was a view that its design was out of character with its surroundings. The bridge is now probably a better known icon of the city than is the neighbouring fortress-prison.

Between the towers there is a walkway. Soon after the structure's opening it was noted that there was a tendency for undesirable elements to gather there. As a result, the aerial span was closed and remained so for many years.

The bridge's road sections can be lifted up to enable maritime vessels to pass. On some days they are raised and lowered several times. Originally, hydraulic machinery provided the means for doing this. In 1976 the equipment was replaced by an electrified system.

Location: The River Thames, SE1 2UP. Downriver of London Bridge.

See Also: TEA Ig Nobel Prize Winners
Website: www.towerbridge.org.uk

The 78: On 30 December 1952 the driver of a southbound No. 78 double-decker bus suddenly appreciated that the bridge's road sections were being raised. He was presented with the predicament of either braking, in which case his vehicle might not stop in time and would therefore fall into the Thames, or of accelerating, in the hope that it would be able to make it over the opening gap, again facing the prospect that the bus might still end up in the river. He chose the latter course and succeeded in landing his charge on the other portion of the rising roadway.

See Also: BUSES

Waterloo Bridge

When the construction of the John Rennie the elder-designed Waterloo Bridge (1817) had been started in 1811, it had been intended that the structure would be known as the Strand Bridge. However, the Duke of Wellington's defeat of Napoleon intervened. An Act of Parliament was passed in 1816 that changed the crossing's name to Waterloo Bridge.

The original structure was demolished in 1934, a temporary one having been put in place beside it. The construction of its replacement was started in 1937. However, the process was retarded by the outbreak of the Second World War. The new crossing was not completed until 1945. It is known as the *Women's Bridge* because the workforce that finished it was largely female. Stones from the old structure were used to build part of the foundations of Heathrow Airport.

From the central section of the bridge it is possible to have one of the most scenic panoramas of London.

Location: The River Thames, WC2E (EB) and SE1 8(XT). Upstream from Blackfriars Bridge.

See Also: GALLERIES The Royal Spanish Art Collection

Waterloo Sunset: Ray Davies's *Waterloo Sunset* (1967) is London's *de facto* anthem. Originally, the pop song was about Liverpool; the 'dirty old river' was the Mersey. The Beatles' release of *Penny Lane* prompted the tunesmith to adapt his composition so that it had a London setting. The 'Terry' referred to in the lyrics is popularly held to have been the movie actor Terence Stamp. His brother Chris, who co-managed The Who, was a friend of the songwriter.

It is reputed that Mr Davies has declared that the day that he finished *Waterloo Sunset* was the saddest one of his life. This was because he appreciated that he would never create a better composition than the one he had just completed.

Westminster Bridge

The Horseferry ferry was the property of the Archbishops of Canterbury. The prelates resided in Lambeth Palace on the southern side of the river. The first written reference to the ferry dates from the 16thC. Westminster Bridge was opened in 1750. The span was constructed despite the City of London having made clear its concerns about its own possible loss of revenues from London Bridge's tolls.

Location: The River Thames, SW1A 2(JR). Downstream of Lambeth Bridge.

THE BRITISH LIBRARY

The British Museum British Library

The British Library is one of the great libraries of the world. While its holdings are smaller than the national libraries of the United States and Russia, it outstrips them in many areas through its having been an acquiring institution for longer than they have.

The Library developed out of a number of manuscript collections. The Cottonian Library was assembled by the Cotton family during the late 17thC. It was presented to the nation at the behest of Sir John Cotton. The material was housed successively in Cotton House in Westminster, Essex House off the Strand, and Ashburnham House in Westminster. The Harleian Collection of Manuscripts was assembled initially by Robert Harley the 1st Earl of Oxford and then by his son the bibulous, bibliophile 2nd Earl. In 1753 the latter's daughter, the Duchess of Portland, sold the material to the government for £10,000. The purchase was authorised by the British Museum Foundation Act.

The Round Reading Room (1857) was built in the Museum's central courtyard. It was created principally through the efforts of the Chief Librarian Sir Antonio Panizzi. Karl Marx's favoured seat was O7 and Lenin's L13.

In 1973 the British Library became a separate institution from the British Museum. The latter's library departments had been merged with a number of other national libraries.

Location: Great Russell Street, Bloomsbury, WC1B 3DG. On the northern side.

See Also: THE BRITISH MUSEUM
Website: www.bl.uk

The King's Library

Lord Lumley was the great book collector of Elizabethan England. His library was bought by Henry Prince of Wales, King James I's eldest son. Thereby, it became the core of the first Royal Library.

For an author or a publisher to establish ownership of the copyright of a book or a literary work it had to be registered at Stationers' Hall in the City of London. Under the Statute of Anne (1711), the Royal Library was entitled to receive one copy of every published work that was pre-

sented. In 1757 King George II gave the Royal Library to the British Museum. Along with the donation, the right of receipt was also transferred to the institution.[1]

George's grandson and successor, King George III, built up a new Royal Library. The latter's son, King George IV, gave this collection to the Museum in 1823. Construction work had to be carried out on the institution's building Bloomsbury so that the material could be accommodated.

Location: Stationers' Hall, Stationers Hall Court, EC4M 7DR. Between Nos. 28 and 30 Ludgate Hill.

See Also: GALLERIES The Royal Collection

Website: www.stationers.org

Copyright and Acquisitions

By law, a copy of every printed literary item (including dress patterns) published in Britain must be deposited with the British Library. This is part of the legal deposit process. There have long been mutterings from within the Library that large swathes of romantic fiction and vanity publishing are a positive drain upon the institution in view of the costs of their initial processing and subsequent storage. (The university libraries of Cambridge, Oxford, and Trinity College in Dublin, and the national

[1]   The legal requirement for all licensed printing to be 'Entered at Stationers' Hall' ended in 1911.

libraries of Wales and Scotland are able to claim copies of books, *etc.*, but are not statutorily obligated to preserve them as is the Library.)

A Treasury grant assists the Library in its purchase of other books and items. The institution also acquires material through donation.

In 2006 the British Library announced that it was shifting its collecting strategy in order to prepare itself for the growth of cultural and intellectual output that it was anticipating would be generated in India and China during the forthcoming years. At the time, the Library possessed over 150 million items.

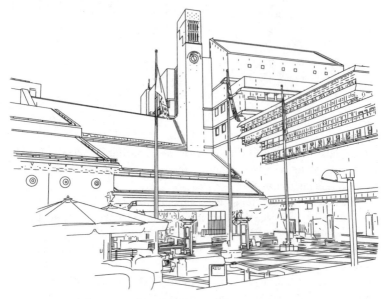

The British Library Building St Pancras

The British Library Building project was given the go-ahead in the late 1970s by a Labour government. The design was created by Colin St John 'Sandy' Wilson. He had first become involved in the scheme in 1962. His plan was inspired by the work of the Finnish architect Alvar Aalto, who had reinterpreted Modernism in an organic manner. Construction began on the St Pancras site in 1980. The work was due to be completed by 1989. The Library opened in 1998. The edifice is deeper than it is tall. Wilson viewed the prospective users' experience of the building as being an important factor. Its interior is better liked than its exterior is.

Location: No. 96 Euston Road, St Pancras, NW1 2DB.

THE BRITISH MUSEUM

Sir Hans Sloane was an Irish-born physician. During the first half of the 18thC he enjoyed an immense annual income that he derived from the fees that he charged his patients. It rose to be higher than that of most of his aristocratic clients. In 1702 his friend William Courten bequeathed to him some curios. These acted as the nucleus for what became a major collection of artefacts. In 1712 the doctor bought the Manor of Chelsea. He used the manor house as a home for his antiquarian and natural historical items.

In 1753 Sir Hans died. He left his collection to the nation upon the condition that a sum of £20,000 - far less than its current value - was paid to his heirs. Parliament sanctioned the purchase and the items were acquired. Two years later the proceeds from a state lottery were used to buy Montagu House in Bloomsbury. In 1759 the British Museum opened there.

From the early 19thC through to the early 20thC, the Museum's building was continuously being extended and remodelled. The institution took to ejecting portions of itself. In 1881 its natural history collection was moved to South Kensington where the material evolved into being the Natural History Museum. In 1973 the British Museum's library became part of the British Library. The latter moved to King's Cross in 1997.

An oddity of the British Museum is that only a small proportion of the items in its collection were made in the British Isles.

Locations: The British Museum, Great Russell Street, WC1B 3DG. On the northern side.

No. 4 Bloomsbury Place, WC1A 2QA. On the northern side, at the eastern end. (This was Sloane's home from 1695 to 1742.)

See Also: THE BRITISH LIBRARY The British Museum British Library; MUSEUMS; MUSEUMS The Natural History Museum

Website: www.britishmuseum.org

Dr Dee's Mirror

Dr John Dee was a 16thC scholar and astrologer whose clients included Queen Elizabeth I.

Dr Dee's Mirror is an obsidian artefact was made by the Aztecs or one of their subject peoples. The reflectiveness of the object's surface was created by means of bat droppings. The excrement has the capacity to be used as a very fine abrasive. This is because it contains the skeletons of insects.

Through the means of long-distance trade, the stone item made its way into the possession of Dee.

Horace Walpole's novel *The Castle of Otranto* (1764) was the first work of Gothic fiction. The author was fascinated by the man. In 1771 he acquired the fellow's Mirror. It is now owned by the Museum.

Mutilated Blocks of Art

In 1687 the Ottoman Empire and Venice were at war with one another. The former's forces used the Parthenon in Athens as a gunpowder dump. This exploded. The building was severely damaged by the blast.

At the start of the 19thC the 7th Earl of Elgin was the British government's Envoy Extraordinary in Constantinople. The authorities there granted him, in his private capacity, the right to salvage sculptures and architectural details from the ruin. The noble returned to Britain with the Elgin Marbles. After years of bargaining, he sold the stones to the British Museum in 1816.

Byron witnessed the removal of the Marbles from the Parthenon. He disliked his fellow peer. He referred to him in his poem *Childe Harold's Pilgrimage* (1812).

> Let Aberdeen and Elgin still pursue
> The shades of fame through regions of Virtu;
> Waste useless thousands on their Phidian freaks,
> Mis-shapen monuments, and maimed antiques;
> And make their grand saloons a general mart
> For all the mutilated blocks of art.[1]

The Marbles have been the cause of a long-running dispute between the Museum and the Greek government. The latter believes that the stones should be in Greece, while the former states that, in international law, it has full and clear legal ownership of them.

It is commonplace to find people in Britain who would be happy to see the Marbles go to Athens. An uncommented aspect of the matter is that through the relative mobility of people of Greek cultural identity during the travails of the 20thC, a large proportion of modern Athenians - if not the majority - are descended from people who would have regarded 5thC BC Athens as either their enemy or their oppressor.

The Classical Athenians were generous and inclusive towards one

---

[1]   Canto ii, Stanza 15, Line 1.

another. However, their culture was xenophobic with regard to anyone who was not of their number. In 484 BC a massive vein of silver-bearing ore was discovered at Laurium close to Athens.[1] The state's citizens voted to use the resulting wealth to invest in their navy. This new military strength was used to create a ruthless *de facto* protection racket against non-Athenian Greeks. It compounded the income that was derived from the mines and enabled the Acropolis to be enhanced in a magnificent manner. Historically, it had been a widely held view amongst the citizen body that conspicuous consumption could have adverse social consequences. This opinion was reflected by the fact that their state had placed a set of sumptuary laws upon its statute book. During the Parthenon's construction many Athenians voiced their opposition to what they regarded as being the excessive grandeur of the structure.

In the early 19thC the southern portion of what is now Greece became independent of the Ottoman Empire; this it achieved with the support of Britain, France, and Russia. Prince Otto of Bavaria became the new nation's first monarch; he Hellenised his name to become King Otho. The German arrived in the country in 1833. He was accompanied by a group of Bavarian advisers. Initially, it was this circle that directed the state's affairs. In large part, these men had been shaped by the Clas-

[1] In the early 20thC the mines were still being worked.

sical instruction that they had received as children and youths. Under their guidance, Greece set herself upon a course of trying to recreate something of the glory of 5thC BC Athens. Therefore, the Parthenon became a symbol of Greek identity in a way that it had not been before. This development was an instance of informal colonialism deriving from the nature of education in Western Europe rather than being a case of native cultural self-expression.

As Otho's reign progressed, his subjects began to chafe at the Bavarians' domination of their political life. A decade after the king had acceded to the throne, there was a *coup d'état*. The monarch continued to be the nation's sovereign but his counsellors were ousted from power. However, the idea of trying to recreate something of the grandeur of the Periclean era was not jettisoned. The colonialist concept metamorphosed into being a nationalist one. However, even at the time, to many ethnic Greeks this would have appeared to have been profoundly anachronistic. For examples of contemporary Greek cultural and commercial dynamism they would have looked to the Levantine cities of Alexandria, Constantinople, and Smyrna.

Reading: Nick Doumanis *A History of Greece* Palgrave Macmillan (2009). A book that argues that modern Greek identity was forged in part through the interaction of Greeks with foreign cultures. The professor seems to favour the transfer of the Marbles to Athens.

William Westermann *The Slave Systems of Greek and Roman Antiquity* American Philosophical Society (1955). The quality of life of the Athenian-owned mining slaves was better than was to be the case under the Romans. This was because skilled work was respected more by the former than by the latter.

The Portland Vase

The Portland Vase is a 24cm-tall, white and cobalt blue cameo glass vessel that was probably made in the 1stC BC. The figures upon its exterior have been the subject of numerous interpretations. One of the most plausible of these contends that they refer to the rupture between Mark Anthony and Augustus that finished the Roman Republic. The former's desire for Cleopatra caused him to abandon his wife Octavia, who was Augustus's sister.

Augustus defeated his brother-in-law at the naval battle of Actium (31 BC). Subsequently, he became the first emperor. However, he was assiduous in trying to portray himself as being the servant of the old state. One passion that he proved to be unable to mask was that he was obsessed by beautiful vases. It was an aspect of his character that was widely known.

The Vase is believed to have been unearthed close to Rome during the 1550s. The first known contemporary written reference to it dates from 1601. In 1782 it was purchased in the city by Sir William Hamilton. He paid £1000 for it. The diplomat was not wealthy enough to be able to keep it. He was acting as a *de facto* dealer. Two years later he sold it and three other items to the Duchess of Portland for £2000. Following her grace's death, the vessel was acquired by her son the 3rd Duke of Portland.

In 1785 the peer lent the Vase to Josiah Wedgwood for a year. The potter dedicated considerable time and effort to trying to create reproductions of it. Wedgwood's friend the physician Erasmus Darwin devoted a section his epic poem *The Botanic Garden* (1791) to the vessel. This literary work was issued commercially by Joseph Johnson. For the book, the publisher commissioned William Blake to produce an engraving of the Vase.

The vessel was loaned to the British Museum by the 4th duke in 1810. 35 years later William Mulcahy, a student who had abandoned his studies at Trinity College Dublin, visited the institution. There, he deliberately smashed the Vase. He was apprehended by the establishment's staff. The youth claimed that he was called William Lloyd. It was apparent that while he had undergone some form of mental crisis in the short-term, he was not insane.

The vandal was charged under the Malicious Damages To Properties Act. An ambiguously drafted portion of the measure was open to being interpreted in a way that implied that its provisions applied only to items that were worth less than £5. Therefore, the prosecution opted to act against him not with regard to the Vase itself but rather in respect to the damage that he had caused to the case in which it had been displayed. The court found the youth guilty and ordered him to pay the Museum £3 in compensation or undergo two months' hard labour in Tothill Fields Prison.

Mulcahy had had only 9*d* upon his person at the time of his arrest. As he had not revealed his true identity and had no known associates, it seemed that he would have to serve out his sentence. However, within two days his fine had been paid anonymously. The money was accompanied by a poorly-spelt note. This claimed that the benefactor was a lawyer who was seeking to salve his conscience. It declared that he was doing so in part for the way in which he had used his professional expertise to act unfairly against others.

While the youth had been being interrogated, he had let slip that he had been a student at Trinity. This lead, in conjunction with an accurate description of his person, enabled the Museum authorities to establish his true identity. It was appreciated that his widowed mother and his tutor brother did not have the financial means to begin to make good the financial loss that the 4th duke had suffered. His grace, upon first being informed of the incident, had proven to be compassionately inclined. He had expressed his concern for the youth's mental state. Upon learning of the Mulcahy family's modest material circumstances, the peer opted to let rest the matter of his own recompense.

The Vase was restored by John Doubleday. His achievement led to the item becoming even more celebrated than it had been before its shattering.

The 7th Duke of Portland sold the vessel to the Museum in 1945 for a sum that was far below the object's contemporary valuation. Three years later a member of the public approached the institution to try to learn what the significance might be of some objects that he had inherited. They were just over three dozen chips of glass. That they might be noteworthy was indicated by the fact that a case had been made to house them. Within it, each shard had its own compartment.

Eventually, it was appreciated that the fragments had been left over from Doubleday's reassembly of the Vase. The restorer had wanted them to be preserved. However, he had died. A colleague of his had then taken it upon himself to ensure that they were kept safely. The fellow had commissioned the building of the box. However, the official had also expired. Subsequently, the case's builder had not sent the fragments and their container to the Museum. They and the box had passed down to his heirs, one of whom had finally approached the institution.

By the mid-20[th]C it was apparent that the restoration was not aging well. Therefore, the Museum's staff decided that the Vase should be reassembled and that the shards should be reincorporated into it. However, the locations of only three of them could be ascertained. The rest were returned to their case.

A degree of physical tension exists between the two layers of glass. To relieve this to a degree and thus reduce the likelihood of its shattering, a very fine series of horizontal lines were ground within the vessel. This was probably done before most of the white outer layer was cut away. The purpose of the discreet incisions, and thus the technique, was not appreciated until the late 20[th]C.

See Also: SHOPPING Wedgwood

BUSES

See Also: BRIDGES Tower Bridge, The 78

Bus Shelters

Double-decker buses are operated along the No. 55 bus route. For years it was the case that the roofs of the bus shelters along its course had had decorated potatoes placed upon them. These could not be seen from street level but could be appreciated from the upstairs deck of the 55.
See Also: STREET FURNITURE

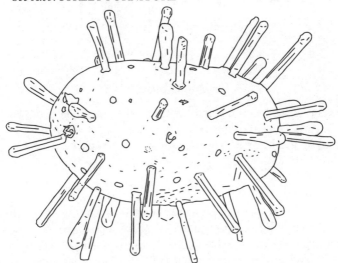

The Edible Bus Route

Starting in Lambeth, a group of guerrilla gardeners have been seeking to create a series of food gardens along the full length of the route of the No. 322 bus.
Website: www.theediblebusstop.org

The Green Line

The Green Line bus services have operated principally in those areas that are beyond metropolitan London's outer edge.

76	100 towards Blackfriars	172
Night Bus **N11**	Night Bus **N15**	Night Bus **N21**
Night Bus **N26**	Night Bus **N47**	Night Bus **N76** **N551**

Night Buses

Night buses tend to run along what were the older, longer bus routes. In the early 1990s the courses' daytime services were split into shorter lengths so that the vehicles operating along them could keep more closely to their timetables.

Routemasters

'Bill' Durrant was put in charge of London Transport's bus policy in the 1930s.[1] In the post-war era London Transport appreciated that cars were becoming more comfortable to travel in. The public body responded to this development by trying to improve the passenger experience for people who were riding on its vehicles. In 1951 Mr Durrant assembled a team at LT's Chiswick Works to develop the Routemaster, a bus that would address the matter.

The band that he assembled included Eric Ottaway, who during the conflict had worked in the London Aircraft Group. This experience had enabled him to develop expertise with regard to the manufacturing of lightweight structures. Colin Curtis was appointed to design the mechanical aspects of the vehicle.[2] Douglas Scott was given responsibil-

---

[1]   During the Second World War Mr Durrant used his mechanical engineering expertise to design the Centurion tank.

[2]   Somewhat curiously Mr Curtis's love of buses had been engendered by a

ity for styling both the bus's external appearance and its interior design.

The Routemaster's aluminium body was fixed onto a chassis-less structure that was composed of small subframes. This arrangement made the bus a quarter of a ton lighter than its antecedent had been. Therefore, it could be run more economically than had been the case with the previous generation of vehicles. Its internal layout enabled it to seat more passengers than its predecessors had been able to. For the drivers the power steering, hydraulic braking, independent suspension on each wheel, and automatic transmission made the bus easy to drive. Its maintenance could be conducted swiftly thereby enabling it to spend more time on the road than its forerunners had been able to.

The first prototypes went into service in 1956. Two years later commercial production started. It ended in 1968. By then 2876 Routemasters had been built.

At the end of 2005 the final regular Routemaster service - the 159 - ended. Subsequently, two 'heritage' routes were established to meet demand from the public to have the opportunity to travel on the bus.

Thomas Heatherwick designed the Modern Routemaster. It was launched in 2012.

Website: www.routemaster.org.uk

Steps To Health

In the years that followed the Second World War Britons began to die of heart attacks in unprecedented numbers. 'Jerry' Morris was the Director of the Medical Research Council's Social Medicine Unit. He led an investigation of the level of coronary seizure rates that members of different occupations were subject to.

In 1949 Dr Morris noticed that his data had revealed that age-for-age bus drivers had markedly higher rates of heart attacks than did the vehicles' conductors. The former were sedentary, whereas the latter climbed at least 500 steps every working day. This was the first clear evidence of there being a relationship between people being physically active and their reducing the likelihood of their suffering a cardiac arrest. The physician's study had involved thousands of men. However, he was wary of treating the link as being proof of a connection. His initial findings were corroborated by data that was derived from postal workers. This demonstrated how stationary ones, such as counter clerks, had more heart attacks than did the postmen who spent their working days delivering letters and parcels.

childhood accident. While he had been cycling, one of the vehicles had run him over.

Morris's paper *Coronary Heart-Disease and Physical Activity of Work* was published in *The Lancet* in 1953. The idea that exercise and health might be associated with one another can be traced back in the history of medicine to Hippocrates (*c*.460-*c*.370 BC), however, it was the physician's article that provided the first scientific evidence of the correlation between them. In the United Kingdom its findings were met with widespread disbelief. Newspapers poured derision upon its conclusion and the large majority of cardiologists chose to ignore the research. However, the value of the work was appreciated in the United States and with time it was given its due in Britain.

For a subsequent study, London Transport supplied the doctor with information about the different sizes of trousers that were worn by its bus drivers and conductors. This data revealed that the latter tended to be thinner than the former. However, Morris was able to establish that body shape was not the factor that determined the level of risk but rather it was the degree of vigorous physical exercise that a person undertook.

Locations: Central Middlesex Hospital, Acton Lane, NW10 7NS.

The London School of Hygiene & Tropical Medicine, Keppel Street, WC1E 7HT. The Unit migrated from the Central Middlesex Hospital to the London Hospital in 1956. Eleven years later it settled at the School. Formally, Dr Morris retired in 1978. However, he continued to work until a few weeks before his own death in 2009.

Website: www.lshtm.ac.uk

Sunken Buses

The vehicle manufacturing business Leyland Motors agreed to sell 42 buses to Fidel Castro's Cuban regime. The deal was supported by two successive British Prime Ministers - Sir Alec Douglas-Home and Harold Wilson. However, the United States government took against the proposed transaction and chose to regard it as being a breach of the trade embargo that it had imposed upon its southern neighbour.

In 1964 the buses were loaded onto the East German freighter the *MV Magdeburg* at Dagenham. The boat set sail. However, off Broadness Point, the *Yamashiro Maru*, a Japanese vessel, collided with her. The German craft sank, taking her cargo with her. Leyland bore the financial loss. No inquiry was conducted into what had happened. A view developed that the CIA had been responsible for the Nipponese ship's action. The pilots' logs disappeared.

The buses were salvaged from the deep. This was done by pumping hundreds of thousands of ping-pong balls into their interior spaces.

CAMDEN TOWN

Camden Market

In the late-1960s the Greater London Council decided to build the London Motorway Box, an inner city ring road system. Part of the eight-lane motorway would have passed through Camden Town. Dingwalls was an old packing case factory that stood be the Regent's Canal next to Camden Lock. Eric Reynolds and a couple of his associates bought the tail-end of the building's lease. They were gambling that the scheme would not be implemented. They divided the structure into a series of retail and workshop units that were made available at low rents. Peter Gross opened a restaurant, Le Routier, and a music venue, Dingwalls. Initially, the market was held just on Saturdays. The Box project was cancelled and in 1976 the mart was granted permission to also trade on Sundays. By the early 1980s it had become a feature of London weekend life. By the end of the decade it was a renowned tourist attraction.

Location: Camden Lock, NW1 8AF

Reading: Caitlin Davies *Camden Lock and The Market* Frances Lincoln (2013)

See Also: CARNABY STREET; FOOD MARKETS, FORMER; PORTOBELLO MARKET; STREET MARKETS East End Street Markets, Brick Lane Market

Websites: www.camdenlockmarket.com www.camdenlock.net

Compendium

The Compendium bookstore was founded in 1968 by Diana Gravill and Nicholas Rochford. It was the UK's premier independent-alternative bookshop. Its shelves were the spawning ground of a series of book subject categories that are now grist-to-the-financial-mill of bookstores, *e.g.* Alternative Medicine, Black Studies, and Women's Studies. It closed in 2000.

Location: No. 234 Camden High Street, Camden Town, NW1 8QS. On the eastern side, to the south of the canal bridge.

The Electric Ballroom

William Fuller was a Kerryman. As a teenager he settled in Camden

Town and became involved in the building trade. He was a keen amateur boxer and wrestler.

Camden's Buffalo Club was an Irish dance hall. However, it was plagued by fights that stemmed from rivalries within the Irish community. The police closed it because it had become too violent. Fuller persuaded the force to allow him to run it. In 1941 an aerial bomb hit Camden Town Underground Station. Much of the adjoining row of buildings had to be demolished. Fuller bought the site and enlarged the dance hall.

The Kerryman was to expand his entertainment venue business within Britain and Ireland. He was also active in the demolition trade, engendering the comment 'What Hitler did not knock down, Bill Fuller did'. He moved to the United States where he opened his first Irish ballroom in Manhattan in 1956. He bought the Fillimore East and the Fillimore West music venues. In the 1960s he became a well-known figure in Las Vegas. In an era when many of the city's casinos were Mafia-controlled, he was one of the few promoters who was able to arrange for bands to perform there.

In 1978 the Buffalo Club reopened as The Electric Ballroom. The Pogues were a band who applied the punk spirit to Irish folk music. Fuller allowed the group to use the venue as a rehearsal space. He would watch its members practice and then cook them a meal. He still owned the building when he died in 2008.

Location: Nos. 184-185 Camden High Street, NW1 8QP. On the eastern side.

Website: www.electricballroom.co.uk

The London Motorway Box

In 1967 the Conservatives took control of the Greater London Council. The local government authority embraced a plan for London that the Ministry of Transport had drawn up. This set out the construction of a system of circular motorways. Of these, the London Motorway Box would have been the innermost. It was envisaged as being an eight-lane, 30 mile-long elevated ring road. The North London districts that it was to have passed through included: Notting Dale, Primrose Hill, Dalston, and Hackney Wick. Hammersmith Bridge was to have been replaced.

For it to have been built, 20,000 homes would have had to have been demolished. The limitations of 1960s urban planning were beginning to be appreciated. In addition, the proposed scheme would have razed several middle class neighbourhoods. Within these, community

groups sprang up spontaneously. They articulated the discontent of their members.

Following the calling of the February 1974 general election, the project was abandoned. It had become too much of a political liability. By then, a number of construction projects had already been executed: the Barrier Block in Brixton's Coldharbour Lane,[1] the East Hill portion of Trinity Road in Wandsworth, the West Cross Route that runs north of Shepherd's Bush Roundabout, and the East Cross Route near Bow.

Prior to the scheme's cancellation numerous properties in Dalston had been compulsorily purchased. The district's subsequent decline was believed by some to have derived from the impact of this occurrence upon the local economy.[2]

See Also: FOOD MARKETS, FORMER Covent Garden

---

[1]   The Barrier Block was designed so as to keep out noise and pollution from the anticipated motorway. In 1995 the Conservative Prime Minister John Major chose to make a disparaging remark about the building. Subsequently, *The Guardian* newspaper revealed that he had been a member of the Lambeth Council Planning Committee that had granted approval for its construction.

[2]   By 2014 parts of Dalston had become sought-after addresses. This was as a knock-on consequence of Shoreditch and the inner East End having become fashionable.

CARNABY STREET

See Also: CAMDEN TOWN Camden Market; PORTOBELLO MARKET; SHOPPING Pedestrianised Shopping Streets

In the 1960s Carnaby Street became a destination in its own right. The thoroughfare's importance to the era's changes derived principally from the boutiques that were opened along its length. These furnished affordable fashion for young men. Even people who could afford to shop elsewhere used its stores. However, there was a second element present - the Greek tailors who worked on its side streets. They were quick to adapt their traditional skills to the new trends, such as fashioning finger-tip-length moleskin jackets. Several of the stores came to be run by the tradesmen's younger, hipper relatives.

In 1968 Lord Kitchener's Valet opened an outlet on Carnaby Street. Like its parent on the Portobello Road, this sold old uniforms and military-style jackets. (It closed in 1977.)

There are now numerous independent shops in the area to the east of the Street.

Location: Carnaby Street, W1F 7(DE).

Website: www.carnaby.co.uk

The Official Monster Raving Loony Party

David Sutch found his initial fame as a rock singer ... of sorts. Musicians who played on his records included artistes of the calibre of Jeff Beck, Keith Moon, and Noel Redding. That their work during concerts was being recorded for commercial release was not always something that the vocalist informed them of at the time.

Sutch was managed by the Midlands-based hairdresser-turned-musical entrepreneur Reg Calvert. In 1963 a sex scandal prompted John Profumo, the War Secretary, to resign both from the Cabinet and as the MP for Stratford-upon-Avon. Calvert had a country home[1] that was located close to the town. The *impresario* suggested to his client that he should stand in the ensuing by-election. The performer participated in the contest as the candidate of the National Teenage Party. The campaign was run by the entrepreneur and his wife Dorothy.

It was Mrs Calvert who wrote Sutch's manifesto. This included a

---

[1]   Clifton Hall, near Rugby.

proposal for the pedestrianisation of Carnaby Street, something that was to come about. As did her call for the lowering of the voting age from 21 to eighteen. She had married her husband when she had been eighteen-years-old and regarded it as having been absurd that she had had to wait another three years until she could cast a ballot.

Sutch formed the Official Monster Raving Loony Party in 1983 to fight the Bermondsey Parliamentary by-election. The organisation became an ornament of the British electoral system. By deed poll he changed his own name to Screamin' Lord Sutch.

In 1991 Stuart Hughes was returned to the East Devon District Council for Sidmouth's Woolbrook Ward. Thereby, the hotelier became the Monster Raving Loony Party's first elected representative. (The West Country has a long tradition of being independently inclined in its politics.)

Location: No. 2 Lord North Street, SW1P 3LB. The Institute of Economic Affairs. Mr Calvert was shot dead by Major Oliver Smedley, who was one of the think-tank's founders.

Websites: www.loonyparty.com www.omrlp.com

CITY OF WESTMINSTER

JOHN STEPHEN
1934-2004

FOUNDER OF CARNABY STREET AS WORLD CENTRE FOR MEN'S FASHION IN THE 1960s

John Stephen

Vince Man's Shop sold dandified, ready-to-wear clothes and Levi jeans. The Newburgh Street establishment was opened in the mid-1950s by Bill Green, a photographer who specialised in creating pictures of body-builders that had homoerotic overtones. His initial customers were mostly gay men. The singer and writer George Melly once declared that it was the only outfitters where 'they measured your inside leg each time you bought a tie'. The store's reputation for selling stylish clobber spread beyond the homosexual community.

John Stephen worked as a shop assistant in Vince's for a while. The Glaswegian then opened His Clothes on Beak Street. The premises were badly damaged by a fire. In 1959 he and some partners opened Carnaby Street's first men's boutique at No. 41.[1] He created a look that used skinny trousers, tight skinny jackets, and fitted shirts. He went on to run several shops along the thoroughfare concurrently. Some of them were physically sited next to each other. He knocked holes through their adjoining walls so that people did not need to go back out onto the pavement in order to move from one of his boutiques to the next. At one point, he had nearly a hundred outlets across the country and had a number of international licensing deals. Over the years he scaled down his operations but remained active as a retailer.

Locations: His Clothes, No. 41 Carnaby Street, W1F 7DX.

Vince's Man's Shops, No. 15 Newburgh Street, W1F 7RX.

TIME & LIFE
BUILDING

Swinging London

In April 1966 the American magazine *Time* published a feature that was entitled *London: The Swinging City*. The piece's principal author was Piri Halasz, an Anglophile staff writer who was far more interested by politics than she was by fashion. She created the article with the help of colleagues in the publication's New York and London offices. Originally, it had been intended for the periodical's *Modern Living* section. However, a fortnight prior to going to press, *Time*'s managing editor, Otto Fuerbringer, took the decision to run the material as a cover story.

Location: No. 1 Bruton Street, W1J 6TL. On the south-western corner of the junction of New Bond Street. The magazine has since vacated the building.

Websites: http://piri.home.mindspring.com www.timelife.com

---

[1]   Ed Glinert *West End Chronicles* (2007) 233-4

THE CHAPELS ROYAL

The Chapels Royal are Anglican places of worship that exist outside the dicoesan structure of the Church of England. They are part of the Royal Household.

See Also: CHURCH OF ENGLAND CHURCHES The Temple Church; HALLS The Banqueting House; PALACES; THE TOWER OF LONDON The Chapel Royal of St Peter ad Vincula

Website: www.royal.gov.uk/theroyalresidences/thechapels royal/thechapelsroyal.aspx

The Queen's Chapel

Construction of the Queen's Chapel was started with the belief that the building would be a private chapel for the Roman Catholic *Infanta* Maria of Spain, whom it was anticipated would marry the Prince of Wales. However, the negotiations for the nuptials broke down and the anticipated betrothal did not occur. In 1625 the now King Charles I married Henrietta Maria, a French princess who was also a Catholic. The building was completed for her two years later.

During the 18thC and 19thC the building hosted Lutheran services.

Location: Marlborough Road, SW1A (1NP). On the eastern side.

WINSTON CHURCHILL

For much of his time in the Commons, Winston Churchill was distrusted by many Conservative MPs. This was because in 1900 he had started his Parliamentary life as one of their number, but four years later he had become a Liberal, and in 1924 he had reverted to being a Tory. He is reputed to have remarked 'Anyone can rat, but it takes a certain amount of ingenuity to re-rat.'

As a domestic politician Churchill made numerous errors during the course of his career. While he was serving as Home Secretary, he earnt the lasting hatred of large portions of the working class; he was regarded as having authorised the use of the Army against striking miners at Tonypandy in 1910 (the troops arrived after members of the Metropolitan Police had largely dispersed a crowd of strikers). As Chancellor of the Exchequer, he withdrew Britain from the gold standard and was widely blamed for the economic events that followed. His handling of the General Strike of 1926 was poor. In 1935 he opposed the Government of India Act. The following year he backed King Edward VIII during the Abdication Crisis.

Britain entered the Second World War in September 1939. Churchill was appointed to serve as First Lord of the Admiralty. In April 1940 a military expedition was mounted that sought to assist Norway. The Commons debated the venture on 7-8 May. In order to try to scare the government, when the House divided on the matter, many Conservatives either voted against it or abstained. These MPs did not anticipate that Prime Minister Neville Chamberlain would resign and they certainly did not want to see him replaced by a man whom they regarded as being a political adventurer. The premier left office on 10 May and the First Lord succeeded him. The new premier knew that large sections of his own party regarded him with hostility.

Until 1940 Private Offices had existed within the service departments but not in Downing Street. At the Admiralty Churchill had had one. When he became Prime Minister, he took it with him to guard against the possibility that his actions might be undermined by some of the No. 10 civil servants who might have felt that they had a greater loyalty to the previous incumbent than they had to him.

Chamberlain was appointed to serve as Lord President of the Council. During the summer of 1940 he supported Churchill steadfastly.

Had he not done so then the new premier might not have survived in office.

Churchill had served as the First Lord of the Admiralty from 1911 to 1915. During the First World War he had been the leading figure behind the attempt to force Turkey out of the conflict. This had involved the landing of a body of Allied troops upon the Dardanelles. The Turkish Army had repulsed the expedition. The episode had been a disaster for the Allies. It had instilled in the politician a sincere belief that the Chiefs of Staff should never be overridden in the execution of strategy. During the Second World War he never did so. This prompted a generation of historians to downplay his role in determining how the hostilities were conducted. It has been argued[1] that the reason why he never overruled the Chiefs was because they concurred with the overall approach that he had set in place. It was he who held back from opening the Western Front until the Nazis had been worn down upon the Eastern one and had overcommitted themselves to the Mediterranean theatre.

Location: No. 28 Hyde Park Gate, SW7 5DJ.

Website: www.chu.cam.ac.uk/archives/home.shtml

The ChurchillWar Rooms

The Churchill War Rooms were a shallow bunker from which Winston Churchill oversaw the British and Imperial military effort. The complex's construction had been started by the Chamberlain government in 1938. The facility was officially opened four days before Britain entered the conflict. During the war the burrow was continuously enlarged. By the end of the hostilities it was several acres in extent. It had steel roofs and lay beneath ten feet of reinforced concrete. However, it would probably not have been able to withstand a direct hit by an aerial bomb. In addition, there was always a strong risk that it might be flooded from below.

Despite the Rooms' purpose, Churchill was by no means given to cowering in the complex. Atavistic urges caused the premier to be enthralled by air raids. Often during them, he would wander through St James's Park bellowing out challenges to the Luftwaffe bombers overhead. He preferred to sleep above ground. Upon one occasion, he went to his bedroom in the Rooms, changed into his nightclothes, and climbed into his bed. He then stated to the detective who was his bodyguard that he had fulfilled the undertaking that he had made to his wife that he would go to bed in the Rooms and that he was going to get up and go upstairs in order to slumber.

[1]   By Carlo d'Este.

CHURCHILL WAR ROOMS

Churchill made his telephone calls to President Roosevelt from a cubicle-sized room that had a lock that could be switched so that externally it read either 'engaged' or 'vacant'.

Physically, Churchill was a brave man. Had the Nazis swept into Britain, it is improbable that the premier would have allowed himself to be hunted down in his bunker. If he had been forced to make his last stand in Westminster he would have done so from a pill-box in Parliament Square that had been camouflaged to look like a W.H. Smith bookstall.

The Rooms were opened to the public in 1984.

Location: The Clive Steps, King Charles Street, SW1A 3AQ.

See Also: MUSEUMS The Imperial War Museum; PERIOD PROPERTIES

Website: ww.iwm.org.uk/visits/churchill-war-rooms

Ditchley Park

Chequers is the prime ministerial country house. Its location in Buckinghamshire was known to the Luftwaffe'. Therefore, Churchill often used to invite himself to stay at Ditchley, the Oxfordshire home of Ronald Tree and Nancy Lancaster.[1] Not all of the Tree family took pleasure in the premier's capacity to give forth of his opinions at great length irrespective of the desire of those who were in his presence to retire for the night...or what might be left of it.

Website: www.ditchley.co.uk (The Ditchley Foundation seeks to promote Anglo-American relations. It has owned the house since 1958.)

French Trousers

Tim Clarke spent most of his working life as a ceramics specialist at Sotheby's the auction house. During the Second World War, he won a

---

[1]   Ditchley is a few miles north of Blenheim Palace, which had been Churchill's birthplace.

medal for removing a Frenchman's trousers. After the fall of France, the political situation in the Middle East had become fluid and it was uncertain as to whether the French authorities in the region would ally themselves to the Free French or to Vichy France. Clarke's military duties in Syria brought him into contact with a French officer whose loyalties were unclear. The auctioneer felt that the situation was of sufficient seriousness to warrant his detaining the man. He did this by debagging the fellow. When Brigadier-General de Gaulle heard of the incident he wanted Clarke to be court-martialled. However, at that particular juncture, Churchill regarded the Free French commander as being particularly irksome and so instead had Clarke gonged with a military MBE.

Locations: No. 4 Carlton Gardens, SW1Y 5AD. De Gaulle's headquarters.

Nos. 34-5 New Bond Street, W1A 2AA. Sotheby's.

Pamela Harriman

Pamela Harriman married Churchill's eldest son, Randolph, in October 1939. Her personal vitality and her capacity for adultery did much to foster the Anglo-American alliance during the Second World War. She was able to help persuade a number of President Roosevelt's senior emissaries that there was plenty of fighting spirit left in Britain. (Subsequently, she moved to the United States, became an American citizen, and involved herself in Democratic Party politics. She served the Clinton Administration as a diplomat.)

Historiography

The first wave of Churchill scholarship was dominated by Martin Gilbert's multi-volume biography of the man. This was published over the years 1966-1988. During the 1990s John Charnley and Clive Ponting produced revisionist studies. In the 2000s a third wave of books appeared. These tended to admire the politician.

CHURCH OF ENGLAND CHURCHES

See Also: BELLS; THE CHAPELS ROYAL; FOOD MARKETS Billingsgate Market; THE GREAT FIRE; HERITAGE; ST PAUL'S CATHEDRAL; WESTMINSTER ABBEY

Websites: http://anglicansonline.org/uk-europe/england/dioceses/london.html www.southwark.anglican.org www.london.anglican.org

All Saints Margaret Street

A deist chapel was opened on Margaret Street in the mid-18thC. Subsequently, the building was used as a proprietary chapel. During the 1840s it became a centre of the Tractarian Movement. The architect William Butterfield was commissioned to design a Gothic Revival style church on the site that reflected the congregation's High Church beliefs. As a young man, the architect had embraced Augustus Pugin's injunction to study Gothic design. Initially, his work had been derivative, however, with time he had forged his own approach. Through his work on All Saint's, Butterfield succeeded in freeing the Gothic Revival manner from the limiting confines of historical English Gothic. He did this by both importing approaches that had been used in European Gothic and using colour freely. The process of construction proved to be highly fraught both for the architect and for his clients. The building was consecrated in 1859. Butterfield found that some of the doctrinal views that were expressed within All Saints were worrying to him. As a result, he did not worship there although, as the edifice's architect, he continued to be involved with it until his death.[1]

Locations: No. 7 Margaret Street, W1W 8JG.
No. 4 Adam Street, WC2N 6AA. Butterfield's office.
See Also: PARLIAMENT The Palace of Westminster
Website: www.allsaintsmargaretstreet.org.uk

Chelsea Old Church

In 1528 Sir Thomas More had the southern portion of All Saints Chelsea rebuilt as his private chapel. The church's mid-20thC appearance derives

---

[1]   Butterfield's other London churches included St Matthias Stoke Newington (1853) and St Alban the Martyr Holborn (1862).

from the building having been struck by an aerial bomb in 1941. The 13thC exterior is commemorated on items of stationery that can sometimes be seen attached to the noticeboard by the building's entrance.

Location: Petyt Hall, No. 64 Cheyne Walk, SW3 5LT.

Website: www.chelseaoldchurch.org.uk

The Fifty New Churches Act of 1711

London's rapid physical growth at the start of the 18thC caused concerns to be expressed that the people who were living in its newer suburbs did not have ready access to Anglican places of worship. The Fifty New Churches Act of 1711 sought to furnish the wherewithal to build churches to serve their religious needs.

See Also: ROYAL STATUES Queen Anne, Queen Anne's Gate

The Friends of the City Churches

The Friends of the City Churches organisation was set up in 1994 in response to the Templeman Report. The document had stated that the City only needed four churches. The Friends thought otherwise.

Website: www.london-city-churches.org.uk

The Grosvenor Chapel

The Grosvenor Chapel (1730) was built in order to try to meet the religious needs of the growing population of Anglicans who lived upon the Grosvenor family's recently developed Mayfair estate. The building was a private undertaking. Its design was to become the model for numerous churches in New England.

The corpse of the notorious 18thC politician, controversialist and libertine John Wilkes was interred in the Chapel in 1797.

In 1829 the original 99-year lease on the site expired. The proprietary chapel became a chapel of ease for the Parish of St George's Hanover Square.

Location: South Audley Street, W1K 2PA. On the eastern side.

Website: www.grosvenorchapel.org.uk

St Andrew Undershaft

The Church of St Andrew Undershaft did not burn down during the Great Fire of 1666. However, by then the building was in a dilapidated physical condition. As a result, extensive restoration work was carried out upon it during the 1680s.

Location: St Mary Axe, EC3A 8(BS). On the eastern side of the junction with Leadenhall Street.

St Anne Soho

The Church of St Anne's Soho (1686) was destroyed by aerial bombing in 1940. The building's tower (1717) survived.

The church's garden, formerly its graveyard, is several feet above street level. This raised condition derives from the fact that many thousands of parishioners have been buried in it since the church was built in the late 17[th]C.

The detective fiction writer Dorothy L. Sayers was a churchwarden of St Anne's. Following her death, her corpse was cremated and her ashes were then scattered in the churchyard.

Location: No. 55 Dean Street, Soho, W1D 6AF.

Reading: Steven Johnson *The Ghost Map: A Street, An Epidemic and The Two Men Who Battled To Save Victorian London* Penguin (2008). A book that gives weight to the Rev Henry Whitehead's contribution to Dr John Snow's epidemiological achievement. As the local cleric, Whitehead had the community's trust. This was a major boon to the physician's research.

Website: http://stannes-soho.weebly.com

St Bride's Church

St Bride's was one of the four churches that rang out the City of London's curfew. During the 16[th]C the parish became associated with the printing industry. The Great Fire of 1666 destroyed the medieval St Bride's. A new building (1678) was designed for the site by Sir Christopher Wren.

During the 19[th]C and 20[th]C the church tended to the spiritual needs of members of the newspaper industry. In 1940 the building's structure was severely damaged by an aerial bomb. Subsequently, an archaeological investigation revealed that its crypt had been built above the remains of a Roman house. The church was reconstructed. In 1957 it was rededicated.

DVD: David Meara *Cathedral of Fleet Street* (2007).

Location: St Bride's Passage, EC4Y 8AU. At the eastern end.

See Also: WEATHER Lightning

Website: www.stbrides.com

Wedding Cakes: St Bride's Church's spire (1703) inspired William Rich (*d*.1811), a local pastry cook, to devise the tiered wedding cake.

Website: www.stbrides.com

St Clement Danes

The Church of St Clement Danes survived the Great Fire of 1666 unscathed. However, its structural infirmity led to the building, with the exception of its tower, being demolished. The new edifice (1680) was designed by Sir Christopher Wren. An extension (1720) to the tower was the work of James Gibbs.

Location: Strand, WC2R 1DH.

The Royal Air Force: From 1919 to 1955 the Royal Air Force's administrative headquarters was located in Adastral House, which was on the eastern corner of the junction of Aldwych and Kingsway. St Clement Danes was severely damaged by aerial bombing during the Second World War. The armed service contributed £150,000 towards the cost of the rebuilding work. The reconstruction was completed in 1958. The RAF holds commemoration services in the church. The building is also frequently used for the weddings of air force officers.

Website: www.raf.mod.uk/stclementdanes

St George's Bloomsbury Way

The Church of St George's Bloomsbury Way (1731) was erected under the Fifty New Churches Act of 1711. The building was designed by Nicholas Hawksmoor. In large part, it was constructed because the respectable parishioners, who inhabited the newly, developed northern portion of the Parish of St Giles-in-the-Fields, disliked having to pass through a notorious, thief-infested rookery, on their way to and from St Giles's.[1]

Location: Bloomsbury Way, WC1E 6DP.

See Also: CLASS

Website: www.stgeorgesbloomsbury.org.uk

St George: St George (*d.c.*303) was a Christian martyr who died at Lydda (in present-day Turkey). During the 6thC stories of his supposed exploits began to be attached to him. By the 12thC he had become associated with the slaying of a dragon. This development may have derived from the myth of Perseus, who is supposed to have fought a sea monster near the city.

St George became known to the English as a result of the Crusades. In the 14thC King Edward III made him the national saint. George was popular internationally. He is also the patron saint of Ethiopia, Georgia

---

[1] The rookery was the setting for William Hogarth's print *Gin Lane* (1751). The district was effectively destroyed by the construction of New Oxford Street (1849).

(the country), Istanbul, Russia, portions of Spain, and the Italian cavalry.
See Also: THE CITY OF LONDON The Sentinel Dragons

St Helen's Bishopsgate

St Helen's Bishopsgate was the City church that the great merchants favoured for the interring of their corpses. The likes of Sir John Crosby (*d.*1476) and Sir Thomas Gresham (*d.*1579) chose to have their remains lodged there.

Location: Great St Helen's, EC3A 6AT.
See Also: HALLS Crosby Hall
Website: www.st-helens.org.uk

St James's Piccadilly

St James's Piccadilly (1684) was erected to serve the neighbourhood that the Earl of St Albans had developed upon his St James's Fields estate. Although Sir Christopher Wren-designed and constructed dozens of churches, St James's was the only one that he ever built upon a new site.

In the early 18thC St James's was the most fashionable church in London; three of its vicars became Archbishops of Canterbury.

Location: No. 197 Piccadilly, W1J 9LL. On the southern side, opposite the southern end of Swallow Street.
Website: www.sjp.org.uk

St Margaret's Westminster

St Margaret's Westminster was founded in the 12thC by an Abbot of Westminster to provide for the spiritual needs of the Abbey's tenants and servants. In 1189 Pope Clement III exempted the church from the jurisdiction of the Bishop of London. In 1614 the House of Commons made St Margaret's its church. In 1840 the parish reverted to being part of the Diocese of London.

Location: St Margaret Street, SW1P 3JX. On the corner of the junction with Parliament Square.
See Also: WESTMINSTER ABBEY
Website: www.westminster-abbey.org/st-margarets

St Martin-in-the-Fields

The Church of St Martin-in-the-Fields (1726) was designed by James Gibbs. He combined a steeple with a Classical portico. The former rises out of the roof of the latter in a manner that was unprecedented. The innovative disposition was highly controversial. King George I endorsed the novelty by opting to become one of St Martin's churchwardens. Subsequently, the architectural arrangement became a commonplace feature of ecclesiastical buildings.

Royal births are recorded in the register of St Martin-in-the-Fields.

On the northern side of the chancel was the Royal Box. Opposite it sat the Lords of the Admiralty.

In 1829 St Martin's churchyard was cleared away to make space for Duncannon Street to be constructed in. Among those whose corpses had been buried there were: the orange vendor and royal mistress Nell Gwynne, the highwayman Jack Sheppard, the painter William Hogarth, the artist Sir Joshua Reynolds, and the furniture maker Thomas Chippendale.

Pat McCormick was the Vicar of St Martin-in-the-Fields from 1927 until his death thirteen years later. It was he who associated the church with homeless people. This is an identification that it actively maintains.

One past incumbent[1] has pointed out the way in which St Martin's possesses a number of paradoxes. It is called 'in-the-Fields' but is patently in the middle of the metropolis; it is the royal family's parish church yet it furnishes aid for people who are homeless; it is the Admiralty's official church, however, it is where the Peace Pledge Union was founded in 1934; and it was named after one of the patron saints of France but it is located by Trafalgar Square, which takes its name from the naval battle at which Napoleon's fleet was defeated decisively.

Location: St Martin's Place, WC2N 4JJ.

See Also: TRAFALGAR SQUARE; WESTMINSTER ABBEY Memorials and Graves, Doctors

Website: www.stmartin-in-the-fields.org

The Rector of Stiffkey: Harold Davidson was appointed as a curate of St Martin-in-the-Fields in 1905. The following year he was made the Rector of Stiffkey in Norfolk. However, he made frequent trips back to the metropolis, where he spent much of his time associating with prostitutes.

Eventually, his conduct brought him to the notice of the church authorities. In 1932, he was tried by the Norwich Consistory Court, which had been convened in London. Five charges had been brought against him. He was convicted of them and defrocked.

Davidson opted to exploit his notoriety in order to earn a living. In 1937 Skegness Amusement Park featured him in a display that was 'inspired' by *The Book of Daniel*. He was mauled by his co-performer (a

---

[1]   The Rev Nicholas Holtam, who in 2011 became the Bishop of Salisbury.

lion). He died in hospital while being treated for his injuries.

St Mary-le-Bow

St Mary-le-Bow (1087) was the first stone church to be built in London.[1] The main body of the medieval structure was destroyed by the Great Fire of 1666. However, its crypt survived the conflagration. It is the oldest ecclesiastical structure in the City. The church (1673) that stands above it was designed by Sir Christopher Wren.

Location: St Mary-le-Bow, Cheapside, EC4M 9DQ.

See Also: BELLS Bow Bells

Website: www.stmarylebow.co.uk

St Mary-le-Strand

A church stood on the site of the Church of St Mary-le-Strand as far back as 1147. The Church of the Nativity of Our Lady & The Innocents was pulled down by the 1st Duke of Somerset (*d*.1552). Its stones were used to help build the Lord Protector's mansion Somerset House. The churchless parishioners were allowed to worship in the Savoy Chapel.

St Mary-le-Strand (1717) was the initial place of worship to be built under the Fifty New Churches Act of 1711. It was the first public building that James Gibbs had designed. (The architect was a Roman Catholic but kept quiet about the fact. This was because of the prevailing sectarianism that then existed in some *strata* of contemporary society.)

Location: Strand, WC2R 1BA. To the north of King's College.

See Also: ROYAL RESIDENCES Somerset House

Website: www.stmarylestrand.org

St Olave's Hart Street

St Olave's Hart Street was named after Olave II Haraldssön, who fled from his native Norway after the King of Denmark had seized the Norwegian throne. In 1013 the exile helped the Saxon King Aethelred II the Unready to defeat the Danes who then controlled London Bridge. Two years later Olave - who during his lifetime was nicknamed 'the Fat' - returned to Norway to claim its throne, pledging himself to rid the country of paganism. He secured a greater ascendancy within Norway than anyone had been able to achieve previously. In 1164 he was canonised. He became the Scandinavian nation's patron saint.

The civil servant and diarist Samuel Pepys worshipped at St Olave's Hart Street. He used its Navy Office pew. That the church survived the

---

[1] The Saxons' churches had been wooden.

Great Fire of 1666 was due in large part to his efforts. He ensured that all of the wooden structures that were close to it were removed before the conflagration could reach them.

The corpse of Pepy's wife was interred beneath the church's nave in 1669, as was that of the official in 1703.

The Clothmakers' Company's original City church was St Dunstan-in-the-East. The building was destroyed by an aerial bomb in 1941. Subsequently, the guild transferred its affiliation to St Olave's. (The roofless St Dunstan's is now a pleasant, small park.)

Locations: St Olave Hart Street, EC3R 7NB. To the west of the junction with Seething Lane.

St Dunstan-in-the-East, St Dunstan's Hill, EC3R 8(HL).

See Also: THE GREAT FIRE OF LONDON The Fire, Surviving Churches

Website: www.sanctuaryinthecity.net/st-olaves.html (www.ahbtt. org.uk/history/st-dunstan-in-the-east)

St Paul's Covent Garden

The 4th Earl of Bedford developed the suburb of Covent Garden. He disliked the prospect of the expense of erecting a place of worship for the inhabitants of the new district. The peer commissioned Inigo Jones to design one. St Paul's (1633) was the first Anglican church to have been built in London since the Reformation. The earl wished to keep down its construction costs. Therefore, he instructed the architect to make sure

that it was plain as a barn, to which Jones replied that his lordship would have 'The handsomest barn in England.' The church was consecrated in 1638 and given its own parish in 1645.

St Paul's has long had a close association with the acting profession.
Location: Bedford Street, WC2E 9ED.
Website: www.actorschurch.org

St Paul's Knightsbridge

St Paul's Knightsbridge is a fashionable church. Many of its incumbents have gone on to become bishops. The Rev Donald Harris was its Vicar from the mid-1950s until the late 1970s. The clergyman was given to referring to his wealthier parishioners as 'trout'. Whenever he was due to be visited by one of them in the late afternoon he was given to declaring 'Trout for tea!' Strangely enough, he was not raised to the episcopal bench.

Location: No. 32a Wilton Place, SW1X 8SH. On the eastern side.
Website: www.stpaulsknightsbridge.org

St Stephen Walbrook

St Stephen Walbrook's medieval building was destroyed by the Great Fire of 1666. The church was reconstructed (1679) by Sir Christopher Wren. He used its design as an opportunity for experimenting with some of the ideas that he subsequently employed in the creation of St Paul's Cathedral.

Sir John Vanbrugh (*d*.1726) paid his fellow architect the compliment of choosing to have his own corpse interred in St Stephen's.

In the mid-1980s controversy was generated when it was proposed that a ten-ton, marble altar, that had been sculpted by Henry Moore, should be installed in St Stephen Walbrook. The Rev Dr Chad Varah had to take the matter before the Court of Ecclesiastical Causes. The body ruled that the church could receive the work.

Location: No. 39 Walbrook, Bank, EC4N 8BN.
Website: http://ststephenwalbook.net

The Savoy Chapel

The Queen's Chapel of The Savoy is the last physical remnant of the Savoy Palace. The present building (1864) was erected after a fire.

Location: Savoy Street, WC2R 0DA. On the western side.
See Also: PALACES, DISAPPEARED & FORMER The Savoy Palace
Websites: www.duchyoflancaster.co.uk/duties-of-the-duchy/ the-queens-chapel-of-the-savoy www.royal.gov.uk/
MonarchUK/Honours/RoyalVictorianOrder.aspx

Southwark Cathedral

The Church of St Saviour is an example of 13thC Gothic architecture. In 1897 the building was redesignated to be Southwark Cathedral. The first Bishop of Southwark was enthroned in 1905.

Location: Montague Close, London Bridge, SE1 9DA.
Website: http://cathedral.southwark.anglican.org

The Temple Church

The Temple Church is one of only four surviving round churches in England. It was built for the Knights Templars in the 12thC. It was modelled upon Jerusalem's Dome of the Rock. During the Reformation King Henry VIII took possession of the building. In the early 17thC King James I gave the freehold of its northern half to the Middle Temple and the one of its southern section to the Inner Temple. Members of the two Inns sit on separate sides of the nave from each other. The Crown retained the right to appoint the Temple Church's Master (chaplain). It is still a royal peculiar that functions outside of the control of the Diocese of London.

Location: Inner Temple Lane, Temple, EC4Y 7BB.
See Also: CHAPELS ROYAL
Website: www.templechurch.com

The Temple Church

THE CITY OF LONDON

See Also: BRIDGES; THE LORD MAYOR OF LONDON; MUSEUMS The Museum of London; ROMAN REMAINS; THE THAMES The City of London and The Thames

Website: www.cityoflondon.gov.uk/things-to-do/visiting-the-city/Pages/default.aspx www.cityoflondon.gov.uk/_layouts/col/ shop.aspx

The Freemen of London

Freemen of the City of London used to have a number of trading privileges within the settlement's walls. These gave them substantive commercial advantages over people who did not possess their status. The first recorded instance of the freedom being conferred dates from 1237. As part of the process of receiving it, an individual had to pay a hefty fee. During the late Middle Ages the money from these disbursements was a major source of income for the City Corporation. As a result, bestowal of the privilege was supervised by the City Chamberlain, whose principal role was to oversee the body's finances.

By the early 19thC the Corporation was the most efficiently run local authority in Britain. Therefore, when Parliament passed the Municipal Corporations Act of 1835 the City was not subjected to any major reforms. However, there was a growing general view that free trade brought the country material benefits. Therefore, the practice of settlements' freemen possessing commercial privileges was regarded as being against the broader national interest. Therefore, the measure ended most of these rights. In addition, it terminated the practice by which admission to London's freedom had been restricted to members of the livery companies. As a result, it became possible for the honour to be bestowed upon people as the result of patrimony and nomination. Liverymen who became freemen did retain a distinction from people who received the distinction but who were not members of a guild. The former were entitled to term themselves 'Citizens of London', whereas the latter were not.

Long ago the money from the freemen's fees ceased to be important to the Corporation's finances. Since the 19thC it has been assigned to the City of London Freemen's School in Ashtead, Surrey.

Each year the freedom is bestowed upon about 1700 people. The connection of some of them to the City of London can be held to be somewhat tangential. The status is conferred during ceremonies that are held in the Guildhall. These occasions are conducted by officials from the Chamberlain's Court. The recipient is required first to swear a short declaration about how s/he will conduct himself as a freeman and then to sign *The Freeman's Declaration Book*. S/he then receives a vellum document that sets out her/his status.

The freemen of the City of London still enjoy a number of historic privileges. The best known one of these is their right to drive sheep across London Bridge. Historically, it covered all livestock. That sheep have continued to be associated with the freedom stems from the centrality of the animal to the pre-modern English economy - it furnished wool that could be exported. Anyone who was not a freeman of the City had to pay a toll to take stock over the bridge or through the settlement's gateways. Therefore, the freemen held a commercial advantage over non-freemen. In the interests of avoiding traffic congestion, the right is not something that the former exercise at will. However, from time-to-time, with clearance from the City of London Police, sheep drives do occur. These are usually conducted in order to raise money for charity.

There are other freedoms. Should the death penalty be reinstated, freemen who may be convicted of murder would have the right to be suspercollated by a silken rope. How this might come to pass may stem from the combination of a couple of their other privileges. It is reputed that, within the Square Mile, they are allowed both to draw a sword and to be drunk and disorderly.

Locations: The Guildhall, Guildhall Yard, Gresham Street, EC2P 2EJ. London Bridge, SE1 9RA.

Website: www.cityoflondon.gov.uk/ about-the-city/ history-and-heritage/Pages/freedom-of-the-city.aspx (www.clfs.sch.uk) (wwwfreemenlondon.org - a North American body)

Good Numbers

Each year the new Lord Mayor is sworn in at the Royal Courts of Justice on the Strand. Another annual City of London ceremony takes place within the complex. Through this, the Corporation acknowledges that properties that it holds the leases of are owned ultimately by the Crown. A billhook and a scythe are paid for the Moors estate in Shropshire and six horse shoes and sixty-one nails for a property known as The Forge, which is located within the Parish of St Clement Danes. The procedure involves the City Solicitor leaving the Square Mile and going to the courts. There, s/he in the Office of the Queen's Remembrancer, s/he hands over the agricultural tools in recompense for the Salopian estate. Next, the Remembrancer asks the Solicitor, 'How many shoes have you?' The Solicitor counts out the six horse shoes and replies, 'Six shoes.' The Remembrancer responds, 'Good number.' The Remembrancer then asks the Solicitor how many nails does s/he have. The Solicitor counts out the nails and states, 'Sixty-one nails.' The Remembrancer replies, 'Good number.'

Location: The Royal Courts of Justice, Strand, WC2A 2LL. On the northern side to the east of the Aldwych.

See Also: THE LORD MAYOR OF LONDON The Lord Mayor's Procession

The Guildhall

The Guildhall is where the City of London is governed from. It is also where the City Corporation holds many of its principal events, such as banquets and elections.

The building takes its name from the Knighten Guild, a religious body. In the 11[th]C the group was granted a number of privileges by King Edward the Confessor. It was dissolved during the following century. When the original hall had been built is unknown. The present one dates from the 15[th]C.

Location: Guildhall Yard, Gresham Street, EC2P 2EJ.

See Also: HALLS; THE LORD MAYOR OF LONDON The Silent

Ceremony
Website: www.guildhall.cityoflondon.gov.uk

The Impact of The Great Fire
Upon The Governance of The City of London

The rebuilding of the City after the Great Fire of 1666 placed the Corporation's finances under immense pressure. In 1694 an Act of Parliament was used to bankrupt the local authority. Subsequently, one of the means that the Corporation utilised to raise money was to auction off a number of its principal civic offices, *e.g.* the City Marshal and the Keeper of Newgate.

Following the Jacobite Rebellion of 1745 the Crown rewarded the City's population for their loyalty. Control of the settlement's daily government was switched from the oligarchic Court of Aldermen to the more open and democratic Court of Common Council.

As the century progressed the local authority bought back the offices it had auctioned off. By the time that Sir Robert Peel proposed setting up the Metropolitan Police Force (1829), the City was able to take the stance that it did not wish to have a constabulary that derived its powers from a House of Commons that was itself in need of being reformed (which was to happen by means of the Great Reform Act of 1832).

In 1837 the Corporation was the only local government body in England that the Municipal Corporations Commission regarded as not being in need of improvement.

See Also: THE GREAT FIRE OF LONDON The Rebuilding of London; THE POLICE The City of London

The Remembrancer

The City of London office of Remembrancer was created in 1571 to act as a conduit between the City and the Crown. Initially, a large part of the position's purpose was centred upon reminding the latter of the amount of money that it had borrowed from the former. It oversees the Corporation's relationship with the government and Parliament. The office also supervises elections that are held within the City and ceremonial occasions such as the Lord Mayor's Procession.

The Remembrancer is allowed a seat on the floor of the House of Commons 'Under the Gallery'. This area is located behind the Serjeant-at-Arms's position. It lies beyond the Chamber's Bar. This presence derives from her/his role as a Parliament Agent (a lawyer who specialises in Parliamentary matters). The City official is not allowed to participate in the House's proceedings. However, s/he is permitted to examine legislation that may affect the City of London while the measures are still being drafted. These privileges are exercised at the discretion of the Speaker of the Commons.

See Also: THE LORD MAYOR OF LONDON The Lord Mayor's Procession; PARLIAMENT The Commons, The Commons Chamber, The Treasury Bench Ceremonialists

Meaty Rumblings: The character of the City's constitution came near to breaking point in 1994 when two separate elements felt driven to apply pressure upon the Corporation. Regulations that had originated in the European Union had required alterations to be made to the Victorian halls of Smithfield Meat Market. The local authority sought to pass on the cost of the building work to the meat traders by raising their rents. The dealers objected to this and threatened to take control of the Corporation by due electoral process in the City elections that were due to be held in June 1994.

This threat was particularly effective because the dealers were able to associate themselves with BP. The oil multinational's argument with the authority was that - despite being one of the City's largest individual employers - its opinions were not being given the weight by the Corporation that the company regarded as being appropriate. The two allies threatened to overturn the existing order by packing the ballot with voters who were sympathetic to their views. Such electors could have been enfranchised by means of a legal ruse that would have involved the sub-letting of property into units that had a minimum £10 rating value.

Before the year had ended the traders and the local government body reached an agreement over the rents. Therefore, the former withdrew their threat to overrun the latter by democratic procedure.

Location: Smithfield Market, West Smithfield, EC1A 9PQ.

The Sentinel Dragons

By the side of the principal roads into the City of London there are a series of plinths. Upon these are pedestals that are topped by individual dragons. The creatures look outwards from the settlement. Their purpose is to deter undesirables from entering it. With one claw, each of the fire-sneezers supports a shield. The devices sport the City's coat of arms. This was derived from the Cross of St George. In view of the fact that the knight became venerable for slaying a dragon, this situation is analogous to statues of Queen Marie Antoinette and King Louis XVI extolling the efficaciousness of Dr Guillotin's splendid chopping device.

Some might take the view that the local authority is subjecting its sentinels to degrading terms of service.

See Also: CHURCH OF ENGLAND CHURCHES St George's Bloomsbury Way, St George; STREET FURNITURE

Stratford Place

In 1439 Westminster Abbey granted the City of London the right to pipe water from the springs at Bayswater. The upwellings were inspected regularly by the Lord Mayor of London and various City dignitaries. A banqueting house was erected on what is now Stratford Place for the use of the officials after they had made their visits.

Location: Stratford Place, W1N 9(AE). On the northern side of Oxford Street, opposite Bond Street Underground Station.

CLASS

See Also: CHURCH OF ENGLAND CHURCHES St George's Bloomsbury Way; DEPARTMENT STORES; MEMORIALS The Cenotaph, Revolutionary Sod; TEA The Marquise Bethinks; WESTMINSTER ABBEY Memorials and Graves, Doctors

The College of Arms

The College of Arms issues coats of arms both to individuals and to corporate bodies. The institution is part of the Royal Household. Its officers conduct heraldic and genealogical research for which they charge fees.

In the Middle Ages heralds organised tournaments. The knights who attended these would have had their coats of arms emblazoned upon their shields. The heralds developed expertise about these emblems. Since the right to sport bearings was often dependent upon descent, the officials went on to become knowledgeable about genealogy.

In 1420 the royal heralds started acting as a corporate body. The College of Arms was founded in 1484. It was given a property at Coldharbour on Upper Thames Street. The following year King Henry VII seized the throne. He repossessed his predecessor's grant and conferred it upon his mother. The College was reincorporated in 1555.

The institution is overseen by the Earl Marshal. This office is held by the Dukes of Norfolk in a hereditary manner. Their graces' supervision was challenged by the heralds. In 1673 the issue was decided clearly in the Earl Marshal's favour. The heralds perform roles in some of the state ceremonies that are overseen by the official, such as coronations, the State Opening of Parliament, and State Funerals.

Location: Queen Victoria Street, EC4V 4BT. On the north-western side of the junction with Peter's Hill.

See Also: CORONATIONS Hereditary and Feudal Office-Holders; PALACES St James's Palace; PARLIAMENT The State Opening of Parliament

Website: www.college-of-arms.gov.uk

Gentlemen Executioners: The executioner Jack Ketch (*d*.1686) was given to terming himself an 'Esquire'. This was because one of his predecessors, Gregory Brandon, had been granted a coat of arms in 1616. It is believed

that the responsible official at the College had known neither Brandon's trade nor his reputation.

Cricket

At some county cricket grounds the 'gentlemen' and the 'players' used to have separate changing rooms from one another. On the scorecards the formers' initial would be placed before their surnames, while the latters' would be placed after theirs.

In 1932 Wally Hammond, a professional, switched to amateur status so that he could captain the England side. Two decades later Len Hutton declined to follow this example. He became the first professional player to lead the national team. In 1962 amateurism was abolished within the sport.

Locations: Lord's Cricket Ground, St John's Wood, NW8 8QN. Middlesex County Cricket Club.

The Oval, Kennington, SE11 5SS. Surrey County Cricket Club.

Websites: www.lords.org www.kiaoval.com

Sloane Rangers

In the October 1975 edition of the magazine *Harpers & Queen* there was an article that popularised the concept of the Sloane Ranger. In 1982 *The Official Sloane Ranger Handbook* was published.

Location: Sloane Square, Chelsea, SW1W 8(AN).

See Also: PUBS The Sloaney Pony

COLUMNS

See Also: ARCHES; THE GREAT FIRE The Rebuilding of London; MEMORIALS; ROYAL STATUES Queen Anne Queen Anne's Gate; STATUES

The Duke of York's Column

The Duke of York was the second son of King George III. The soldier-prince was neither a dashing commander nor a victorious one. Rather, he was a thorough administrator whose extensive labours did much to improve both the lot of the ordinary individual soldier and the standing of the Army in society.

In line with the old military tradition of 'being volunteered', the money for building his grace's Column (1834) was raised by every officer and soldier in the service forfeiting one day's pay. The duke's gaze is reputed to rest upon what was then the War Office building in Whitehall. His Royal Highness died deeply in debt. One wag commented that on top of his Column his statue would be out of the reach of his creditors.

Within the Column there are a set of steps. It used to be possible for members of the public to ascend these. This access ended after too many people had declined to use the same method to descend by.

Location: At the junction of Carlton House Terrace, SW1Y 5AF, with Waterloo Place, SW1Y 4(AU).

The Monument

St Margaret Fish Street Hill was the first church in the City of London to burn down during the Great Fire of 1666. Its parish was united with that of St Magnus the Martyr. The Monument (1677) was erected on what had been the site of St Margaret's.

The 202ft-tall column has 311 steps within it. The base is 202ft from the site where the Fire broke out. Its location made it the domi-nating presence visually to anyone who was travelling northwards over the pre-1831 London Bridge.

The structure commemorates not so much the occurrence of the Fire as the success of Londoners in rebuilding their city within the space of a few years. People who ascended the column were able to look down upon on what had been achieved.

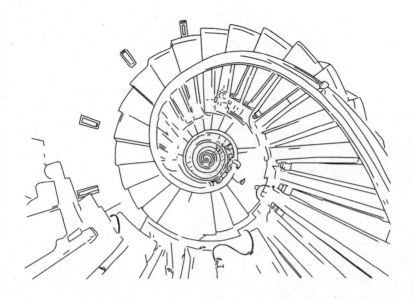

The Monument was designed jointly by Sir Christopher Wren and Robert Hooke. The pair had their own agenda with regard to its construction. They ensured that it had the scope to be used as an instrument for a number of scientific experiments that they were interested in performing. However, the impact of vibrations caused by passing traffic meant that many of these were never carried out.

One matter upon which the two men differed from one another was as to what should be placed upon the structure's summit. Wren believed that it should be capped by a statue of King Charles II, while Hooke was of the opinion that it ought to be a flaming urn that would symbolise the Fire. The latter carried the matter. The gilt crown adds a further 42ft to the column's height.

The railings at the top of the Monument were put in place in 1842 in order to prevent suicides.

Location: The Monument, Monument Street, EC3R 8AH.

See Also: ARCHES The Temple Bar; BRIDGES London Bridge; THE GREAT FIRE The Rebuilding of London; VISITOR ATTRACTIONS The London Eye

Websites: www.themonument.info www.cityoflondon.gov.uk/ things-to-do/visiting-the-city/attractions-museums-galleries/ Pages/ default.aspx

GALLERIES, PALACES & TEA

Nelson's Column

At the Battle of Trafalgar (1805) the naval commander Lord Nelson vanquished a combined Franco-Spanish fleet. The victory gave Britain and her allies the initiative in their struggle against Napoleon. It was widely celebrated at the time. However, the construction of Nelson's Column (1849) did not begin until 1839, 34 years after the sea battle had taken place. That a structure was erected owed something to inter-service rivalry and the building of the Army-funded Duke of York's Column (1834). Nelson's admirers were able to exploit the prior completion of his grace's support to commission a structure that was taller than it.

The statue of Nelson that stands on top of the Column is over seventeen-feet-tall. The commander's actual height was nearer to five feet (1.52m) than it was to six (1.83m).

Locations: Trafalgar Square, WC2N 5DS.

No. 103 New Bond Street, W1Y 6LG. On the western side, to the south of the junction with Blenheim Street. Nelson's home during his 1798 shore-leave.

See Also: TRAFALGAR SQUARE

Landseer's Lions: There are four sculpted lions at the Column's base.[1]

Sir Edwin Henry Landseer was an animal artist who was not interested in simply painting his subjects. He felt a need to set them in the context of a narrative, of which the picture would be a record of the key dramatic moment. *Alpine Mastiffs Reanimating A Distressed Traveller* (1820), which was set in the St Bernard Pass, created the myth that St Bernards have a collar around their necks from which hangs a small barrel that contains brandy.[2] The spirit was supposed to help revive travellers who had been caught in the snow.

In 1857 Landseer was offered the commission of fashioning the lions that were to be sited at the foot of Nelson's Column. He accepted the task knowing full well that he had a limited knowledge of sculptural technique. He spent a decade working on the project. When the leonine quartet was unveiled in 1867 his work was greeted as being a success. However, by then, critical opinion had swung in favour of the Pre-Raphaelites and Aestheticism so that Landseer's own style of painting was passing out of fashion.

Following the announcement of the artist's death, wreaths were placed around the lions' manes.

---

[1]   Sea-lions would have had a more maritime air to them, if a less formal one.

[2]   A strain of mastiffs had been bred so that they looked like the true St Bernard, which had become extinct.

Seven Dials

Seven Dials is a junction where several roads converge. The original Seven Dials column stood at its centre. The development of the surrounding district had been initiated by Thomas Neale, who was the Master of the Mint during the 1690s.

With time, the area came to regarded as being a slum and a thieves' den. In 1773 the column was taken down. This was an attempt at social engineering; it was thought that the structure provided a gathering place for anti-social personages. (It does not seem to have been considered that by dismantling it the space for such elements to assemble in was being enlarged.) The structure went on to lead a peripatetic life. Finally, it was re-erected on Weybridge Green in deepest, darkest Surrey.

The column that was raised at Seven Dials in 1989 is a replica of the original one.

Location: Seven Dials, WC2H 9(DD).

See Also: ROYAL STATUES Queen Anne St Paul's Cathedral

CORONATIONS

Every English and British sovereign since King Harold (*d*.1066) - with the exceptions of King Edward V (*d*.1483) and King Edward VIII (*d*.1972) - has been crowned in Westminster Abbey.

Location: The Sanctuary, SW1P 3PA.

See Also: ROYALTY; WESTMINSTER ABBEY

Website: www.westminster-abbey.org/our-history/royalty/ coronations

The Coronation Chair

The Coronation Chair in Westminster Abbey is the oldest dated piece of furniture in Britain. It was made by the king's painter Walter of Durham. The Chair was first used in 1399 when King Henry IV was crowned. It has been part of every coronation since the 14thC, with the exception of that of Queen Mary I (*d*.1558). She considered the seat to have been tainted by the Protestantism of her predecessor - and younger brother - King Edward VI. The Chair has left the Abbey only three times: for the installation of Oliver Cromwell as Lord Protector (1653) in Westminster Hall, and for safety during the two World Wars.

Website: www.westminster-abbey.org/visit-us /highlights/ the-coronation-chair

Hereditary and Feudal Office-Holders

A handful of court offices are hereditary. The coronation provides these officials with roles to execute. The Earl Marshal is central to the ceremony's organisation. The office has long been in the possession of the Dukes of Norfolk. Many of their graces have been Roman Catholics. The coronation can be said to be one of the most Anglican of ceremonies, as one portion of it involves the new sovereign swearing to act as the Defender of the Faith.

During the ceremony, the hereditary Champion calls upon anyone who wishes to dispute the new sovereign's claim to the throne to fight him (the Champion). The office has long been held by the Dymoke family of Scrivelsby, Lincolnshire.

The Dukes of St Albans are the Grand Falconers. Their graces are descended patrilineally from one of King Charles II's illegitimate sons by Nell Gwynne. In 1953 the 12th duke proposed taking a live falcon to Queen Elizabeth II's coronation. He was told that he should bring either a stuffed bird or nothing. Given these two alternatives, his grace opted for a third one of his own creation and did not attend the ceremony.

Some roles are executed by people who have inherited or acquired particular lordships of manors. The Lordship of Worksop carries with it the right to support the sovereign's right arm at her/his coronation (provided that the Earl Marshal's Court of Claims has judged the holder of the lordship to be 'fit and proper' to do so). In 1994 the title was sold at auction. It was bought for £40,000 by John Hunt, a retired businessman.

See Also: CLASS The College of Arms; PARKS St James's Park, Birdcage Walk; PARLIAMENT The State Opening of Parliament

Website: www.royal.gov.uk/TheRoyalHousehold/OfficialRoyalposts/EarlMarshal.aspx www.royal.gov.uk/TheRoyalHousehold/OfficialRoyalposts/LordGreatChamberlain.aspx

In Most Respects

The 7th Earl of Harewood was a music-loving cousin of Queen Elizabeth. He had progressive artistic tastes. At his suggestion, Buckingham Palace commissioned the composer Benjamin Britten and the librettist William Plomer to write an opera to mark the 1953 coronation. The pair opted for the subject of Queen Elizabeth I. The resulting composition, *Gloriana*, was premiered during the summer of 1953. The piece was about a raddled and cantankerous despot. It did not chime with the upbeat note that the Palace had been seeking to strike.

It is reputed that upon one occasion Her Majesty remarked of her kinsman, 'Funny thing about George. You know, in most respects he's perfectly normal.'[1]

Location: No. 2 Orme Square, W2 4RS. Harewood's townhouse at the time of the coronation.

Oil

Sir Theodore Turquet de Mayerne (*d*.1655) was a Geneva-born Huguenot.

---

[1]   During the Second World War the future earl fought in Italy. He became a prisoner-of-war in 1944. He was soon identified as being a nephew of King George VI. He was taken to Colditz, where the *Prominenten* prisoners were held. He used his time there to develop his musical education by reading Sir George Grove's multi-volume reference work *A Dictionary of Music & Musicians*. When the conflict ended the aristocrat was on the letter 'T'. Many years later, when he was asked what his incarceration had been like, he replied that it had not been too bad and that the food had been better than it had been at Eton.

He studied at the University of Montpellier, which was then a stronghold of Protestantism. It was he who furnished the recipe for the oil that is still used to anoint British monarchs during their coronations.

Location: Lindsey House, Nos. 91-104 Cheyne Walk, SW10 0DQ. The knight-physician's home.

The Regalia

In 1303 the Crown Jewels were moved from Westminster Abbey to the Tower of London, where they were deposited in the Wardrobe Tower.

During the English Republic of 1649-1660 the regalia was either melted down or sold off. (In the Civil Wars the City of London had supported Parliament against King Charles I; the survival of large quantities of medieval guild plate testifies to the efficacy of backing the winning side during a conflict.)

The monarchy was restored in 1660. By then, the anointing spoon, the ampulla (a vessel for oil) and some individual jewels were all that survived of the Crown Jewels. The goldsmith Sir Robert Vyner oversaw the preparation of the regalia that was used during the coronation of King Charles II the following year.

The Royal Collection's jewels date largely from the end of the 19thC after Queen Victoria had had herself made Empress of India (1877) and South Africa's diamond and gold mines had started disgorging. Prior to that era the royal family had hired the precious stones that they had sported during coronations. These had then been set in the crowns temporarily.

Location: The Tower of London, EC3N 4AB.

See Also: MUSEUMS The Ranger's House Greenwich Park; THE TOWER OF LONDON Captain Blood

Websites: www.royal.gov.uk/MonarchUK/Symbols/TheCrown Jewels.apsx   www.hrp.org.uk/TowerOfLondon/stories/crownjewels

The Stone of Scone

The Stone of Scone - or Stone of Destiny - is an unprepossessing 336 *lb* (152 *kg*) lump of yellow sandstone that became a talisman of Scotland's nationhood. There are folk traditions that are associated with it that claim that it came from Ireland or the Middle East. In 1296 King Edward I of England took the Stone south of the border. He installed it in Westminster Abbey the following year.

In December 1950 the rock was taken from the Abbey by four young Scots who were members of the Scottish Covenant Association, an organisation that was seeking home rule for Scotland rather than full independence.[1] The following April, the block was recovered from the high altar of the ruined Arbroath Abbey and returned south.

In 1996 the Stone was moved to Edinburgh Castle in Scotland. It was intended that it would be brought back temporarily to Westminster Abbey for future coronations.

Website: www.westminster-abbey.org/visit-us/highlights/ the-coronation-chair

The Tower of London

During the Middle Ages and the Early Modern period it was customary for a monarch to sleep in the Tower of London on the night before her or his coronation in Westminster Abbey. Oliver Cromwell stripped the fortress-prison of most of its royal-associated furnishings. As a result, the tradition was not continued following the restoration of the monarchy in 1660.

Location: The Tower of London, EC3N 4AB.

See Also: PALACES, FORMER & DISAPPEARED

---

[1]   The theft has come to overshadow the fact that the Association managed to organise a petition that collected two million signatures that sought home rule.

DEPARTMENT STORES

Most of London's department stores grew out of extant drapery shops. During the second half of the 19thC a number of factors combined to assist their development. Foremost among these were the example of the Great Exhibition of 1851 and the opening of Le Bon Marché store in Paris the following year. The latter had demonstrated how a vast array of goods could be displayed within a single building. In addition, advances in glass and gas technology meant that wares could be presented in a more attractive manner than had been the case up until then and that shops could be lit more brightly than they had been.

In the later 19thC the stores' clientele shifted from being predominantly the aristocratic residents of the West End to being the middle classes of the mushrooming suburbs and the Home Counties beyond them. These new customers would travel into London for the day by train. Their purchases were price sensitive. The resulting lower profit margins forced the retailers to expand their product ranges in order to maintain their profitability. Larger businesses required bigger premises.

The Oxford Street department stores, notably Selfridges, are sited in the section of the road that lies to the west of Oxford Circus.

Locations: Oxford Street, W1N 9(HA) and W1R 5(FB).

Regent Street, W1R 7(FB) and W1R 5(TB).

See Also: ARCADES; CLASS; PUBS Gin Palaces;
SHOPPING

Websites: http://oxfordstreet.co.uk   www.regentstreetonline.com

Debenhams

Debenhams grew out of a drapery shop that was established on Wigmore Street in 1778. In 1813 William Debenham joined the partnership. Five years later the firm opened its first non-London outlet in Cheltenham.

In 1919 Debenhams acquired Marshall & Snelgrove. Seven years later the Debenham family allowed their controlling interest in the business to be bought out. In the post-1945 era the company was by far the largest owner of provincial department stores in Britain.

Location: Nos. 334-348 Oxford Street, W1C 1JG. (The former Marshall & Snelgrove premises.)

Website: www.debenhams.com

Fortnum & Mason

Hugh Mason had a shop in St James's Market. His lodger William Fortnum worked as a servant in the royal household. The perks of the latter's position included the right to dispose of any candles that had not been finished. Mason sold these in his store. In 1707 the pair set up a stall in Piccadilly on the site of the present-day shop. (Members of the Fortnum family continued to serve in the royal household.)

Fortnum & Mason's reputation was aided by the Great Exhibition of 1851. The store's food displays were one of the sights that many visitors included upon their itinerary of London.

Fortnum & Mason's hampers became standard fare for Britain's ruling classes during the 19thC, whether it was for fighting wars in distant lands or for having a day at the races.

In 1896 the American entrepreneur Henry J. Heinz chose the store to be the first outlet for his canned foods in Britain.

Location: No. 181 Piccadilly, W1A 1ER. On the southern side, to the east of Duke Street St James's. To the west of Hatchard's.

Website: www.fortnumandmason.com

Harrods

In 1849 Henry Charles Harrod acquired a small grocer's shop in the village of Knightsbridge. Twelve years later his son Charles Digby Harrod purchased the business from him. The store benefited from the westward growth of London from Belgravia. By the 1880s, Harrods was employing a hundred shop assistants. In 1883 its building was destroyed by a fire. The emporium was rebuilt with remarkable speed.

In 1889 Harrod *fils* sold the enterprise to a limited liability company. Two years later Richard Burbridge was appointed to be the store's general manager. He took the business upmarket. In 1898 Harrods installed the first escalator in London. It has been claimed that at its top an attendant dispensed brandy to those customers who had been overcome by the experience of the ride.

Eric Newby, the author of *A Short Walk In The Hindu Kush* (1958), attributed his desire to wander the Earth to his mother having taken him along with her on her visits to Harrods. To him the wonders that were to be found overseas were hinted at both by the contents of the Food Hall and by the displays of silk.

For several years Roland 'Tiny' Rowland, the head of the Lonrho conglomerate, had a running public conflict with the al Fayed brothers, over the Egyptians' 1985 purchase of Harrods and the House of Fraser department stores business. The dispute was 'officially' ended in 1993 when the al Fayeds and Mr Rowland joined together in lowering a pair of sharks that the Egyptians had had hung in the Food Hall - the larger shark had been symbolically eating the tail of the smaller one. In 2010 the sibs sold the business to a Middle Eastern investment concern.

After dark the store's external structure is lit by thousands of light bulbs. It is a delightful sight, especially so when it is come across unexpectedly.

Location: Nos. 87-135 Brompton Road, Knightsbridge, SW1X 7XL. On the southern side, to the north-east of Hans Road.

Website: www.harrods.com

A Simian Transportation: The Kangaroo Gang was a loose collective of criminals that centred upon half-a-dozen gifted Antipodean shoplifters. The group coalesced in the early 1960s because its operation enhanced the capacity of its members to rob London's numerous upmarket shops.

The Gang's activities included stealing specific items to order. There is a story that upon one occasion, a client commissioned some of its members to pinch a young chimpanzee from the Harrods Pets' Department. The criminals appreciated that in order for them to be able to execute the theft successfully they would have to have a means of transporting the ape during the time that it would take them to walk from the Department to the street outside. There was a real risk that during this passage the animal would draw attention to them by shrieking. They could not gag the beast for fear of killing it. They needed a means to normalise any possible piercing utterances that it might make.

The solution to the problem proved to be simple. The shoplifters started their heist by going to the store's Baby & Toddlers' Department. There, they stole a perambulator. This they wheeled to the Pets' Department, where they filched the simian, securing it firmly within the pram. They then made a leisurely exit out onto the public thoroughfare.

Reading: Adam Shand *The Kangaroo Gang: Arthur 'The King' Delaney* Allen & Unwin (2010).

Harvey Nichols

Benjamin Harvey (*d*.1850) opened a linen shop in Knightsbridge. This enterprise grew to be the Harvey Nichols department store. The business has been on its present site since 1880.

In 1991 Harvey Nichols was bought by Dickson Concepts, a company that was owned by Dickson Poon, a Hong Kong-based businessman. Five years later Harvey Nichols opened a second department store in the Yorkshire city of Leeds. Other outlets followed in Birming

-ham, Bristol, Dublin, Edinburgh, and Manchester.

Location: Nos. 109-125 Knightsbridge, SW1X 7RJ. To the east of the junction with Sloane Street.

Website: www.harveynichols.com

The House of Fraser

The House of Fraser was built up as a department store business by Sir Hugh Fraser 1st Bt (*d*.1966), a Glaswegian. His son, the 2nd baronet, was also a gifted retailer. However, in the 1970s the business was hit hard both by the development of specialist rivals, such as Mothercare and Laura Ashley, and by the impact upon consumers of the oil price rises. Sir Hugh *fils*'s interest switched to compulsive gambling. The business passed out of the control of the Fraser family.

Location: No. 318 Oxford Street, W1C 1HF.
Website: www.houseoffraser.co.uk

The Army & Navy Stores: The Army & Navy Stores department store business was established as a co-operative for military personnel and their families. It enabled them to buy goods at prices that were lower than those that were being charged in the West End's *emporia*. In 1872 the firm's store was opened in Victoria. In 1918 - to offset its falling membership[1] - the co-operative opened its outlets to the general public. In 1976 House of Fraser bought the business.

In 2005 the Army & Navy assumed its parent's name. 'A&N' can still be seen above the black-edged Howick Place street entrances to the southern portion of the store.

Location: No. 101 Victoria Street, SW1E 6QX.

Peter Jones

In 1868 Peter Jones opened a draper's shop in Hackney. Nine years later he acquired premises at Nos. 4-6 The King's Road, Chelsea. In 1906 the store was bought for £20,000 cash by John Lewis, a former employee who had become a competitor. Without Mr Jones's presence, the Sloane Square store began to decline. To reverse this state of affairs, Mr Lewis made over the Chelsea business to his own eldest son John Spedan Lewis. However, Lewis *père* insisted that his offspring should first work a full day at the John Lewis store on Oxford Street before attending to the affairs of its Sloane Square sister.

Lewis *fils* suffered a bad riding accident in 1909. It took him two years to recuperate from it. While doing so, he considered the future of the business that he was going to inherit. He developed his own ideas about retailing and then used his control of Peter Jones to implement them. As a result, he and his father fell out with one another. The son went to work in Sloane Square full-time.

When John Lewis made a private visit to the Chelsea store, he was favourably struck by what he saw there. Both men now possessed an appreciation of the achievements of the other. They were soon reconciled. Eventually, John Spedan Lewis was given control of all of the Lewis family's retailing businesses.

Location: Sloane Square, Chelsea, SW1W 8EL.

Website: www.johnlewis.com/our-shops/peter-jones

John Lewis

John Lewis worked as a buyer in Peter Robinson's store in Chelsea's Sloane Square before setting up on his own as a retailer. In 1864 he opened his first shop on the western corner of the junction of Oxford Street and

---

[1]   The First World War finished the same year.

Holles Street (the site is now covered by part of the company's flagship outlet). Using retained profits, he built the business up into one of the avenue's principal department stores.

In 1897 Lewis acquired Cavendish Buildings on the southern side of Cavendish Square. He did this with the intention of enlarging his premises northwards so that the shop floor would run through from Oxford Street to the square. People who lived in townhouses on the latter opposed his plan because they were concerned that the change would commercialise its character. The issue went to law and, when Lewis defied a court injunction on the matter, it led to his spending a brief spell incarcerated in Brixton Prison. On appeal, the retailer carried the question and extended his store.

John Spedan Lewis, Lewis's son, was interested in the subject of employee-ownership. In 1929 he transferred his shares to a trust 'for the happiness of all its members'; the John Lewis Partnership was set up to take control of those assets. When the trust was established it was set to expire 21 years after the death of the final descendant of King Edward VII who had been alive at the time of its creation. The only one left is Queen Elizabeth II.

Location: No. 300 Oxford Street, W1A 1EX. On the eastern side of the junction with Old Cavendish Street and Holles Street.

See Also: CHARLES DICKENS Jarndyce *vs.* Jarndyce

Websites: www.johnlewispartnership.co.uk www.johnlewis.com

Lights Out: Despite having a home in Mayfair, the BBC Radio music producer Bernie Andrews was notorious for his frugality. He was given to returning light bulbs to John Lewis if he was of the opinion that they had lasted insufficiently long.

Liberty & Company

Arthur Lasenby Liberty started his retail career as a sales assistant in *Messrs.* Farmer & Rogers, a Regent Street emporium. In 1862 he visited the International Exhibition that was being held in South Kensington and was struck by the potential that products from East Asia, and particularly those made in Japan, might have as retail items. He persuaded his employers to stock some and was proven to have been right. However, he was denied a partnership in the firm. Therefore, he decided to set up in business for himself.

In 1875 Liberty opened his store. He was soon taken up by the fashionable world. The stylistic innovations that he made included the use of pastel colours. The retailer became an important figure in the era's decorative arts movements. His tastes influenced the Pre-Raphaelite painters and the Aesthetic Movement. For the original production of Gilbert & Sullivan's *Patience* (1881) the costumes were made from Liberty fabrics.

The distinct character of Liberty's premises derive from the combination of the flair of the firm with the conservatism of its landlord the Crown Estate. It is reputed that the timber beams in the building's façade were cannibalised from the naval vessel *H.M.S. Impregnable*.

Location: Great Marlborough Street, W1B 5AH. On the southern side of the western end.

See Also: ST PAUL'S CATHEDRAL The Crypt
Website: www.liberty.co.uk

Selfridges

Harry Gordon Selfridge was an American[1] who had made his reputation as the general manager of Marshall Field's retail department in Chicago. He believed that the British knew how to make goods but not how to sell them. He arrived in London in 1906 with a plan to build the finest store that the metropolis had ever seen. Sam Waring, of the Waring & Gillow furniture store, backed Selfridge financially on the condition that the retailer would not sell any furniture.

In 1909 the Selfridges department store opened on Oxford Street. It revolutionised Britain's shopping. Its innovations included: a credit scheme, a bargain basement, annual sales, inventive window displays, and its allowing the public to inspect goods at their own leisure. The 1920s were the establishment's golden era. In 1928 the world's first sale of a television set took place in the store.

While Selfridge's wife Rose had been alive his personal conduct had been orderly and conventional. However, following her death in 1918, he had taken to cultivating an exotic private life and spending money freely. He had moved into Lansdowne House, a splendid townhouse in Fitzmaurice Place. In the economic downturn of the 1930s the retailer found himself to be unable to operate so effectively. In 1939 the company's board compelled him to resign. His final years were spent living in straitened circumstances in Putney.

Locations: No. 400 Oxford Street, W1N 9(HE). On the eastern side of the junction with Orchard Street.

Lansdowne House, Fitzmaurice Place, W1J 5JD.
See Also: SHOPPING Whiteley's
Website: www.selfridges.com

---

[1]   Selfridge was to become a British citizen.

CHARLES DICKENS

Website: www.dickensfellowship.org

Detective Fiction

The creation of the Metropolitan Police's detective department in 1842 has led to it being possible to make a case for the character of Mr Nadgett, in Charles Dickens's *Martin Chuzzlewit* (1844), being the first proper private detective in English literature.

Jonathan Whicher, who conducted the Road Hill House inquiry, became the model for Collins's character Sergeant Cuff. The man's achievements also informed Charles Dickens's *The Mystery of Edwin Drood* (1870).

The Dickens House Museum

Following the success of *The Pickwick Papers* (1836) Charles Dickens was able to afford the £80 *p.a.* rent for No. 48 Doughty Street. The writer and his family moved into the house in 1837. While they were living there, he wrote both *Oliver Twist* (1838) and *Nicholas Nickleby* (1839). In 1839 the Dickenses moved to No. 1 Devonshire Terrace, which was a larger property.

In 1923 the Dickens Fellowship bought both Dickens's house in Doughty Street and one of the properties that neighbours it. Two years later The Dickens House Museum opened.

Location: No. 48 Doughty Street, WC1N 2LX. On the eastern side, to the south of Guilford Street.

See Also: MUSEUMS

Website: www.dickensmuseum.com

Jarndyce vs. Jarndyce

From 1733 until 1883 the Court of Chancery sat in Lincoln Inn's Old Hall (1492). The fictional lawsuit of Jarndyce *vs.* Jarndyce in Dickens's novel *Bleak House* (1853) is meant to have been heard there. The writer modelled it upon the real, decades-long Thelusson case. The merchant Peter Thelusson (*d*.1797) had died in possession of a fortune of over £600,000. He had left it tied up in a legal settlement that was intended to operate

until the time of the death of his final surviving great-grandson. The large amount of money that was involved prompted litigation between his descendants. The matter was determined finally by a ruling that the House of Lords made in 1857. This was four years after *Bleak House* had been published.[1]

Location: Lincoln's Inn, WC2A 3TL.

See Also: DEPARTMENT STORES John Lewis; HALLS Lincoln's Inn The Old Hall; PALACES, DISAPPEARED & FORMER The Savoy Palace; ROYAL STATUES King William III St James's Square

Website: www.lincolnsinn.org.uk/index.php/history-of-the-inn/historic-buildings-ca/the-old-hall

The Old Curiosity Shop

The shop that Dickens's novel *The Old Curiosity Shop* (1841) referred to was probably one in Orange Street. Its site is now occupied by a statue (1910) of the actor Sir Henry Irving that was sculpted by Thomas Brock.

Location: Orange Street, WC2H 7(HH). At the southern end of Charing Cross Road.

See Also: PERIOD PROPERTIES The Old Curiosity Shop

Please, Sir!

Under the provisions of the St Paul Covent Garden Poor Relief Act of 1775 a workhouse was built in fields that lay to the west of the northern portion of Tottenham Court Road. For the St Paul's vestrymen, the building physically placed the parish's most needy souls at a distance from their own homes and businesses.

The property accommodated elderly people. It was constructed on an H pattern. A burial ground was created at its back. The building was extended several times, thereby covering its graveyard. It became so large that it could house several hundred residents at a time.

There is no clear written evidence to indicate that Dickens used the complex as the basis for the institution in *Oliver Twist* (1838). However, the writer spent two spells in his youth, totalling five years, living nine doors along the street from the workhouse in a property that stood on the corner of Cleveland Street with Tottenham Street. It is improbable

---

[1]   The settlement of the case seems to have prompted the members of one branch of the Thelusson family to refurbish their residence at Brodsworth near Doncaster in Yorkshire. Subsequently, the property was not changed. As a result, it is one of the few surviving examples of unaltered High Victorian country house interior decoration.

that the establishment did not inform in part his creation of the novel.

In 1856 Joseph Rogers was appointed to be the establishment's medical officer.[1] He proved to be a reformer. In 1868 the workhouse combined with the one that was run by St Martin-in-the-Fields to become the Strand Union. As a result of Dr Rogers's efforts the enlarged institution was redesignated an infirmary in 1873. In 1913 it merged with a number of others to become part of the City of Westminster Union. The building was acquired by the Middlesex Hospital, which used it as a working hospital while its own principal site was being rebuilt. It then served a variety of medical uses. Until 2006 it was the out-patients department.

Locations: Strand Union Workhouse, No. 44 Cleveland Street, W1T 4JT. On the eastern side, to the south of the junction with Howland Street.

No. 22 Cleveland Street (formerly No. 10 Norfolk Street), W1T 4(HZ). (Dickens's former home.)

No. 33 Dean Street, W1D 4PW. Dr Rogers's home. On the western side, south of the junction with Bateman Street.

Reading: Ruth Richardson *Dickens and The Workhouse: Oliver Twist and The London Poor* Oxford University Press (2012).

Websites: http://clevelandstreetworkhouse.org/dickens
www.workhouses.org.uk

---

[1] The physician took the position because nearly all of his paying patients had died during a cholera outbreak. (It was the one that John Snow studied.)

DOWNING STREET

Downing Street was built for Sir George Downing 1st Bt, who was the Secretary of the Treasury from 1667 to 1671.

No. 10 Downing Street

In 1732 King George II offered No. 10 Downing Street to his then 1st Lord of the Treasury (Prime Minister) Sir Robert Walpole as a personal gift. The politician appreciated the jaded way in which some backbench MPs might choose to interpret such an instance of royal generosity. Therefore, he accepted the house on condition that the property was given to him in his official capacity and not to him in his private one. As a consequence, when the knight fell from power in 1742, he left No. 10 for his successors as premier to occupy.

The street *façade* of the property belies what has become in reality a small office block that houses the Prime Minister's Private Office. Some premiers have used the building purely as a place of work, preferring to continue to reside in their own grander townhouses.

There are two front doors to No. 10. This means that one can be maintained while the other one is in use. Neither of them has a keyhole. The portal is always opened from within.

Locations: No. 10 Downing Street, SW1A 2AA. To the west of Whitehall.

No. 5 Arlington Street, SW1A 1RA. Walpole's own townhouse.

See Also: ROYALTY The Constitution, The Prime Minister and The Sovereign

Website: www.gov.uk/government/history/10-downing-street

No. 11 Downing Street

No. 11 Downing Street is the official residence of the Chancellor of the Exchequer (the finance minister). Until the early 19thC a number of Prime Ministers served as both First Lord of the Treasury and Chancellor. After 1835 it became the usual practice for the two offices to be held separately from one another.

Since the mid-19thC Chancellors have taken their Budget speeches to the House of Commons in the Budget box. This is a battered wood and leather case that is believed to have been made for the Liberal politician

William Gladstone. On the morning of each Budget it is customary for the Chancellor to appear upon the steps of No. 11 bearing the box. This is held up by the politician. At the official's side stands her/his spouse. The practice started following the Chancellorship of the Conservative politician George Ward Hunt. He presented his only Commons Budget Speech in 1869. When he rose to address the Chamber he realised that he had left his speech at home.

It is customary for the Chancellor to have an alcoholic drink while s/he delivers the Budget speech. However, some refrain from doing so and instead opt for a non-alcoholic refreshment.

As a residence, No. 11 is physically far more spacious than No. 10 is. Whereas the premier's private quarters are now confined to a flat at the top of the latter, the former is still a townhouse.

See Also: PARLIAMENT The Commons, Money Bills

The Downing Street Gates

Until 1990 it was possible for members of the public to walk into Downing Street. Margaret Thatcher the Prime Minister developed a degree of paranoia. A set of gates was built at the cul-de-sac's junction with Whitehall. A few months later the premier was ousted from power - by her own party.

Early the following year her successor as prime minister, John Major, was presiding over a weekly Cabinet meeting when the members of an IRA cell parked a van at the junction of Horse Guards Avenue and Whitehall. From there, they launched a series of mortars towards No. 10. One of these exploded in the property's garden. The house's staff regarded the incident as being an 'annoyance'.

See Also: STREET FURNITURE Gates

EXHIBITING GALLERIES

See Also: GALLERIES

The Dairy

Frank Cohen's future wife Cherryl was the daughter of a dealer in *objets d'art*. Among the items that the man peddled were limited editions of L.S. Lowry prints. He was a skilled salesman and every time that the youth called by the man would sell him a print.

Cohen made a fortune through building up a DIY stores business that was based in England's North-West. Subsequently, he became one of the United Kingdom's principal private collectors of contemporary art. The British artists whose works he purchased included Frank Auerbach, Edward Burra, and Tracey Emin. He kept his collection in a storage facility that was in Wolverhampton. There, in 2007 Mr Cohen opened the Initial Access exhibition space to display works that he owned. The shows that were mounted were poorly attended.

Nicolai Frahm is a Dane who has lived in London since the late 1990s. His collection is strong in post-war European abstract works. The two men joined forces to open a London gallery in the former Express Dairies depot off Wakefield Street. The space mounted its first exhibition in 2013.

Location: No. 7a Wakefield Street, WC1N 1PG.

Websites: http://dairyartcentre.org.uk www.initialaccess.co.uk

The Hayward

The Hayward (1968) is an art gallery that hosts temporary exhibitions. The Brutalist style building forms part of the South Bank arts complex. It was named after Sir Isaac Hayward, a Labour politician who had led the London County Council from 1947 to 1965.

Location: Belvedere Road, SE1 7(GF).

Website: www.haywardgallery.org.uk

Archigram: The Hayward was designed by Norman Engleback of the London County Council's Architecture Department. He was assisted in the task by Warren Chalk and Ron Herron. The pair were members of Archigram, a six-strong Futurist group.

The sestet were a diverse bunch. No two of them had come from the same town or had attended the same university. Their ages ranged over a decade. The three younger men had set up a journal and had invited the older fellows to contribute to it. The projects that they outlined in the publication tended to be a margin more realistic than were the contemporary fantastical works that were being envisaged in France and Italy.

See Also: ZOOS London Zoo

Mother Knows Best: The painter David Hockney was close to his mother Laura. She was a Yorkshirewoman who knew her own mind and who was given to expressing it. During one of her visits to London, he took her to an exhibition of conceptual art that was being staged at The Hayward. One of the pieces that was being displayed was an installation by the artist Barry Flanagan. It consisted of a coiled rope. Mrs Hockney indicated her view of the work by asking 'Did he make the rope?'

Upon another occasion someone enquired of Mrs Hockney whether she was proud of her son's achievements. She gave a gushing reply. However, it included a number of references to the contributions that he had made to local government in their native Bradford. These mystified the questioner until it was appreciated that she was talking about Paul, her first-born child. Unlike David, he had stayed in the town and had served as its Lord Mayor in 1977.

Websites: www.hockneypictures.com www.barryflanagan.com

The Photographers' Gallery

The Photographers' Gallery is an independent gallery that is focused upon displaying photographic works. It was founded by Sue Davies in

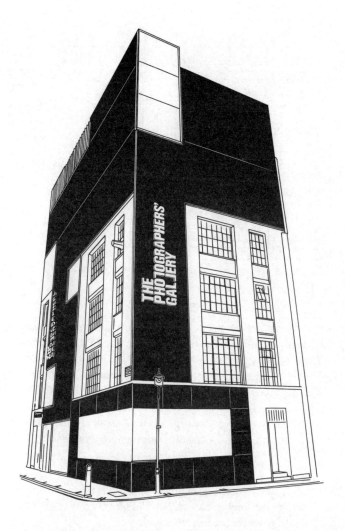

1971. Its first home was at No. 8 Newport Street, which previously had been a Lyons Tea Bar.

In 2012 the gallery reopened in a former warehouse in Ramillies Street that is located close to Oxford Circus. The building had been extended vertically. Its facilities include three floors of galleries, a print sales space, a bookshop, and a café.

Location: Nos. 16-18 Ramillies Street, W1F 7LW.

Website: http://thephotographersgallery.org.uk

Raven Row

Raven Row is a not-for-profit art gallery that is supported by a member of the Sainsbury family. The building has a fine 18thC shop front.

Location: No. 56 Artillery Lane, E1 7LS. On the southern side, a couple of buildings to the east of Artillery Passage.

See Also: GALLERIES The National Gallery; PERIOD PROPERTIES

Websites: www.ravenrow.org www.6a.co.uk (6a Architects is the architectural firm that adapted the building into a gallery.)

The Royal Academy of Arts

The Royal Academy started staging loan exhibitions in 1870.
Location: Burlington House, No. 50 Piccadilly, W1J 0BD.
Website: www.royalacademy.org.uk

Sensation: One of the institution's most notable shows was *Sensation* (1997). This was composed of works by members of the Young British Artists movement (the YBAs). The displayed items came solely from the collection of Charles Saatchi.

See Also: GALLERIES The Saatchi Gallery

The Royal Academy Summer Exhibition: Each year, during June, July, and August, the Academy holds its Summer Exhibition. Amateurs and professionals alike tender works for consideration by the Hanging Committee. This body is composed of Academy members. It whittles down the submissions to a number that can be hung and that should be hung. The exhibited works can be purchased.

The first annual show was held in 1769.

Location: Burlington House, Piccadilly, W1J 0BD.

Website: www.royalacademy.org.uk/exhibitions/summer

The Serpentine Gallery

The Serpentine Gallery mounts temporary exhibitions of modern and contemporary art. Its principal building (1934) was constructed as a tea room. The Arts Council opened the space as an exhibiting gallery in 1970.

The Serpentine Sackler Gallery (2013) was designed by Zaha Hadid. It is located to the north-east of the northern end of the bridge that crosses the Serpentine. The architect created the building by adapting an early 19thC armoury building.

Location: Kensington Gardens, W2 3XA.

Website: www.serpentinegallery.org

The Whitechapel Art Gallery

The Whitechapel Art Gallery (1901) hosts temporary exhibitions of modern art. It was founded by Canon Samuel Augustus Barnett, the Vicar of St Jude's Whitechapel, and his wife Henrietta. Charles Harrison Townsend designed its home. John Passmore Edwards provided funds towards meeting the costs of constructing the building.

On 26 April 1937 Luftwaffe aircraft attacked the Spanish town of Guernica with incendiary bombs. It was the first instance of military airplanes being used to make a premeditated attack upon a civilian population. *The Times* journalist George Steer arrived in the settlement a few hours after the assault had taken place. His description of what had happened was published in both his paper and *The New York Times*. It revealed that the German Air Force was an active participant in the Spanish Civil War. This carried the implication that the Nazis were using the conflict as an opportunity for training the Luftwaffe for a future conflict.

Pablo Picasso painted *Guernica* (1937) in protest at the assault.[1] In

---

[1] Picasso is supposed to have painted *Guernica* with an appreciation that it would remain a powerful work when it was reproduced through the medium of black and white photography. Newspapers were unable to print colour photographs in the 1930s.

1938 Roland Penrose organised a touring exhibition of the work. The Whitechapel Gallery and the Stepney Trades Union Council made the arrangements that enabled the picture to be brought to London, where the gallery displayed it.

In 1956 the Whitechapel mounted the Independent Group's *This Is Tomorrow* exhibition. The show launched the Pop Art movement globally. The term 'Pop Art' probably derived from Richard Hamilton's collage *Just What Is It That Makes Today's Home So Different, So Appealing* (1956). The elements within the work included a bodybuilder holding a lollipop. The word 'Pop' appeared upon the confection.

Under Bryan Robertson's leadership, the exhibitions of foreign artists that the gallery staged included ones of paintings by contemporary American artists such as Jaspers Johns and Robert Rauschenberg.

In 1964 the Whitechapel mounted the *New Generation* show. The British artists whose work was displayed included: Patrick Caulfield, David Hockney, John Hoyland, Paul Huxley, Alan Jones, and Bridget Riley.

Robertson stepped down from his post at the Whitechapel in 1969. Subsequently, it had a succession of directors. The gallery experienced a decline in its standing. Its reputation for being at the forefront of contemporary British art was overtaken by those of the Institute of Contemporary Arts and the Hayward.

Nicholas Serota was appointed to be the Director of the Whitechapel in 1976. Previously, he had headed the small Oxford Museum of Modern Art, which was also an exhibiting gallery. There, his successes had included mounting the first retrospective of Howard Hodgkin's paintings. Under Serota's leadership the Whitechapel's standing began to revive. The gallery took to displaying work by the likes of Gilbert & George, as well as mounting shows of foreign schools such as the German Neo-Expressionists. A number of traditionally-minded art critics disliked its progressive outlook and took to voicing their opposition to it in the media.

The Whitechapel's renewed standing amongst artists was witnessed by the way in which a number of them gave works to it that could be sold at auction. The money that was raised was used to help to pay for a redevelopment of the gallery's building that was carried out in 1984-5.

The Whitechapel acquired its next door neighbour the former Whitechapel Library and expanded into it in 2009. Thereby, the gallery doubled its size.

Location: Nos. 80-82 Whitechapel High Street, E1 7QX.
Website: www.whitechapelgallery.org

FISH & CHIPS, ETC.

Eel Pie

Pie and mash is usually served with a light green parsley liquour.

There have been a number of London pie'n'mash shop owning dynasties - the Cookes, the Kellys, and the Manzes.

The shops that have survived tend to be located in the poorer sections of the city. However, the dish is also reputed to be a frequent feature on the menus of some of Essex's golf clubs.

A. Cookes: The A. Cookes business was founded in 1899 by Alfred Cooke. The firm has been trading from its Goldhawk Road premises since 1934.
  Location: No. 48 Goldhawk Road, Shepherd's Bush, W12 8DH.
  Website: http://cookespieandmash.com

G. Kelly: G. Kelly trades in Bow. The business was founded by Samuel Kelly. Its original shop was on Bethnal Green Road.
  Location: No. 526 Roman Road, Bow, E3 5ES.
  Website: http://gkellypieandmash.co.uk

M. Manze: The M. Manze premises on Tower Bridge Road are London's oldest pie and mash shop. The business was opened by Robert Cooke in 1891. Eleven years later it was purchased by Michele Manze, a native of Italy's Amalfi coast who had settled in Bermondsey. By 1930 the Manze chain had fourteen outlets. The family are still active in the business. Not only do they still run several of the Manze shops but they also supply eels and pies for Cockney-themed evenings and other social occasions.
  Location: No. 87 Tower Bridge Road, SE1 4TW. On the western side, to the north of the junction with Rothsay Street. The flagship M. Manze shop.
  Website: www.manze.co.uk

Fish & Chips

Fish and chips became a widely eaten dish in the mid- to late 19thC. This was because the development of the railway system meant that fish that had been landed at ports on England's east coast could be transported to London in a matter of hours. It was still fresh upon its arrival in the city. The practice of covering a fillet of fish with batter and then deep frying is

thought to have derived from Ashkenazim Jewish cuisine.[1] This is held to have become allied to a supposedly Huguenot tradition of deep frying pieces of potato.[2] In 1860 Joseph Malin opened what was probably London's first fish and chip shop in the East End.

While the dish is widely available in central London in pubs and fast food outlets, there are not many fish and chip shops left there. *Bona fide* chippies are often given punning names, such as *The Dining Plaice* and *The Friar's Inn*.

Locations: *Fish Central*, King Square, Nos. 149-155 Central Street, EC1V 8AP. On the western side, to the north of the junction with Lever Street.

Golden Union Fish Bar, No.38 Poland Street, W1F 7LY. On the western side of the northern end. (www.goldenunion.co.uk)

The Rock & Sole Plaice, Nos. 45-7 Endell Street, WC2H 9AJ. On

---

[1]   The Sephardim community were given to eating fried fish fritters (*pescardo frito*).

[2]   Belgians claim that during the winter of 1680 the River Meuse froze so solidly that locals were no longer able to catch fish. With no fish to fry they took to frying potatoes instead, thus creating the chip. The first written reference in English to preparing potatoes in such a manner was in Alexis Soyer's *Soyer's Shilling Cookery for The People*. (1854).

the north-western corner of the junction with Shorts Gardens. (www.rockandsoleplaice.com)

Reading: Panikos Panayi *Fish & Chips: A History* Reaktion Books (2014).

Phoebe Stubbs (ed.) *A Guide To London's Classic Cafes and Fish & Chip Shops* Black Dog Publishing (2012).

John Walton *Fish & Chips and The Working Classes* Continuum (1992).

Website: www.federationoffishfriers.co.uk (The National Federation of Fish Fryers)

Oysters

Formerly, oysters were a commonplace food. In steak and oyster pie, they were used to make the steak go further. The bivalves changed into being an expensive delicacy because the British oyster population was severely undermined both by disease and by a succession of hard winters.

In Britain it has traditionally been said that oysters should only be eaten during a month that has an 'r' in its name.[1]

See Also: ARCADES The Burlington Arcade

Seafood

Tubby Isaacs: Tubby Isaacs is a stall that sells jellied eels and seafood. The business was founded in 1919.

There is a story that the late Mr Isaacs used to work with his brother Barnie. However, the sibs fell out with one another. Barnie left the stall and opened his own one a few yards further up the street. The two men did not exchange a word for decades.

Location: Goulston Street, Aldgate, E1 7TP. At the southern end, on the eastern side.

---

[1] Some people choose to sport boaters rather than bowlers during the r-less season.

FOOD MARKETS

See Also: FOOD MARKETS, FORMER; STREET MARKETS
Farmers' Markets

Borough Market

Borough Market is reputed to be the oldest municipal fruit and vegetable market in London. It is the successor of one that was held on London Bridge in the 13thC. In 1756 the management of it was transferred from the City of London to the Parish of St Saviour's Southwark (now Southwark Cathedral).

In the late 1990s both Brindisa, a Spanish food business, and Neal's Yard, a whole food retailer, established presences in Borough. This prompted the market trustees to make an effort to establish a quality food retail mart in addition to the wholesale operation. Subsequently, Borough Market became a tourist attraction.

The wholesale market takes place in the early morning. The retail one is held during the late morning and afternoons from Thursday to Sunday.

Location: Stoney Street, Southwark, SE1 9AH.
See Also: BRIDGES London Bridge; THAMES Wharves
Website: www.boroughmarket.org.uk

FOOD MARKETS, FORMER

See Also: CAMDEN TOWN Camden Market; FOOD MARKETS;
STREET MARKETS

Billingsgate Market

London's fish trade moved from Queenhithe Dock to Billingsgate Market in Lower Thames Street in the 14[th]C during the reign of King Edward III.

The modern fish market was established by an Act of Parliament in 1699. The quay was used for landing a range of non-piscine goods, notably coal. However, as London's population gradually moved out of the City of London, fish became the principal commodity that was traded within Billingsgate.

In 1982 the market moved eastwards to a thirteen-acre site in West India Dock on the Isle of Dogs.

Location: No. 16 Lower Thames Street, EC3R 6DX.

Website: www.oldbillingsgate.co.uk

Market Porters: Billingsgate's porters were renowned for their colourful language ('colourful' that is if you can appreciate a range of blue hues). The Church of St Magnus-the-Martyr (1676) stands nearby. It has been claimed that Sir Christopher Wren designed small windows for its eastern wall so that worshippers there would not have to hear the market workers' profanities.

See Also: CHURCH OF ENGLAND CHURCHES

Covent Garden

In 1536, during the dissolution of the monasteries, the Russell family acquired the garden of a convent that had been sited to the north of the Strand. Their townhouse, Bedford House, was built between the road and what is now Covent Garden piazza. In the 17thC London was grew westwards. In order to try to profit from this expansion, the 4th Earl of Bedford decided to develop the property. He hired Inigo Jones to act as his planner-architect for a new suburb that was built upon the land. In 1671 King Charles II granted the 1st Duke of Bedford the right to have a daily fruit and vegetable market in Covent Garden.

The 6th Duke commissioned the Central Market Building's (1830). erection The Jubilee Hall was added in 1908. A decade later the 11th Duke sold Covent Garden to the Covent Garden Estate Company Ltd., a private enterprise. The market's second market building was created in 1933 in order to take advantage of the then low bank interest rates.[1]

Covent Garden was acquired in 1962 by the Covent Garden Market Authority, a government agency. Four years later the body bought from British Rail a 68-acre site at Nine Elms in inner, south-west London. This became New Covent Garden Market. In 1974 the original Covent Garden Market was closed. The Greater London Council paid £6m for the twelve-acre property. The site became the subject of a conflict between the local authority's planners, who wished to raze the buildings on it, and members of the public. The latter won.

The restored Covent Market Buildings were re-opened in 1981.

Location: Covent Garden, WC2E 8HB.

See Also: CAMDEN TOWN The London Box

Website: www.newcoventgardenmarket.com

Leadenhall Market

The Sir Horace Jones-designed Leadenhall Market (1881) is a covered retail market. Its name was derived from the Neville family's townhouse. This building had had a roof that was covered by lead.

In the mid- and late 1370s the *condottiere* Sir John Hawkwood transferred funds to his agents in England by means of Italian merchants who were based in Bruges. The money was used to buy a number of properties in London and Essex. The widow of Sir John Neville sold the

---

[1] In taxi slang old Covent Garden Market was 'The Flowerpot.'

reversion of Leadenhall to the warlord's agents. In 1377 non-Londoners were given permission to vend cheese and butter on the property.

In 1409 Hawkwood's heirs sold Leadenhall to the wealthy mercer, moneylender, and City official Richard Whittington. The Corporation of the City of London bought the site from him two years later. The property developed into being a retail food market. Meat was the principal commodity that was sold there.

In the 19[th]C the carcasses of wild birds, such as skylarks, could still be bought in the market.

Location: Leadenhall Market, EC3V 1LT.

Website: www.cityoflondon.uk/things-to-do/visiting-the-city/food-drink-and-shopping/leadenhall-market

Spitalfields Market drain covers

Spitalfields Market

In 1682 John Balch, a Huguenot silk-weaver, was granted a charter to hold a market in Spitalfields. The Goldschmidt family bought the mart from him. In 1856 Robert Horner, a horticultural wholesaler, purchased the site from them. He invested heavily in its buildings. It was only then that Spitalfields grew into being a large market. In 1920 the City of London acquired the property. During the subsequent decade the Corporation made major improvements to the site's facilities.

In 1991 the fruit and vegetable market relocated to Temple Mills, Waltham Forest. The following year a new, general Sunday market opened on the Spitalfields site.

Location: No. 105a Commercial Street, Spitalfields, E1 6BG.

See Also: PORTOBELLO MARKET; STREET MARKETS East End Street Markets

Website: www.spitalfields.co.uk

GALLERIES

See Also: EXHIBITING GALLERIES; MUSEUMS

The Courtauld Gallery

The Courtauld Collection was born out of a visit that the textiles magnate Samuel Courtauld made to an exhibition that was mounted at the Burlington Fine Arts Club in 1922. This seeded in him an interest in art. Nine years later he founded The Courtauld Institute. This was the first academic body in Britain that taught art history as a discipline in its own right. It became part of the University of London.

Courtauld's personal collection bore the hallmarks of the systematic caution of an experienced businessman. It has been opined that the works that he owned reveal little of the person. He bought according to informed advice. He made no spectacular purchases - never spotting an underrated painter - but then he made no major blunders - the collection did not have any weak paintings or weak artists represented. He bought art from the previous century in a mature market.

The Collection is strong in the fields of the French Impressionists and the Post-Impressionists. Courtauld was the leading British collector of these two schools. While he was still alive the businessman gave the Institute part of his personal collection. His will left it much of the rest. The Collection has acted as a magnet for subsequent bequests.

For many years The Courtauld resided in a building that was located on Woburn Square. In 1990 the Institute moved into the northern wing of Somerset House.

Location: Somerset House, Strand, WC2R 0RN. On the southern side, opposite the western end of The Aldwych.

Website: www.courtauld.ac.uk www.courtauld.ac.uk/gallery/index.html

Dulwich Picture Gallery

Noël Desenfans married Margaret Morris. Using her dowry, the Frenchman and his friend Francis Bourgeois, a Swiss, established a picture dealership in Charlotte Street.

In 1790 Stanislaus Augustus King of Poland commissioned the two men to assemble a collection of pictures that could serve as the basis for a national gallery of Poland. Bourgeois and Desenfans devoted them-selves to the task. They toured Europe in order to acquire works of art that were of an appropriate calibre. However, in 1793 the kingdom was diminished when much of her territory was stripped away from her by her neighbours Austro-Hungary, Prussia, and Russia. Two years later the troika engaged in a further partition and the country disappeared both physically and as a legal state. The two dealers decided to try to sell the collection as a complete entity. The parties that they approached included the British government. It proved to be unreceptive to the idea of a state gallery being established.

The pair decided to try to transfer the works of art to an institution. In 1807 Desenfans died. Bourgeois continued to seek to dispose of the collection as a whole. He approached the British Museum. In the wake of the French Revolution, the body was wary of the dealer's relatively populist approach towards the displaying of art. He responded to this attitude by concluding that the Museum would not be an appropriate recipient.

In 1811 Bourgeois bequeathed the collection to Alleyn's College of God's Gift 'for the inspection of the public'. He left £2000 for the con-struction of a gallery in which the works could be displayed. This was designed by his friend Sir John Soane. Using an Egyptian catacomb as his basic model, the knight created a series of interlinked rooms that had overhead skylights. The Dulwich Picture Gallery was Britain's first public art gallery. It proved to be an architectural template that others were to draw upon.

The College underwent a major reorganisation in 1995. As a result, Dulwich Picture Gallery became an independent body.

Locations: Dulwich Picture Gallery, Gallery Road, Dulwich, SE21 7AD.

Hallam Street, W1N 5(LH). Formerly, Charlotte Street.

See Also: MUSEUMS The John Soane Museum; WILLIAM SHAKE-SPEARE The Rose Theatre

Website: www.dulwichpicturegallery.org.uk

The Estorick Collection of Modern Italian Art

Eric Estorick was an American academic sociologist who became a writer. In the 1940s he spent time in the United Kingdom and married a Briton. While the couple were on honeymoon in Italy, he became fas-cinated by the creations of the Futurist movement and started to collect Modern Italian works of art. In the mid-1950s he began to deal in art.

The Italian government expressed an interest in purchasing Estorick's personal collection. Prior to his death, he set up the Eric & Salome Estorick Foundation to own all of his and his wife's Italian works of art. In 1994 a property was purchased to house the Foundation's collection.

Location: No. 39a Canonbury Road, N1 2DG. The entrance is in Canonbury Road.

Website: www.estorickcollection.com

The Guildhall Art Gallery

In the wake of the Great Fire of 1666, a panel of judges played an important role in facilitating London's rebuilding. They assessed the validity of the property claims that were being made. As an expression of gratitude for the justices' work, the City of London commissioned a series of portraits of them. These paintings became known as the *The Fire Judges*. They acted as the kernel around which the Guildhall Art Gallery collection developed. The Corporation went on to acquire portraits of monarchs and individuals who had rendered the City major service.

In 1941, during the Second World War, the Gallery's collection was removed from London for safekeeping. Three weeks later aerial bombs destroyed the works' emptied home. Post-1945, the Gallery's acquisitions became focussed upon London subjects.

The new Guildhall Art Gallery opened in 1999.

Location: The Guildhall Art Gallery, Guildhall Yard, EC2V 5AE.

See Also: THE GREAT FIRE OF LONDON The Rebuilding of London

Website: www.cityoflondon.uk/things-to-do/visiting-the -city/attractions-museums-and-galleries/guildhall-art-gallery-and- roman-amphitheatre/Pages/Guildhall%20Art%20default.aspx

The National Gallery

The National Gallery (1838) houses the national collection of Western Art.

After making a Grand Tour of Europe in the 1780s, Sir John Leicester decided to focus his art purchases on contemporary British works. In 1823 he offered his paintings to the government as the nucleus for a state collection. The then Prime Minister Lord Liverpool declined the tender. The same year John Julius Angerstein, an insurance tycoon and a major art buyer, died. The idea of establishing a national gallery by buying the man's collection was promoted by both King George IV and the art patron Sir George Beaumont. The following year the government acceded to their lobbying. The foundation of the National Gallery was aided by the Austro-Hungarian state's timely repayment to Britain of a war loan. The institution effectively came into being when the House of Commons voted money for the purchase of 38 paintings from Angerstein's estate. Beaumont added to these some works from his own collection. The body was housed during its first decade in a building on Pall Mall on the site of what is now the Reform Club.

In 1834 the Gallery moved into its present home. Given the building's prominent location, it is a relatively unimposing structure. William Wilkins, its architect, was under considerable pressure to produce an 'economic' edifice; he was required to use the columns that Henry Holland had created for Carlton House even though they were inappropriate for his design. When the structure had been completed, it engendered numerous adverse comments. Initially, the Gallery occupied just part of the site, the rest of it accommodated the Royal Academy of Arts.[1]

In 1837 John Constable's *The Cornfield* (1826) became the first work by a living British artist to enter the Gallery's collection. The painting was bought for the institution by a subscription. In 1854 the government purchased Burlington House in Piccadilly. It was decided that the building should house the Academy and a number of learned societies. This gave the Gallery considerably more space in which to display its works. During the following year Parliament made its first grant to the body of money that it could spend on acquisitions. With the opening of the Tate Gallery in 1897 much of the National Gallery's British collection was transferred there.

The family wealth of the brothers Sir John, Simon and Timothy Sainsbury derived from a supermarkets business. In 1985 the sibs offered to finance the construction of an extension of the Gallery building. The Sainsbury Wing (1991) houses the institution's Early Renaissance collection.

Location: Trafalgar Square, WC2N 5DS. The northern side.

Reading: The Rev Nicolas Holtam *The Art of Worship: Paintings, Prayers and Readings for Meditation* Yale University Press (2011). Prior to his being appointed to be the Bishop of Salisbury in 2011, the Rev Holtam was the Vicar of St Martin-in-the-Fields, which is one of the Gallery's neighbours.

See Also: EXHIBITING GALLERIES Raven Row; STATUES The National Gallery Statues; TRAFALGAR SQUARE The National Gallery

---

[1] Initially, the National Gallery was a far shallower building. Over the years, through a series of extensions, the institution has slowly spread itself northwards.

Passage
Website: www.nationalgallery.org.uk

John Julius Angerstein: John Julius Angerstein arrived in London from Russia at the age of fifteen. He was apprenticed to the firm of Thomson & Peters, a merchant house that specialised in the Russian trade. Upon his coming of age, the youth became an insurance underwriter. He went on to dominate Lloyd's of London, moulding much of the market's character according to his own will.

Locations: Woodlands Art Gallery, No. 90 Mycenae Road, Greenwich, SE3 7SE. Angerstein's rural retreat still exists.[1]

No. 99 Pall Mall, SW1Y 5(ES). Angerstein's townhouse.

The Duke, 007, and The Bus Driver: In 1812 the Spanish painter Goya was commissioned to paint the Duke of Wellington. Most of the portrait was done in a series of sittings. The artist took it away for finishing. However, the general's military career progressed from glory to glory. He was awarded a succession of medals and honours that he felt should be incorporated into the work. The artist acted as he was instructed to. However, he found some of the discs hard to paint, notably the Order of the Golden Fleece. Upon viewing the finished work, his grace chose to give it to a distant relative.

In 1961 the National Gallery put Goya's *The Duke of Wellington* on display. Nineteen days later the painting was stolen. The movie version of *Dr No* (1962) features a moment in which James Bond, while he is

---

[1]   Angerstein had a hypochondriac streak to his character. One of the rooms of the Greenwich house was fitted with air flutes so that its temperature could be maintained at a constant.

being ushered through the evil scientist's underwater lair at Crab Key, notices the missing picture. In 1965 *The Duke* was recovered from the marginally less exotic environment of the left luggage office of New Street Railway Station in Birmingham. Kempton Bunton, a disabled, retired bus driver, claimed somewhat improbably to have been the cat burglar who had taken it.

See Also: GALLERIES The Royal Spanish Art Collection; THE POLICE New Scotland Yard, Art Theft

Website: www.nationalgallery.org.uk/paintings/ francisco-de-goya-the-duke-of-wellington

Super-sized Over The Centuries: The National Gallery's collection includes a *Last Supper* that was painted by Ercole de' Roberti (*c*.1451-1496). In 2010 *The International Journal of Obesity* published an academic paper that had been written by the brothers Brian and Craig Wansink, respectively a food economist at Cornell University and a religious studies professor at Virginia Wesleyan College. The article analysed 52 pictures of the subject that had been created over the course of a thousand years. The size of the depicted food portions was compared to that of the accompanying heads. The former relative to the latter increased by 70% over the millennium.

Website: www.nature.com ijo/index.html

The National Portrait Gallery

The National Portrait Gallery was founded at the prompting of the historian the 5th Earl Stanhope. In 1859 the institution opened in Great George Street. Its present building (1895) was paid for by the philanthropist William Henry Alexander, the site having been provided by the government. Its rooms are arranged in chronological order and can be seen progressively while descending through the building.

Location: St Martin's Place, WC2N 4JH. On the western side.

See Also: GALLERIES The Royal Spanish Art Collection, The Duke and The Bus Driver

Website: www.npg.org.uk

The Royal Collection

See Also: THE BRITISH LIBRARY The King's Library

King Charles I's Collection: King Charles I had poor political judgement - he was to lose a civil war and then have his head chopped off - but he did have an excellent eye for paintings. He built up one of the great art collections of 17thC Europe. The monarch's sophisticated, aesthetic self-indulgence was one of the traits that separated him from his political critics.

In July 1649, following the establishment of the English Republic, the debonced sovereign's goods were sold off at Somerset House. The French and Spanish Crowns had representatives present who bought on behalf of their respective courts. Oliver Cromwell retained a number of major works including Mantegna's *Triumphs of Caesar* series (1486-1505).

The monarchy was restored in 1660. King Charles II indicated that he required those items of his father's collection that were still in the British Isles to be returned to the Crown.

See Also: THE BRITISH LIBRARY; ROYAL STATUES King Charles I, Charing Cross

The Queen's Gallery: King Charles II, in honour of his father, tried to restart the Royal Collection. He commissioned the painter Sir Peter Lely to buy drawings that had been created by Leonardo da Vinci, Michael-angelo, Raphael, and Hans Holbein.[1] These were stored in a bureau and were forgotten about. Over forty years later, during the reign of King George II, the desk, which by then was in Kensington Palace, was re-opened and the trove discovered.

George II's heir-apparent, Frederick Prince of Wales, was an active art buyer. He purchased the notable collection that had been assembled by the physician Dr Richard Mead (*d*.1754). The prince's son, King George III, bought on a sufficiently large-scale that his failures in judgement did not stop a solid body of works being amassed. Prince Albert (*d*.1861), Queen Victoria's husband, had the Royal Collection put in order.

The Queen's Gallery opened to the public in 1962. It displays works of art that are part of the Royal Collection.

Location: Buckingham Palace, Buckingham Palace Road, SW1A 1AA.

See Also: PALACES Buckingham Palace

Website: www.royal.gov.uk/theroyalresidences/queensgallery buckinghampalace/ thequeensgallerylondon.aspx

The Royal Collection Trust: The Royal Collection Trust is the sovereign's trading business. It was set up so that the Royal Collection could be managed without the use of public funds. The body has a subsidi-

---

[1]   These had largely been owned by the 14th Earl of Arundel (*d*.1646). He had been one of the great collectors of early 17thC England.

ary, Royal Collection Enterprises. This administers souvenir sales and admissions at Buckingham Palace, the Queen's Gallery, and Windsor Castle. The Trust's profits are spent on restoration work at the castle and on the Royal Collection.

See Also: PALACES Historic Royal Palaces

Websites: www.royalcollection.org.uk www.royal.gov.uk/ the%20 collection%20and%20collections/overview.aspx

The Royal Spanish Art Collection

Originally, much of the Wellington Museum's collection hung in the royal palaces of Spain. In 1808 Napoleon placed his own brother Joseph upon the Spanish throne as a puppet king. This caused the country's peoples to rise up against the French. This popular rebellion gave the world the term 'guerrilla' warfare, guerrilla coming from *guerra*, the Spanish word for war. Quite apart from the strategic value of tying down some of the emperor's forces on the Iberian peninsula, the uprising struck a note of sympathy in Britain - of a nation rising up against its oppressors. Using Portugal as a base, the British pursued active military operations in Spain. In 1809 the Duke of Wellington was appointed to lead the expeditionary force that was fighting there.

In 1813 the commander defeated Joseph at the Battle of Vittoria. In the French army's baggage train was a large proportion of the Spanish royal art collection. His grace offered to return the works to King Ferdinand VII. However, the rightful monarch declined the tender and instead gave them to the peer as a gesture of thanks.

Location: Apsley House, No. 149 Piccadilly, W1J 7NT. To the east of Hyde Park Corner.

See Also: BRIDGES Waterloo Bridge; GALLERIES, The National Gallery, The Duke and The Bus Driver

Website: www.english-heritage.org.uk/daysout/properties/ apsley-house/art-collection

The Saatchi Gallery

Charles Saatchi was a renowned figure in the advertising industry during the 1970s and 1980s. Early in the latter decade he was inspired by a series of sewn-up slashed canvases that had been created by Lucio Fontana to devise a campaign for the Silk Cut cigarettes brand.[1] This proved to be highly effective. In a variety of permutations, it ran for over twenty years.

[1]   Saatchi's colleague Paul Arden also developed an interest in Contemporary Art. He entered into negotiations with Camden Council in an attempt to purchase an installation art piece. It turned out to be a water mains repair.

The space for the original Saatchi Gallery (1985) on Boundary Road, St John's Wood, was found by the architect Max Gordon. Appropriately, the building was a former paint factory. The works that were displayed there initially were by artists such as Cy Twombly.

In 1991 the Saatchi Gallery started exhibiting Richard Wilson's *20:50* (1987). The oil piece is the only work that the gallery has displayed continuously. It is no longer possible for visitors to stand at its centre as the artist had envisaged originally.

In 1997 the Royal Academy of Arts mounted the *Sensation* exhibition of Young British Artists art. The institution used works that were sourced solely from Saatchi's collection.

The Saatchi Gallery moved into a space in County Hall in 2003. The following year there was a fire at the Momart warehouse in Leyton. At the time, a major part of the collection was being stored in the East London facility. The pieces that were destroyed included Jake and Dinos Chapman's *Hell* (2000) and Tracey Emin's *Everyone I Have Ever Slept With, 1963-1995* (1995). In 2005 the Gallery vacated County Hall. Three years later it moved into the Duke of York's Headquarters in Chelsea. The building had fifteen galleries. These had 70,000 sq ft of floor space.

Location: The Duke of York's Headquarters, No. 31 Kings Road, Chelsea, SW3 4RP.

Website: www.saatchigallery.com

Tate Britain

The National Gallery had only been in existence for a few years when opinion began to gather behind the view that there should be an institution that displayed only British art. The idea took several decades to come to fruition. The first substantive step towards its achievement was the Chantrey Bequest (1877). This was set up by the sculptor Sir Francis Chantrey. He bequeathed his fortune so that ultimately it entered the care of the Royal Academy of Arts. The body was charged with using it to purchase works of art that had been created in Britain.

The sugar refining magnate Sir Henry Tate had a gallery at Park Hill, his house in Streatham, South London. In 1890 he proposed to the

National Gallery that, upon his death, it should receive his collection. The institution replied that it did not want it as a whole but that it was prepared to take selected items from it. The businessman was unhappy with this response. Therefore, he approached the Chancellor of the Exchequer, G.J. Goschen, and offered all of his art works and a building in which to house them if the government would provide the land upon which a new institution could stand. The site of the former Millbank Penitentiary was furnished.

Initially, The Tate Gallery (1897) operated under the supervision of the National Gallery. Works that had been acquired by the Bequest were housed at Millbank. In 1919 the National's British collection was moved to the institution, although the former retained some of the best Turners and Constables.

The Tate grew to be increasingly independent. During the 1950s it became an autonomous body. The institution did not feel that it should confine itself to just acquiring British art. It developed collections of both Modern American painting and 20thC European Art.

The Clore Gallery (1987) was erected to house works by the artist J.M.W. Turner. The building was designed by 'Big Jim' Stirling. In 1988 Nicholas Serota took up the Directorship of the Tate Gallery. Previously, he had led the Whitechapel Gallery. There, he had revived the exhibiting space's reputation. Following his assumption of office at the Tate, it soon became apparent that he intended to place the institution upon a footing that was far more focused upon living artists than had been the case up until then.[1] The gallery had acquired a degree of notoriety for the way in which its curators had chosen to largely ignore the works that had been being created by contemporary painters such as Francis Bacon and Lucian Freud.

In 1989 the businessman Dennis Stevenson both joined the Board of the Tate Trustees and was elected by its members to serve as their Chairman and thus the gallery's. The Conservative government disliked the fellow's progressive reputation and indicated that it would veto the choice. However, Serota proved to be able to avail himself of the influ-

---

[1]   Serota had started his association with the Tate during his early twenties by joining the Young Friends of the Tate organisation. He had been elected to serve as the group's chairman. Under his direction, it had established an innovative outreach programme that had sought to involve the local disadvantaged communities that lived in districts near to the gallery. However, the Tate Trustees had become anxious about this development. They had instructed the Young Friends to terminate the effort. Serota and his colleagues had declined to do so and instead had chosen to resign *en masse*.

ence of the public relations executive Tim Bell, who was close to Prime Minister Thatcher, to imply to her that with age Stevenson might have moderated his outlook. This possibility seems to have been accepted by the premier and the appointment was allowed to go ahead. Stevenson and Serota soon developed a good working relationship with one another. As a result, the Trustees proved to be supportive of a series of initiatives that the director put forward.

Under the administrative regime that had preceded Serota, the Tate had staged exhibitions of works by Jennifer Bartlett and Julian Schnabel. Some people had concluded that in doing so the gallery had been manipulated by the artists' dealers, who, some claimed, had utilised the shows to increase interest in the pair and thereby drive up the prices of their creations. The institution had incurred considerable hostile criticism in the media over the matter. Serota sought to develop a relationship between the Tate and Charles Saatchi, the principal patron of the Young British Artists movement. However, since the advertising mogul sold art as well as buying it, the director appreciated that there was a need to defend the gallery from further adverse comments about its having become too susceptible to commercial interests. Therefore, the institution and the collector did not develop a rapport. As a result, the Tate did not embrace the YBAs as swiftly as many had hoped that it might.

The Tate Prize had been established in 1984 as an honour not only for artists but also for art critics, art historians, and curators. As such, it had proven to be of limited interest to the general public. In 1991 Serota persuaded his fellow jury members to refocus the award so that it could only be bestowed upon artists who were aged under 50. This change helped the gallery to embrace the YBAs. The following year Damien Hirst was included on its short-list. In 1993 the award was conferred upon Rachel Whiteread. Two years later Hirst received it. By then the Prize had developed a strong media profile.

Location: No. 52 Millbank, SW1P 4RG.

Website: www.tate.org.uk/visit/tate-britain

Tate Modern

The Tate Trustees concluded that the Tate Gallery should house its international modern and contemporary art works in a separate building. The Sir Giles Gilbert Scott-designed Bankside power station (1963) had been decommissioned in 1981. The idea that the Tate could acquire the former electricity generating facility was first promoted to it by an architectural historian who was concerned about the survival of the structure.

Its ground level covered an expanse that was of a similar size to the footprint of the Tate. The prospect that the institution could acquire the site became financially viable because the National Lottery was established. A strand of the latter's profits had been earmarked to finance projects that would commemorate the then forthcoming millennium.

The Swiss architectural practice of de Meuron & Herzog was awarded the contract to design the building's conversion. The firm had a reputation for appreciating the needs of artists. A distinctive feature of its plan had been not to subdivide the turbine hall by means of mezzanines and walls but rather to leave it as a single vast exhibition space that could prompt the creation of works that could be displayed in it.

The Tate Modern building was formally opened by Queen Elizabeth in 2000. The monarch has a reputation for not being interested in modern art. She inaugurated the gallery with the words 'I declare the Tate Modern open' and then left. (A few months later she opened the British Museum's Great Court. Upon that occasion she spoke for quarter of an hour about the worth of the museum.)

Location: No. 25 Sumner Street, SE1 9JZ. To the south of the southern end of the Millennium Bridge (aka the Wobbly Bridge).

Websites: www.herzogdemeuron.com www.tate.org.uk/visit/tate-modern

THE GHERKIN

No. 30 St Mary Axe is popularly known as The Gherkin.

For many years Peter Rees worked in the Department of the Environment's Historic Areas Conservation Division. There, his achievements included the creation of the single pale yellow line for heritage districts. It was an alternative to the painting of double yellow lines. In 1985 he was appointed to be the City of London's Controller of Planning.

In 1992 the IRA placed a bomb in St Mary Axe that killed three people and severely damaged the Baltic Exchange building, an important centre for the global shipping trade that had a Grade II* listing. Both Mr Rees and English Heritage were insistent that the Exchange should be restored to its previous condition. The market's members were of the view that this would be too expensive and sold the site to Trafalgar House, a conglomerate that had a property development division. In 1995 the company submitted a design for a modern building that incorporated a repaired version of the Exchange's trading floor. The City authorities approved the scheme. However, no prospective tenants were prepared to commit themselves to renting space in the proposed office block. Meanwhile, the remains of the old Exchange hall that had survived the blast were deteriorating physically.

In spring 1996 English Heritage and Rees gave up their plan of retaining something of the old Exchange building. They agreed that it could be demolished subject to its being replaced by 'a contemporary scheme of real quality...by an architect of international repute'. The developers then availed themselves of a provision in the City planning regulations that allowed for the construction of tall buildings if they were located a mile or so away from St Paul's Cathedral[1] - the St Mary Axe site lay within this strip of land.

In autumn 1996 Norman Foster unveiled a plan for a 385m-tall, 92-storey Millennium Tower glass finger that would have been topped by rabbit's ear-like wings. The design was too extreme for Rees. However, the Corporation felt that it was under pressure to preserve the City's position in the financial world. The development of Canary Wharf in East London and the ambitions of Frankfurt in Germany, where Foster

---

[1]   This provision had been utilised to enable Tower 42 (the NatWest Tower as many people still call it) to be developed.

30 ST MARY AXE

built by **Swiss Re**

had designed the Commerzbank Tower (1997), were providing alternative locations for financial businesses that had large workforces.

In summer 1996 Swiss Re had bought M&G Re, a reinsurance business that operated from six separate buildings across the City. The former wanted to draw all of the latter's operations together on a single site. Canary Wharf provided a means for it to do so. The St Mary Axe location had the additional attraction of being within easy walking distance of the Lloyd's of London Building. In January 1997 Swiss Re agreed to buy the site provided that it came with planning permission for a towerblock. Foster assigned Ken 'The Pen' Shuttleworth to lead a team to produce a new scheme.

The thinking behind The Pen's design was informed by an awareness of a need to neutralise opposition. He endeavoured to lessen the building's impact upon its immediate environment by opting for a circular shape. This would prevent the structure from funnelling wind at street level. He then sought to conceal some of its height by curving the roof towards its central axis. In essence, he was trying to create an edifice that would not draw attention to itself within its immediate vicinity.

Rees liked the work that he saw being done and even began making suggestions of his own; he proposed that the building should be heightened so that it might be able to complement Tower 42 more effectively, while at the same time slimming its own girth. Shuttleworth, to add light and create a sense of height, decided to create light wells by cutting out six segments on each floor. It was realised that, by twisting their appointment, external air pressure upon the building could be utilised to bring fresh draughts into it, thereby cutting down on the need for air conditioning and providing a barber's pole motif for the edifice's exterior. Rather than topping the structure with chimneys and boilers, Shuttleworth exiled these to a neighbouring site and instead designed a glass-

THE GHERKIN

domed top that included a bar and a restaurant. The hemisphere was a shape that had been featured in a number of other buildings that the Foster practice had created.

In summer 2000 the City of London's planning committee sanctioned the plan for the 590ft (180m), 41-storey skyscraper. Its popular name soon emerged as being 'The Gherkin'. Subsequently, the City's Court of Common Council endorsed the committee's approval of the scheme. In autumn 2002 the structure was topped out. It was reported that because of the economic downturn, Swiss Re was only going to occupy half of the building - floors two to eighteen. Originally, the company had planned to use all of it.

In late 2003 Shuttleworth left the Foster practice after Norman Foster had taken exception to an interview that he had given to *Building* magazine. Subsequently, The Pen founded Make, an employee-owned architectural group. In autumn 2004 The Gherkin won the Stirling Prize architectural award. Subsequently, it was reported that, in a book about Foster's work, a photograph of practice members, that had been taken in 2002, had been altered so that Shuttleworth was no longer to be seen standing next to his former boss.

There is a story that Swiss Re did not like the way in which 'The

Gherkin' moniker had become attached to the building. Therefore, the company sent out a memo to its tenants that asked them not to refer to it by the name in their dealings with outside parties. It is reputed that an employee of one of the occupants sent back a reply that 'The Gherkin' was being used affectionately and that the insurer should not get itself into a 'pickle' over the matter.

In 2007 Swiss Re sold the building to a property business.

Locations: No. 30 St Mary Axe, EC3V 1LP.

No. 13 Fitzroy Street, W1T 4BQ. Make's offices. On the western side, north of the junction with Howland Street.

Riverside, No. 22 Hester Road, SW11 4AN. Foster's offices.

Reading: Charles Jencks *The Story of Post-Modernism: Five Stories of The Ironic, Iconic and Critical In Architecture* Wiley (2011). Lord Foster's output is regarded as being essentially that of a Modernist. The Gherkin is a PoMo building.

Jonathan Speirs (1958-2012), Mark Major & Anthony Tischhauser *Made of Light: The Art of Light & Architecture* Birkhäuser, Basel (2005). The architectural firm of Speirs + Major is noted for its expertise in lighting design. No. 30 St Mary Axe is one the buildings that it has illuminated.

See Also: ST PAUL'S CATHEDRAL The Cathedral and The Second World War

Websites: www.30stmaryaxe.com www.fosterandpartners.com www.makearchitects.com www.speirsandmajor.com

THE GREAT FIRE OF LONDON

The Fire

The Great Fire broke out during the early hours of 2 September 1666 on Pudding Lane in the premises of Farriers, the Bakers to the King. Aided by easterly winds, the conflagration spread quickly. Only nine lives are known to have been lost to it. 89 churches, 44 guild halls, and over 13,000 houses were destroyed. 80,000 people were left homeless. Only about 75 acres of the City remained unburnt.

The Great Fire is believed to have stopped at Pye Corner. A small gilt figure of a boy on the corner-house of Cock Lane, Smithfield, marks the spot. A plaque attributes the Fire to 'the Sin of Gluttony'.

Locations: The Monument, Monument Street, EC3R 8AH.

The Golden Boy, Pye Corner, Smithfield, EC1A 9BU. On the northern side of the junction of Cock Lane with Giltspur Street.

Surviving Churches: Among the churches that survived the Fire were: All Hallows by the Tower, St Botolph-without-Aldersgate in Aldersgate Street, and St Olave Hart Street.

Location: St Olave, No. 8 Hart Street, EC3R 7NB. To the west of the junction with Seething Lane.

See Also: CHURCH OF ENGLAND CHURCHES St Olave's Hart Street; PERIOD PROPERTIES City of London Hostelries

The Rebuilding of London

Much of the capital for the physical rebuilding of London was released by ground landlords agreeing to forego the income that they would have received otherwise. This enabled tenants to spend this money upon constructing new properties. As a result, a number of the City's social institutions experienced a severe drop in their incomes. Therefore, they became less active than they had been. In turn, in the late 17[th]C and early 18[th]C, Londoners became more inclined to set up new organisations and societies that sought to address contemporary social concerns.

To help raise finance for rebuilding the City, its Corporation was empowered to levy a tax upon all coal that was brought into the Port of London. 51 churches replaced the 89 that had been destroyed.

Mount Terrace in Whitechapel takes its name from an artificial hill that was created in part by rubble collected after the Fire (its lower portion consisted of defensive ramparts that had been put up during the Civil Wars of the 1640s).

Following the conflagration, King Street[1] and Queen Street were created to provide an approach to the Guildhall from the River Thames. They also furnished the City with a firebreak.

Locations: King Street, EC2V 8(EA).

Mount Terrace, E1 2BB.

Queen Street, EC4N 1(SR).

Reading: Leo Hollis *The Phoenix: St Paul's Cathedral and The Men Who Made Modern London* Weidenfeld & Nicolson (2008). An account of how London was reborn in the 60 years that followed the Fire. The book argues that the ideas of Nicholas Barbon, John Evelyn, Robert Hooke, John Locke, and Christopher Wren created the framework for the redevelopment of the City and that their concepts interlocked in the rebuilding of St Paul's Cathedral.

See Also: THE CITY OF LONDON The Impact of Great Fire Upon The Government of The City of London; COLUMNS The Monument; GALLERIES The Guildhall Art Gallery; ST PAUL'S CATHEDRAL; STREET FURNITURE Paving

---

[1]   King Street was named in honour of King Charles II.

THE GUNPOWDER PLOT

The Gunpowder Plot of 1605 was a scheme by a small group of Roman Catholics to assassinate King James I and the people who were attending the State Opening of Parliament. The conspirators sought to do this by renting space in the cellars beneath the legislature. There, they amassed barrels of gunpowder. The plan was revealed as the result of Francis Tresham, one of the conspirators, advising Lord Monteagle, a relative of his who was due to attend the ceremony, not to go to it. The peer informed the authorities of his suspicions and a search soon revealed the explosives.

Location: Parliament Square, SW1P 3AD.

See Also: CORONATIONS Hereditary and Feudal Office-Holders; PARLIAMENT The Palace of Westminster; PARLIAMENT The Commons, Robert Maxwell; PARLIAMENT The State Opening of Parliament

Website: www.parliament.uk/about/living-heritage/evolutionofparliament/parliamentaryauthority/the-gunpowder-plot-of-1605

The Catesbys

The Catesby family have made something of a habit of forfeiting their estates, having done so in 1265, 1485, and 1605. In the last instance it was Robert Catesby's involvement in the Plot that did for them. Technically, the resulting Act of Attainder continued to be in operation until the 1970s. Its provisions legally prohibited the family's members from voting. However, by then the Catesbys were unaware that the measure was still in force and had been leading ordinary civil lives for several generations.

Location: Nos. 64-67 Tottenham Court Road, W1P 9PA. A building that housed a furniture retailing business that members of the family owned in the 20thC. There is a big C on its corner with Goodge Street.

The Observing of 5 November

Since King James I's reign it has been a tradition to mark 5 November and Parliament's delivery from the Gunpowder Plot with bonfires. The observance, despite its origins, has long been free of any sectarian char

acter.

In the 18thC the marking of 5 November was not solely about the discovery of the Plot. William of Orange had landed in Britain at Torbay on 5 November 1688, thus starting the Revolution of 1688. The Dutchman was the thinly disguised hero of Nicholas Rowe's play *Tamerlane* (1701). For more than a century the dramatic work was performed in commemoration of the prince's arrival.

Lord Robert Grosvenor was a progressively-minded Whig who held strong Low Church Anglican beliefs. In 1857 the MP was the principal figure behind a number of changes that Parliament made to the Church of England's calendar. These included abolishing the services of thanksgiving that marked the Plot, King Charles I's martyrdom, and the restoration of the monarchy in 1660.

These reforms seem to have derived from the politician's sincere belief that the remembrances were no longer appropriate. However, they also indicated that he was not afraid of the mob.[1] In 1850 the government had allowed the Roman Catholic Church to establish a legally recognised hierarchy in Britain. This development had triggered a number of pope-burnings. These occasions had involved effigies being paraded through the streets of London and then set alight. Grosvenor's calendar reforms passed smoothly through the legislature. No popular reaction

---

[1]   Two years earlier Grosvenor had sponsored a Sunday Trading Bill. This measure had triggered a popular protest movement. A crowd of 150,000 people had gathered in Hyde Park to signal their opposition to it.

was triggered. It turned out that most of the people who had made up the large crowds that had attended the conflagrations had done so in order to partake in a traditional form of entertainment rather than because they had possessed ardent sectarian opinions.

Fireworks did not become a feature of the observance of 5 November until the High Victorian era when the government ended its own monopoly upon the manufacture of gunpowder. The introduction of the Fireworks Code in 1976 led to some varieties of firework being phased out. As a result, most children take a greater interest in Hallowe'en than they do in the 5th.

See Also: PARKS Hyde Park, Speakers' Corner; WEATHER Wind, The Protestant Wind

Searching Parliament's Cellars

On the eve of the State Opening of Parliament, the Yeomen of the Guard carry out a ceremonial search of the building's cellars. The custom is meant to derive from the discovery of the Gunpowder Plot of 1605. The first recorded instance of such a rummage dates from 1641, which was a time when political tensions were mounting prior to the outbreak of the Civil Wars. (The Yeomen's task has been made relatively easy by the fact that the palace's subterranean chambers are no longer rented out.)

See Also: MILITARY CUSTOMS

HALLS

See Also: THE CITY OF LONDON The Guildhall; HERITAGE Harmondsworth Great Barn

The Banqueting House

The Banqueting House (1622) is the principal visible remnant of White-hall Palace. The building was designed for King James I by Inigo Jones. In 1698 a fire destroyed almost all of the complex. The House survived. Subsequently, it was used as a royal chapel.

Originally, the building's exterior was dressed with a warm, honey-coloured sandstone. In the 1830s it was remodelled so that it acquired its present neoclassical character. The masonry that was used to cover it had a bleak grey colour. Over the years, a number of the buildings along Whitehall were clad to resonate with it. As a result, much of the street developed an arid, impersonal tone.

In 1890 the House became the home of the Royal United Services Museum. The government took back the building for official use. In 1963 it was opened to the public. It is still sometimes used as a venue for diverse state occasions.

Location: Whitehall, SW1A 2ER. On the eastern side, south of the junction with Horseguards Avenue.

See Also: THE CHAPELS ROYAL; PALACES, DISAPPEARED & FORMER Whitehall Palace; WEATHER Wind, The Protestant Wind

Website: www.hrp.org.uk/banquetinghouse

Crosby Hall

Crosby Hall (1475) is a hall with a hammerbeam roof. The structure was the Bishopsgate home of Sir John Crosby, a prominent merchant who was a member of the Grocers' Company. For a while, it was the residence of the Duke of Gloucester, who ascended the throne as King Richard III.

In 1907 the building was transplanted to Chelsea Embankment so that it could become part of a hostel for women students. In 1995 planning permission was granted for a river front mansion that incorpo-rated Crosby Hall. The new, old style, brick building varies from the old, externally unexceptional looking Hall.

Locations: No. 38 Bishopsgate, EC2N 4AF.

Danvers Street, Chelsea, SW3 5(AY).

Lambeth Palace The Great Hall

Lambeth Palace is the London residence of the Archbishops of Canterbury. Its Great Hall was where the episcopants would receive and entertain their notable visitors.

Following the Civil Wars of the 1640s, the Hall was demolished and its materials were sold off. The monarchy was restored in 1660. The structure was rebuilt for Archbishop William Juxon. The room was given a Gothic hammerbeam roof, which even then was deeply anachronistic.

Location: Lambeth Palace Road, SE1 7JU. To the north of the eastern end of Lambeth Bridge.

Website: ww.archbishopofcanterbury.org/pages/lambeth -palace-library.html

Lincoln's Inn The Old Hall

Lincoln's Inn's Old Hall was built at the end of the 15thC.

Location: Lincoln's Inn Fields, WC2A 3TL. To the east.

See Also: CHARLES DICKENS Jarndyce vs. Jarndyce

Website: www.lincolnsinn.org.uk/index.php/history-of-the-inn/ historic-buildings-ca/the-old-hall

Westminster Hall

The construction of the Palace of Westminster had been initiated by King Edward the Confessor. Westminster Hall was built at the end of the 11thC as a Norman extension to the complex. Initially, the chamber was used to hold banquets in.

From the late 13thC until 1825, the chief courts of English law sat in Westminster Hall during the legal term. At other times, they convened in a variety of other sites.

In 1834 the Palace burned down. The Hall survived the conflagration. Subsequently, it was decided to relocate the superior courts closer to the Inns of Court. The Royal Courts of Justice complex (1882) was built on the Strand in order to provide them with permanent year-round accommodation. The facility received the courts that had previously been housed in the Hall, Lincoln's Inn, and the Doctors' Commons.

Location: Palace of Westminster, Parliament Square, SW1P 3AD.

See Also: PARLIAMENT The Palace of Westminster

Website: www.parliament.uk/about/living-heritage/building/ palace/westminsterhall

HERITAGE

See Also: ARCHES; CHURCH OF ENGLAND CHURCHES; MUSEUMS; PALACES; PERIOD PROPERTIES; ROMAN REMAINS; ROYAL RESIDENCES

Blue Plaques

London's principal streets contrast with those of most other major European cities in that very few of them are named after individuals. This is paralleled by the way in which none of the city's bridges over the Thames are named in honour of a monarch or a prime minister. A blue plaque is fixed to a building's exterior to commemorate someone of note who has lived there. The person who is being so marked needs to have been dead for at least a couple of decades.

The scheme to fasten the plaques was created by the Royal Society of Arts. In 1867 the first one was fastened to No. 24 Holles Street to commemorate the birthplace of the poet Lord Byron (*d*.1824). Technical difficulties led to its being brown in colour. Subsequently, blue was used. The building that the plate was mounted upon has been demolished.

In 1901 the London County Council assumed responsibility for the scheme. In 1965 the local authority was superseded by the Greater London Council. With the latter's abolition in 1986, administration of the programme passed to English Heritage. Subsequently, it was expanded to operate nationally.

Location: No. 24 Holles Street, W1G 0(BN). Towards the southern end of the western side.

Website: www.english-heritage.org.uk

Prince Henry's Room

The London County Council (General Powers) Act of 1898 granted the London County Council the capacity to buy and restore places of historical interest. The first site that it acquired was Prince Henry's Room.

The Room had been part of an inn that was probably rebuilt while King James I's first-born son, Henry (*d*.1612), was Prince of Wales. The establishment changed its name to *The Prince's Arms*.

Location: No. 17 Fleet Street, EC4Y 1AA. On the southern side.

See Also: INNS & TAVERNS; PERIOD PROPERIES

Website: www.cityoflondon.gov.uk/about-the-city/history-and-heritage/our-buildings-in-the-city/Pages/prince-henrys-room.aspx

The Prince of Wales: In 1284 the Welsh chieftans approached King Edward I. They asked him to choose as their prince a man who had been born in Wales, who spoke no English. The monarch presented them with his infant son as the first ever Prince of Wales. The future King Edward II had been born in Caernarvon Castle and was far too young to be able to articulate anything intelligible in any language.

Websites: www.princeofwales.gov.uk www.royal.gov.uk/MonarchUK/Symbols/HonoursofthePrincipalityofWales.apsx

London Open House

London Open House raises awareness of architecture and the built environment through a series of activities. The one of these that has the highest public profile is the co-ordination of a weekend each September when members of the public are given access to notable and interesting buildings that they would not normally be able to see the interiors of. The initial one was held in 1992.

Website: www.londonopenhouse.org

Lost London

The Euston Arch: Euston Railway Station was the London terminus of the London & Birmingham Railway's London to Birmingham railway. It was the first purpose-built station in a capital city. The Euston Arch (1837) furnished it with a grand entrance. The Doric-style archway became known as 'The Gateway to the North'. The 70ft (18.5m) tall, 44ft (10.9m) deep structure was designed by Philip Hardwicke. Its fluted arches were eight and a half feet in diameter.

In the late 1950s British Rail made a decision to rebuild the station. The Arch could have been moved to a nearby site. However, the rail authority stated that it regarded the cost of such an operation as being too high for it to be justifiable. The declaration triggered a popular opposition. The issue of whether or not the portal should be demolished went before the Cabinet. The body ruled that the structure could come down. In 1962 it was dismantled.

The campaign to try to preserve the archway inspired the birth of the modern conservation movement in Britain. After the rebuilding of Euston, St Pancras Railway Station was next on British Rail's list for redevelopment. It was planned that the terminus and the neighbouring King's Cross one would be merged into a single facility. However, the poet and architectural writer John Betjeman led a successful defence of the station and its hotel.

Dan Cruickshanks, an architectural writer of a subsequent generation, engaged in a prolonged quest to unearth the physical remains of the Arch. During the course of 1993 and 1994 he made a number of finds. Some of the structure's Doric detailing was unearthed in the stonework of a terrace that a Mr Frank Valori had built for himself at his house in Kent. He had been the contractor who had demolished the structure. Subsequently, Mr Cruickshanks discovered that 24 of the portal's stones had been used to fill in a chasm in the bed of the River Lea's Prescott Channel in East London. These were recovered.

In 2014 the Secretary of State for Transport stated that the government wanted the Euston Arch to be re-erected as part of the southern terminus of the proposed HS2 high-speed railway line.

Locations: Euston Railway Station, NW1 2DU. The Arch was located next to where the station's indicator board is.

No. 43 Cloth Court, EC1A 7LS. On the western side of the junction with Cloth Fair. Betjeman's home.

See Also: ARCHES; BRIDGES The Albert Bridge

Website: www.eustonarch.org. (The Euston Arch Trust)

The National Trust

The National Trust for Places of Historic or Natural Beauty was founded in 1895 by the social reformer Octavia Hill, Sir Robert Hunter, who was the Solicitor to the Post Office, and Canon Hardwicke Rawnsley, a Lakeland clergyman. The government had indicated that it would not involve itself in the preservation of beauty spots and ancient monuments. Therefore, the trio set up the organisation to try to protect open spaces from urban and industrial engulfment.

The National Trust's first acquisition was made in 1895 - Dinas Oleu, a cliff-top above Barmouth in West Wales. In the 1920s the growth of interest in architecture, particularly in Georgian buildings, gave the Trust a new range of ambitions. In 1931 it was given Montacute, a grand country house in Somerset. Looking after such a stately home whetted the Trust's institutional palate. However, the body's senior management appreciated that it would be organisational suicide to accept such buildings without having the financial means to underwrite the support of their fabric. Thus was born the Country Houses Scheme. Under this, a family may give their house to the Trust, and retain for themselves and their heirs the right to live in it, so long as they hand it over with an endowment of investments or property that provides for its structural upkeep and maintenance. The National Trust has become one of the largest property owners in the United Kingdom. It has more than 500,000 acres of land.

The prolonged agricultural depression between the two World Wars, as well as the economic crash and death duties, helped part much of the aristocracy from the outright ownership of their ancestral seats. In the 1950s and 1960s the growing leisure use of cars meant that an increasing number of people were able to visit the Trust's sites. This led to the body becoming a mass membership organisation. It has been referred to as the 'paramilitary wing of the middle class'.

Websites: www.nationaltrust.org.uk www.jamesleesmilne.com

Period Groups

The Georgian Group: The Georgian Group is focussed on the period 1700-1837. The organisation was founded in 1937 by the 3rd Baron Derwent, Angus Acworth, and the travel writer Robert Byron as part of The Society for the Protection of Ancient Buildings. They had become alarmed at the rate at which Georgian buildings were being demolished. London had recently lost Norfolk House in St James's Square and much of The Adelphi.

The Group has statutory amenity society status. If the implementation of a planning application will have any impact upon a listed Georgian building, structure, or space then it has to be consulted about the matter.

Location: No. 6 Fitzroy Square, W1T 5DX.

Website: www.georgiangroup.org.uk

The Twentieth Century Society: The Twentieth Century Society (C20) concerns itself with post-1914 design and architecture.

In 1979 The Hayward Gallery hosted an exhibition on the 1930s. The same year The Thirties Society was founded by Marcus Binney, John Harris, and Simon Jenkins. They set it up because none of the existing amenity socities were interested in trying to save Sir Edwin Cooper's Lloyd's of London building (1928). The following year its members were outraged by the demolition of the Wallis, Gilbert & Partners-designed Firestone Factory (1929) on the Great West Road.

The Society's interests were not restricted to the Thirties. In 1992 it was renamed The Twentieth Century Society.

Location: No. 70 Cowcross Street, EC1M 6EJ.

Website: www.c20society.org.uk

The Victorian Society: The Victorian Society is focussed upon Victorian and Edwardian buildings. The organisation was founded in 1958 as a result of the efforts of Anne Lady Rosse. Its inaugural members included John Betjeman and the architectural historian Nikolaus Pevsner.

Location: No. 4 Priory Gardens, Bedford Park, W4 1TT.

See Also: PERIOD PROPERTIES Linley Sambourne House

Website: www.victoriansociety.org.uk

Richmond Hill

The view south-westwards from the brink of Richmond Hill features the River Thames in the foreground and its flood plain beyond. This vista has been painted the likes of Joshua Reynolds and J.M.W. Turner.

In 1898 the Cunard family bought the Marble Hill estate on the Thames's northern bank with the intention of developing the property for housing. One of the attractions for the purchasers would have been the fine eastward view of Richmond Hill. A local movement that opposed this proposed development mushroomed into being.

The activists succeeded in securing the passage through Parliament of the Richmond, Ham & Petersham Open Spaces Act. This measure made it illegal for there to be any developments that might impair the view from the hill. The arrangement was facilitated by the 9th Earl of Dysart, the owner of Ham House. He transferred a swathe of meadows to the control of Richmond Council. A Board of Conservators was established. In return, the Scottish peer secured a number of economic rights over some other properties that he retained.

The Marble Hill estate was acquired by London County Council.

See Also: THE THAMES

Website: http://thames-landscape-strategy.org.uk

The Society for The Protection of Ancient Buildings

The Society for The Protection of Ancient Buildings was founded in 1877 by William Morris and several members of the Pre-Raphaelite group.

The Ancient Monuments Protection Act of 1900 was sponsored by the Conservative MP David Lindsay, the courtesy-titled Earl of Balcarres, who was the Honourable Secretary of the Society. The measure was supplemented was by the Ancient Monument Protection Act of 1910 and the Ancient Monuments Consolidation & Amendment Act of 1913. The latter was the first British law to address building conservation.

Location: No. 37 Spital Square, E1 6DY.

Website: www.spab.org.uk

SHERLOCK HOLMES

In 1891 Arthur Conan Doyle was practising as a physician at No. 2 Devonshire Place. As a newcomer to the district, he had relatively few patients. He used the time between appointments to write what proved to be the first of the Sherlock Holmes stories. He based the detective upon both the person of Dr Joseph Bell, who had taught him medicine at Edinburgh University, and the character of C. Auguste Dupin, the French detective whom Edgar Allen Poe had created in the story *The Murders in the Rue Morgue* (1841). Holmes fused sensationalism and science, while raising deduction to a new level. However, the initial story was rejected by a series of publishers before it was accepted.

Doyle's second most successful series of novels featured Professor Challenger. The hero was modelled upon his friend the journalist Bertram Fletcher Robinson. The two men first met one another in 1900 while they were on-board a troop ship that was returning from the Second Boer War. It was Robinson who told the writer the tale of the Black Shuck. This became the basis for *The Hound of The Baskervilles* (1902).

In 1902 Doyle was knighted in acknowledgement of the propaganda work that he had performed during the conflict. He came to the view that Holmes was overshadowing his other works, such as his historical saga *The White Company* (1891) and the epistolary novel *A Duet, With An Occasional Chorus* (1899). The following year he killed off the character at the Reichenbach Falls. Workers in the City of London took to wearing mourning *crêpe* on their top hats. The *Strand* magazine promptly lost 20,000 of its subscribers.

Locations: *The Sherlock Holmes*, No. 11 Northumberland Street, WC2N 5DA. On the corner of Northumberland Street with Craven Passage. The pub has a collection of items that are associated with Conan Doyle and his most popular literary creation. The material is reputed to be a vestige of the Festival of Britain of 1951.[1]

No. 2 Devonshire Place, W1G 6HJ.

No. 2 Upper Wimpole Street, W1G 6LD. A plaque at the address

---

[1]   The original name of *The Sherlock Holmes* was *The Northumberland Arms*. Northumberland House, the Percy family's townhouse, occupied what is now Northumberland Avenue.

was unveiled by Dame Jean Conan Doyle in 1994.

No. 12 Tennison Road, South Norwood, SE25 5(RT).

See Also: THE POLICE

Website: www.sherlock-holmes.org.uk

221b Baker Street

No. 221b Baker Street was the supposed residence of Sherlock Holmes. It is reputed that the Abbey bank, which for many year occupied a site that included No. 221, employed a person to reply to the detective's correspondence.

Location: No. 221 Baker Street, NW1 6XE.

Mycroft Holmes

There is a theory that Conan Doyle based Holmes's older brother Mycroft upon Oscar Wilde, giving him the Irishman's size, lethargy,[1] and Hellenism as characteristics. The two writers had met one another early in their respective literary careers and had become friends.

Location: The Langham Hotel, No. 1c Portland Place, W1B 1JA.

The Sherlock Holmes Society of London

In 2008 The Sherlock Holmes Society of London issued the two volume *Holmes and Watson Country: Travels In Search of Solutions*. The publication was the first collection of Holmesian writing.

Website: www.sherlock-holmes.org.uk

---

[1]   Doyle was *sportif*.

HORROR FICTION

Frankenstein

In 1815 Mount Tambora, a volcano in the Dutch East Indies, erupted. This had the effect of disrupting weather systems globally. 1816 became known as 'the year without summer'. During it, Percy Bysshe Shelley, Mary Wollstonecraft Godwin, and Mary's sister Claire Clairmont visited Lord Byron at the Villa Diodati on the shore of Lake Geneva in Switzerland. Also resident at the property was the baron's physician John Polidori. At the peer's prompting, the party set themselves to writing short stories about supernatural phenomena. Mary Godwin's tale drew upon contemporary debates in the scientific world about whether electricity could be used to generate life in lifeless flesh.

At the end of the year Godwin and Shelley married one another. With the poet's encouragement, she worked up her story into a full-length novel. *Frankenstein; or, The Modern Prometheus* (1818) was published anonymously. 500 copies were printed. As the work passed through different editions, its text underwent a series of adjustments. This was because its author sought to maintain and develop its appeal. In 1831 her name appeared upon it for the first time.

Mary Shelley identified Byron with the Creature. It was 'Deformed, rejected, and fatally destructive'. In 2012 it emerged that the copy of *The Modern Prometheus* that the novelist had given to the poet had been discovered in the library of the late Douglas Jay. He had been a senior Labour politician and minister.

Locations: No. 87 Marchmont Street, WC1N 1AL.

No. 38 Great Pulteney Street, W1F 9NU. Polidori's home.

See Also: WEATHER Clouds; WEATHER Deadly and Anonymous

A Moving Example: Luigi Galvani's ideas were known to the Mary Shelley group. The scientist's nephew Giovanni Aldini had played a leading role in promoting them.

George Forster had been convicted of having wilfully drowned his wife and daughter in a stretch of canal at Paddington. The killer had been executed in Newgate Prison on 18 January 1803. While his corpse had still been warm, it had been taken to the nearby Royal College of Surgeons. There, before a gathered audience, Aldini had applied an electric current

MARCHMONT ASSOCIATION

Percy Bysshe Shelley
1792–1822
Poet & Radical Thinker
&
Mary Shelley
1797–1851
Author of Frankenstein
lived in a house
on this site
1815-16

to it. Its muscles had been seen to spasm. This had been done in order to demonstrate that electricity plays a role in the functioning of the body.

Location: No. 32 Old Bailey, EC4M 7HS. At the northern end of the eastern side. The site of Newgate Prison.

Reading: Andy Dougan *Raising The Dead: The Men Who Created Frankenstein* Birlinn (2008). A book about scientists who used electricity in order to try to understand life.

Vampires

Bloodsuckers-By-Appointment: Vampires do not form part of the folk traditions of Britain. However, upon occasion immigrants who have lived in the country have maintained a firm credence in the creatures' existence. The German-born King George II believed them to be real. Upon one occasion the politician Sir Robert Walpole made a remark that indicated that he did not share the view. This incensed the monarch, who expressed his opinion upon the matter in no uncertain terms.

Dracula: Bram Stoker worked as a civil servant in his native Ireland, however, he harboured literary ambitions. He broke into the theatrical world by working as an unpaid drama critic. He became known to the actor Sir Henry Irving. In 1878 the thespian invited Stoker to become his business manager.[1]

In 1890 Stoker started compiling notes for a Gothic adventure in which a vampire was encountered by a British adventurer. In it, the anti-hero comes to Britain, lands at Whitby, and is slain by the hero. The project was perhaps inspired by the vampire-lesbian novel *Carmilla*

---

[1]   In 1878 Stoker married Florence Balcombe, a Dublin beauty. Oscar Wilde had been one of her other suitors.

(1872) that had been written by the Irish author Sheridan Le Fanu. The 'shape shifting' aspect of Stoker's count was drawn from Irish folklore, while the poet Lord Byron may have made an indirect contribution through *The Vampyre* (1819), which had been written by his physician John Polidori.[1] The name Dracula was derived from Vlad Dracula (Vlad the Impaler), the soubriquet of Prince Vlad III of Wallachia (*d*.1476).

Stoker was well aware that many novels were adapted for theatrical performance. Therefore, he was careful to tailor the character of Dracula so that it could easily be moulded into a role for Irving. However, the actor declined to take the bait and no stage adaptation of the book was mounted during its author's lifetime. The volume sold well but it did not provide the writer with the financial independence that he had been hoping for.

Location: No. 18 St Leonard's Terrace, Chelsea, SW3 4QG. Stoker's home.

See Also: THEATRES The Lyceum

Websites: www.blood.co.uk www.thedraculasociety.org.uk (The Dracula Society was founded in 1973 by the actors Bernard Davies and Bruce Wightman)

Tolerance of The Other: Christianity is central to *Dracula* (1897). The vampire perverts the faith by rising from the dead and drinking blood. Initially, the novel plays with 19thC Protestant stereotypes of Roman Catholicism. However, the work is essentially ecumenical in its nature. Dr van Helsing is expressly a Catholic. He uses the crucifix and the host to counter the count and teaches others, whom the book's early readers would almost certainly have taken to be Protestants, to use them.

---

[1] Polidori's sister was Frances Rossetti, the mother of the Rossettis. (*See Also*: *WOMBATS* in *BEANS, BEARS & PIRACY*)

INNS & TAVERNS

See Also: HERITAGE Prince Henry's Room; PUBS

Coaching Inns

From the 17thC to the early 19thC London's coaching inns played an important role in the social and economic life of the city and its environs. They acted as a mixture of hotel and embarkation point for travellers to other parts of Britain. Often the inns had a strong association with a particular part of the country. By departing from the inn businessmen and gentry who came to London knew that they had a good chance of travelling with people whom they knew or knew of. While, people who originated from a region, but who, through work or official service, had to live in the metropolis, would often spend some of their leisure time frequenting the public rooms of their 'local' inn to hear news from home and/or to eat regional delicacies.

District Names

A number of districts in London acquired their names from inns or pubs: The Angel in Islington derives its moniker from *The Angel Inn*, New Cross from *The New Cross Inn*, and Swiss Cottage from *The Swiss Cottage* pub.

See Also: PUBS Pub Names

The George Inn

The George Inn is the best surviving (if incomplete) example of a coaching inn in London. Southwark's inns became doomed with the opening of London Bridge Station (1837). Yet, *The George* has survived as a pub.

Location: No. 77 Borough High Street, SE1 1NH. On the eastern side.

Reading: Pete Brown *Shakespeare's Local* Maxmillan (2012). A history of the inn.

The Star & Garter

No. 100 Pall Mall stands on what was the site of *The Star & Garter* tavern. In the 18thC it was one of the inns where gentlemen and aristocrats from the same region or county as one another could, if they so chose, meet on

The George Inn

a given day of the week while they were in London.

Location: No. 100 Pall Mall, SW1Y 5HP. On the southern side, to the west of Carlton Gardens.

The Wicked Lord Byron: The Nottinghamshire Club used to meet at *The Star & Garter*. In 1765, while attending a gathering there, the 5th Baron Byron fell into an argument with his cousin William Chaworth over the game on their respective estates. The disagreement escalated into being a duel in which his lordship mortally wounded his kinsman.

The baron was tried by his peers in the House of Lords and found guilty of manslaughter. However, as a noble, he was discharged under the statute of privilege.[1]

See Also: PARLIAMENT The Lords

---

[1] The 5th Baron was a great-uncle of the poet Byron.

JACK THE RIPPER

Over a period of three months, starting in August 1888, five women, four of whom were prostitutes, were killed within a square mile of Whitechapel. Their corpses were mutilated in a grotesque manner. The first of the Ripper's victims, Mary Ann Nichols, was slain in Whitechapel on 31 August 1888. The other women whom he is known to have murdered were: Annie Chapman in a yard off Hanbury Street on 8 September; Elizabeth Stride in Beaver Street also on 8 September; Catherine Eddowes in Berner Street on the 30th of the same month; and Mary Jane Kelly in Miller's Court on 9 November. After the slayings, the killer sent confessions to the police. He signed himself as 'Jack the Ripper'. The attacks ended as suddenly as they had begun. The Met's inability to solve the crimes prompted the Police Commissioner to resign in disgrace.

It is known that the killer was left-handed.

Suspects

Paul Chapman: Philip Sugden's *The Complete History of Jack The Ripper* (1994) was the first book that applied academic rigour to the subject of Jack the Ripper. Dr Sugden's favoured candidate was George Chapman, a Polish-born doctor's assistant. However, the writer regarded the case against the man as being unproven.

The Duke of Clarence: Albert Victor Duke of Clarence & Avondale, a younger son of the Prince of Wales (King Edward VII), is a suspect. He was an eccentric who was given to wearing capes and deerstalkers.

Montague Druitt: One of the favoured candidates for Jack the Ripper is Montague Druitt, a schoolmaster whose brother was a doctor in the East End. Although the former had been a student at the University of Oxford, he moved in the same social circles as many of the Apostles, a group of former Cambridge graduates. Many of them were bisexual or homosexual. Their sex lives were often carried out under assumed identities and in clandestine manners. That they should have extended their protection to Druitt was not unreasonable in view of what light his public exposure might have thrown upon their own activities. The police investigation was wound up after the teacher's corpse had been retrieved from the Thames in December 1888.

KEW GARDENS

See Also: PARKS

The Royal Botanic Gardens

The Royal Botanic Gardens is the most congenially verdant portion of the British state. The land was once a royal rural retreat.

In 1728 Queen Caroline acquired the Kew Park estate. The property was used by the royal family as an informal residence. Her daughter-in-law Princess Augusta enlarged it. The latter commissioned the architect Sir William Chambers to design several structures for it. Of these, the China Pagoda (1761) survives.

Augusta's son, King George III, took a keen interest in Kew. He had Sir Joseph Banks and William Aiton advise him about its gardens. These started to be treated in a more botanical manner than had been the case previously. In 1771 the plant collector Francis Masson was hired to search out new plants for it. A decade later the monarch bought the neighbouring Dutch House property. In 1797 Banks was formally appointed to be Kew's Director. He is reputed to have stated that the gardens might become a great 'botanical exchange house for the empire'.

Queen Victoria acceded to the throne in 1837. Not having been raised at Kew, she did not have the same degree of identity with the estate that her three predecessors had had. In 1840 the property became the national botanical garden; this was done with an appreciation of the economic ramifications that botany could have. The following year William Hooker was appointed to be Kew's Director. Under his leadership, the grounds were extended so that they covered 300 acres (120 *ha*.). The Palm House (1848) was designed by Decimus Burton. It was the first large building to be constructed from wrought iron.

Kew's Joseph Banks Centre for Economic Botany opened in 1990.

Location: Kew Road, Richmond, Surrey, TW9 3AB.

Reading: John Gascoigne *Science In The Service of Empire: Joseph Banks, The British State and The Uses of Science In The Age of Revolution* Cambridge University Press (1998).

See Also: MUSEUMS The Natural History Museum; ROYAL RESIDENCES

Website: www.kew.org

Rubber

In the mid-19thC the burgeoning global railway industry became a major market for rubber. The material was used to manufacture hoses and springs for rolling stock, as well as buffer springs in *termini*. Henry Wickham's first commercial activity in Latin America was an attempt to supply London's milliners with exotic feathers that were sourced from Nicaragua's tropical forests. In Brazil Wickham became the first Briton to learn how to tap rubber.[1] He tried to establish a plantation in the country. The venture failed.

In 1876 Wickham smuggled 70,000 rubber tree seeds out of Brazil. At the time, it was not technically a crime to export them. However, in order to try to develop an image of himself as a maverick individual, he chose to foster a myth that he had had to steal them. He gave the seeds to Kew. Three months later almost 3000 of them were dispatched to botanical gardens in Singapore and Sri Lanka.

Wickham had hopes that the superintendency of one of the principal colonial gardens would be conferred upon him. Joseph Hooker, the Director of Kew, secretly vetoed any such appointment. The adventurer was given £700 as a reward. He also received shares in a commercial rubber business. However, these were to prove to be worthless. Subsequently, he was knighted and received some further financial acknowledgement of his achievement.

In 1913 the first non-Brazilian rubber crop was harvested. Within six years the British Empire was supplying 95% of the world's demand for the commodity. The market for Brazilian wild rubber collapsed.

Reading: Joe Jackson *The Thief At The End of World: Power and The Seeds of Empire* Duckworth (2008).

William Woodruff (1916-2008) *The Rise of The British Rubber Industry During The Nineteenth Century* Liverpool University Press (1958).[2]

See Also: TEA Robert Fortune

---

[1]   The rubber tree (*Hevea brasiliensis*) was native to the Amazon Basin.

[2]   A footnote in the book states that Professor Woodruff had been able to find only one 19thC article on contraceptives. This had been entitled *Questionable Rubber Goods*.

THE LORD MAYOR OF LONDON

The first Lord Mayor of London was Henry FitzAlwyn. He held the office from 1192 until his death in 1212. Three years later King John granted to London the right to elect its own chief magistrate. The monarch did this in an attempt to secure the City's support for himself in his struggles against the barons. However, a few weeks later the noblemen compelled him to sign *Magna Carta*.

If an individual wishes to serve as Lord Mayor s/he must be an alderman who has already been a sheriff.[1] It is the usual practice for the most senior alderman who has not served in the mayoralty to be chosen. The vote takes place in the Guildhall. The electorate is made up of the City's liverymen. Usually, about a thousand of them participate. The matter is determined by a show of hands. If the vote is close then there is a ballot. The last time that there was one was in 1894.

Within the City, the Lord Mayor has precedence over everyone except the sovereign. Each mayor holds office for a single year, from November to November.

The new Lord Mayor hosts a banquet at the Guildhall. This is usually attended by the current Prime Minister and several senior members of the government. The occasion is often used by an invited politician as an opportunity for making a key-note speech about the state of the economy.

See Also: THE CITY OF LONDON

Website: www.cityoflondon.gov.uk/about-the-city/who-we- are/ key-members/the-lord-mayor-of-thecity-of-london/Pages/ default.aspx

The Lord Mayor's Coach

In 1711, while going to swear his oath of office, Sir Gilbert Heathcote, the Lord Mayor-elect, fell off his horse and broke one of his legs. Since then it has been the custom for the mayor-elect to make the journey by coach.

The Lord Mayor's coach was built by Joseph Berry in 1757 to a design that had been created by the architect Sir Robert Taylor. The Court of Aldermen furnished the £1065 that it cost to build. In 1777 the vehicle became the property of the Court of Common Council. It is still used for the Lord Mayor's Procession. Most of the time it is on exhibition

---

[1]   S/he does not need to have been a common councilman.

in the Museum of London.

Location: The Museum of London, No. 150 London Wall, EC2Y 5HN.

See Also: THE LORD MAYOR OF LONDON The Lord Mayor's Procession; MUSEUMS The Museum of London

Website: www.lordmayorsshow.org/procession/coach.html

The Lord Mayor's Procession

On the second Saturday of November, the new Lord Mayor assumes the post. In order to do so s/he travels from the Guildhall in the City of London to the Royal Courts of Justice on the Strand. The latter lies just outside of the Square Mile. This journey is known as the Lord Mayor's Procession. Until 2006 the Lord Mayor's coach was pulled by horses that earned their daily keep by delivering beer within the City. At the Courts, the Lord Chief Justice, the most senior judge in England and Wales, swears the official into office.

By the 2010s the Procession had come to involve several thousand people. As a result, it was about three-miles-long. Therefore, it extended over a greater distance than exists between the Guildhall and the Courts.

Location: The Royal Courts of Justice, Strand, WC2A 2LL. On the northern side, to the east of the Aldwych.

See Also: THE CITY OF LONDON Good Numbers / THE CITY OF LONDON The Remembrancer

Website: www.lordmayorsshow.org

The Mansion House

Until the 18thC there was no official residence for the Lord Mayor. The dignitaries fuflfilled their entertaining duties either in livery companies' halls or in their own homes. The Stocks Market was chosen to become the site for the mayoralty's permanent residence. George Dance the elder-designed the proposed Mansion House. Its foundation stone was laid in 1739. Sir Crisp Gascoyne was the first Lord Mayor to reside in the building (1752).

The Lord Mayor possesses powers to act as a magistrate. The Mansion House has its own court room and cells. Nine of these are for men and one - 'the birdcage' - is for women. The building's banqueting room became known as the Egyptian Hall. Its columns were derived from the work of Palladio (*d.*1580) but were held to be 'Egyptian' in character.

Location: Bank, EC4N 8BH. On the south-western side.

Website: www.cityoflondon.gov.uk/about-the-city/history-and
-heritage/our-buildings-in-the-city/Pages/History-of-the-Mansion-
House.aspx

The Silent Ceremony

On the day before the Lord Mayor's Procession the formal transfer of
jurisdiction from one Lord Mayor to the next occurs in a ceremony that
is held in the Great Hall of the Guildhall. During it, the incoming official
is vested with a series of symbolic items. These include a mace, a purse,
a seal, and a sword. The individuals who present the objects endeav-
our to avoid showing any disrespect towards her/him. Therefore, they
do not display their backs to her/him. This means that, once they have
handed over their article, they walk away backwards. The only speech
that is involved in the 90-minute-long procedure is a brief declaration
that the new mayor makes. As a result, the occasion is known as the
Silent Ceremony.

Location: The Guildhall, Guildhall Yard, EC2V 5AE.

See Also: THE CITY OF LONDON The Guildhall; ROYAL
STATUES Queen Anne, St Paul's Cathedral

Website: www.cityoflondon.gov.uk/events/Pages/
event-detail.aspx?eventid=1253

MAPS

The A-Z

Alexander Gross was a Hungarian *émigré* who established a map-publishing business in London. The venture was successful. He had the financial means to be able to send his daughter Phyllis to Roedean School. There, she proved to be gifted at art. However, her father's firm failed and he went bankrupt. He moved to the United States. Phyllis had to leave the school. In 1927 she married an artist called Richard Pearsall. They lived in Spain. The marriage failed. She then moved to London and supported herself by painting portraits. However, she found the city's art world to be highly affected and soon became disenchanted by it.

Some friends of Mrs Pearsall invited her to visit them. She had not been to their home before. Her means were limited and therefore she sought to walk there. She became lost and arrived at her destination long after she had intended to. Subsequently, she realised that the last time that a street map of London had been published had been in 1919. The city had undergone a large number of changes since then. She resolved to create one and publish it. She walked the streets for eighteen hours a day and compiled an index of over 20,000 cards that she placed in a set of shoeboxes that she kept underneath her bed. In 1936 she published *London A-Z Street Atlas*. This proved to be a success and she set up the Geographers' A To Z Map Company. She was able to employ a draughtsman who previously had worked for her father.

Mrs Pearsall withdrew from the day-to-day management of the Company during the late 1950s to lead a congenial life that consisted in large part of writing and painting. In 1962 she relocated the firm's offices from the Gray's Inn Road to Sevenoaks. As a committed Christian, she believed that a business should be a social entity as well as a commercial one. In 1965 she set up the Geographers' Map Trust and vested her shares in the business in it. This was in order to protect its employees from any possible takeover and to enable them to benefit from the venture's successes. She continued to act as the Company's chairman until her death.

The West End section of the CrossRail system was bored in 2013. The tunnelling machine that did the work was named Phyllis in honour of Mrs Pearsall.

Locations: No. 24 Gray's Inn Road, WC1X 8HP. On the eastern, towards the southern end.

No. 3 Court Lane Gardens, Court Lane, Dulwich, SE21 7DZ. Mrs Pearsall's home.

The Radcliffe Line

The cost of fighting the Second World War had effectively bankrupted the United Kingdom. The expense of maintaining British rule over India was no longer bearable. There was a view that South Asia's large contribution to the war effort should be rewarded. In addition, the United States wanted Britain to wind up her empire.

A decision was taken that British India should be divided into two independent countries: India and Pakistan. The latter was to consist of what is now Pakistan and Bangladesh (East Pakistan). It was hoped that by India being a predominantly Hindu country and Pakistan an overwhelmingly Muslim one, sectarian tensions within them would be reduced. The Indian Independence Act of 1947 made provision for setting up two commissions that were charged with demarcating the two borders that were to separate India from the two portions of Pakistan. Both bodies contained equal numbers of representatives of the Indian National Congress and the Muslim League. All of them were trained lawyers.

Sir Cyril Radcliffe was an intellectually distinguished British barrister. During the Second World War he had served as a temporary Whitehall civil servant. He had become the Ministry of Information's Director-General. The knight was appointed to be the chairman of both of the commissions. In large part, he was selected because he had had no involvement in the administration of British India. It was believed that his prior ignorance of the realities of the subcontinent would be an aid to his being impartial.

Following the official's arrival in India, he was given five weeks in which to determine the two states' mutual borders. In order to ensure that a speedy result was secured, a decision had been made that neither commission should be supported by anyone who had expert knowledge of the issues that they were to be dealt with. The South Asian members of the bodies proved to be highly sectarian in their conduct. Therefore, Radcliffe himself had to decide the binding responses to most of the knotty issues that had to be addressed. Physically, he found the subcontinent's climate hard to endure. Therefore, he worked in a state of considerable physical unease.

The resulting frontiers became known as the Radcliffe Line. It ran through numerous densely populated areas rather than skirting them. Many millions of people found that their religious identity meant that they were on the *wrong* side of the Line. A wave of sectarian violence was launched against many of them. Therefore, one of the largest human movements in history ensued; over thirteen million people are believed to have fled from their homes. Many hundreds of thousands of them - probably over a million - were murdered while they were in transit.

Before returning to Britain, Radcliffe destroyed all of his papers that related to the Line. He had been of the view that whatever decisions were made people would suffer. However, there was nothing inevitable about the scale of the slaughter. The British state could have ended its rule of India in other ways. When the knight appreciated what had happened, he had the grace to decline to accept his official salary for the work he had performed.

Locations: The India Office, Whitehall, SW1A 2AH. In 1947 it was on the western side, to the south of the junction with King Charles Street.

No. 5 Campden Hill Gate, Duchess of Bedford Walk, W8 7QH. Viscount Radcliffe's final London home.

William Smith's Map

William Smith was born a member of an impoverished Oxfordshire family. A bright lad he was hired to assist a road surveyor. His ability led to his being appointed to survey the best route for a proposed canal venture. The need to take into consideration how much work would have to be done to excavate the route underscored his interest in geology. He was commissioned to assess the potential of a mine, which gave him - quite literally - a deeper appreciation of his subject. He worked across the country advising landowners and businessmen on how they could use their land more efficiently. Through these commissions he deepened his knowledge of Britain's substrata.

Smith made the unprecedented decision to synthesise what he knew about Britain's geology onto a single map and to add to this information about what he had not yet seen. It would be the first geological map to be made of the whole country. The project took many years and helped to devastate his finances. His creation was finally published in 1815.

The Geological Society had been founded in 1807. Smith's map fell foul of a dilettantish clique that then had the prevailing influence within the body. As a result, his chances of making good his fortune were curtailed. In 1819 he left London and withdrew to Yorkshire. However, within the organisation an intellectually more rigorous group began to emerge. They recognised the man as one of their own number. A process of reassessment began. In 1831 the Society's highest honour - the Wollaston medal - was bestowed upon him.

Smith's original map is now one of the Society's most prized possessions.

Locations: Burlington House, No. 50 Piccadilly, W1J 0BD. The Geological Society's current home.

The Grand Connaught Rooms, Nos. 61-5 Great Queen Street, WC2B 5DA. The site of the Society's original home.

Reading: Simon Winchester *The Map That Changed The World* Viking (2001). A biography of Smith.

Website: www.geolsoc.org.uk

The Underground Map

The individual Underground lines were developed by different groups of investors. By 1912 they were - with the exception of the Metropolitan Line - all owned by the same company, the Underground brand was established and its first map created. This and the subsequent early maps of the system were geographically correct. This meant that information for the central area was crowded, with stations' names sometimes being illegible, while on the peripheries they were arranged relatively sparsely.

In 1931 Harry Beck of the London Underground Signals Office drew the world's first diagrammatic underground railway map. This distorted the central area by enlarging its share of the chart. Mr Beck had developed the idea in his spare time. He offered it to London Transport's management. They rebuffed the design. He presented it to them again the following year. This time, they had it tested upon members of the public, who responded positively towards it.

Beck conveyed the copyright of the map to London Transport in 1937. The following year the two parties had their first spat over it. Their subsequent relations were fractious. In 1947 he resigned from London Transport. In 1960 a new edition of the map caused his relations with the body to rupture permanently.

Location: London Transport, No. 55 Broadway, SW1H 0BD.
See Also: MUSEUMS The Design Museum

MEMORIALS

See Also: ARCHES; COLUMNS; ROYAL STATUES; ST PAUL'S CATHEDRAL Monuments; STATUES; STATUES Eros, The Belgian Years; WESTMINSTER ABBEY Memorials & Graves
Website: www.pmsa.org.uk (The Public Monuments & Sculptures Association)

The Albert Memorial

The ornate Albert Memorial (1876) commemorates Prince Albert, Queen Victoria's consort. Despite having no official constitutional position, he had sought to defend the monarchy's interests whenever he could do so reasonably. He had been aided in this effort by the fact that the queen bore him nine children. As a result, she had been physically indisposed for much of the time. She had been willing to allow him to act as her *de facto* deputy.

In 1861 the consort had travelled to Cambridge by train in order to admonish their oldest son the Prince of Wales (the future King Edward VII) for the way in which he had been conducting himself. During the journey Albert had contracted a cold. This had developed into being a case of double pneumonia. The condition had proven to be fatal.

From seven proffered designs Victoria chose one that had been created by Sir George Gilbert Scott. The Memorial was paid for jointly by a government grant and by a public subscription that was organised by the Royal Society for Arts. William Gladstone, the prime minister, chose to quibble about the details of the contract under which it was to be built. This delayed the project's start.[1]

The 14ft-tall (5.4m) prince holds in his hands a copy of the catalogue of the Great Exhibition of 1851.[2]

Location: Kensington Gardens, SW7 2AP. On the southern side, opposite The Royal Albert Hall.

[1]   The premier's wife is reputed to have once said to him 'If you were n't such a great man you would be very boring.'

[2]   The architect Sir William Tite MP had been prominent in the campaign that had prevented Scott from giving the new Foreign Office Building a Gothic *façade*. Tite had called for it to be given an Italianate one instead. However, Sir William was not inclined to comprehensive opposition to either Scott or the Gothic style. In 1863 he publicly applauded the man's use of it for the Albert Memorial.

The Albert Memorial

The Cenotaph

In the centre of Whitehall is The Cenotaph (1920). This structure commemorates the dead of the 1914-1918 and 1939-1945 World Wars. It was designed by the architect Sir Edwin Lutyens and was first erected in plaster as a saluting point for the Allied Victory March of 1919. It was then rebuilt in stone and unveiled on 11 November 1920.

Location: Parliament Street, SW1A 2(NH).

See Also: MILITARY CUSTOMS; MILITARY CUSTOMS Remembrance Sunday; MUSEUMS The Imperial War Museum; WESTMINSTER ABBEY Memorials and Graves, The Unknown Warrior

Websites: www.cwgc.org (The Commonwealth War Graves Commission) www.twgpp.org (The C.W.G. Photographic Project)

Revolutionary Sod: The First World War and its immediate aftermath witnessed one of the principal socio-economic revolutions of British history. A sign of this was the manner in which belawned cemeteries for the burial of the slain were created. The graves were not located according to rank. The corpse of a colonel could be laid to rest next to that of a private.

However, Britain was Britain. There was a difference in the way that the lids of the soldiers' coffins were fastened shut. The officers' ones were secured with screws whereas those of the ranks were sealed by nails that were hammered into them.

During the conflict officers were proportionately more likely to be killed than were members of the ranks. This was because the formers' uniforms were distinctive and they were armed with revolvers rather than with rifles. Therefore, Axis snipers were able to identify them on the battlefield and shoot them.

Reading: David Crane *Empires of The Dead: How One Man's Vision Led To The Creation of WWI's War Graves* Collins (2013). A biography of Sir Fabian Ware, the founding Director of the Commonwealth War Graves Commission.

See Also: CLASS

Charing Cross

In 1290 Queen Eleanor of Castille, King Edward I's consort, died at Harby in Nottinghamshire. Her body was carried back to London so that it could be interred in Westminster Abbey. The queen had been immensely popular with ordinary people. Therefore, each night of the journey, while her corpse was lying in state, large crowds paid their respects to it.[1] The night before Eleanor's remains were received by the Abbey, the procession rested upon what was to become the site of Charing Cross. The following year, the king commemorated his late wife by commissioning the erection of a stone cross at each of the sites where the train had stopped overnight.[2]

The Charing Cross cross fell victim to the English Civil Wars; it was demolished by the Puritans in 1647. In 1675 an equestrian statue of King Charles I (1633) was erected upon its site.

Location: Trafalgar Square, WC2N 5DS. The traffic island that stands between the square and the top of Whitehall.

See Also: ROYAL STATUES King Charles I; WESTMINSTER ABBEY Royal Graves

The Charing Cross Monument: The Charing Cross Monument (1863) was created for the South Easterrn Railway Company. It was erected to complement the Charing Cross Hotel (1864) which was designed by Edward Barry.

Location: Charing Cross Station, Strand, WC2A 2LL. The forecourt.

The Queen Victoria Memorial

The 82ft-tall (25m), 2300 ton marble Queen Victoria Memorial (1911) stands in front of Buckingham Palace.[3] It was created by the sculptor Thomas Brock, whom King George V knighted when the structure was formally unveiled.[4]

Location: Buckingham Palace, SW1A 1AA.
See Also: ARCHES Marble Arch

The Scott Memorial

Perhaps the most archetypal British explorer was Robert Falcon Scott (*d*.1912). He failed to return from the South Pole.[5] In part, this was

---

[1]   The fact that your average medieval peasant does not get the chance to gawp at a dead queen every day may have played a part in compounding her posthumous popularity.

[2]   Crosses were erected at: Lincoln, Grantham, Stamford, Geddington, Northampton, Stony Stratford, Woburn, Dunstable, St Albans, Waltham (the nearest extant one), Cheapside, and Charing Cross.

[3]   In the taxi trade's slang the Memorial is known as 'the Wedding Cake'.

[4]   Ben Weinreb & Christopher Hibbert (eds.) *The London Encyclo-paedia* Macmillan (1983) 648-9

[5]   An uncharitable interpretation ascribes Scott's death to his failure to use dogs. In the last resort, they could have acted as an unexciting alternative to

because his trip was a portion of an expedition that was focussed on science. Among the items that were retrieved from his final camp were fossils that proved that formerly Antarctica had had a climate in which leafed plants had been able to grow.[1]

In terms of image-building Scott did have one advantage - he had married the sculptress Kathleen Scott. The statue of the explorer that stands in Waterloo Place was crafted by his widow.

Locations: The Scott Memorial, Waterloo Place, SW1Y 4(AU).

No. 56 Oakley Street, SW3 5HB. Scott's home.

---

mutton. (*Chapter 9: Zebras, Unhappy Marriages and The 'Anna Karenina' Principle* in Jared Diamond's *Guns, Germs & Steel: The Fates of Human Societies* (1997).)

[1]   One of the scientists who asked him to look out for such rocks was Marie Stopes. She was then a palaeobotany lecturer at the University of Manchester. (Her lasting fame was to derive from her subsequent activities in another field.)

MILITARY CUSTOMS

See Also: THE GUNPOWDER PLOT Searching Parliament's Cellars; MEMORIALS The Cenotaph

The Beating Retreat

The Beating Retreat is a musical event that is performed on two evenings each June. It grew out of a custom that took place each evening in military camps. This involved closing the strongholds' gates and lowering their flags.

The musicians who perform are drawn from the bands of the Household Division.

Location: Horse Guards Parade, SW1A 2NS.

Websites: www.householddivision.org/beating-retreat www.royal parks.org.uk/parks/st-jamess-park/st-jamess-park-attractions/royal-marines-beating-retreat

The Changing of The Guard

The Changing of The Guard takes place in front of Buckingham Palace. The ceremony involves the New Guard exchanging duties with the Old Guard. The ritual is accompanied by music that is played by a regimental band.

When the sovereign is resident in the palace, four sentries are present at the front of it. When s/he is away, there are two.

Location: Buckingham Palace, SW1A 1AA.

Websites: www.army.mod.uk/events/ceremonial/23241.aspx www.householddivision.org.uk/beating-retreat

The Constable's Dues

Roughly once a year, depending upon naval vessel movements, the Constable's Dues ceremony takes place at the Tower of London. Royal Navy sailors deliver a barrel of rum to the fortress-prison's Constable. This is to pay for the service's access to the Pool of London.

Location: The Tower of London, EC3N 4AB.

See Also: THE THAMES The Pool of London; THE TOWER OF LONDON The Ceremony of The Keys

Remembrance Sunday

Remembrance Sunday occurs on the Sunday that is closest to 11 November. Members of the royal family, the government, the opposition, and representatives of Commonwealth countries lay poppy wreaths around the Cenotaph. The flower was chosen as the symbol for remembrance because after the First World War it was the first plant to spring up on the former battlefields of Belgium and France. It is taken to represent regeneration. At 11 *a.m.* a two-minute-long silence in memory of the fallen begins.

The politician the 1st Marquis Curzon devised most of the Remembrance Day ceremonies.

Location: Parliament Street, SW1A 2(NH).

See Also: MEMORIALS The Cenotaph; ROYALTY The Sovereign and The Prime Minister, Marquis Curzon

Websites: www.royal.gov.uk/royaleventsandceremonies/ remembranceday.aspx www.britishlegion.org.uk/remembrance/ the-nation-remembers/remembrance-sunday

The Royal Hospital Chelsea

The Royal Hospital Chelsea was founded in 1682 by King Charles II to provide material support for soldiers who had had to retire from the Army through age or infirmity. The building was designed by Sir Christopher Wren.

Location: Royal Hospital Road, Chelsea, SW3 4SR.

Website: www.chelsea-pensioners.co.uk

Ceremonies: Three annual ceremonies take place at the Hospital. The Cake Ceremony involves free cake and beer. These are provided by the Returned Services League of Australia. The Founder's Day Ceremony commemorates when, following the Battle of Worcester (1651), King Charles II hid in an oak tree. Each 29 May (Oak Apple Day) the institution's Grinling Gibbons bronze (1676) of the monarch is covered with oak leaves and a parade is held in front of a royal guest.[1] Every December the Cheese Ceremony takes place. It dates back to 1692 when a London cheesemonger presented the Hospital with a Gloucestershire cheese.

Website: www.rsl.org.au

Royal Salutes

On 22 April the Queen's Birthday is marked in Hyde Park by a 41-gun

---

[1]   Royal Chelsea Hospital's statue of King Charles II was put up in 1692.

salute. This is performed by the King's Troop Royal Horse Artillery. The first 21 firings signify that it is the sovereign's birthday that is being marked. The subsequent twenty indicate that the discharge is being performed in a royal park.

With the outbreak of the Second World War in 1939 the Horse Artillery Batteries were mechanised. Following the return of peace, King George VI expressed a desire that something of the regiment's equine tradition should be preserved. As the result of this wish, a permanent saluting battery unit was established. The following year the sovereign visited the Troop's St John's Wood's Barracks. There, he bestowed its name upon it.

When the regiment is on parade with its guns, it occupies the place of honour on the right of the line. This position gives it precedence over all of the other regiments that are present.

Location: Hyde Park, W2 2UH.

See Also: ARCHES The Marble Arch; ROYALTY

Websites: www.army.mod.uk/artillery/regiments/24679.aspx www.royal.gov.uk/RoyalEventsandCeremonies/GunSalutes/ GunSalutes.aspx www.royalparks.org.uk/parks/green-park/green-park-attractions/gun-salutes

Trooping The Colour

Each year, on the Saturday nearest 11 June, Horse Guards Parade hosts the Trooping The Colour ceremony. The event marks the sovereign's Official Birthday. The custom originated in the military practice of trooping (carrying) flags and banners in front of soldiers. This was done in order to familiarise them with the colours around which they would be expected to rally on the battlefield. The ceremony was first performed in 1755. It has taken place regularly since 1805.

Location: Horse Guards Parade, SW1A 2NS.

See Also: ROYALTY

A Week's Winter Fodder

The office of Commander-in-Chief of the British Army was conferred upon George Duke of Cambridge in 1856. He was a cousin of Queen Victoria. Initially, his grace proved to be a reformer. However, with the passage of the years, he became set in his ways.

During the second half of the 19thC there were developments in international military practice. There were also technological changes to weaponry. Therefore, a body of public opinion came to believe that the service should be modernised. In this light, the Household Cavalry was regarded by many people as being an anachronism. Cambridge waged a vigorous campaign against Army reform. He lost a number of his political battles but he also won some of them as well. He was of the firm belief that regimental traditions and history were an important factor in engendering *esprit de corps*.

The duke died in 1904. Three years later an equestrian statue of him was unveiled in Whitehall. Subsequently, an informal military custom developed. Each Christmas Eve members of either the Blue & Royals or of the Lifeguards are on duty at Horse Guards. On New Year's Eve soldiers of the other regiment are. On the former day men from the unit that is serving attach a feedbag to the head of the horse. This contains straw. They also place sawdust between the animal's hooves. These are marks of gratitude to his grace for the role that he played in the Household Cavalry's survival. Seven days later soldiers from the other regiment remove the bag.

Location: Whitehall, SW1A 2(EU). Between The Old War Office and Horse Guards.

See Also: STATUES Two Too Many Beers

MUSEUMS

See Also: THE BRITISH MUSEUM; CHARLES DICKENS The Dickens House Museum; GALLERIES; HERITAGE

The Design Museum

The Design Museum is a museum of contemporary design. It was established with the support of the designer and restaurateur Sir Terence Conran. In 1989 the institution opened in a former banana warehouse on Shad Thames.

In 2014 it was the case that changes were being made to the former Commonwealth Institute building site on Kensington High Street. This was so that it could become the new home of the Museum. At its Shad Thames premises the institution had only hosted exhibitions. However, it was intending to display a permanent collection of its own in its new West London abode.

Locations: No. 28 Shad Thames, SE1 2YD.

No. 250 Kensington High Street, W8 6NQ. On the northern side, to the west of the south-eastern portion of Holland Park.

See Also: MAPS The Underground Map; MUSEUMS The Geffrye, Museum of The Home; MUSEUMS The Museum of Brands, Packaging & Advertising; MUSEUMS The Victoria & Albert Museum; THE THAMES Warehouses; THEATRES The Donmar Warehouse

Websites: http://designmuseum.org www.oma.eu (The additions and the alterations to the former Commonwealth Institute building were designed by the OMA. Rem Koolhaas is one of the firm's partners.)

The Fan Museum

The Fan Museum possesses over 3000 fans, some of which date back to the 11[th]C, as well as fan-related ephemera. The collection was amassed by Helene Alexander. The Museum was opened to the public in 1991.

Location: No. 12 Croom's Hill, SE10 8ER.

Website: www.thefanmuseum.org.uk

The Geffrye, Museum of The Home

As a young man Robert Geffrye was admitted to the Ironmongers'

Company. He became wealthy through being a merchant in the East India trade. He served as the Lord Mayor of London in 1686 and was knighted. In 1715, under the terms of his will, an almshouse was founded in Hackney to house needy members of his livery.

In 1911 the building was sold to the London County Council, which used it to house a collection of furniture. This evolved into being the Geffrye Museum. It has eleven period rooms that would have existed in the homes of middling people over the period from 1600 to the present.

Location: No. 136 Kingsland Road, E2 8EA.

See Also: MUSEUMS The Design Museum

Website: www.geffrye-museum.org.uk

The Grant Museum

The Grant Museum is a small natural history museum that is part of University College. Its collection includes the remains of a number of animals that have become extinct, *e.g.* the dodo, the quagga (a variety of zebra), and the thylcacine (the Tasmanian tiger).

Location: The Rockefeller Building, No. 21 University Street, WC1E 6DE. On the southern side of the eastern end.

Website: www.ucl.ac.uk/museums/zoology

The Last Dodo: The last recorded sighting of a dodo was made in 1662 by Volkert Evertsz, a Dutchman.

In 2003 the scientific journal *Nature* published a statistical analysis by researchers at the Royal Botanic Gardens Kew and the Woods Hole Oceanographic Institute in Massachusetts on the probable extinction date for the dodo. This indicated that the likeliest point was 1690 but that the species may have survived until as late as 1797.

The Horniman Museum & Gardens

In 1840 John Horniman invented a machine that could package goods in sealed packets. He opted to apply it to the tea trade. His sons William Henry and Frederick John Horniman entered the firm, which, in 1868 became W.H. & F.J. Horniman & Company. By the 1890s it was the biggest tea business in the world.

As a child, Frederick collected curious objects. As he grew older the amount he could spend increased exponentially. He used travellers and missionaries as agents for acquiring artefacts. In time, he started to journey extensively himself. In 1868 he purchased Surrey House in Forest Hill. Eventually, the tea magnate's collection became so large that he moved out of the property and into the neighbouring Surrey Mount.

In 1890 he opened Surrey House as a public museum. In 1901 an extension was completed that consisted of two large galleries and a tower. These were designed by Charles Harrison Townsend. Soon afterwards the house, its grounds, and Horniman's collection were given to the London County Council to hold on behalf of the people of London.

In 1903 the Museum acquired a public aquarium. Horniman's son, Emslie Horniman, presented the institution with the financial means to build a lecture hall and a library.

In 1918 J. Lyons acquired control the Horniman tea business.

Location: No. 100 London Road, Forest Hill, SE23 3PQ.

See Also: TEA

Website: www.horniman.ac.uk

The Hunterian Collection

The surgeon John Hunter collected physiological specimens. His home in Leicester Square had to be extended so that it could accommodate the artefacts. He requested in his will that the assemblage should be offered to the government for purchase. In 1799 the state made £15,000 available to buy it. The Collection was then passed on to the Company of Surgeons.

By the first half of the 20thC the Royal College of Surgeon had the finest physiological museum in the world. However, a large part of it was destroyed during the Second World War as the result of its home being struck by an aerial bomb.

The paintings in The Hunterian include three Stubbs and a Zoffany.

Locations: No. 28 Leicester Square, WC2H 7LE.

The Royal College of Surgeons, Nos. 35-43 Lincoln's Inn Fields, WC2A 3PE.

See Also: VISITOR ATTRACTIONS Madame Tussaud's; WESTMINSTER ABBEY Memorials and Graves, Doctors

Website: www.rcseng.ac.uk/museums/hunterian

The Imperial War Museum

Ludgwig Mond (*d*.1909) was born and raised in Germany. During the mid-19thC Germans were at the forefront of both pure chemistry and its application. Mond proved to be highly gifted at both disciplines. The professors under whom he studied included Robert Wilhelm Bunsen of burner fame. Mond, during his early adulthood, worked in his homeland, The Netherlands, and the United Kingdom. He opted to settle in the last and was to become a British citizen.

Soda was used in the manufacture of commodities such as glass, paper, soap, and textiles. In the early 1870s Mond met the Belgian chemist Ernest Solvay. The latter was seeking to refine the ammonia-soda process for producing it. The prevalent Leblanc technique was inefficient and generated a number of unwanted by-products. Mond founded a business that processed these into chemicals that had commercial value.

When it became apparent that Solvay's research might be successful, Mond was in a financial position to be able to buy from him the British rights to his process. With John Tomlinson Brunner, he set up Brunner, Mond & Company to exploit them. The firm established a plant in Cheshire. There, Mond improved the effectiveness of the technique. The business became the world's largest manufacturer of alkalis. He and Brunner were to become millionaires. The latter, who had the more public role of the pair, was to be dubbed the 'Chemical Croesus' by *The Times* newspaper. Brunner, Mond sought to treat its employees well. The business furnished them with leisure facilities and good homes, as well as having them work only an eight-hour day.

Mond continued to research applied chemistry. The advances that he made included devising a technique for producing ammonia from the nitrogen that was present in solid fuel. As the result of an unanticipated laboratory observation, he created a process for refining pure nickel. In 1900 he established the Mond Nickel Company. The Swansea-based enterprise used energy from coal that was mined in South Wales to refine nickel from ores that had been dug in Ontario.

Despite his fortune having come from the application of scientific techniques, Mond always believed that scientific education should be focused upon pure science. Among the many benefactions that he made was a gift in 1896 of £100,000 to The Royal Institution of Great Britain. The money was used to purchase a property in Albemarle Street that stood next door to the body's premises. The building was fitted out as a research facility. It was named the Davy-Faraday Laboratory. The scientist-tycoon became a leading purchaser of Early Italian paintings. He bequeathed the majority of his collection to the National Gallery.

Mond had two sons Robert and Alfred. They were to be active in the businesses that their father had founded. The former was the more scientifically-inclined of the pair. He became an able chemist who was granted a number of patents. However, in the discipline, he was not of the same calibre as his father had been. With time, he came to act principally as a manager of researchers who were working on the application of chemistry.

Robert suffered a bout of illness. In order to recover his health, he travelled to Egypt to take advantage of its warm wintertime climate. There, he developed an interest in Egyptology. His wealth enabled him to financially back a number of excavation and preservation projects. The archaeologists whom he helped support included Howard Carter. Sometimes, the chemist participated in fieldwork. He bought Ancient Egyptian artefacts with a taste that was both informed and discerning. Some of the items he displayed in a 'Pharaoh Room' that he created in his London townhouse. The majority of them were given to universities and museums. His interest in collecting extended to other spheres, notably model soldiers. They were a passion that lasted for much of his adult life.

Alfred's ambitions were political. Therefore, he studied law at university and became a barrister. He spoke with an accent that preserved some of his parents' German-derived inflections. At his father's wish, he became a director of Brunner, Mond and soon afterwards the enterprise's managing director. He proved to be an able business leader and developed a high degree of scientific literacy. He believed that worker/employer relations should be characterised by co-operation rather than by confrontation. He was elected to serve as a Liberal MP in 1906.

The First World War began in 1914. Two years later David Lloyd George assumed the leadership of the government. The new premier appreciated that Alfred had proven his organisational talents in the commercial world. Therefore, he appointed his fellow Liberal to serve as First Commissioner of Works.

By the mid-19thC it had become apparent that many of the new industrial processes that had been developed were having a deleterious impact upon the people who lived in close proximity to sites where they were being used. The Metropolitan Buildings Act of 1844 had been designed in part to address this reality. However, the measure had only covered a defined physical area of the metropolis. Silvertown in East London had been located outside of this zone. Therefore, in 1894 Brunner, Mond & Company had established a facility in the district to make soda crystals and caustic soda. Production of the latter stopped in 1912. This meant that the facility had spare capacity.

The senior judge Lord Moulton was a former Liberal MP. He was a gifted mathematician and as a barrister had specialised in Patent Law. He was adept at dealing with a wide range of scientific information. Following the start of the war, he was appointed to head a committee that advised the government on its supply of high explosives. The body soon evolved into being the Explosives Supply Department.

The crude TNT that was imported from the United States was of variable quality. The chemist Herbert Humphrey, with the aid of two Brunner, Mond employees, devised a vacuum process that enabled benzoic to be used to purify the explosive to a single standard. Moulton learnt of the spare processing capacity at Silvertown. He asked the company to use it to refine the explosive. The firm's senior managers did not welcome the request. Their reasons for doing so were threefold. They understood the riskiness of the technique. They appreciated the unpleasant physical effects that their workers would suffer as a result of handling the chemical. And they knew that the district in which the plant was located was densely populated.

Ultimately, however, Brunner, Mond complied with the official's wish. TNT purification was commenced in East London in autumn 1915. Subsequently, the company developed a dedicated facility at Rudheath in Cheshire for the process. This was sited in a location that was physically much more isolated than its southern sister was. Its refinement capacity was greater than that of the London plant. However, the demand for the explosive was such that the latter continued to be operated.

On 19 January 1917 approximately 50 tons of TNT detonated within the Silvertown works. 69 people were killed instantly and hundreds of others were injured. Several hundred buildings were either flattened or rendered beyond repair. Tens of thousands of others were damaged by the blast. A second explosion was triggered in a gasholder that stood on the southern side of the Thames in the South Metropolitan Gas Company's East Greenwich Gas Works.

For Alfred the disaster would have underscored the impact that the hostilities were having upon Britain. Perhaps, drawing on the examples of how his father and his brother were not only collectors but also public benefactors, he started considering how the nation should commemorate the conflict. In his official capacity, he had already been approached by Charles ffoulkes, the Curator of the Tower of London, with a suggestion that materials that related to the conflict should be gathered. The following month the minister proposed to Lloyd George that a national war museum should be set up. In March the War Cabinet resolved that a body should be established to hold items about the Great War (the First World War).[1]

The minister-industrialist was appointed to chair a committee that oversaw the amassing of artefacts for the intended institution. It soon came to be appreciated that the British war effort was not just a national one but an imperial one to which the colonies were making large contri-

---

[1]   An official report into the Silvertown explosion accused Brunner, Mond of negligence. The document was not made public until the 1950s.

butions. Therefore, the proposed body's name became the Imperial War Museum. It was constituted under the provisions of the Imperial War Museum Act of 1920. Later that year it opened in the Crystal Palace.

The Museum's founding Director was Sir Martin Conway. He was an academic art historian who had become a contemporary celebrity and who had been elected to be an MP. His numerous achievements included being an experienced mountaineer. He was interested in portraying masculinity as being something that was apart from the everyday.

Peace had been re-established in 1918. Most of the world's principal trading nations had opted to try to rebuild their economies by means of protectionism. As a Liberal, Alfred had been associated with his party's broadly pro-free trade stance. However, in the new global environment, he re-examined his outlook with regard both to business and politics. He came to believe that Britain and her empire should respond in kind. He and a large proportion of the Parliamentary Liberal Party became increasingly inclined to identify themselves with the Conservatives. In 1926 he changed parties. This switch was part of a trend that rendered the Liberals a political force of the second order.

Alfred convinced himself that Britain's principal industrial enterprises should be amalgamated with one another to form combines. These could then be rationalised. He stated publicly that the national economy should be directed by the senior managers of a few vast corporations. In 1926 Brunner, Mond merged with Nobel Industries, and two other companies to form Imperial Chemical Industries (ICI). Three years later Mond Nickel became part of the International Nickel Company of Canada.

The newspaper proprietor Lord Rothermere had bought the former Bethlehem Royal Hospital (Bedlam). His intention had been to raze its building (1815) and then use its grounds as a space in which to create a park for the people of Lambeth. The Museum's need for a new home prompted him to transfer the building to it.[1] By then, his original plan had progressed to the extent that the complex's two wings had been demolished. The institution moved to the site in 1935.

Just prior to the creation of Imperial Chemical Industries, IG Farben had been established in Germany through the merger of six major chemicals companies with one another. Following the Second World War, the colossus was split up. The subsequent success of the daughter enterprises proved that Alfred's argument had been wrong. In the 1990s ICI finally divided itself up into a series of separate businesses. Of these, the jewel

---

[1]   The surrounding land is called Geraldine Mary Harmsworth Park in honour of the peer's mother.

was its pharmaceuticals operation. In 1993 this was demerged as Zeneca Group (later AstraZeneca). In 2008 Akzo-Nobel acquired the rump ICI.

Alan Borg served as the Museum's Director from 1982 to 1995. He is reputed to have once remarked that the institution's name was formed from 'the three most off-putting words in the English language'.

The Museum has a number of satellites: The Churchill War Rooms, *H.M.S. Belfast*, IWM Duxford in Cambridgeshire, and IWM North in Manchester.

Locations: The Imperial War Museum, Lambeth Road, SE1 6HZ. On the southern side of the junction with St George's Road.

Crescent Wharf, North Woolwich Road, Silvertown, E16 2(BG). Close to the junction with Mill Road. (Next to City Airport.)

Kensington Town Hall, Hornton Street, W8 7NX. On the western side, to the south of the junction with Holland Street. Professor Conway's London home was The Red House, which stood on the site.

No. 35 Lowndes Square, SW1X 9JN. Alfred Mond's home. At the southern end of the western side.

No. 9 Millbank, Westminster, SW1P 3GE. ICI's headquarters.

No. 57 Onslow Square, SW7 3LR. Moulton's home. The centre of the north-western side.

The Institute of Mechanical Engineers, No. 1 Birdcage Walk, SW1H 9JJ. The Explosives Supply Department's First World War home.

See Also: WINSTON CHURCHILL The Churchill War Rooms; GALLERIES Military Art; MEMORIALS The Cenotaph; THE TOWER OF LONDON The Royal Armouries

Websites: www.iwm.org.uk

www.akzonobel.com

www.brunnermond.com

The Museum of Brands, Packaging & Advertising

The Museum of Brands, Packaging & Advertising uses household products to portray the history of consumer culture. It evolved out of the Robert Opie Collection.

Location: No. 2 Colville Mews, Notting Hill, W11 2AR. At the western end.

Reading: Robert Opie *Remember When: A Nostalgic Trip Through The Consumer Era* Bounty Books (2007).

See Also: MUSEUMS The Design Museum

Websites: www.robertopiecollection.com

www.museumofbrands.com

The Museum of Childhood

In 1866 a prefabricated building was transferred from the South Kensington Museum's site to Bethnal Green where it was re-erected. The Bethnal Green Museum's functions as an outpost of its mother institution were various.

Following the First World War, Arthur Sabin was appointed to be the satellite's Curator. In the 1920s he started to focus the institution upon artefacts that were related to children. In 1974 its parent body, the (now) Victoria & Albert Museum, designated it as being a museum of childhood.

Location: Cambridge Heath Road, E2 9PA.

See Also: MUSEUMS The Victoria & Albert Museum; MUSEUMS Pollock's Toy Museum; SHOPPING Hamleys

Website: www.museumofchildhood.org.uk

The Museum of London

The Museum of London came into being because Donald Harden, the Director of the London Museum, and Norman Cook, the Director of the Guildhall Museum, concluded that the city would be served best by their institutions merging with one another. Both men struggled hard for their joint vision to come into being. Formally, they had both retired from their positions before the Museum opened in 1976.

In 2008 The Museum had 17,000 skeletons in its possession.

Locations: No. 150 London Wall, EC2Y 5HN.

No. 1 Warehouse, West India Quay, E14 4AL.

See Also: THE CITY OF LONDON; THE LORD MAYOR OF LONDON The Lord Mayor's Coach; ROMAN REMAINS

Websites: www.museumoflondonarchaeology.org.uk
www.museumoflondon.org.uk/london-wall

The Natural History Museum

The nucleus of the British Museum's natural history collection was amassed by Sir Hans Sloane (*d.*1753). In 1781 the institution was given the Royal Society's repository. In 1820 it received the botanical collection of Sir Joseph Banks.

The anatomist and palaeontologist Richard Owen[1] was appointed in 1856 to be the first superintendent of the Museum's natural history department. He divided it into botany, entomology, mineralogy, palaeontology, and zoology sections. Three years later he proposed to the government that the institution should divest itself of the material, which should become the core of a new natural history museum. In 1860 the Museum's trustees voted to hive off the department into an autonomous body.

A site in South Kensington was purchased in 1863. The following year a competition was held to determine who would design the new museum's home. Captain Francis Fowke of the Royal Engineers won this with a Renaissance style plan. However, he died. Owen, during his early career, had advanced himself by identifying with reactionary political elements. Times had changed and society was again progressively inclined. The importance of the museum to him prompted him to work with anyone who would forward the project. He proved to be fortunate in obtaining support for the scheme from the Liberal prime minister William Gladstone.

Alfred Waterhouse - a very charming architect[2] who had developed his own early career by working for a nexus of wealthy northern Liberals - was commissioned to oversee the construction of Fowke's plans. However, the man went on to redesign the project, declaring that a building in the South German Romanesque manner should be constructed. Owen supported this choice. The opposition of Queen Victoria to the change had to be overcome. It was. However, the scheme then became the subject of a degree of a politicking. During the early 1870s construction of the edifice finally began.

---

[1]   Sir Richard Owen coined the word 'dinosaur'.

[2]   It was said that Waterhouse's smile earned him an extra £1000 a year.

The Natural History Museum finally admitted the public in 1881.[1] Three years later Owen retired.

The Museum's Darwin Centre opened in 2009. There is a theory that the institution was extended in order to keep the more embedded curators on their toes. Some of them had been beginning to believe that they knew their way around the building.

Locations: The Natural History Museum, Cromwell Road, SW7 5BD. On the western side of the junction with Exhibition Road.

No. 61 New Cavendish Street, W1G 7LP. Waterhouse's home.

Reading: Richard Fortrey *Dry Store Room No 1: The Secret Life of The Natural History Museum* HarperPress (2007). Fortrey worked at the Museum as a palaeontologist.

See Also: THE BRITISH MUSEUM; KEW GARDENS The Royal Botanic Gardens; MUSEUMS; ZOOS

Website: www.nhm.ac.uk

An Artificial Protuberance: Rosie is a stuffed, one-horned Indian rhinoceros. In 2012 the Museum replaced her horn with an artificial one. This was because there had been a trans-European wave of thefts of the protuberances. Over fifty had been sawn away from exhibits. This fashion derived from the misapprehension that keratin, the protein of which the outgrowth is composed, is an aphrodisiac. (Should the prong-chompers still be desperate for an alternative source of the substance they can always try chewing their own fingernails.)

Website: www.cites.org (The Convention on International Trade In Endangered Species)

Ornamentations: Over the years 1875-8 Waterhouse drew designs for over 300 animal sculptures. Members of the Museum's staff checked them for their anatomical accuracy. The mouldings were made by a Monsieur Dujardin. Terracotta was used because of the large scale of production. However, the employment of this material was contentious. The art critic John Ruskin held that craftsmanship was essential to social responsibility and beauty. He had played a leading role in the design of the University of Oxford's Museum of Natural History (1861). That building's stone ornamentation had been carved *in situ*. However, the Ruskinians opted to approve of Waterhouse's semi-industrial approach.

Along the western wing's front were placed figures of extant creatures and along its eastern one representations of extinct ones. The arches of the Central Hall have reproductions of 78 monkeys climbing on them.

---

[1] In taxi slang the Natural History Museum is the 'Dead Zoo'.

Website: www.oum.ox.ac.uk

Piltdown Man: Charles Dawson was a country solicitor and amateur archaeologist. He was known to nurse ambitions of being elected to be a member of the Royal Society. In 1912 he unearthed some head bones in a gravel pit at Piltdown in Sussex. The material seemed to furnish evidence of their having been a 'missing link' between apes and men.

The remains had been stained to make them appear to be far older than they in fact were. They had been fractured in such a way that it was not possible to ascertain whether the jawbone actually complemented the skull.

In the 1950s it was established that the cranium had come from a modern man and the jaw from an orang-utan. The effect of the hoax was to muddy the waters of evolutionary anthropology.

Martin Hinton, a Curator of Zoology at the Natural History Museum, is a possible candidate for the creation of the Piltdown Man. He was known both to have carried out a number of hoaxes and to have developed a grudge against Arthur Smith Woodward, the institution's Keeper of Palaeontology.

Another candidate for the mischief-maker is Sir Arthur Conan

NATURAL HISTORY MUSEUM

Doyle, the creator of Sherlock Holmes. He had a country home that was sited near to Piltdown. However, it was probably Dawson who was the perpetrator.

Website: www.nhm.ac.uk/nature-online/science-of-natural-history/the-scientific-process/piltdown-man-hoax/Piltdown-hoax-revealed

Too Small: In 1932 the Museum recruited Leslie Bairstow, a specialist on the fossils of the North-East English coast. He stayed with the institution until he reached retirement age. His career was spectacularly unproductive - with the exception of a letter that appeared in the cycling magazine *Happy Days*. After he had left, it was discovered that in his office he had had a collection of boxes in which he had stored string. One of these contained very short pieces. It was labelled 'Too small to be of use'.

The Ranger's House, Greenwich Park

The Ranger's House (1723) was built as a private residence. In 1815 the Crown bought it. The building now houses the Wernher Collection.

In the early 1870s Julius Wernher joined Jules Porgès's London and Paris-based diamond trading business. The young German soon became trusted by his employer and was sent out to South Africa's Kimberley diamond field to represent the firm. The smallness of the claims there and the chaos that this generated meant that there was scope for well-organised, properly financed companies to manage a consolidation process. In 1880 Wernher founded Compagnie Française des Mines du Cap to participate in the aggregation.

Four years later Alfred Beit joined the Porgès firm. The new partner had good relations with Cecil Rhodes, who controlled De Beers. Wernher was thus able to establish a constructive dialogue with Rhodes, who, in 1887, bought 'the French Company'. The previous year gold had been discovered in Witwatersrand. Wernher, Beit & Company, as the Porgès business had been renamed, proved to be able to establish itself as one of the operators that dominated the field.

Wernher used part of his vast wealth to purchase Medieval and Renaissance works of art. His son Derrick married Theodora Anna Romanov, a member of the wider Russian imperial family. The princess had inherited a notable collection of artefacts. These, together with Sir Julius's treasures, were displayed to the public at the family's Luton Hoo estate. In 1991 the property was sold. Subsequently, the collection was provided with a home in The Ranger's House.

Locations: The Ranger's House, Chesterfield Walk, Greenwich Park, SE10 8QX. Towards the southern end of the western side.

No. 82 Piccadilly, W1J 7(BP). Wernher's townhouse.

See Also: CORONATIONS The Regalia; PARKS Greenwich Park

Website: www.english-heritage.org.uk/daysout/properties/ rangers-house-the-wernher-collection

The Science Museum

In 1898 a Parliamentary Select Committee recommended that the South Kensington Museum should be divided into scientific and artistic sections - the Science Museum and what was to become the Victoria & Albert Museum. In 1913 the former body moved westwards across Exhibition Road to its present site.

Location: Exhibition Road, SW7 2DD. On the western side, to the north of the junction with the Cromwell Road.

Website: www.sciencemuseum.org.uk

The Sir John Soane Museum

The Sir John Soane Museum (1813) building was designed and built as a townhouse by the architect Sir John Soane, who lived in it until his death. Previously, he had resided at No. 12 (1792), which he had also created.

In 1833 Sir John obtained an Act of Parliament that still preserves Nos. 13-14 Lincoln's Inn Fields as a public museum. The knight stipulated that his collection of paintings, sculptures, books, and architectural fittings should be neither disturbed nor augmented. Thus, the Museum has retained its original character. It possesses William Hogarth's original paintings for *The Rake's Progress* (1735) series of etchings.

Soane was fixated by a shape that was akin to that of a pocket handkerchief that is being pulled down at its corners. He used it for the ceiling of the dining room of his house in Lincoln's Inn Fields and for his own grave in the graveyard of St Pancras Old Church.[1]

Locations: No. 13 Lincoln's Inn Fields, WC2A 3BP. On the northern

---

[1]   Giles Gilbert Scott used the motif for the K2 telephone box's (1927) roof.

side. Towards the western end.

Pitshangar Manor, The Green, Ealing, W5 5DA. Soane's country house.

St Pancras Old Church, Pancras Road, NW1 1UL. His grave.

See Also: GALLERIES Dulwich Picture Gallery; STREET FURNITURE Telephone Boxes

Website: www.soane.org

A Staff Contribution

It has been claimed that one employee of a certain, world-renowned museum made a singular contribution to the institution's collection.

Somewhere in or near London is a large warehouse in which the museum stores many of the artefacts that it is not displaying. In order to check that nothing untoward is happening, people patrol the building. There is a story that it used to be the institution's practice to have single individuals perambulate the facility. One gentleman embarked upon his rounds. He did not return. It came to be assumed that he had taken some alternative employment and had not informed the institution's personnel department of his departure from the body's service.

Time passed. One day another member of staff came across a desiccated cadaver that not only did not have an acquisition number attached to it but which was wearing contemporary clothes. Thereafter, the museum instigated a policy of always having its workforce patrol the repository in pairs.

The Victoria & Albert Museum

The Victoria & Albert Museum is a museum of the applied arts.

Sir Henry Cole and Prince Albert set up the Museum of Manufactures (1852). It resided in Marlborough House. Its collection incorporated that of the Central School of Practical Art. It received a number of exhibits that had been bought by the government at the end of the Great Exhibition. In 1853 the institution changed its name to the Museum of Ornamental Art. Four years later it was merged with the School of Design (founded in 1837) to form the South Kensington Museum. The site became known as the Brompton Boilers.

In 1884 the National Art Library opened within the Museum. Fifteen years later, the latter, after a heavy hint from Queen Victoria, renamed itself in honour of her and her late husband.

The V&A's collections contain works of fine art. Its possessions include drawings by Raphael and paintings by John Constable, as well as numerous statues. The institution has a number of satellites. These include the Museum of Childhood in Bethnal Green.

Location: Cromwell Gardens, SW7 2RL. On the eastern side of the junction with Exhibition Road.

See Also: MUSEUMS The Design Museum; MUSEUMS The Museum of Childhood; PUBS Pub Names, The Black Lion

Website: www.vam.ac.uk

The Wallace Collection

The art and artefacts that the Wallace Collection holds date from the Renaissance and Early Modern periods. Within Britain, the institution's best-known item is Frans Hals's painting *The Laughing Cavalier* (1624).

The 4th Duke of Manchester commissioned the construction of Manchester House (subsequently Hertford House) (1788) because he believed that it would be conveniently sited for duck hunting. In 1797 the property was leased by the 3rd Marquis of Hertford. The peer married an illegitimate daughter of the Marchesa Fagnani. Both the 4th Duke of Queensberry and George Selwyn believed themselves to be the father of the marchioness. Therefore, they both left her large bequests.[1] Thereby, the Seymour-Conway family's fortune was increased.

The marquis spent much of his life residing in Europe. He utilised the opportunities created by France's political instability to become a major purchaser of *ancien régime* art and artefacts. In his later years the peer had a dissipated lifestyle. As a consequence characters in novels that were written by Benjamin Disraeli and William Makepeace Thackeray were modelled upon him.

The 4th marquis was raised by his mother largely in Paris. He lived principally in France and devoted himself to collecting objects of beauty. His tastes were broader and deeper than those of his father had been. He too availed himself of the buying opportunities that were engendered by the country's domestic travails.

In 1848 a series of revolutions occurred across Europe. These made the peer appreciate the benefits of Britain's relative stability. In 1850 he began to store items in Hertford House. He never married. Sir Richard Wallace was his illegitimate son by a Mrs Agnes Jackson. While the peer never acknowledged his paternity of Wallace, he left him his collection and his fortune. Following the death of the knight's widow, Lady Wallace (*d.*1897), Hertford House became a public museum.

Location: Hertford House, Manchester Square, W1M 5(AE). On the northern side between Manchester Street and Spanish Place.

Website: www.wallacecollection.org

---

[1]   Among the items in the Wallace Collection is a bust of King Charles I that was sculpted by Louis François Roubiliac. Formerly, this was a possession of Selwyn. Among his contemporaries, the MP and junior government minister had a reputation for having an excessive interest in executions. The monarch had been beheaded in 1649.

THE OLYMPICS

In 1612 Robert Dover staged an Olympicks in the Cotswolds. The event included one sport the essence of which seems to have been to try to break your opponent's shins with a heavy wooden stick before he broke yours with his.

In 1850 William Penny Brookes mounted a form of olympic games for the villagers of Wenlock. This proved to be a link in the concatenation of events that led to the staging of the first modern Olympic Games in Athens in 1896.

Website: www.olympic.org (The International Olympic Committee)

The 1908 London Olympics

Mount Vesuvius erupted prior to the 1908 Olympics. Rome cancelled her plans to host the Games. A committee of five Britons stepped into the breach.

In Shepherd's Bush a 140-acre plot of land was being developed by Imre Kiralfy as The White City exhibition site. The *impresario* recognised how the sporting event could raise the profile of his venue. Therefore, he made it available to the organising group. He built the White City stadium in return for being granted 75% of the receipts.

The sports included motor boat racing and tug-of-war. 21 countries sent competitors. The Austro-Hungarian Empire despatched three separate teams: Austria, Hungary, and Bohemia.[1] Australasia was composed of both Australia and New Zealand. The Games took place from April to October. There was a fortnight in which many of the principal events were held. The two weeks proved to be very heated because of Anglo-American rivalry. Team America, which included a number of Irishmen, was highly professional in its approach.[2]

Running lanes had not yet been introduced for the 400m race. The

---

[1]   With regard to securing medals, Hungary was to do better than Bohemia did. The l atter was to outperform Austria. (Mr Kiralfy was a Hungarian by birth.)

[2]   The Games' organisers failed to procure either a Swedish flag or an American one. By c ontrast the Japanese standard was flown. No Nipponese athletes participated in the competition.

TUG OF WAR

1   GREAT BRITAIN I
2   GREAT BRITAIN II
3   GREAT BRITAIN III

event was staged under British rules. These barred athletes from block ing their fellow competitors. However, in the United States, the practice was regarded as being acceptable. In one of the qualifying heats Wyndham Halswelle, a Briton, set a new Olympic record. The other three runners in the final were Americans. During it, he was brazenly blocked by one of them. The presiding officials disqualified the cheat and ordered that the race should be re-run in lanes. In an expression of misplaced solidarity the other two American athletes declined to accept the decision. Therefore, they did not turn up at the scheduled time. The only person to do so was Halswelle. Despite there being no one for him to vie against, it was ruled that the race had to be run. He complied with the authorities' wishes and ran it alone. It was a unique occasion in Olympic history. He was awarded the gold medal for the event.

The finishing line for the marathon was in the stadium. The first runner to enter the arena was Dorando Pietri, an Italian. He was clearly in a state of extreme exhaustion. He started to run the wrong way around the track. A number of officials - who may well have included Sir Arthur Conan Doyle in their number - intervened and directed him past the finishing line. An American runner finished second. Team America protested at the way in which Pietri had been assisted. As a result, the Italian was disqualified.

The United Kingdom had the single largest haul of medals. This outcome was aided by the fact that several of the events had
only Britons competing in them, while others had more than one United Kingdom team contest them. Sailing and tennis were events that had particularly large numbers of British entrants.

Upon their return to the United States, the American athletes paraded a 'British lion' on a chain.

The 1908 Olympics had been far better organised than any of the previous events had been. The Americans were upset at how it had gone. Therefore, they pressed for reforms. These two factors helped to give the

MEDAL WINNERS

GREAT BRITAIN	56 GOLD	51 SILVER	38 BRONZE
U.S. OF AMERICA	23 GOLD	12 SILVER	12 BRONZE
SWEDEN	8 GOLD	6 SILVER	11 BRONZE
FRANCE	5 GOLD	5 SILVER	9 BRONZE

Games the organisational rigour that was to enable them to re-emerge following the carnage of the First World War.[1]

Location: (Nos. 1-3) Ariel Way, Shepherd's Bush, W12 7SL. To the north of the Shepherd's Bush Green. The Westfield London shopping centre stands on the south-eastern portion of the White City site.

Not The Winning: Ethelbert Talbot the Episcopalian Bishop of Central Pennsylvania attended the 1908 Lambeth Conference of the Anglican Communion. On 19 July he preached a sermon in St Paul's Cathedral as part of a service that was held for Olympic officials and athletes. The views that the prelate expressed prompted Pierre de Courbertin of the International Olympic Committee to coin the epithet that 'The important thing in the Olympic Games is not the winning but the taking part.'[2]

Location: St Paul's Cathedral, St Paul's Churchyard, EC4M 8AD.

The 1948 London Olympics

The near bankrupt British government was not inclined to finance the 1948 Games. They became known as the Austerity Olympics. The contemporary shortage of building materials meant that only two new structures were created for them. These were a small stand at the Herne Hill Velodrome and Olympic Way, a road that leads towards Wembley Stadium, the dog racing track that acted as the principal venue. The neighbouring ice rink was adapted to serve as a swimming pool.

Competitors were asked to bring their own towels. Many of the <u>athletes who participated</u> in the event did so in homemade kit. Male

[1] At the 1912 Stockholm Olympics America won the most gold medals (25). Sweden secured one less but received the most overall medals (65). Britain came third. The demonstration sports that the hosts included were those old Nordic favourites *kasta varpa* and *stångstörtning*.

[2] During the Stockholm Olympics Baron de Courbertin was awarded its gold medal for poetry for his *Ode To Sport*. He had submitted the work pseudonymously.

athletes were lodged on military bases, while female ones were accommodated in hotels and hostels. Halal kitchens were established to meet the dietary requirements of Muslim participants.

The British, with regard to their own athletes, were severe about the issue of professionalism. Denis Watts, the AAA triple jump champion, was barred from participating in the Games because prior to them he had applied for a job as a physical education teacher in a school.

The innovations that the Nazis had introduced for the 1936 Berlin Olympics had included a torch relay from Olympia in Greece to the Olympiastadion, the German Games' principal venue. Despite the circumstances in which the practice had been created, the organisers of the London ones chose to re-employ it. This decision enabled it to evolve into being one the core aspects of the competition's opening.

At the Herne Hill Velodrome the cycling races overran. The track did not have any floodlights. The competition was able to continue because some of the spectators had driven to the event. They used their car lights to illuminate the circuit.

It was the first Olympics in which a photofinish was used - for the men's 100m.

The medals table ended with America coming first with 38 golds, Sweden second with sixteen, and Britain twelfth with three.[1] The star of the Games was the Dutch sprinter 'Fanny' Blankers-Koen. She won four gold medals. She was pregnant at the time. The Briton Jim Halliday secured a bronze in the weightlifting. He had survived being interred in a prisoner-of-war camp in the Far East. Upon being released three years earlier, he had weighed 4½ stone (28.6kg).

The Games cost £732,000 to stage. A profit of £29,420 was made. £9000 tax was paid upon this.

The Olympics were complemented by the Stoke Mandeville Games that were held in Aylesbury. This event was to evolve into being the Paralympics.

Location: Olympic Way, HA9 0NP.

The 2012 London Olympics

London was awarded the opportunity to host the 2012 Olympics in large part because of the organisers' commitment to creating a legacy that would benefit the city after the Games had been staged.

Of the permanent buildings that were constructed for the Games the Aquatic Centre was designed by Zaha Hadid Architects, the Velo-

[1]   Two for rowing and one for sailing. (In the Olympics, Britain has tended to do well in what can be termed 'sports for rich people'.)

drome by Hopkins Architects Partnerships, and the Olympic Stadium by the Populous architectural practice.

Reading: Iain Sinclair *Ghost Milk: Calling Time On The Grand Project* Hamish Hamilton (2011). Mr Sinclair is a respected writer who has lived in Hackney for many years. He has long entertained doubts about the value of *grand projets* such as the Olympics, the Thames Gateway, and the Millennium Dome. He was not hostile towards the 2012 Games *per se*. Rather, he possessed a profound appreciation of the districts that were changed by them.

Websites: www.teamgb.com (The British Olympic Association) www.londonlegacy.co.uk (The London Legacy Development Corporation) www.london2012.org www.gov.uk/organisations/ Olympic-delivery-authority (The Olympic Delivery Authority) www.olympic.org/London-2012-summer-olympics

www.zaha-hadid.com (The Hadid practice designed the Evelyn Grace Academy in Brixton and the Serpentine Sackler Gallery in Kensington Gardens.)

www.hopkins.co.uk (The Hopkins Architects Practice's other buildings in London include: the Evelina Children's Hospital on the St Thomas's site, Westminster Underground Station, the Ticket Office at Buckingham Palace, the Lawn Tennis Association's National Tennis Centre in Roehampton, and the masterplan for the Victoria & Albert Museum, as well as a number of developments within the institution.)

http://populous.com (The structures that Populous has designed in London include: Arsenal's Emirates Stadium, the O2 Arena within the Millennium Dome, and the sliding roof that can cover the All England Tennis Club's Centre Court at Wimbledon.)

The Orbit: The ArcelorMittal Orbit viewing structure was devised by the sculptor Anish Kapoor and the designer and engineer Cecil Balmond. Both men had been born in South Asia. They had chosen to live and work in London because of the city's capacity for flux. They sought to reflect this adaptability in the structure's flowing form. They derived it by reworking the five Olympic rings.

The architect who oversaw the physical realisation of The Orbit was Kathryn Findlay. Her own *avant-garde* design work was described as being Organic Modernist, DigiThatch, and Future-Rustic. She had studied at the Architectural Association in the 1970s. There, her tutors had included Peter Cook of the Archigram group of architectural thinkers.

See Also: VISITOR ATTRACTIONS

Website: www.arcelormittalorbit.com

The Paralympic Games: The UK television rights for the Paralympic Games were held by Channel 4. Following the Olympics but before the start of the Paralympics, the station ran a poster campaign that featured British paralympians. The images bore the strap line 'Thanks For The Warm-up'.

We Have n't Either: Sir Tim Berners-Lee was raised in East Sheen in South-West London. As a child, he initially taught himself electronics by tweaking his model train set.

In the late 1980s Berners-Lee was working for Cern (the European Organisation for Nuclear Research) in Switzerland. In 1989 he submitted a proposal to his line managers about there being scope for a universal, linked information system to operate on the Internet. The scheme became the World Wide Web.

Sir Tim is not burdened by being recognised by members of the public. He was featured in the opening ceremony of the 2012 London Olympics. This involved him programming on a NeXT computer. He had used a similar machine to code the Web. One of the commentators who was working for America's NBC television channel responded to the sight by declaring 'If you have n't heard of him, we have n't either.'

Websites: All of them. Every last one.

PALACES

See Also: THE CHAPELS ROYAL; HERITAGE; PALACES, DIS-APPEARED & FORMER; PARLIAMENT The Palace of Westminster; PUBS The Board of Green Cloth; ROYAL RESIDENCES; ROYALTY

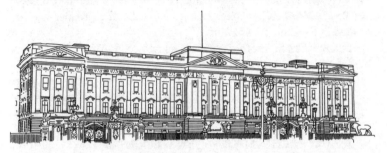

Buckingham Palace

King George III was one of the few pre-20thC examples of a male British sovereign who had a virtuous domestic life.[1] In 1761 the monarch bought Buckingham House from the Sheffield family. In 1775 he gave the building to his wife Queen Charlotte.[2] The couple occupied it as their private residence; their official one continued to be St James's Palace. In 1818 the queen bequeathed the House to their son the Prince Regent.

The prince acceded to the throne as King George IV. In his new position he concluded that Carlton House, his pet architectural project in London, was no longer grand enough for him. During the 1820s Buckingham House was remodelled by John Nash. The architect went over budget. Upon the accession of George's younger brother, King William IV, the man was replaced on the scheme by Edward Blore. However, the work was not finished during the new monarch's reign.

Queen Victoria had been raised in Kensington Palace. Following her accession in 1837 she moved into Buckingham Palace. She made it the principal royal residence in London. Her husband Prince Albert died in 1861. She spent most of the rest of her reign living away from the metropolis. She was able to do so because of the development of teleg-

---

[1]   Edward VI was another. He died young.

[2]   In turn, Queen Charlotte gave up Somerset House, the traditional palace of the royal consorts.

raphy and railways. The former enabled her to keep abreast of affairs in almost real time and the latter meant that she could swiftly return to the city whenever she needed to be there in person.

During the late 1860s and early 1870s there was a strong wave of republicanism in England. This started waning in 1872 after the monarch attended a service of thanksgiving at St Paul's Cathedral. This was held to express gratitude for the Prince of Wales's recovery from a case of typhoid. The residual popular image of the sovereign is one that was largely created for her during the later years of her rule by the Conservative Prime Minister Benjamin Disraeli. In 1877 the premier had her crowned as the Empress of India.

In a way that his mother, Victoria, had not, King Edward VII appreciated that the public and ceremonial aspects of the monarchy were important to its maintenance. At his death he left the institution in a more vital condition than it had been at his accession. His son, King George V, was to retain his throne while several of their kinsmen were to lose theirs.

Location: Buckingham Palace, SW1A 1AA.

See Also: ARCHES Marble Arch; GALLERIES The Royal Collection, The Queen's Gallery; ROYALTY The Constitution, The Marquis Curzon; ROYALTY Royal Garden Parties

Websites: www.hrp.org.uk   www.royal.gov.uk   www.royal.gov.uk/TheRoyalResidences/BuckinghamPalace/BuckinghamPalace.aspx

Death In The Gardens: In 1996 it was reported that a fox had either killed or scared to death six flamingoes that lived on an ornamental pond in the Palace gardens. This was in spite of the fact that the grounds were surrounded by a brick wall that was topped by barbed wire.[1]

See Also: THEATRES St Martin's Theatre, A Deathbed Undertaking

Historic Royal Palaces

Historic Royal Palaces is a charity that was set up in 1998 to manage the Tower of London, Kensington Palace, The Banqueting House, Hampton Court Palace, and Kew Palace.

See Also: GALLERIES The Royal Collection, The Royal Collection Trust

Website: www.hrp.org.uk

---

[1]   Llamas have a reputation for being inclined to attack foxes. As a result, some sheep farmers put them in with their flocks as a means of protecting lambs from being predated by foxes. However, the average llama might well regard Buckingham Palace Gardens as being a giant *smörgåsbord* rather than as a field of valour upon which to perform deeds of chivalry for flamingo-kind.

Kensington Palace

In 1689 the 2nd Earl of Nottingham sold Kensington House to King William III and Queen Mary II. The building became known as Kensington Palace. The Dutchman resided in it in order to be close to London. For him, its principal attraction was that it was located to the west of the city. Therefore, it was exposed to the prevailing westerly winds. Thus, the quality of its air was better than that of the metropolis. This afforded the monarch some relief from the asthma with which he was afflicted.[1] The architects Sir Christopher Wren and Nicholas Hawksmoor designed extensions to the residence, as well as making a number of alterations to it.

The Palace was the principal royal seat until 1760. Since then, it has been used as a place to park assorted royal relatives in. The young Princess Victoria lived there prior to her accession to the throne in 1837.

Location: Kensington Gardens, W8 4PX.

See Also: PARKS Kensington Gardens; WEATHER Wind, The Protestant Wind

Websites: www.hrp.org.uk/KensingtonPalace   www.royal.gov.uk/TheRoyalResidences/KensingtonPalace/KensingtonPalace.aspx

The State Apartments: In 1889, upon the occasion of Queen Victoria's 70th birthday, the State Apartments of Kensington Palace were opened to the public. In 1912 the complex was used to accommodate the London Museum. Two years later the latter moved to Lancaster House and the former were again closed. In 1923 they were re-opened.

Location: Kensington Palace, Kensington Gardens, W8 4PX.

St James's Palace

In the Middle Ages the ground upon which St James's now stands was marshland. Therefore, it was physically isolated from London. As such, it was taken to be well-suited for providing the location for a lepers' hospital.

King Henry VIII (*d*.1547) acquired the property and had a house built upon it for his second wife Anne Boleyn.

Whitehall Palace burned down in 1698. Therefore, King William III needed a formal home that was located conveniently for both Westminster and Kensington Palace, where the actual court resided. Thus, St James's became the statutory royal residence. The palace was used for court functions such as *levees*. Queen Anne and her two Hanoverian successors t ended to follow the Dutchman's example of living in a

---

[1]   Hampton Court Palace, several miles to the west, was William III's favourite English residence.

private capacity at Kensington Palace while using St James's for official occasions.

During the early 1810s John Nash restored and remodelled the Palace. The last members of the royal family to live in the complex for many years were two of King George III's sons - the Duke of York and the Duke of Clarence (the future William IV). Following George IV's accession in 1820, the new monarch supplied his two younger sibs with the financial wherewithal to start building their own grandiose townhouses (Lancaster House and Clarence House) on The Mall.

Queen Victoria acceded to the throne in 1837. She made Buckingham Palace the principal royal residence in London. A number of court functions were transferred to it. However, St James's continued to be the Crown's seat. All foreign ambassadors who are posted to London officially reprresent their home governments at the Court of St James's. (High Commissioners - the representatives of Commonwealth countries - are accredited to the government.)

Location: Cleveland Row, SW1A 1NP. On the corner with Marlborough Road.

See Also: CLASS The College of Arms; PARKS St James's Park

Website: www.royal.gov.uk/TheRoyalResidences/StJamess Palace/StJamessPalace.aspx

PALACES, DISAPPEARED & FORMER

See Also: CORONATIONS The Tower of London; PALACES; ROY-AL RESIDENCES; ROYAL RESIDENCES, DISAPPEARED; THE TOW-ER OF LONDON

Bridewell Palace

Bridewell Palace was built in 1523 for King Henry VIII. The complex extended southwards towards the River Thames. In 1553 his son King Edward VI gave the property to the City of London to house the Royal Bridewell Hospital. The institution received its royal charter the same year. It had a variety of functions during its history, including being an orphanage. It evolved into being a prison.

Location: No. 14 New Bridge Street, EC4V 6AG. The gateway (1802) of the former Bridewell Palace.

Chelsea Palace

King Henry VIII had Chelsea Palace built for his third wife Jane Seymour. However, she died after having given birth to their son the future King Edward VI. In 1543 he gave the property to his sixth wife, Catherine Parr.

Location: Nos. 19-26 Cheyne Walk, Chelsea, SW3 5QZ.
Reading: Alison Weir *The Six Wives of Henry VIII* Vintage (2007).

Greenwich Palace

Humphrey Duke of Gloucester (*d.* 1447) was the younger brother of King Henry V. The prince built a palace at Greenwich. He called it Bella Court. Following his death the property passed to the royal family. It was renamed the Palace of Placentia and became one of the principal royal residences. Queen Elizabeth I was born there.

King James I commissioned Inigo Jones to build The Queen's House (1617) for his consort Queen Anne of Denmark. In 1635 the architect adapted the building for the use of Queen Henrietta Maria. She was the wife of King Charles I, who was the son of James and Anne.

Following the restoration of the monarchy in 1660, King Charles II decided that the palace should be rebuilt. He appointed John Webb to

design a replacement. Most of the old complex was demolished. However, only a small portion of the architect's design was erected.

At the instigation of Queen Mary II the construction of Greenwich Hospital, a home for old and injured seamen, commenced during the 1690s. It provided a naval equivalent to the Royal Hospital Chelsea, which housed elderly and infirm ex-soldiers.

In 1873 the Royal Naval College moved into the Royal Hospital for Seamen building. In 1934 the National Maritime Museum was established on a neighbouring site to the south. The College became part of the Joint Services Command & Staff College. In 1998 it left the site.

The palace's current occupants include portions of both the Trinity Laban Conservatoire of Music & Dance and the University of Greenwich.

Location: Greenwich Park, SE10 9NF.

See Also: PARKS Greenwich Park

Websites: www.ornc.org (The charity that cares for the site) www.grenhosp.org.uk (Britain's oldest naval charity) www.gre.ac.uk (Greenwich University) www.trinitylaban.ac.uk (Trinity Laban Conservatoire)

Rotherhithe Manor House

King Edward II (*d.*1327) owned a manor house in Rotherhithe. With time, the site came to be covered by a tobacco wharf. When this was demolished the remains of the medieval structure were discovered. Portions of its gatehouse have been left uncovered.

Location: *The Angel*, No. 101 Bermondsey Wall East, Rotherhithe, SE16 4NB. Opposite.

The Savoy Palace

The Savoy Palace dates from the mid-13thC. King Henry III had a troubled relationship with his barons. Needing all of the allies that he could secure, the monarch gave the property to Peter Earl of Richmond & Savoy, a kinsman of his wife. After the complex had passed through various hands, it returned to the Crown at the end of the 14thC.

In 1505 King Henry VII endowed the Palace as a Hospital. However, the institution did not flourish. In 1553 King Edward VI suppressed it and gave the buildings to the City of London to help to endow the Bridewell. Three years later Queen Mary I, who was inclined to be against most things that her brother and predecessor had been for, refounded the Hospital. However, it fared no better than it had previously. A diverse array of activities came to be carried out on the site. In 1697 the right of sanctuary that it had enjoyed was taken away from it.

The institution was suppressed for a second time in 1702. Its buildings fell into disrepair while the Crown and the Duchy of Lancaster engaged in a protracted dispute with one another about which of them owned the property. In 1772 the matter was finally resolved. The Duchy took possession of the Savoy Chapel and the outer ring of the site, while the Crown took control of the inner portion. The only part of the Hospital that survives is its chapel. The rest of the land was developed for other uses during the course of the 19[th]C.

Location: Savoy Hill, WC2R 0DA.

See Also: CHURCH OF ENGLAND CHURCHES The Savoy Chapel; CHARLES DICKENS Jarndyce *vs.* Jarndyce

The Duchy of Lancaster: King Henry IV acceded to the throne in 1399.

Since then the Duchy of Lancaster has been held by the reigning sovereign. This meant that the 18th C disagreement was really between different facets of the Crown. What lent weight to the matter was that those two aspects were maintained by their own separate, mutually-antagonistic bureaucracies.

The Duchy furnishes much of the Privy Purse's income. The latter provides money that covers those expenses that the sovereign incurs through acting as the head of state that are not expressly met by the Civil List.

Website: www.duchyoflancaster.co.uk

Bona Vacantia: *Bona vacantia* ('unowned goods') is the Polari-sounding, Common Law principle that covers property that has no owner. Under it, if a person dies without leaving a will and has no known relatives then her/his possessions pass to the Crown. The exceptions to this are when s/he is a resident either of the County Palatine of Lancashire or of Cornwall. Her/his property becomes the possession of either the Duchy or the Duchy of Cornwall respectively. The money that is raised consequently is given to Duchy-related charities upon a discretionary basis.

Websites: www.duchyoflancaster.co.uk/duties-of-the-duchy/ bona-vacantia.aspx www.duchyofcornwall.org/management andfinances_bonavacantia.htm (www.bonavacantia.gov.uk)

The Loyal Toast: The loyal toast in Lancashire is to 'The Queen, Duke of Lancaster'.

Whitehall Palace

The property that became Whitehall Palace was acquired by the Archdiocese of York in the middle of the 13th C. It served as the London residence of successive Eboracan archbishops. In 1514 Cardinal Wolsey was elected to lead the province. He used the position's considerable revenues to spend lavishly upon the complex's development and ornamentation. In 1529 King Henry VIII had the arch-prelate convey York Palace to the Crown, renamed it Whitehall, and moved the court's principal London residence there from Westminster.

The complex's feasting hall was consumed by a conflagration in 1619. King James I had Inigo Jones and John Webb design a new palace for him. Jones's Banqueting House proved to be the only part of the plan that was ever built.

In 1698 a sheet was left too close to a fire to dry. It caught alight and

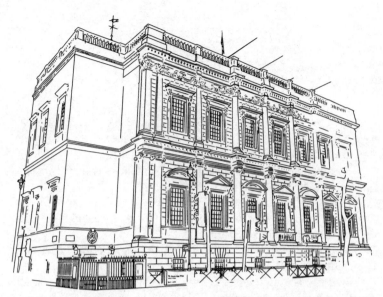

led to Whitehall Palace burning down. All that remained of the complex was the Banqueting House and King Henry VIII's Wine Cellar.[1] Subsequently, the Crown granted out leases of plots of the site to members of the aristocracy. Townhouses were built upon the divisions.

There is a model of the old palace in The Museum of London.

Location: Whitehall, SW1A 2EU. On the eastern side.

See Also: HALLS The Banqueting House; STREET FURNITURE Street Signs, Whitehall's End; WEATHER Wind, The Protestant Wind

Website: www.british-history.ac.uk/report.aspx?compid =67775

---

[1]   The Wine Cellar now lies underneath the Ministry of Defence Building.

PARKS

See Also: KEW GARDENS; SQUIRRELS

John Evelyn's *Fumifugium* (1661) may have been the first book to have been written about pollution. In it, he argued that green spaces should be created so that London's smoke could dispel.

Reading: Jill Billington (illus.) Sandra Lousada *London's Parks and Gardens* Frances Lincoln (2003).

John C. Hopkins (1953-2013) & Peter Neal *The Making of The Queen Elizabeth Olympic Park* John Wiley (2012). Mr Hopkins oversaw the creation of the 250-acre park.

Malcolm Tait & Edward Parker *London's Royal Parks* Royal Parks Foundation/Think Publishing (2006).

Websites: www.londongardenstrust.org (London Parks & Gardens Trust) www.royalparks.gov.uk

Battersea Park

Battersea Fields was a stretch of open land that Londoners had long used for assorted scurrilous purposes, such as duelling and enjoying themselves. In large part, the mischief and the merry-making were focused upon *The Red House* tavern.

The Battersea Park Act of 1846 enabled the Commission for Improving the Metropolis to purchase the Fields for the creation of a park. The ground was laid out under the supervision of Her Majesty's Commissioners for Woods. Its marshy soil was consolidated with earth that had been excavated during the construction of the Victoria Dock in East London. The leisure ground was opened to the public in 1853.

The park contains a children's zoo and in its south-western portion a wooden adventure playground.

Location: Battersea, SW11 4NJ.

Websites: www.batterseapark.org www.batterseaparkzoo.co.uk

Green Park

Green Park was enclosed in the 16[th]C by King Henry VIII. In the following century King Charles II designated the land a royal park. At 53-acres it is the smallest of the royal parks in central London. It does not have any flowerbeds in it, hence its name.[1]

Location: Piccadilly, SW1A 1EE. To the south of the road's western section.

See Also: STREET FURNITURE Gates, The Green Park Gates

Website: www.royalparks.gov.uk/parks/green-park

Constitution Hill: Between the wall that runs along the north-eastern side of Buckingham Palace's grounds and Green Park lies Constitution Hill. The road used to be known as St James's Hill. In almost any other country its new name would refer to a momentous political development. In Britain, with its diffused constitution, the name records King Charles II's (*d*.1685) partiality for taking a 'constitutional' stroll for the sake of his health. (The incline is so slight that 'Hill' is an overstatement. It isn't even much of a slope.)

Location: Constitution Hill, SW1A 2BJ. Runs along the southern side of Green Park

See Also: ROYALTY The Constitution; STATUES The National Gallery Statues

Milkmaids' Passage: Milkmaids' Passage is a privately-owned alley that runs to the north of Lancaster House. The passageway enters the southern end of the eastern side of Green Park. Its name probably recalls the practice by which people who were promenading in the park or along The Mall could buy a drink of milk that was fresh from the udder.

Location: Milkmaids' Passage, SW1A 1(BB).

See Also: TEA White

Greenwich Park

In 1675 King Charles II commissioned the construction of the Royal Greenwich Observatory. The complex was built upon the crest of the hill that overlooks the northern portion of Greenwich Park.   In   the 18[th]C the park was opened to the public.

Location: Greenwich Park, SE10 9NF.

See Also: MUSEUMS The Rangers House; PALACES, DISAPPEARED & FORMER Greenwich Palace

Hyde Park

Together, Hyde Park and Kensington Gardens make up the largest of the central London parks. They furnish almost a rectangular mile of greenery.

---

[1]   However, in spring numerous daffodils make their presence known.

The estate from which Hyde Park was created had belonged to West-minster Abbey until 1536. King Henry VIII acquired it then through an exchange of properties. The monarch turned the land into a deer park.[1] It is not altogether clear when it was opened to the public. This develop-ment probably happened in the 1630s at the behest of King Charles I.

For many years a wall enclosed the park. In the early 19thC it was replaced by iron railings.

The south-western portion of the park hosted the Great Exhibition of 1851.

Location: Hyde Park, W1 7AQ. East of Kensington Gardens and west of Park Lane.

Website: www.royalparks.org.uk/parks/hyde-park

Speakers' Corner: Lord Robert Grosvenor was a scion of one of the wealthiest of the great aristocratic dynasties. For most of his political career the MP was on the progressive wing of the Whig party; when Garibaldi was to visit London in 1864 it was to be Lord Robert who was to host a banquet that was to be held to honour the Italian. Grosvenor's religious beliefs were an ardent form of Low Church Anglicanism. In Parliament, the social issues that he and the similarly-minded Tory Lord Shaftesbury co-operated with one another on included the placing of statutory limits upon the number of hours that people could work in a factory during a single week.

Grosvenor sponsored the Sunday Trading Bill of 1855. The measure sought to prevent shops from opening on Sundays. The passage of the Factory Acts had not been universal in their impact upon the working lives of ordinary people. For many Londoners, the Sabbath was still the only day during which they could shop for the necessities that sustained them. Therefore, there was popular opposition to the measure.

A mass rally was held in the north-eastern corner of Hyde Park. At the time, there was no legal right of assembly. That the crowd gathered where it did was probably so that it could be accommodated physically. However, the site could also be seen and heard from Grosvenor House, the family townhouse where the MP lived when he was in London. He had taken the precaution of leaving the metropolis. Subsequently, he withdrew the Bill.

In 1866, as part of a popular movement that was demanding a broadening of the electoral franchise, large rallies took place in Hyde Park. The Second Reform Act of 1867 extended the right to vote to with-in the (male) population.

---

[1]   Deer remained a feature of the park until the middle of the 18thC.

As a consequence of the demonstrations, Park Lane was widened. The road's railings were set back within what was then the park's perimeter to make room for the road to be broadened.

The Parks Regulation Act of 1872 furnished the right of public assembly. Speakers' Corner was established in the north-eastern corner of Hyde Park. The site has no immunity from the laws respecting slander or incitement to cause a breach of the peace.[1]

Locations: Hyde Park, W2 2UH. The north-eastern corner.[2]

Grosvenor House, No. 35 Park Street, W1K 7(TN). Between Mount Street and Upper Grosvenor Street. On the western side.

See Also: THE GUNPOWDER PLOT The Observing of 5 November; STREET MARKETS East End Street Markets, Petticoat Lane

Kensington Gardens

During the 16thC Hyde Park and Kensington Gardens became a private royal park.

After the opening of the former to the public in the 1630s, Kensington Gardens, her western sister, continued to be the sovereigns' private domain. The park's current character was determined in large part by Queen Caroline (*d*.1737), King George II's consort. Her ambitions extended to incorporating the eastern sib within the Gardens and thus closing the land to the public. She asked the then prime minister, Sir Robert Walpole, whether the scheme would prove to be expensive. He replied that it could be done...for 'The price of two Crowns.'[3]

When the court was at Richmond, George II permitted the Gardens to be opened to 'respectably dressed' people on Saturdays. The Broad Walk became a fashionable promenade where Society could parade itself to itself.

King William IV (*d*.1837) opened the park to the public throughout the year.

Location: West of Hyde Park, W8 4PX. To the north of Kensington Road.

See Also: PALACES Kensington Palace

Website: www.royalparks.gov.uk/parks/Kensington-gardens

The Regent's Park

In the 16thC King Henry VIII used Marylebone Park as a hunting ground.

[1]   The speakers' stepladders and portable platforms give the impression that they are taking a break from papering the parlour.

[2]   In taxi slang Speakers' Corner is referred to 'Spouters' Corner'.

[3]   The crown was a coin that was worth five shillings (25p).

Subsequently, the Crown granted a long lease on the property. Therefore, the land passed out of its direct control.

The 4th Duke of Portland surrendered Marylebone Park back to the Crown in 1811. The Prince Regent felt that, in addition to Carlton House, he needed a summer palace. Therefore, he instructed the architect John Nash to devise a scheme in which the land would be turned into aristocratic housing. At its hub would be the desired aestival residence. In the consequent disposition, and in accordance with contemporary planning practice, a social range of lodging was to have been built. This was so that those who helped keep life gracious for the leisured class should be close at hand.

The prince's palace only ever proved to be a fancy.

Just eight of the 56 great villas that Nash envisaged were built.[1] Some of the octet are located along the park's Inner Circle, while the rest stand on its Outer one. One of the conditions of the mansions' Crown Estate leases is that their grounds should be opened to the public on certain days each year.

On the park's western, southern and eastern peripheries bestuccoed cliffs of Regency terraces were constructed. Nash left its northern side open thereby retaining vistas of both Hampstead Hill and Highgate Hill.

Location: The Regent's Park, NW1 4NR.

Reading: Ruth Rendell *The Keys To The Street* Arrow (1997). The crime novel is set in the Regent's Park. Ms Rendell wrote it because she had become interested by the open spaces that had been created in the park by the great storm of 1987.

Ann Saunders *Regent's Park: A Study of The Development of The Area From 1086 To The Present Day* Bedford (1981). Second edition.

See Also: ROYAL RESIDENCES, DISAPPEARED Carlton House

Website: www.royalparks.gov.uk/parks/regents-park

The Crown Estate Paving Commission: The Crown Estate Paving Commission is a public body that was set up in 1813. Legally, it has always been a separate entity from the Crown Estate. The Commission has two areas of responsibility. Firstly, it supervises aspects of Regent's Park, such as the space's street furniture and the opening and shutting of its gates. And secondly, in the streets that neighbour the park, that stand upon Crown Estate property, the body manages a range of activities such as rubbish collection and vehicle parking.

Location: No. 12 Park Square East, Regent's Park, NW1 4LJ.

Website: www.cepc.org.uk

---

[1]   Rob Humphreys *The Rough Guide To London* Rough Guides (2008) 351

THE ROYAL PARKS

C.E.P.C.

St James's Park

St James's Park is the oldest of the royal parks in central London. Originally, it was a marshy meadow that was owned by the Hospital of St James, an institution that housed lepers. In 1532 the land was drained and laid out for King Henry VIII as a deer nursery that linked St James's Palace to Whitehall Palace.

The park was King Charles II's (*d.*1685) pleasure ground. The French landscape designer André Le Nôtre joined up a set of ponds to one another to create a rectangular body of water. The monarch used this for swimming in. His interest in ornithology is commemorated by the name Duck Island.

In the late 1820s the architect John Nash turned the formal lake into the informal one that dominates the centre of the park.

Possibly the most picturesque view in London is the eastwards one from the centre of the bridge that crosses the body of water. The crossing was designed by Eric Bedford, the Ministry of Works's Chief Architect. (He was also architect of the Post Office Tower (1964).)

Location: Horse Guards Road, St James's Park, SW1A 2BJ.

See Also: PALACES St James's Palace

Website: www.royalparks.gov.uk/parks/st-jamess-park

Birdcage Walk: The Birdcage Walk aviary was established by King James I (*d.*1625). It was enlarged by his grandson King Charles II.

Until 1828 only members of the royal family and the Grand Falconer could have their carriages driven along Birdcage Walk.

Location: St James's Park, SW1A 2BJ. The southern side.

See Also: ARCHES; CORONATIONS Hereditary and Feudal Office-Holders; ZOOS The Royal Menagerie

St James's Park Lake and Duck Island: The wide variety of species of bird that are present on St James's Park Lake owes much to King Charles II's (*d*.1685) interest in ornithology. Many were effectively exiles from their native habitats as he himself had been for over a decade after his father Charles I had lost the Civil Wars of the 1640s.

There have been pelicans on the lake in St James's Park since the 1660s. The colony is descended from a gift of some of the birds that was made by a Russian Ambassador.

Charles II appointed Charles de Marquetel de St Evremond to be the Governor of Duck Island. This absurd position honoured the popular exiled French poet without antagonising the French court.

Charles's nephew King William III shared his interest in ornithology. The latter had a hide on Duck Island that he used for bird-watching.

Location: St James's Park, SW1A 2BJ. The southern side.

PARLIAMENT

See Also: ROYALTY
Reading: Clyve Jones *A Short History of Parliament: England, Great Britain, The United Kingdom, Ireland and Scotland* Boydell Press (2009).

The Palace of Westminster

In the 11[th]C the principal residence of King Edward the Confessor, the last of the Anglo-Saxon kings, was built in Westminster. Parliament meets in the building that is its successor. Legally, the site is still a royal palace.

New Palace Yard is on the plot's north-western corner. It takes its name from a late 11[th]C plan that never progressed beyond the completion of Westminster Hall (1099).

In the 14[th]C, during the reign of King Edward III, the two Houses of Parliament began to develop identities that were distinct from one another. The Commons's sessions were held in the Chapter House of Westminster Abbey. The Lords remained in the palace, meeting in a chamber in the complex's southern portion.

In 1512 the Palace was damaged by a fire. The subsequent repairs that were carried out to its structure were only partial. In 1530 King Henry VIII saved himself the expense of further building work by moving the court a couple of hundred yards downstream to York Palace, which he renamed Whitehall Palace. He left behind the legislature and the judiciary.[1]

On 16 October 1834 a fire was organised so that some redundant tally sticks could be destroyed.[2] It ran out of control. Most of the surviving medieval complex burned down. The artist J.M.W. Turner took sketches of the conflagration. Subsequently, he worked these up into a painting.[3] The only parts of the old palace to survive were the

---

[1] Until 1882 the principal courts for England and Wales sat in Westminster Hall during the legal term.

[2] The sticks were pieces of wood that were used to record payments that had been made to the Treasury. Notches were cut into them to record the amount of money that had been received. In 1826 they had been superseded by the use of indented cheques.

[3] Turner's picture is in the Philadelphia Museum of Art. (www.philamuseum. org/collections/ permanent/103831.html)

Cloisters, the Jewel Tower, St Mary Undercroft (St Stephen's crypt), and Westminster Hall.

See Also: CHURCHES OF ENGLAND CHURCHES All Saints Margaret Street; THE GUNPOWDER PLOT; HALLS Westminster Hall; PALACES

Website: www.parliament.uk/about/podcasts

Pugin and Barry: A competition was held for the design of the Palace's successor. There were 97 submissions. Charles Barry's entry was selected. It was a long central range that was set between two pavilions. In essence, it was a large Italianate country house with a Gothic cloak.

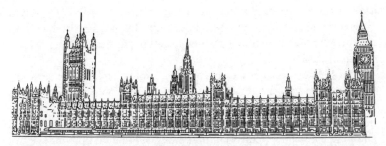

The need for the Palace's heating and ventilation system to be physically accommodated led to the building's external appearance becoming more Gothic in character than it would have been otherwise. Its construction started in 1840.

Four years later Barry put Augustus Pugin in charge of designing the complex's interiors. The latter's decorative work both stressed Parliament's medieval origins and sought to create a level of architectural harmony with Westminster Abbey, which neighboured it to the west. Despite there being no provenance for such, the items that he devised for the building included medieval-style gas lamps and umbrella stands.

Barry treated Pugin appallingly. He excluded the man's name from the published list of his assistants and did not admit that it had been him (Pugin) who had had the idea that St Stephen's Tower should be built.

The Lords moved into their new Chamber in 1847 and the Commons into theirs five years later. The complex was finished in 1888.

The Palace is reputed to be a world apart from London. During the winter the building is said to smell of toast.[1]

In 2012 the Parliamentary authorities marked Queen Elizabeth II's diamond jubilee by changing the name of the tower that houses Big Ben from St Stephen's Tower to the Elizabeth Tower.

Location: Parliament Square, SW1P 3AD.

See Also: BELLS Big Ben;

Website: www.parliament.uk www.parliament.uk/about/living-heritage/building/palace/architecture

The Commons

See Also: WESTMINSTER ABBEY The Chapter House

The Commons Chamber: The government of the day sits to the Speaker's right and Her Majesty's Opposition to her/his left.

There is a line in front of each of the two sets of front benches. They

---

[1] In taxi slang the Houses of Parliament are 'The Gas Works'.

are two sword lengths' distance from one another. No MP is allowed to cross their line while the House is in session. The purpose of the marks is to prevent Members from engaging in acts of physical violence against one another.[1]

In 1941 an aerial bomb struck the Chamber, wrecking it. Prior to then there had not been enough benches in the room to enable all of the House's members to sit in it together. It would have been a simple matter for the space to have been rebuilt so that it could have seated all of the legislators. However, there was a substantial body of MPs, of whom Churchill was one, who believed that the limited number of places helped to engender the Chamber's particular atmosphere. This, they held, influenced the nature of the debates that took place there. In turn, these informed the character of British democracy. The group carried the matter.

After the war, Sir Giles Gilbert Scott, an architect who was deeply versed in the Gothic Revival style, was commissioned to rebuild the room. In 1950 the Lower House returned to the space. There are 427 seats for the 651 MPs. On those occasions when every seat on their side of the House has already been taken, late-arriving Members have to stand behind its rear benches.

Location: The Chamber is to the east of the northern portion of Westminster Hall.

See Also: ST PAUL'S CATHEDRAL The Cathedral and The Second World War

Baiting: Many members of the Commons are seasoned in the art of baiting their fellow Members across the floor of the Chamber.

In 1981 Geoffrey Dickens had a dalliance with a lady who was not Mrs Dickens. In an attempt to try to control the media story, he informed the press of his misconduct. The Conservative MP let slip that he had met the woman at a tea dance. When a journalist asked him how his wife felt about the matter the backbencher then realised that he had not yet told her about it. Thereafter, Dickens, when speaking in the Chamber, was taunted with cries of 'Slow, slow, quick, quick, slow.'

Quentin Davies was fined £1500 under the Protection of Animals Act of 1911 for cruelty to sheep. A flock of the animals starved to death on his property. As a result, whenever the MP rose to speak in the Commons a chorus of baaing would break out.

There is a story that upon one occasion a renowned Labour

---

[1]   The lines are informed by presumption that it is only members of the other side that MPs may wish to assault.

backbencher, while speaking in the Chamber, stated that half of the Conservatives present were liars. The Speaker intervened and instructed him to withdraw the comment. The MP complied with this injunction. He then stated that half of the Tories before him were not given to lying.

Partial Voting: The way in which Commons divisions are held involves MPs walking through one of two doorways. One of these indicates approval for the motion and the other opposition to it. At a given point the two doors are closed in unison. After that time legislators can no longer cast a vote upon the contended issue.

In 1968 there was a division on a Finance Bill. As the portals were being shut the Labour MP Walter Harrison forced his way through one of them. Iain Macleod, a Conservative, challenged the validity of the man's participation in the proceedings. Harrison stated that at the crucial juncture he had been three-quarters in the Chamber and that subsequently he had pulled in after him the leg that had been external to it. The presiding Chairman declared the matter to have been carried by 22¾ votes to 22.

The Treasury Bench Ceremonialists: The Treasury Bench is the front row of seats on the governing party's side of the Commons Chamber. It is used by ministers. However, on certain ceremonial occasions, the MPs who represent the City of London and Westminster also sit on it. This custom derives from a historic practice that was enjoyed by the City's MPs. It symbolised the important role that the settlement played in Britain's national life.

See Also: THE CITY OF LONDON The Remembrancer

The Members' Lobby: Access to the Members' Lobby only became limited to MPs and certain journalists after a terrorist attack took place there in 1884. The Lobby reporters include the representatives of national daily newspapers and weeklies, provincial newspaper chains, and assorted radio and television journalists. At any given juncture a couple of hundred media workers have access to the space. Anything that is said by a Member in the Lobby has an automatic anonymous attribution given to it unless the politician wishes to be associated with the statement. The purpose of this informal rule is to encourage MPs to speak more freely than they might do so otherwise.

See Also: THE POLICE New Scotland Yard, The Special Branch

Fleet Hares and Provincial Tortoises: In terms of media manipulation, it is reputed that during the 20thC politicians were most wary of those journalists who worked for provincial newspapers. This was because Fleet Street papers had to be distributed nationally overnight, therefore, their journalists had to meet very tight deadlines. *Ergo*, if a politician wished to leak an item, the national reporters had only a short time in which to write it up and therefore they did not necessarily have the opportunity in which to assess its true character. For an individual national daily to fail to publish the story would have made it appear to be lacklustre in comparison to its rivals. In contrast, the regional rags, with their local distribution networks, did not have to go to press so early. Therefore, their journalists had an extra two or three hours in which to mull over the material and to follow up leads that might cast it in a light that was different from the one in which the originator wished it might be taken.

The Monarch and The House of Commons: In 1642, during the political troubles that preceded the outbreak of the Civil Wars, King Charles I and a troop of soldiers entered the Commons Chamber in order to try to arrest five particularly irksome MPs. The House had been forewarned of the monarch's intended action and the men had already left it before the sovereign arrived. Upon his entry into the room, the king was informed by the Speaker of the Commons that 'The birds have flown.' Since that occasion, the monarch only formally enters the Chamber with the House's permission; a rare instance of such was the visit that King George VI made in 1950 to inspect the repairs that had been carried out after the Chambers's wartime bombing.

(In the late 17thC and the early 18thC the sovereign would sometimes attend a debate in which s/he had a particular interest. Upon such occasions, s/he would be present on an *incognito* basis rather than an official one.)

    See Also: ROYALTY

Money Bills: The principle that money grants should originate in the Commons was assented to by King Henry IV in 1407. The Lower House's control of financial matters was by no means firmly established right away. Nearly 300 years later the Lords still felt able to interfere in money bills upon occasion. Eventually, the two Chambers agreed to accept one another's supremacy of different spheres, the Upper House having justice. It was upon the Commons's ability to hold the government to financial ransom that its eventual political dominance over its sib was to be based.

    See Also: DOWNING STREET No. 11 Downing Street

Parliamentary Privilege: During the early 20thC Horace de Vere Cole was Britain's most renowned practical joker. One day he was walking up Bury Street with his associate the MP Oliver Locker-Lampson. The Parliamentarian boasted that, as a member of the Commons, he could not be arrested. Unobserved, de Vere Cole slipped his own wallet into one of his companion's jacket pockets. The conversation moved on and the hoaxer, judging that circumstances had reached the right condition, challenged Locker-Lampson to a race up the street. The legislator accepted and both men started running towards Piccadilly. De Vere Cole fell behind and shouted out 'Stop, thief!' A policeman whom he had seen walking down the road tackled the Parliamentarian. De Vere Cole exclaimed that the man had stolen his wallet. This was duly recovered from Locker-Lampson's person. Upon hearing of the incident, Winston Churchill felt prompted to comment that de Vere Cole was 'a very dangerous man...to his friends.'

Location: Bury Street, SW1Y 6(AL).

St Stephen's Chapel: One of the means by which the Reformation was wrought was the Chantries Act of 1547. The measure required that all religious services must be held in public places. This was done so that the state could monitor their doctrinal orthodoxy. As a result, all private chapels were deconsecrated, including those that were within royal palaces. The Palace of Westminster's St Stephen's Chapel became a secular room.

That year the Commons moved their meetings back into the Palace, taking up residence in St Stephen's. The House's seating arrangement is reputed to be descended from the lay-out of the chapel's choir stalls. The custom of MPs bowing to the Speaker's chair is thought to derive from the seat having been placed where the altar had been. The returning MPs had known the room as a chapel. Therefore, they were accustomed to paying obeisance in that direction.

Liquid Refreshment

The Kremlin: Until the 1987 general election there was a tendency for the Labour MPs who sat for constituencies in North-Eastern England to be modestly-educated, trades union-sponsored men who were native to the region. At Westminster, they tended to drink together in *The Strangers' Bar*, which, as a result, was nicknamed *The Kremlin*.

It is reputed that within the *Bar*, by its entrance, there used to be a sign that had the words 'Way Out' printed upon it. It had been secured a few inches above the ground.

See Also: PUBS

Robert Maxwell: Robert Maxwell was a newspaper owner who died in mysterious circumstances in 1991. At the time, the finances of his business empire were imploding. However, during the 1960s he had been a Labour MP. While he had been the Chairman of the House of Commons Catering Committee, he had managed to generate a profit for it. He had achieved this rare feat by selling the Chamber's excellent wine cellar...to himself.

See Also: THE GUNPOWDER PLOT

Taunting The Tourists: The Palace has a terrace that overlooks the River Thames. During the summer a bar is erected upon it. Lord Fitt was a widely respected life peer. It is reputed that, whenever he was drinking there and saw a sight-seeing boat passing by on the river, he would hold up in one hand a fullish glass, use his other one to point towards it, and shout out, 'It's all free, you know!'

See Also: THE THAMES The Embankment and Sir Joseph Bazalgette

The Lords

Parliament is a younger institution than the House of Lords is. As a body, the latter can trace its history back to 1095. King William II summoned England's nobles to attend a meeting that he had convened at Rockingham Castle in Northamptonshire. The purpose of this gathering was to try to resolve a dispute between himself and Anselm the Archbishop of Canterbury. The first English Parliament was not to be held until 140 years later.

See Also: INNS & TAVERNS The Star & Garter, The Wicked Lord Byron; THEATRES St Martin's Theatre, A Deathbed Undertaking

Dinner Gong: The Rt Rev Maurice Wood (*d*.2007) Bishop of Norwich was an episcopal member of the Chamber. He became known as 'Dinner Gong' Wood. This was because it was reputed that, whenever he rose to speak in the Chamber, a large proportion of the peers present would stand up and go to the tea rooms.

The Dreamtime: There is a story of an early twentieth-century Cabinet minister who dreamt that he was addressing the House of Lords. He awoke in its Chamber to discover that he was due to do so.

Umbrellas: In 1923 the composer and dilettante the 14th Baron Berners went to the House of Lords to assume his seat. He never went to the Chamber again, claiming that, while he had been there, a bishop had stolen his umbrella.

See Also: WEATHER Umbrellas

Whipped Herring: Whips are responsible for enforcing cohesion within their parties.

The 13th Earl Ferrers was a hereditary peer who was active in the proceedings of the House of Lords. He served in a number of Conservative governments in a variety of junior and middle-ranking posts. During the early 1970s he was a whip. The then Chief Whip was the 2nd Baron Denham. Upon one occasion, after the latter had left the Palace at the end of a working week, the earl placed a dead herring in one of the drawers of his superior's desk. On the Monday the baron returned to an office that smelt high. Upon discovering the fish he screamed. He proceeded to conceal it within Ferrers's bureau. With time the earl, in his turn, unearthed the rotting remains of the piscine vertebrate. Upon doing so he threw it at Denham who hurled it back at him. The underling then bided his time before secreting the carcass in his colleague's brief case.

The House of Lords Act of 1999 reduced the number of hereditary peers who sat in the Chamber from several hundred nobles to 92. This rump was chosen electorally by the House's members. Ferrers topped the ballot.

The Woolsack: There is a throne in the Lords. It is used solely by the monarch. The Lord Chancellor, in her/his capacity as the Speaker of the House, sits upon the Woolsack, which stands upon the floor of the Chamber. The arrangement is believed to have originated during the reign of King Edward III (*d*.1377). The seat's name is a reminder of how important the wool trade was to Medieval England's economy.

The State Opening of Parliament

Each autumn the State Opening of Parliament marks the start of the Parliamentary session. Present at it, in their official capacity, are an array of exotically titled officials from both the Palace of Westminster and the Royal Household, *e.g.* the Howard Pursuivant Extraordinary and Bluemantle Pursuivant. The ceremony starts with Black Rod formally summoning the Commons's members from their Chamber to hear the Queen's Speech in the House of Lords. In this address, the government's intended legislative programme for the forthcoming Parliamentary session is arrayed. The sovereign reads it out while sitting upon the throne.[1]

See Also: CLASS College of Arms; GUNPOWDER PLOT

---

[1]   During the Opening the Vice-Chamberlain of the Royal Household, a government whip, is 'held hostage' in Buckingham Palace. This is done in order to ensure the monarch's safe return from the legislature.

PERIOD PROPERTIES

See Also: WINSTON CHURCHILL The Churchill War Rooms; EXHIBITING GALLERIES Raven Row; HERITAGE; HERITAGE Prince Henry's Room; THE THAMES Strand-on-the-Green

The Adam Room

The Adam Room (1788) on the eleventh floor of the Lloyd's of London Building (1986) is used by insurers for important meetings. It was designed by the Scottish architect Robert Adam as the dining room of Bowood House, the Wiltshire mansion of the 1st Marquis of Lansdowne.

The property was demolished in 1955. However, before this happened, the Room had been bought by Lloyd's and dismantled. It was then incorporated into the body's then home. Subsequently, it was taken to pieces a second time and then reassembled within the Richard Rogers-designed tower.

Location: Lloyd's of London Building, Leadenhall Street, EC3M 7JJ.

Bankside

It was long maintained that Sir Christopher Wren (*d*.1723) lived at No. 49 Bankside (opposite) during the construction of St Paul's Cathedral. Despite the property's fine northward view of the building, this was probably not the case.

Gillian Tindall's book *The House By The Thames* (2006) is a history of the house.

Location: No. 49 Bankside, SE1 9JE. East of Tate Modern.

Berry Brothers & Rudd

The wine merchants Berry Brothers & Rudd have bow-fronted premises on St James's Street. The business was founded in 1698.

Location: No. 3 St James's Street, SW1A 1EG. On the eastern side of the road, at its southern end.

Website: www.bbr.com

Carlyle House

Thomas Carlyle disowned his Scottish Calvinist background and chose

No. 49 Bankside

to immerse himself in German literature. However, this latter activity was done within the mental framework of the former so that the writer translated authors such as Johann von Goethe without partaking of the rationalism of the Enlightenment. Thereby, he developed an outlook that was informed by their philosophical outlook but which was divorced from its mainspring. He viewed novels as being too light a literary form but wrote works of history in a florid style that bore witness to his extraordinary imagination.

In 1834 Carlyle and his wife moved to Cheyne Row. Towards the end of the year, at the suggestion of John Stuart Mill, he started writing a work about the French Revolution that was informed by the Romantic perspective, portraying both the magnificence and the horror. He sought to create a work of art rather than a work of fact. By describing the essence of what had been, he would be dealing with the present and the future. He was trying to display how the old order had been stripped of its redundant trappings and that there was no possibility of the past being returned to.

In spring 1835 Carlyle lent the manuscript to Mill. Subsequently, the latter appeared at the Carlyles' door in Cheyne Row in a state of distress. He told Carlyle that a maid had mistaken the script for waste paper and had thrown it upon a fire. Only four sheets had been retrieved from the blaze. There was no second copy, Carlyle had systematically destroyed his notes after completing the chapter that each batch of research had been the basis for. He continued with the project, writing out a new version of what had been destroyed. The book was published in 1837.

Carlyle believed that the failure of the Chartist movement to secure reform beyond the repeal of the Corn Laws derived from its lack of an effective leader. He was of the opinion that without direction, popular movements were limited to being able only to sweep away an old order. He was interested in trying to identify those aspects of nature and per-sonality that were the foundation of the unconscious. He believed that some figures incorporated core spiritual truths in both their deliberate and their unconscious actions.

The author tried to write a work about Oliver Cromwell (*d*.1658). In late 1843 Carlyle chose to burn the manuscript. Instead, he worked on a collection of the Lord Protector's letters and speeches. In 1851 he identified in King Frederick the Great of Prussia (*d*.1786) the subject that he had been looking for. In 1865 his *History of Frederick the Great* was completed.

Location: No. 24 Cheyne Row, SW3 5HL. The property became a museum within fifteen years of Carlyle's death.

Website: www.nationaltrust.org.uk/carlyles-house

City of London Hostelries

See Also: THE GREAT FIRE The Fire, Surviving Churches; PUBS

The Hoop & Grapes: The foundations of *The Hoop & Grapes*, in Aldgate High Street, date from the 13[th]C. The pub is the only surviving 17[th]C timber-framed structure of its kind in the City of London. In the wake of the Great Fire, the Rebuilding of London Act of 1666 barred the use of the construction technique.

Location: No. 47 Aldgate High Street, EC3N 1AL.

The Old Shades: The Old Shades wine house in Martin Lane was probably built in the early 1660s. It survived the Great Fire.

Location: No. 6 Martin Lane, EC4R 0DP.

The Coram Foundation's Governors' Court Room

No. 49 Mecklenburgh Square houses the headquarters of the Thomas Coram Foundation child welfare organisation. The building contains a re-assembly of the 18th C Foundling Hospital's Governors' Court Room.

Location: No. 40 Brunswick Square, WC1N 1AZ.

Website: www.coram.org.uk

No. 18 Folgate Street

Dennis Severs was a Californian who moved to England in 1967. A dozen years later he bought No. 18 Folgate Street, a derelict 18th C Spitalfields townhouse. He restored the property's rooms in a variety of 18th C and 19th C styles. His creation can be visited.

Location: No. 18 Folgate Street, E1 6BX.

Reading: Dennis Severs (1944-1999) *18 Folgate Street: The Life of A House In Spitalfields* Random House (2002).

Website: www.dennissevershouse.co.uk

Fournier Street

The Spitalfields silk industry sprung up in the early 17th C. Following the Revocation of the Edict of Nantes in 1685, there was a large influx of Huguenot silkweavers into the district. The weaving attics of their houses had deep rear windows so as to admit as much light as possible. Fournier Street is a surviving example. In the second half of the 19th C the industry began to decline. There were still silkweavers working in Bethnal Green during the 1930s.

Location: Fournier Street, E1 6QE.

Fribourg & Treyer

'Fribourg & Treyer, Tobacconists To His Majesty and Purveyors of Foreign Snuffs to the Royal Family' was a business that was established in 1720. The shop was constructed *c*.1770.

The Fribourg & Treyer business closed in 1981. The premises are now occupied by a gift shop.

Location: No. 34 Haymarket, SW1Y 4HA. On the eastern side at the northern end.

Reading: George Evans *The Old Snuff House of Fribourg and Treyer...34 St James's, Haymarket, 1720-1920* Macbeth (1921).

Leighton House

Frederick Leighton was a leading painter of the late 19thC. Leighton House (1864) was built for him both as a home and as a studio. The building's most noted room is its Arab Hall (1877).

In 1896 Leighton was the first British artist to be ennobled. He 'enjoyed' the distinction of holding the shortest-lived peerage in history. He died on the day after he had been made a baron. He had no child to inherit the title. Therefore, it was extinguished. Four years later the property became a museum.

Leighton had a habit of trying to educate the models whom he painted. This practice informed George Bernard Shaw's play *Pygmalion* (1913).

Location: No. 12 Holland Park Road, W14 8LZ.

Website: www.rbkc.gov.uk/subsites/museums/leightonhouse museum.aspx

New Bond Street

Lucie Campbell: Lucie Campbell, Fine Jewels occupies the former premises of Tessiers, itself a jewellery business that had acquired the site in 1856. When the shop is closed, its windows are still covered by wooden shutters.

Location: No. 26 New Bond Street, W1S 2JY.

Website: www.luciecampbell.com

No. 143 New Bond Street: No. 143 New Bond Street is a shop that has a fine period front. The words 'Savory & Moore', a chemist's business, can be discerned above the doorway's lantern. The premises are occupied by a store that sells Ralph Lauren's childrenswear.

Location: No. 143 New Bond Street, W1S 2TP.

The Old Curiosity Shop

The Old Curiosity Shop dates from 1567. It is the oldest retail shop in England. During the 19thC the premises adopted the name of Charles Dickens's 1841 novel. The building did not have any link to the writer.

Location: Nos. 13-14 Portsmouth Street, WC2A 2ES. On the eastern side.

See Also: CHARLES DICKENS The Old Curiosity Shop

The Old Operating Theatre

The Old Operating Theatre, Museum & Herb Garret was an early 19thC operating theatre that was built as part of St Thomas's Hospital. After St Thomas's moved westwards away from Southwark, the room was used for storing herbs in. It fell into disuse and was forgotten about for many years. Thereby, it survived intact.

The theatre was discovered in 1956, almost a century after it had been sealed shut.

Location: No. 9a St Thomas Street, SE1 9RY. On the northern side.
Website: www.thegarret.org.uk

Linley Sambourne House

Linley Samboune (*d*.1910) was an illustrator. He bequeathed No. 18 Stafford Terrace to his son Roy who never redecorated the property. Eventually, it passed to the latter's niece Anne Countess of Rosse. In 1958 she, along with John Betjeman, was one of the founders of the Victorian Society, an organisation that sought to promote an appreciation of Victorian art and design during an era in which both were deeply unfashionable. In 1979 the Greater London Council bought the house. The building is now owned by Kensington & Chelsea Borough. It is administered by the Society.

Location: No. 18 Stafford Terrace, W8 7BH. On the southern side.

See Also: HERITAGE Period Groups, The Victorian Society
Websites: www.rbkc.gov.uk/subsites/museums/
18staffordterrace1.aspx www.victoriansociety.org.uk

The Water House Room

New River House, Thames Water's former headquarters in Sadler's Wells, contains a room from the Water House of 1693. It is now forms part of a private flat.

Location: New River House, No. 173 Rosebery Avenue, Sadler's Wells, EC1R 4(TJ) . On the western side, to the north of the junction with Hardwick Street.

Wilton's

John Wilton was an East End publican. In 1858 he opened Wilton's Grand Concert & Supper Room as a music hall. It catered not only to dockers and sailors but also to upmarket swells who were indulging in an evening's amusement in the East End.

The Methodist Church's aggressive promotion of temperance meant that the sect regarded Wilton's as a particular *bête noire*. As a result, when, in 1880, it learnt that the owner wished to sell the business, it ensured it had funds immediately available to be able to buy the building with. It did so. The church retained the property for several decades. It used it as a soup kitchen and as a mission hall. Eventually, the sect sold it. By then music hall was dead as a popular entertainment.

Paradoxically, it was the Methodists' sustained ownership of the venue that was probably the key factor in the building's survival. Thanks to them in 2008 Wilton's hosted music hall for the first time in over 120 years.

Location: Graces Alley, E1 8JB. On the eastern side of Ensign Street.

Reading: Peter Honri *John Wilton's Music Hall: The Handsomest Room In Town* Ian Henry Publications (1984).

Website: http://wiltons.org.uk

Woburn Walk

Woburn Walk (1822) is a short, pedestrianised street that is lined by small shops that have bow windows.

Location: Woburn Walk, WC1H 0(JJ).

See Also: SHOPPING Pedestrianised Shopping Streets

THE POLICE

See Also: SHERLOCK HOLMES; TRAFALGAR SQUARE Trafalgar Square Police Station

The City of London Police

The City of London had a system of watchmen and constables that dated from medieval times. The arrangement's shortcomings were exposed by the Gordon Riots of 1780. Four years later it was supplemented by the Day Police. This force's members wore blue greatcoats; Jonas Hanway had suggested the colour, arguing that it was both sober and dignified.[1] In 1839 the watch was abolished and the City of London Police force was established under an Act of Parliament.

The force's Commissioner is appointed by the Lord Mayor, the Aldermen, and the Common Council of the City of London. Their choice is subject to approval by the Home Secretary.

Location: No. 37 Wood Street, EC2P 2NQ. On the eastern side.

See Also: THE BANK OF ENGLAND The Bank of England Picket; THE CITY OF LONDON The Impact of The Great Fire Upon The Government of The City of London

Website: www.cityoflondon.police.uk

New Scotland Yard

The Derby Gate New Scotland Yard building (1890) was designed by Norman Shaw.[2] The Met's senior officers were accommodated in offices on the lower floors. The more junior a policeman was the more flights of stairs he had to climb.

In 1958 Joseph Simpson became the Commissioner of the Metropolitan Police. He was the first person to be appointed to the position who had started his policing career in the force's ranks.

---

[1]   When the Metropolitan Police force was created in 1829 it too adopted a blue uniform. In part, the colour was chosen because it was free of military connotations.

[2]   Originally, the site had been intended to accommodate an opera house. However, the cost of sinking foundations into ground that had been claimed from the Thames only recently had proven to be too great and the project had foundered.

In 1967 the Met moved to a building that stands on a site that is between Victoria Street and Broadway. The complex's entrance features a triangle that rotates 14,000 times every day. This is reputed to be known as 'The Whirling Toblerone'. It was designed by Edward Wright. He was a Modernist who was a member of the Independent Group.

In 2012 the Met announced that it was going to sell its New Scotland Yard building. It was planning to move to the Curtis Green Building on the Victoria Embankment.

Locations: Nos. 8-10 Broadway, SW1H 0BG.
Norman Shaw Building, Victoria Embankment, SW1A 2HZ.
Curtis Green Building, Victoria Embankment, SW1A 2JL.
Website: www.met.police.uk

Art Theft: *Reading*: Edward Dolnick *Stealing The Scream: The Hunt For A Missing Masterpiece* Icon Books (2007). Edvard Munch's painting *The Scream* (1893) was stolen from a Norwegian gallery in 2004. Charley Hill of Scotland Yard led the recovery of the art work two years later.

Keith Middlemas (1935-2013) *The Double Market Art Theft and Art Thieves* Saxon House (1975). A book about the art market and art thieves.

See Also: GALLERIES The National Gallery, The Duke and The Bus Driver

The Special Branch: A wave of Fenian terrorism in the 1880s led to the setting up of the Special Irish Branch in 1883. Subsequently, the unit was renamed the Special Branch (SO12).

In 2006 the Special Branch merged with the Anti-Terrorist Branch (SO13) to form the Counter Terrorism Command.

See Also: PARLIAMENT The Commons, The Members' Lobby

Peelers

In 1829 the Metropolitan Police Force (the Met) was legislated into existence at the behest of Sir Robert Peel the Home Secretary. The Force's commissioners established their premises at No. 4 Whitehall. At the back of the building, in Great Scotland Yard, was its adjunct - the first police station. This occupied what had been the servants' quarters.

During their early years the police were deeply unpopular. In 1833, during a disturbance that had broken out at Clerkenwell Green, Robert Culley, an unarmed officer, died as a result of having been stabbed. At the coroner's inquest into his killing, the jury brought in a verdict of 'justifiable homicide' because the force's conduct had been 'ferocious, brutal, unprovoked by the people'. At the subsequent funeral a crowd heckled the parading policemen. However, the Met went on to prove its worth. The government felt able to encourage the creation of local constabularies throughout Britain.

Location: No. 4 Whitehall, SW1A 2(DY).

The River Police

The Marine Support Unit polices the River Thames from Hampton Court to Dartford Creek.

Patrick Colquhoun was a Glaswegian who had precocious success as a tobacco merchant. He became one of his native city's leading figures. As he did so, he developed a reputation for bumptiousness. The American War of Independence (1776-1783) subjected his home town to severe economic strains. Colquhoun took it upon himself to travel to London to petition Parliament and the government for ameliorating measures. Following the re-establishment of peace, it emerged that there had been a permanent shift in the tobacco trade away from the Clyde. Colquhoun's business was no longer viable. He responded to this development by moving to London in order to try to become a professional lobbyist.

At the time, the government's management of Scottish politics was handled by Henry Dundas the Home Secretary. He judged Colquhoun to be someone of consequence and so secured for him an appointment as the stipendiary magistrate for Shoreditch. The former merchant threw himself into his new profession. He developed a programme of social policy that was intended to reduce crime; it was derivative in character. The minister came to appreciate that the justice had both an inflated concept of his own abilities and little real understanding of the complexity of the societal matters in which he was seeking to meddle. The Home Secretary stopped accepting his fellow Scot's requests that they should meet. Colquhoun's response to this situation was to publish his scheme in an anonymous pamphlet - *Treatise on The Police of The Metropolis* (1796). It found a receptive audience. The author soon made his identity known publicly and basked in the the kudos that the publication had generated.

John Harriott aspired to be a gentleman and had several children to provide for. He had tried to establish himself in a succession of careers. Each attempt had failed. In 1797 one of his uncles, who was an influential insurance underwriter, secured for him an appointment as a stipendiary magistrate. The office was based in Shadwell. Merchant vessels that were waiting to unload their goods were anchored on the Thames. The scale of thefts from these craft was a substantial trade in itself. In his new position Harriot was exposed to the problem on a daily basis. He drew up a plan for forming a police force that would operate on the river. However, he was largely unknown and so was unable to persuade anyone in authority or of consequence to take his scheme seriously.

Harriott took the idea to his fellow magistrate Colquhoun. The latter appreciated the potential that it possessed. As a former transatlantic trader himself, he was able to persuade a body of West Indian merchants that they should consider it. This they did. They realised that it might benefit them materially. They controlled one of the largest groupings within the House of Commons. Therefore, the Thames Police Act was soon enacted. The merchants paid the lion's share of the new force's running costs. The government provided some of its funds.

Colquhoun returned to his social policy concerns although these were no longer so focussed on reducing criminality as they had been. In 1798 Harriot assumed the command of the new force. His conduct in office was not without a degree of controversy. He sometimes failed to observe a proper demarcation between the private aspects of his life and the official ones.

The force was based at Wapping Police Station. Subsequently, it established outposts at Blackwall and Waterloo. In 1839 the Marine Police became the Metropolitan Police's Thames Division. In the 1880s the Division was equipped with steamboats. In 1910 it acquired its first motor boat. In 1925 it stopped using rowing boats. In 2001 it was renamed the Marine Support Unit.

Location: Wapping Police Station, Wapping High Street, E1 2NE.
See Also: THE THAMES
Website: www.thamespolicemuseum.org.uk

PORTOBELLO ROAD

In 1739 Admiral Edward Vernon defeated a Spanish force at Puerto Bello in the Caribbean.[1] To mark the victory, a farmstead, in what is now Notting Hill, was named after it. Portobello Road derived its appellation from the property.

A local market existed in the late 1830s. This was dominated by Gypsy horse-traders who had been drawn to the area by the nearby Notting Hill Hippodrome racecourse. In 1841 the track was closed. The repository faded away.

In the 1880s an informal street market grew up. Following the First World War many of the stallholders were ex-servicemen. This factor prompted the authorities to hold back from suppressing it. The London County Council finally licensed the mart in 1927. During the 1930s antiques dealers began to do business in it. After the Second World War the general market of the Caledonian Market in Islington was closed down. Portobello Road received many of the traders who had been working there.

There is a daily street market. On Saturdays the northern section of the road becomes geared to the young and international visitors, while the southern portion tends to be more weighted towards the antiques trade. During the market's first couple of hours, the dealers sell items to one another. At around breakfast time antique collectors begin to appear and as the morning progresses so the ordinary public come to predominate.

Location: Portobello Road, W10 5(SY) and W11 2(DY).

Reading: Blanche Girouard *Portobello Voices* The History Press (2013).

See Also: CAMDEN TOWN Camden Market; CARNABY STREET; FOOD MARKETS Spitalfields Market; STREET MARKETS Bermondsey Market; STREET MARKETS East End Street Markets, Brick Lane Market

Websites: www.portobellomarket.org www.portobelloroad.co.uk www.portobellovillage.com

[1]   'Old Grog's' participation in the major British setback at Cartagena de las Indias, on the northern coast of South America, two years later is not commemorated. Indeed, to most Britons it is completely unknown. The admiral's popularity survived the *débâcle* untarnished. (There had been other British naval successes at Portobello in 1707 and 1726. These too are little known.)

PUBS

See Also: INNS & TAVERNS; INNS & TAVERNS The George Inn; PARLIAMENT Liquid Refreshment; PERIOD PROPERTIES City of London Hostelries; STREET FURNITURE Signs
DVD: *Roll Out The Barrel: The British Pub On Film* BFI (2012).
Websites: www.innsignsociety.com www.pubhistorysociety.co.uk

The Blackfriar

The Blackfriar (1875) is London's only art nouveau pub. The establishment stands on a site where a Dominican monastery stood.

Location: No. 174 Queen Victoria Street, EC4V 4EG. On the corner of New Bridge Street and Queen Street.

Website: www.nicholsonspubs.co.uk/theblackfriar blackfriarslondon

The Blue Posts

There are several *Blue Post* pubs across the West End. Their name commemorates a series of blue posts that marked out the Soho hunting ground.

Locations: No. 28 Rupert Street, Soho, W1D 6DJ; No. 18 Kingly Street, Soho, W1B 5PX; No. 22 Berwick Street, Soho, W1F 0QA (on the south-eastern corner of the junction with Broadwick Street); No. 81 Newman Street, Fitzrovia, W1T 3EU; No. 6 Bennet Street, St James's, SW1A 1RP, on the southern side of the junction with Arlington Street (the name of this *Blue Post* pub dates back to at least 1667 and may commemorate the symbol of two poles that advertised a Bennett Street-based sedan chair hire business).

The Dog & Duck: *The Dog & Duck* is a compact gin palace of a pub.lic house The establishment'ss name is also a relict of Soho's hunting ground heritage.

Location: No. 18 Bateman Street, Soho, W1D 3AJ. On the north-western corner of the junction with Frith Street. (There is a Duck Lane to the west of the Berwick Street *Blue Posts*.)

Website: www.nicholsonspubs.co.uk/thedogandducksoho london

The Board of Green Cloth

The Board of Green Cloth issued alcohol and gaming licences for establishments that were in royal palaces. The body could also grant them within areas that were within a set distance of any of the regal complexes. It was abolished by the Licensing Act of 2003. The Board had been the last surviving Court of the Royal Prerogative.

Location: Gordon's Wine Bar, No. 47 Villiers Street, WC2N 6NE. Formerly, the establishment operated under a Board licence.

See Also: PALACES; ROYALTY; THE TOWER OF LONDON The Star Chamber

Website: http://gordonswinebar.com

Lodged In The Loo: The solicitor David Lavender served as the Clerk of the Board from 1984 to 2000. He was appointed to the position because he had developed an expertise in securing liquor and entertainment licences for West End pubs and restaurants. He had frequently been in conflict with Westminster City Council, which had often opposed his clients' wishes. Upon one occasion, a licence application had had to be submitted to a court by a particular date. When Mr Lavender had arrived at the appropriate address on the day, he had discovered that the establishment had been closed. He had walked around to the back of its premises. There, he had seen that a window of its Gents had been left open. He had thrown the application through the aperture. The following day he had returned to the building. Upon his arrival, he had directed one of its clerks to collect the document. Thereby, he had become able to validate his assertion that the paper had been duly lodged with the body within the required time.

The Castle

The Prince Regent liked to watch cockfights and to bet upon the result of individual clashes. He attended an event that was staged at *The Castle*, a pub in Farringdon. He had a run of bad luck. This meant that he had no money to hand that he could wage upon the encounters' outcomes. The establishment's landlord lent him some cash to cover his embarrassment. The following day the prince sent a messenger with a sum that paid back the loan. Accompanying it was a royal license that allowed the publican to act as a pawnbroker. This enabled the man to take legal possession of items of value as security for the repayment of money that he lent out to gamblers who found themselves to be illiquid.

Location: Nos. 34-35 Cowcross Street, , EC1M 6DB.

Website: www.thecastlefarringdon.co.uk

The Coach & Horses

The Coach & Horses is Soho's most noted watering hole.

Location: No. 29 Greek Street, W1D 5DH. On the northern corner of the junction with Romilly Street, W1.

Reading: Norman Balon with Spencer Bright *You're Barred, You Bastards: The Memoirs of A Soho Publican* Sidgwick & Jackson (1991). Mr Balon was a landlord who possessed an Augean turn of phrase.

Jeffrey Bernard (1932-1997) *Low Life: A Kind of Autobiography* Gerald Duckworth (1993). Mr Bernard was an alcoholic journalist who drank in pub. His dislike of being drunk was outweighed by his fondness for becoming drunk.

Website: www.coachandhorsessoho.co.uk

The French House

In 1914 Victor Berlemont, a Belgian, bought *The Wine House*. He renamed the business *Maison Berlemont* and subsequently *The York Minster*. The pub's clientele has included Brigadier-General de Gaulle. Following *M* Berlemont's death in the 1950s his son Gaston succeeded him as the establishment's landlord. Both *père et fils* sported fine handlebar moustaches.

The French was unusual for a pub in that it stocked and sold absinthe, arrack, and pastis. The reason why the establishment only provides beer in half-pint glasses is because there is so little space behind its bar.

Berlemont *fils* retired in 1989 - on 14 July.

Location: No. 49 Dean Street, W1D 5BG. On the eastern side, south of Old Compton Street.

Website: http://frenchhousesoho.com

Gin Palaces

During the 1820s it came to be appreciated that the new technology of gas lighting could be used to make pubs more attractive places to be in at night than they had been up until then. The first gin palaces are reputed to have been *Thompson & Fearon's* in Holborn and *Weller's* on Old Street.

Locations: *The Princess Louise*, No. 208 High Holborn, WC1V 7BW. On the southern side, to the west of Kingsway.

The Red Lion, No. 2 Duke of York Street, SW1Y 6JP. Western side.

See Also: DEPARTMENT STORES

The Bride of Denmark: The Architectural Press published *The Architects' Journal* and the *Architectural Review*. The basement of the enterprise's

Queen Anne's Gate building contained *The Bride of Denmark*, a pastiche Victorian pub that Hubert de Cronin Hastings (*d.*1986), the firm's proprietor, had built himself (in part).[1] The den derives its name from the statue of Queen Anne (*d.*1714) that stands next to No. 13 Queen Anne's Gate. Her husband was Prince George of Denmark.

Hastings intended that *The Bride* should be an inspiration for contemporary architects who were designing pubs in the prevalent Festival of Britain style. It proved to be popular with those members of the pro-

---

[1]   The ideas that originated from Hastings and his associates included 'townscape.' This concept sought to look at the whole composition of a town rather than just the design of individual buildings.

fession who enjoyed a drink, notably Cedric Price and 'Big Jim' Stirling. Hastings's associate Osbert Lancaster coined the term 'gin palace' to describe ornate Victorian pubs.

Location: Nos. 9-13 Queen Anne's Gate, SW1H 9BU.

See Also: ROYAL STATUES Queen Anne, Queen Anne's Gate

The Punch Tavern: In 1841 *The Punch Tavern* was the birthplace of *Punch*, a magazine that was launched by the engraver Ebenezer Landells and the writer Henry Mayhew. They were reforming Liberals who sought to combine humour and political comment.

As the later 20[th]C progressed, the organ came to be increasingly identified with dentists' waiting rooms. In 1992 the magazine was closed. It was relaunched in 1996 but closed for a second time in 2002. In 2004 The British Library bought *Punch*'s archive.

Location: No. 99 Fleet Street, EC4Y 1DE. A betiled and bemirrored pub. On the southern side of the eastern end.

Website: www.punchtavern.com

The Salisbury: In the late 1950s and early 1960s *The Salisbury* was a favourite haunt of a group of young actors, who were then establishing themselves as leading thespians of the London stage and who would go on to become international movie stars. It was not unknown for them to drink in the pub before, after, and sometimes - if they were appearing in a theatre that was nearby and they were not required to be on stage - during a performance.

Location: No. 90 St Martin's Lane, WC2N 4AP. On the southern side of the corner with St Martin's Court.

Reading: Robert Sellers *Hellraisers: The Life and Inebriated Times of Burton, Harris, O'Toole and Reed* Preface Publishing (2008).

See Also: THEATRES

Website: www.taylor-walker.co.uk/pub/salisbury-covent garden

The Lamb & Flag

The Lamb & Flag pub is a timber-framed building that dates from 1623. The building's exterior is Georgian.

In the 19[th]C the establishment became known as *The Bucket of Blood* because of its association with boxing.

Location: No. 33 Rose Street, WC2E 9EB.

Website: http://lambandflagcoventgarden.co.uk

The Duchess of Portsmouth: The anonymous manuscript *An Essay On Satire* (1679) attacked a range of court figures. The number included

King Charles II, the 6th Earl of Dorset, the 2nd Earl of Rochester (who was also a poet), and the Duchess of Portsmouth, who was the snootiest of the king's mistresses. Close to The Lamb & Flag the poet and playwright John Dryden was almost assassinated by some men who had been hired by her grace to attack him.[1] His survival is commemorated annually in the pub. It is almost certain that Dryden was not the principal author of the *Essay*, which does not bear his flourish. The work was probably composed by the 3rd Earl of Mulgrave, who may have called upon the writer to aid him with some of its lines. Dryden may have been a long-standing target of the duchess. His career as a playwright had been launched in 1663 with the aid of the Duchess of Cleveland, who was another of the king's mistresses.

The Marquis of Granby

The pub name *The Marquis of Granby* is derived from the courtesy-titled Marquis of Granby (*d*.1770), who was the eldest son of the 3rd Duke of Rutland. During the early stages of the Seven Years' War British troops did not distinguish themselves in the European campaigns in which they participated. The general, who was bald, became renowned for charging into battle while not wearing a wig; this gave rise to the phrase 'To go at something bald-headed.' His vitality and his martial successes restored the reputation of the Army as a combatant force.

Granby was given to helping his former non-commissioned officers set themselves up in business. A number of the ex-NCOs became publicans and in gratitude for the help that they had received from their former commander they named their hostelries after him. There are several *Marquises of Granby* in London and it is a pub name that can be found elsewhere in England.

Some of the marquises have proven to be inconstant and have changed their names. *Paxton's Head* in Knightsbridge used to be one.[2] (Nearby Rutland Gate (1838-1856) was built on the site of what had been Rutland House, the family's London townhouse.)

Locations: No. 142 Shaftesbury Avenue, Cambridge Circus, WC2H 8HJ (now *The Ape & Bird* on the corner of Earlham Street and West Street); Nos. 51-52 Chandos Place, Covent Garden, WC2N 4HS; No. 2 Rathbone Street, Fitzrovia, W1T 1NT; No. 41 Romney Street, Westminster, SW1P 3RF; Paxton's Head, No. 153 Knightsbridge, SW1X 7PA.

[1]   *The Lamb & Flag* pub is a wooden-framed building dating from 1623. The building's exterior is Georgian.

[2]   Sir Joseph Paxton was the designer of the Crystal Palace. The structure was erected in the neighbouring Hyde Park to house the Great Exhibition of 1851.

The Only Running Footman In London

A running footman was a liveried servant who ran ahead of a coach to prepare the way for it.

In 1718 the Duke of Wharton set his running man to race against one employed by Captain L ___ over a course from Woodstock Cross to Tyburn. £1000 was waged on the contest's outcome.

During the 18[th]C the spread of the turnpike system improved the quality of roads. This meant that there was no longer the same need for carriages to be so sturdy. As they became physically lighter so they

became faster. Running footmen became increasingly less necessary but continued to exist for a while as a distraction for rich men.

The 4th Duke of Queensberry (*d*.1810) is the last known person to have retained one in his service.

Location: *The Last Running Footman In London*, No. 5 Charles Street, W1J 5DE. A pub.

Website: www.therunningfootmanmayfair.com

The Prospect of Whitby

The pub that became *The Prospect of Whitby* was extant in the 17thC. It took its present name in 1777 from a Whitby-registered ship called *The Prospect*. This had been moored upon the Thames nearby long enough to have become a *land*mark.

Location: No. 57 Wapping Wall, E1 9SP.

Pub Names

A number of London's districts derive their names from inns or pubs.

See Also: INNS & TAVERNS District Names

Reading: Jacqueline Simpson *Green Men and White Swans: The Folklore of British Pub Names* Random House (2010).

The Black Lion: That a toponym came from a pub did not guarantee its permanence. Queensway, above the north-western section of Kensington Gardens, used to be known as Black Lion Lane. Its current moniker was bestowed upon it by Queen Victoria. She had been raised nearby in Kensington Palace. Following her accession to the throne in 1837 she made it known that she thought that the name Queensway was a more appropriate appellation.

Location: *The Black Lion*, No. 123 Bayswater Road, W2 3JH. The pub is on the eastern side of the roads' junction.

See Also: MUSEUMS The Victoria & Albert Museum

Website: www.taylor-walker.co.uk/pub/black-lion -bayswater/c3606

The Sloaney Pony

Sally Cruickshank had a somewhat varied working life. In 1981 she decided that she wanted to run a pub. She became the landlady of *The White Horse* on Parson's Green. Prior to her doing so, she had been warned that the establishment was a rough house. This was because two rival amateur soccer teams both regarded the hostelry as being their local. The presence of 'undesirables' did not trouble her. As far as she was concerned, by the time that she had turned the premises into what she intended to no one would even notice them.

The bitters that were being offered were switched from keg beers to real ales. She served good quality food early in what became London's gastro-pub boom and ensured that *The Horse* had a varied, affordable cellar of wines. The pub began not only to attract far more customers than had been the case previously, it also drew them in from a wider social spectrum. The high proportion of drinkers with RP (received pronunciation) and marked RP accents led to it being nicknamed *The Sloaney Pony*. The moniker blended a measure affection with a degree of derision.

Mrs Cruickshank retired as *The Horse*'s landlady in 1995. At the time, members of Dauntless Athletic, one of the two teams of 'undesirables', were still drinking in the pub.

Location: Nos. 1-3 Parson's Green, SW6 4UL.
See Also: CLASS Sloane Rangers
Website: www.whitehorsesw6.com

The Star Tavern

Paddy Kennedy was a landlord of *The Star Tavern* in Belgravia. In the 1960s he ran the pub in a way that encouraged people from a broad range of social *strata* to drink with one another there. He had a soft spot for the underworld hard man-*cum*-bit part actor John Bindon.[1] The publican allowed the enforcer to rent a small house in Chesham Mews that was attached to the pub. The thug-thespian had an older brother Michael, who was an alcoholic. He was also retiring and bookish by nature. From time-to-time, he would stay with his younger sib at the property.

One winter's night, while Bindon minor was away, Michael died of hypothermia. *Rigor mortis* set in. Subsequently, John returned. It is reputed that he slung the corpse over his shoulder. He then walked to *The Star* with the body, entered the establishment, lent his charge against the bar, and exclaimed 'We're having a wake!'

Location: No. 6 Belgrave Mews West, Belgravia, SW1X 8HT. On the western side of the northern end

Reading: Wensley Clarkson *Bindon: Fighter, Gangster, Actor, Lover - The True Story of John Bindon* John Blake Publishing (2005).

Website: www.star-tavern-belgravia.co.uk

Ye Olde Cheshire Cheese

Ye Olde Cheshire Cheese is a pub that was rebuilt after the Great Fire of 1666. It was one of Dr Samuel Johnson's (*d*.1784) favourite haunts.

Location: Wine Office Court, No. 145 Fleet Street, EC4A 2BU. On the northern side.

Reading: Thomas Wilson Reid *The Book of The Cheese: Being Traits and Stories of 'Ye Olde Cheshire Cheese'* B. A. Moore (1896). 3rd edition.

Website: www.yeoldecheshirecheese.com

---

[1]   Mr Bindon gained entry into the acting world after the director Ken Loach saw him in a pub and invited him to play the role of Tom in the movie *Poor Cow* (1967).

ROMAN REMAINS

London was located by a ford. It stood on raised land that did not flood. These two factors made it attractive to the Romans. Londinium grew to be one of the principal cities of the Western Empire.

The settlement's name was almost certainly an adaptation of an older Celtic moniker. This may have meant 'city by the lake.' The lake would have been a winter-time body of water that would have collected on the low-lying northern portion of the South Bank.

See Also: BRIDGES London Bridge; THE CITY OF LONDON; HERITAGE; MUSEUMS The Museum of London

Boudicca

At the western end of the undercroft of All Hallows by The Tower it is possible to see a layer of ashes. These are some of remains of the Londinium that Boudicca burned down in AD 61.

Location: All Hallows by The Tower, Byward Street, EC3R 5BJ.

Reading: Ian Andrews (ed.) Trevor Cairns *Boudicca's Revolt* Cambridge University Press (1980).

Website: www.ahbtt.org.uk

Elevation

The land in the City of London is approximately 35ft higher than it was in the time of the Romans. (Medieval Londoners must have been assiduous litter louts.)

The Guildhall Amphitheatre

In 1988 excavations were conducted prior to the construction of the new Guildhall Art Gallery. Some Roman walls were unearthed. They had been part of an amphitheatre. It is the only one to have been found in London.

Location: The Guildhall Art Gallery, Guildhall Yard, EC2V 5AE.

Reading: Nick Bateman *Gladiators At The Guildhall: The Story of London Roman Amphitheatre and Medieval Guildhall* Museum of London Archaeology Service (2000).

Website: www.cityoflondon.uk/things-to-do/visiting-the-city/

> *The arena of London's Roman amphitheatre beneath the Guildhall Yard is indicated by the black slate oval inlaid in the yard's paved surface*

attractions-museums-and-galleries/guildhall-art-gallery-and-roman-amphitheatre/Pages/Guildhall%20Art%20deafult.aspx

The Leadenhall Basilica

Leadenhall Market stands above part of what was an eight-acre basilica complex. London was governed from there. The settlement's centre lay immediately to the west of the Market.

Location: Leadenhall Market, EC3V 1LT.

See Also: TRAFALGAR SQUARE The Centre of London

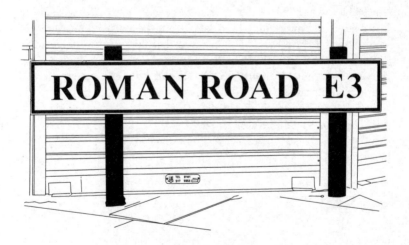

Roman Roads

Kennington Park Road and Newington Causeway: Stane Street linked Chichester to London. As the road approached the River Thames, it ran along the course of present-day Kennington Park Road and Newington Causeway.

Oxford Street: Ermine Street was the Roman road that formed the basis of Oxford Street and the Bayswater Road. It helped to give the West End an east-west axis and to determine the northern edge of Hyde Park and Kensington Gardens.

The Temple of Mithras

In the 3rdC a temple to Mithras was built upon the banks of the Walbrook. In the early 4thC the shrine was rededicated to Bacchus, the Roman deity whose diverse, divine portfolio was centred upon wine.

In the 1950s an excavation of the site was conducted by a Museum of London team that was led by William Grimes, the institution's Director. In 1962 the temple's remains were moved and re-erected at Temple Court on Queen Victoria Street. However the reconstruction was upon the wrong alignment. Subsequently, it was reported that the temple was going to be disassembled and returned to its original position.

Location: Walbrook, EC4N 8(DQ).

Tower Hill Cathedral

In 1995 it was announced that the remains of a Roman building had been discovered on Tower Hill. They dated from the 380s and measured 50 metres by 100. Archaeologists believed that the structure might have been London's first cathedral. If so, it would have been built for the Emperor Magnus Maximus (*d*.388). He had ruled the western Roman world from Britain.

Location: Tower Hill, EC3N 4(DU).

See Also: ST PAUL'S CATHEDRAL

ROYAL RESIDENCES

See Also: HERITAGE; KEW GARDENS The Royal Botanic Gardens; PALACES; ROYAL FAMILY; ROYAL RESIDENCES, DISAPPEARED

Clarence House

Following King George IV's accession in 1820, the new monarch supplied his two younger brothers with the financial wherewithal to start building their own grandiose townhouses (Lancaster House and Clarence House) on The Mall.

George IV died in 1830. Clarence acceded to the throne as King William IV. Like his sib-predecessor, the new monarch was interested in architecture. The sovereign continued to reside in Clarence House. This was because the construction of Buckingham Palace was still a work in progress.

Clarence House was the residence of Queen Elizabeth II prior to her accession to the throne in 1952. It then became the home of her mother Elizabeth the Queen Mother, and subsequently that of Charles, Prince of Wales until he moved to St James's Palace.

Location: Stable Yard Road, SW1A 1AA. To the east.

Websites: www.princeofwales.gov.uk www.royal.gov.uk/The RoyalResidences/ClarenceHouse/ClarenceHouse.aspx

Marlborough House

The Churchill family's lease upon Marlborough House expired in 1817. Despite the heavy hints that they had made, the property reverted to the Crown. Since then the building's uses have included housing assorted royals, the likes of the future King Edward VII (*d*.1910) and his Danish wife the very popular Queen Alexandra, and subsequently their son the future King George V and his wife Queen Mary.

Currently, the House is the headquarters of The Commonwealth Secretariat.

Location: Marlborough Road, SW1A 1DD. On the north-western of The Mall and north-eastern of the Marlborough Road.

Somerset House

In the mid-16thC a series of great mansions spread out westwards from the

City of London along the Thames's northern shore. Of these, Somerset House was owned by the 1st Duke of Somerset. He was the uncle and Lord Protector of the young King Edward VI (Henry VIII's only son). In 1552 the building passed into the Crown's possession.

The property was never used as the sovereign's residence. This may have stemmed from its being located too close to the City for any monarch to have felt comfortable there. Instead, it was a place where royal wives and widows lived.[1]

Queen Charlotte was the last royal consort to dwell in the residence. In 1775 her husband King George III gave her Buckingham House. She moved there.

Sir William Chambers was appointed to reconstruct Somerset House so that it could provide lodgings for various departments of state. It was the first purpose-built set of government offices (1786) in Britain. A number of learned societies were also accommodated within the complex.

The two wings are 19thC additions.

Location: Strand, WC2R 0RN & WC2R 1LA. South of the western end of the Aldwych.

See Also: CHURCH OF ENGLAND CHURCHES St Mary-le-Strand
Website: www.somersethouse.org.uk

---

[1]   Nearby Portugal Street was named in honour of Queen Catherine of Braganza (*d*.1705), the wife of King Charles II.

ROYAL RESIDENCES, DISAPPEARED

See Also: PALACES, DISAPPEARED & FORMER; ROYAL RESIDENCES

Carlton House

The original Carlton House (1709) was built for the Whig politician Baron Carleton. His lordship was a scion of the Boyle family.[1] In 1732 Frederick Prince of Wales bought the property. His widow, Princess Augusta, used it as her London residence until her own death in 1772. Subsequently, their son King George III granted it to his eldest son the future King George IV.

The prince was very interested in architectural matters. He commissioned building work both at Carlton House and on his Pavilion in Brighton. In 1792 his activities in London were given greater scope when he bought the neighbouring Warwick House. Construction on the joint site did not stop until after he had acceded to the throne in 1820.

Carlton House was dismantled in 1826. Many of its materials and fittings were cannibalised for contemporary building projects. Its columns now form part of the central portico of the National Gallery (1837).

Location: Carlton House Terrace, SW1Y 5(AH).
See Also: PARKS Regent's Park

---

[1]   Carleton's nephew was the architect-peer the 3rd Earl of Burlington.

ROYAL STATUES

See Also: ARCHES; COLUMNS; MEMORIALS; STATUES; STATUES The National Gallery Statues

Queen Anne

Queen Anne's Gate: The Queen Anne's Gate statue of Queen Anne was sculpted to commemorate the monarch's part in promoting the Fifty New Churches Act of 1711. The measure sought to provide places of worship for people who lived in the metropolis's fast growing suburbs. The Church of St Mary-le-Strand (1717) was the first of the churches that was completed. The statue was to have been erected upon the top of a column that it was intended would stand in front of the building's entrance. However, during the then on-going War of the Spanish Succession (1702-1713) such an expensive project as the column was regarded as being inappropriate. It was postponed. The queen died in 1714.

Anne had antagonised her successor, King George I, by ending Britain's participation in the conflict earlier than he had wished. Therefore, he was disinclined to look favourably upon any scheme that praised her memory. *Ergo*, the support was never raised. Eventually, the statue was installed in Westminster between the rival Queen Anne's Gate and Park Street developments.

Location: Queen Anne's Gate, Westminster, SW1H 9(AB).

See Also: CHURCH OF ENGLAND CHURCHES The Fifty New Churches Act of 1711; COLUMNS; PUBS Gin Palaces, The Bride of Denmark

St Paul's Cathedral: Sir Christopher Wren's rebuilding of St Paul's Cathedral was completed in 1710 during the reign of Queen Anne. To commemorate the achievement a statue of the monarch was erected in front of the cathedral's western front two years later. That the Francis Bird-sculpted figure's back was facing the building was something that lampoonists seized upon quickly.

With time, the statue's stone became weathered. In the late 19thC a decision was taken by the Corporation of the City of London that it should be replaced by a copy. The present one (1886) was carved by Richard Claude Belt, who had a controversial reputation. In 1886 he was

erected on this spot in the ... *commemorate the complet* ... *AINT PAULS CATHEDR* ... *FRANCIS BIRD Sculpt* ...

convicted of conspiracy to obtain money by false representations. He received a year-long prison sentence with hard labour. The Corporation decided against cutting its losses and instead arranged for materials to be sent into Holloway Prison where the sculptor was serving his time. There, he finished the work. The figure was put in place and duly unveiled to the public. Upon his release he complained that his name was not present on the plinth.[1]

The Bird statue was rescued from a stonemason's yard. It now resides on the South Coast.

Location: St Paul's Cathedral, St Paul's Churchyard, EC4M 8AD.

See Also: COLUMNS Seven Dials; THE LORD MAYOR OF LONDON The Silent Ceremony; STATUES Eros, The Belgian Years

King Charles I

Charing Cross: The equestrian figure of King Charles I (1633) is the oldest of the royal statues that stand in the West End. It was sculpted by Hubert Le Sueur. In terms of scale, the effigy makes the monarch out to have been a taller man than he was (4ft 7in (1.4m)). The compliment is delivered discreetly through the placement of the 6ft (1.83m)-tall representation upon a horse.

Following Parliament's victory in the Civil Wars and the execution

---

[1] Philip Ward-Jackson *Public Sculpture of The City of London* Liverpool University Press 379-80

of Charles in 1649, Oliver Cromwell ordered that the figure should be sold for scrap. John Rivett acquired it and was soon carrying on a lively trade in selling artefacts that he declared had been cast from the statue's metal.

The monarchy was restored in 1660. Subsequently, it emerged that the brazier had carried out a deception. He had buried the effigy in his garden. It was exhumed and sold back to the Crown for £1600, which furnished him with a healthy profit.[1] King Charles II (a genuine 6ft in his hose) had it re-erected (1675) on what had been the site of Charing Cross. The spot had been used for the executions of those regicides,[2] who had not been dead or in exile when he had returned to England.

Location: Trafalgar Square, WC2N 5DS. The traffic island that stands between the square and the northern end of Whitehall.

See Also: GALLERIES The Royal Collection, King Charles I's Collection; MEMORIALS Charing Cross; TRAFALGAR SQUARE

King Charles II

Soho Square: Soho Square was originally called King's Square in honour of King Charles II (*d*.1685). In the gardens that occupy its centre there stands a statue of the monarch. In the 1870s changes were made to the space. During these alterations the figure was removed. Subsequently, he was re-erected at Grimsdyke House (1872) near Harrow. The librettist W.S. Gilbert acquired the property and thus the effigy. His widow returned the sovereign to the square, where he was re-re-erected in 1938.

Location: Soho Square, W1D 3(QD).

See Also: STREET FURNITURE Gates, The Green Park Gates

A Royal Audience: There is a story that in years long past some of the square's park keepers used to entertain themselves by using His Majesty as a regal form of ventriloquists' dummy. They did this by secreting one of their walkie-talkies under his nameplate. Passers-by found that the statue would seek to draw them into conversation. As a variant, the parkies would place the device in a rubbish bin. The receptacle would shout at children if they failed to put their litter in it.

It is reputed that the gentlemen ended the practice because one of their number used a hidden walkie-talkie to bark at a police dog. That there was no obvious source for the noise drove the animal to distraction. The Met made known its views on the matter.

---

[1]   It is to be wondered whether any of the purchasers of the objects supposedly cast from the statue asked for a refund.

[2]   The legal officials who had presided over King Charles I's trial.

CHARLES II

Queen Charlotte

Queen Square: Queen Square (1720) in Bloomsbury commemorates Queen Anne in its name. The statue (1775) that stands in its garden is of Queen Charlotte. Her husband King George III suffered from an undiagnosed case of porphyria. It was assumed that he had succumbed to madness. This led to his spending time living privately in the square in the home of Dr Francis Willis. The physician was renowned for his treatment of the insane.

The square's *The Queen's Larder* pub derives its name from Queen

Charlotte. She rented some space in its cellar so as to have a place in which she could store treats for her husband, while he was residing with the doctor.

Location: No. 1 Queen's Square, WC1N 3AR. At the eastern end of Cosmo Place, on the north side of the junction with the square.

Website: www.queenslarder.co.uk

Queen Elizabeth I

St Dunstan-in-the-West: The statue of Queen Elizabeth I (*d*.1603) that supervises Fleet Street from the Church of St Dunstan-in-the-West was carved in the 16thC. It was created to be part of the decorations that ornamented the City of London's Ludgate gateway. The portal was demolished in 1760. The figure was then placed upon the church's street front.

In 1929 the prominent suffragette Lady Millicent Fawcett set up a trust for Her Majesty's maintenance and repair. This arrangement made her the only statue in London to enjoy a private income.[1]

Location: St Dunstan-in-the-West, No. 184 Fleet Street, EC4A 2HR.

Website: www.stdunstaninthewest.org

King George I

Leicester Fields: In a instance of family point scoring, Frederick, Prince of Wales (*d*.1751) had an equestrian statue of his paternal grandfather, King George I, erected in Leicester Fields (now Leicester Square). The nub of this action was that, in Frederick's view, George I had been a monarch who was worth commemorating whereas King George II, the prince's own father, was not.

The statue proved to have a somewhat chequered history. It was taken down for the last time in 1871. Thereafter, it disappeared in mysterious circumstances.

Location: Leicester Square, WC2H 7(LE).

King George IV

Trafalgar Square: Marble Arch (1827) used to stand in front of Buckingham Palace. King George IV commissioned a statue (1834) of himself that he intended to have placed upon top of it. However, the monarch died before the figure had been finished. The portal was too narrow for the royal family's carriages to pass through. Therefore, a decision was made to relocate the entryway. It was concluded that the

---

[1]   Tom Quinn *London's Strangest Tales: Extraordinary But True Stories* Portico (2008) 320-1

likeness should be installed somewhere else. However, there was no obvious site that suggested itself. As a result, the statue was 'temporarily' placed upon a pedestal in the north-eastern corner of Trafalgar Square. It is still there.

Location: Trafalgar Square, WC2N 5DS.

See Also: ARCHES Marble Arch; TRAFALGAR SQUARE

Queen Victoria

Kensington Gardens: After numerous sculptures having been made of members of various monarchical dynasties, the Saxe-Coburgs produced a sculptor - Princess Louise, a daughter of Queen Victoria. The Royal College of Art acquired its 'Royal' in 1896 as a result of its having had her as one of its students. For many years a statue of the monarch, that the princess had modelled, has stood on the eastern side of the Round Pond in Kensington Gardens.

Location: The Round Pond, Kensington Gardens, W8 7DH.

Reading: Lucinda Hawkesley *The Mystery of Princess Louise: Queen Victoria's Rebellious Daughter* Chatto &Windus (2013).

King William III

Kensington Palace: The thirteen-year-old Prince of Wales (the future King Edward VII) visited France for the first time in 1855. He took a liking to the country. Subsequently, he made a number of trips there that consolidated his Francophilia. He was particularly partial to Paris's bordellos. He became a fluent French speaker and played a leading role in the improvement of Anglo-French relations that occurred during the early years of the twentieth century.

The Kensington Palace statue of King William III (1907) was sculpted by Heinrich Baucke. It was given to Edward by his nephew Kaiser Wilhelm II of Germany. The present has a very precise reading. The Dutchman's adult life had been devoted to resisting French imperialism within Western Europe. The German emperor was trying to appeal to his uncle for their two countries to unite against Britain's centuries old rival France, with which the United Kingdom had recently signed the innovative *entente cordiale* (1904). In 1914 it was to prove to be the case that Britain, France, and Russia were to go to war against Germany.

Location: Kensington Gardens, W8 4PX. In front of Kensington Palace's principal southern front.

Reading: Catrine Clay *King, Kaiser, Tsar: Three Royal Cousins Who Led The World To War* John Murray (2007).

GVLIELMVS.III.

St James's Square: In the early 18thC a proposal was made that a statue to the memory of King William III should be erected in St James's Square. However, it proved to be hard to persuade people to pledge money towards the cost of the figure's creation. Eventually, Samuel Travers MP offered to furnish the funds. In his 1724 will he set out instructions that his heirs should do so. Following his death, his relatives contested the dispositional document that he had left. The resulting litigation was not resolved until 1793.

The William III Monument (1807) was sculpted by John Bacon the younger. The equestrian statue has rather a muddied message. At the time of its erection, Britain was involved in a military struggle against the contemporary imperialism of Napoleonic France. The horse that the monarch's figure is riding is about to step upon a molehill that caused the animal to stumble. The fall, which threw the sovereign to the ground, was popularly believed to have caused his death.[1] Therefore, the mortality of the great opponent of Louis XIV's expansionism is indicated.

Location: St James's Square, SW1Y 4(LB).

See Also: CHARLES DICKENS Jarndyce *vs.* Jarndyce; THEATRES The Theatre Royal Haymarket, Break A Leg

---

[1]   William was asthmatic. He died from pneumonia. He contracted it while he was recuperating.

ROYALTY

See Also: ARCHES Marble Arch; CORONATIONS; MILITARY CUSTOMS Royal Salutes; MILITARY CUSTOMS Trooping The Colour; PALACES; PARLIAMENT; PARLIAMENT The Commons, The Monarch and The House of Commons; PUBS The Board of Green Cloth; SHOPPING Royal Warrants; WESTMINSTER ABBEY

The Constitution

See Also: PARKS Green Park, Constitution Hill

Emergency Powers: In an emergency, the sovereign's residual powers enable her/him to overrule Parliament and to govern by means of Orders of Council.

Under the terms of the Emergency Powers Act of 1964, a state of emergency does not have to exist for the monarch to be able to declare that such a condition is extant.

The Sovereign and The Prime Minister: The prime minister has a weekly audience with the monarch. (The regular encounters between Queen Elizabeth II and her First Ministers furnished the subject of Peter Morgan's play *The Audience* (2013). She liked Harold Wilson in particular.)

The sovereign has two prerogative powers that are potentially of great political import. They are those of appointing premiers and of dissolving Parliament.

See Also: DOWNING STREET No. 10 Downing Street
Website: www.theaudienceplay.com

The Marquis Curzon: For most of the 1st Marquis Curzon's adult life, it was widely assumed that his abilities were such that at some point the politician would serve as prime minister. That the peer had a high opinion of himself is testified to by a rhyme that he composed as a young man, and for which he is now best remembered, 'My name is George Nathaniel Curzon. I am a most superior person.'

In 1923 the marquis was regarded as being the frontrunner to become the next premier. However, instead, King George V chose Stanley Baldwin MP, the peer's Conservative colleague. The monarch told Curzon that he felt it was proper that the prime minister should be in the same House as the mass of the opposition. His lordship sat in the Lords where, at the time, the Labour Party had minimal representation. The sovereign may have done the nation a great service. The peer's haughtiness meant that he was temperamentally ill-equipped to deal with the social unrest that Britain was still experiencing in the wake of the First World War.

There is a story that that upon one occasion Curzon was in a room and felt himself to be in need of some fresh air. He was unable to find a servant to open a window. Therefore, he decided to try to execute the task himself. He realised that he did not know how to do so. After having given the matter some consideration, he picked up a small log that was lying by the fireplace, went to the aperture that he wished to open, and used the piece of wood to break one of its panes.

Location: No. 1 Carlton House Terrace, SW1Y 5AF. On the south-eastern side, to the east of Carlton Gardens. A bronze to 'most superior'.

See Also: MILITARY CUSTOMS Remembrance Sunday; PALACES Buckingham Palace

Corgis et al.

The royal family had kept shih tzus. In 1933 King George VI bought a Pembroke corgi. Thereby, he started the breed's regal association. In 1944 his older daughter, Elizabeth (the future Queen Elizabeth II), was given one called Susan. The princess adored the bitch. She even took her on her honeymoon. (It is believed that the Duke of Edinburgh does not share his spouse's besottedness with the breed.)

At its apogee the royal canine pack was made up of seven animals. The corgis were Flora, Kelpie, Pharos, Phoenix, and Swift and the dorgis (corgi/daschund crosses) were Brandy and Harris. Collectively, they and the Queen Mother's beasts had as bad a reputation as any despot could have wished for. In 1989 Chipper, one of the Queen's dorgis, was assassinated by the Queen Mother's corgis. Five years later news leaked of the sovereign's animals had been 'hounding' a police alsatian. The traffic was not all one-way. In 2003 the Princess Royal's bull terrier Dottie mauled Pharos so badly that the corgi had to be put down.

In 2012 the royal pack consisted of the corgis Holly and Willow and the dorgis Candy and Vulcan.

John Prescott

John Prescott is a Labour politician, who in 1997 was appointed to serve as Deputy Prime Minister. His tendency to mangle the English language when he engaged with it publicly masked to popular view his effectiv-nesss as an administrator.[1] He was able to run a Whitehall super-depart-ment in a way that several of his more media-friendly colleagues proved to be unable to do.

Prescott is by no means a royalist although he has been known to express his appreciation of Queen Elizabeth's social skills. Upon one occasion, to please some members of his constituency party, the MP went to a gathering where the monarch was present. He was placed in the receiving line. As she walked along it, the Labour Party members each bowed or curtsied to her in turn; the politician was resolute that he would engage in no such obeisance. When the sovereign reached him, she whispered something. He could not quite catch what she said. She whispered it again. He leant forward to try to hear what she was saying - a movement that he subsequently realised was not so very dissimilar from a bow.

Royal Garden Parties

The guests at royal summer garden parties are, for the most part, ordinary people from throughout Britain, who have made some form of contribu-tion to society.

Guests have been allowed to take their 18 to 25-year-old daughters since the late 1950s. This was a sop after Queen Elizabeth II stopped the presentation of debutantes at court. In 1993 guests were allowed to take a partner of their choice. There was no specification that the partner had to be of the other sex. The following year the privilege was extended to guests' sons in the 18 to 25-age bracket.

In 1996 it was announced that, for the first time since 1972, the London Borough of Hackney would be sending representatives to one of the parties. The invitations had been sent annually by Buckingham Palace but the borough council, because of its dogmatic 'left wing' agenda, had chosen not to send anyone.

Location: Buckingham Palace, SW1A 1AA.

See Also: PALACES Buckingham Palace

Website: www.royal.gov.uk/RoyalEventsandCeremonies/ GardenParties/Gardenparties.aspx

---

[1]   At least one former mandarin differs on this point.

ST PAUL'S CATHEDRAL

The first St Paul's Cathedral was commissioned by Ethelbert King of Kent in 604. It was probably a wooden structure. The building was consumed by a fire during the same century. A second cathedral was raised upon the site. In 962 Vikings destroyed it. A conflagration burned down a third one in 1067. The recently victorious Normans used this misfortune as an opportunity to mark their arrival. The stone edifice that they created was larger than the current building is.

The dome of Sir Christopher Wren's St Paul's is two separate structures that have up to 60 feet (18.3m) of space separating them from one another. The inner hemisphere, visible from within the cathedral, is made of brick. The outer one is a timber frame that has been covered with lead. Linking them there is a cone-like structure that supports the weight of the lantern that tops the upper, outer skin.

The building was finished in 1710. Wren is reputed to have been the first architect in the history of Christianity who had lived to see the cathedral that he had designed be completed.

Location: St Paul's Cathedral, St Paul's Churchyard, EC4M 8AD.

See Also: BELLS Saved By The Bell; CHURCHES OF ENGLAND CHURCHES; CHURCHES OF ENGLAND CHURCHES St Stephen Walbrook; THE GREAT FIRE OF LONDON The Rebuilding of London; ROMAN REMAINS Tower Hill Cathedral; WESTMINSTER ABBEY

Website: www.stpauls.co.uk

The Cathedral and The Second World War

Prior to the Second World War the Cathedral's exterior had become crowded in by buildings that had been constructed around it. During the conflict the bombs that were dropped by the Luftwaffe created a series of vistas. Some of these have been allowed to survive.

In December 1940 Herbert Mason took a photograph of St Paul's from the west. In this, the Cathedral was framed by clouds of smoke. The picture made the building appear to be unscathed by the bombing raid that had just taken place. The iconic image became renowned for its inspirational quality.

See Also: THE GHERKIN; PARLIAMENT The Commons, The Commons Chamber

The Crypt

Wren was one of the first people to be buried in St Paul's crypt. His son Christopher wrote his epitaph, 'Reader, if you seek his monument, look around you.'

In the western portion of the space, below the centre of the dome, is the burial place of the naval commander Lord Nelson (*d.*1805). The sarcophagus had been designed for Cardinal Wolsey (*d.*1530). The sailor's coffin was made from the mainmast of the French ship *L'Orient*. His corpse is preserved in spirits.

Location: The Crypt's entrance is in the southern transept.
See Also: DEPARTMENT STORES Liberty & Company

Monuments

The only monument in St Paul's that survived the Great Fire of London relatively undamaged was the figure of the Rev John Donne (*d.*1631) in the southern aisle. The poet had been a dean of the cathedral.[1] In the southern transept is a statue (1795) of the prison reformer John Howard (*d.*1790). This was the first new memorial to be admitted to

---

[1]   This seems appropriate enough in view of the survival of St Dunstan in the West in Fleet Street, where Donne had been the Rector.

Wren's building. It had been carved by John Bacon, who also created the second one. This celebrated the lexicographer Dr Samuel Johnson (*d*.1784). The third was by John Flaxman and was to the artist Sir Joshua Reynolds (*d*.1792). Around this, Painter's Corner subsequently developed. Benjamin West, Sir Thomas Lawrence, John Constable, J.M.W. Turner, Sir Edwin Landseer, Sir John Millais, Lord Leighton, and William Holman Hunt are honoured there.

See Also: MEMORIALS; WESTMINSTER ABBEY Memorials and Graves

WILLIAM SHAKESPEARE

The Authorship Debate

In the early 19thC the adherents of Romanticism held that works of art should be regarded as being a spiritual autobiography. However, the few surviving documents that related directly to Shakespeare revealed indisputably that he had been a litigious moneylender. Therefore, some devotees of his canon sought to dissociate the man from his works. German scholars had brought new levels of critical analysis to *The Bible* and to Homer's *Iliad*. These techniques were applied to the Bard's output in the service of the disgruntled votaries' agenda.

Delia Bacon, an American lecturer, came to the conclusion that Shakespeare had not written the plays and the poetry that had been attributed to him. She decided that they had been composed by Francis Bacon.[1] She believed that the lawyer-scientist had found Queen Elizabeth I's reign to be despotic and had written the texts in order to try to propagate a republican creed that had led ultimately to *The Declaration of Independence* (1776). In 1857 she set out her beliefs in a book that she entitled *The Philosophy of The Plays of Shakespeare Unfolded*. Two years later she died in a lunatic asylum.

Bacon's Bacon theory was taken up by numerous enthusiasts in the United States. That the judge-researcher had been known to be interested in cyphers led to Shakespeare's works being closely scrutinised for secreted messages. Orville Ward Owen, a Detroit physician, concluded that copies of the plays in Bacon's handwriting had been placed in waterproof, lead containers that had been cast into the River Severn. The waterway was dredged without any such vessels being recovered. A reaction set in. However, rather than Shakespeare's authorship being reasserted, new alternatives to him were sought. Those who came to be considered included: Christopher Marlowe, the 6th Earl of Derby, and the 5th one of Rutland.

J. Thomas Looney was a schoolmaster from the North-East of England. He espoused the candidature of the 17th Earl of Oxford. He published his claim in the book *Shakespeare Identified* (1920). The work held that the plays had advocated a form of feudalism. In the polemicist's

---

[1] The Bacons were not relatives of one another.

opinion the fact that the peer had died in 1604 did not confound the argument nor did the chronological reality that *Macbeth* had been written two years later and *The Tempest* in 1611. Facts that were seen as supporting the thesis included: Oxford had married his wife when she had been the same age as Juliet had been; his mother had remarried after his father's death, as Hamlet's had; and he had three daughters, as King Lear had had. In 1922 the Shakespeare Fellowship was set up to promote the Oxonian cause. The organisation's members were soon claiming for the earl much of the late 16thC dramatic canon, as well as advocating a range of fanciful theories that connected him to prominent figures of the age.

Looney's supporters came to include Sigmund Freud. The Austrian Anglophile had believed that Shakespeare had written *Hamlet* after his father had died. The drama had been central to his own creation of his Oedipal theory. However, subsequently it had been established that the Bard's pop had been alive when the work had been written. Therefore, Freud had felt compelled to believe that it had been authored by someone other than the actor-manager. Prior to the play's composition, the peer's father had died and his mother had remarried. Therefore, the psycho-analyst became an Oxonian.

The Bacon controversy intrigued the American textiles million-aire George Fabyan (*d*.1935). He owned the Riverbank Laboratories, a private research establishment that included a codes and cyphers depart-ment. The people whom he employed at the facility included the geneti-cist William F. Friedman. Initially, the scientist was prepared to use his analytical skills to support his employer's opinion about the playwright. However, over time Friedman, together with his wife Elizebeth, became an opponent of the theory. The couple's forensic analysis of the idea destroyed the plausibility of its standing.[1]

Websites: http://malonesociety.com (Edmond Malone was a bar-rister who gave up the law in order to become a man of letters. His *An Inquiry Into The Authenticity of Certain... Miscellaneous Papers... Attrib-uted To Shakespeare* (1798) demonstrated that William Henry Ireland had faked a number of supposed Shakespearean documents.) www.shakespearefellowship.org

Individuality

The 18thC poet and satirist Alexander Pope devoted much of his time to translation and literary criticism. He was moved to state that in the

[1] In 1940 Mr Friedman played the leading role in breaking the Japanese state's Code Purple cypher.

works of Shakespeare even those characters that have only a few lines of dialogue sound like no other figure in any of the Bard's other plays.

The Italian Aspect

Little is known about Shakespeare's life. There is not a shred of evidence for what he was doing during the years 1585-1592. Some Italians have claimed that during them he must have been living in Italy. Indeed, there is a school of Sicilians who claim that he was a native of their island.

There is a large Italian aspect to Shakespeare's works. He had a knowledge of Italian literature; some of his sonnets may have drawn on Petrarch's compositions. Thirteen of the plays were set either wholly or partially in Italy. His Venetian and Veronan ones all had contemporary or near-contemporary settings. Thereby, he was able to make indirect comments about the London of his day. The Roman plays, *Anthony & Cleopatra* and *Julius Caesar*, were set in the Classical era.

DVD: Francesco da Mosto *Shakespeare In Italy* BBC (2012).

Reading: Martino Iuvaea *Shakespeare era italaniano* Editorial Agora (2002). The book argues that Shakespeare was really Michelangelo Florio Crololanza, a native of Messina. His family were Calvinists. In order not to be persecuted for their beliefs, they emigrated from Sicily to London.

The Rose Exhibition

Archæological Remains of
Bankside's First Theatre
The Rose Theatre

Philip Henslowe was a Bankside businessman who was active in a variety of trades. His interests included involvement in the local entertainment industry. He owned an animal baiting pit in what is now Paris Gardens.

In 1587 the entrepreneur commissioned the construction of the Rose Theatre upon one of his properties. The fourteen-sided polygon was the first purpose-built theatre in the district. The venue was run principally by his son-in-law the actor-manager Edward Alleyn, who was an associate of Christopher Marlowe.

The theatre appears to have fallen out of use during the first decade of the 17thC. Its remains were identified in 1989.

Location: No. 56 Park Street, Bankside, SE1 9AS.

See Also: GALLERIES The Dulwich Picture Gallery

Website: www.rosetheatre.org.uk

Shakespeare's Globe

The American movie director and actor Sam Wanamaker was the moving force behind the re-creation of The Globe theatre. In 1979 he asked the theatre historian John Orrell to produce a report on what evidence existed that could be used to aid the task. From it a book emerged. For this, Mr Orrell laid Wenceslas Hollar's *Long View* (1644) panorama of London - which included the second Globe (1614) - onto a modern Ordnance Survey map. This proved the accuracy of the drawing. Theo Crosby, a member of the Archigram group of architectural thinkers, became the project's architect. It was he and his wife 'Polly' Hope who created the approach by which the venture became its own contractor. This meant that construction was able to start and to stop according to whether or not there were funds available.

In 1987 construction commenced. Among the things that was learnt during the building process was that modern cattle are not as hairy as their 16th C predecessors had been - their filaments proved to be inadequate for the traditional use of cow and goat hair in plaster. In 1989 the foundations of part of the original Globe were uncovered. These indicated that the building had had twenty sides rather than 24 as had been believed up until then.

The Shakespeare Globe theatre opened to the public in 1997.

The venue's adjacent 340-seat Sam Wanamaker Playhouse (2014) was designed by Jon Greenfield, a long-time Crosby associate. The oak structure's lighting is furnished by beeswax candles. The space is used to help to advance understanding of the Bard's later plays. These were written to be performed in indoor theatres.

Location: No. 21 New Globe Walk, Bankside, SE1 9DT.

Reading: John Orrell (1934-2003) *The Quest for Shakespeare's Globe* Cambridge University Press (1983).

See Also: THEATRES

Website: www.shakespearesglobe.com

Shakespeare's Motor

The half-timbered Morris Minor Traveller estate is commonly known as the Shakespearean car.

Reading: Martin Wainwright *Morris Minor, The Biography: Sixty Years of Britain's Favourite Car* Aurum (2010).

Website: www.mmoc.org.uk (The Morris Minor Owners Club).

SHOPPING

See Also: ARCADES; DEPARTMENT STORES; STREET MARKETS

Angels Fancy Dress

Angels's core business is hiring costumes for theatrical and cinematic use.

In the 1830s Morris Angel started selling upper-class cast-offs from a stall on the eastern fringe of the West End.[1] At the time, it was the accepted practice that actors should provide their own costumes, therefore, they frequented the stand. Mr Angel's business developed to the point where he was able to open a shop. One day the enterprise was set upon a new course when an actor asked if he could rent some clothes rather than buy them.

In 2003 Angels relocated its principal warehouse from Camden to a four-storey building in Hendon. Five years later the business acquired the BBC's costume department. The deal extended the length of the firm's racks from five miles to eight. At the time, the Shaftesbury Avenue outlet extended over six floors. The Angel family still run the business.

Locations: No. 119 Shaftesbury Avenue, WC2H 8AD. On the northern side, to north of Cambridge Circus.

No. 1 Garrick Road, Hendon, NW9 6(AP).

Websites: www.angels.uk.com www.fancydress.com

Charity Shops

Reading: Lettice Wilkinson *Charity Shopping and The Thrift Lifestyle* Marion Boyars Publishers (2009).

The British Red Cross: In 1941 the British Red Cross opened London's first charity shop at No. 17 Old Bond Street.

Locations: No. 17 Old Bond Street, W1S 4PT.

No. 67 Old Church Street, SW3 5BS. A renowned charity shop.

Website: www.redcross.org.uk

---

[1]   'Angels' is also the term for private individuals who finance West End shows during their pre-production stage.

Oxfam:

> *Location*: No. 202B Kensington High Street, W8 7RG.

> *Reading*: Seb Hunter *How To Be A Better Person* Atlantic Books (2009). Mr Hunter's experiences included working in the Oxfam shop on Kensington High Street.

> *Website*: www.oxfam.org.uk/shop/local-shops/ oxfam-shop -kensington

Ede & Ravenscroft

The firm of Ede & Ravenscroft made the robes that were used in 1689 for the coronation of King William III and Queen Mary II.

The business has been selling wigs and gowns to judges and barristers since the 1850s. The supposed purpose of these items is to help maintain respect for authority and status. The Commercial Bar Association has called for their abandonment in Commercial Law cases. In 1993 Lord Chancellor Mackay and Lord Chief Justice Taylor stated that the wigs and gowns would remain in use. The following year the latter declared that wearing wigs in court was the exclusive preserve of barristers. Some solicitors - who had been appearing as advocates - had been seeking to share the right.

> *Location*: No. 93 Chancery Lane, WC2A 1(EU).

See Also: CORONATIONS
Website: www.edeandravenscroft.co.uk

Floris

The Floris perfumery is descended from a barbershop that was opened in 1730 by Juan Famenia Floris, a Majorcan. (At the time, Majorca was a British possession. The island was transferred from Britain to Spain by the Treaty of Versailles (1783), which ended the American War of Independence.)

In 1820 Floris received its first royal warrant.

Location: No. 89 Jermyn Street, SW1Y 6JH. On the southern side.

Website: www.florislondon.com

Hamleys

Hamleys is a department store-sized toyshop on Regent Street. William Hamley, a Cornishman, opened his first shop in High Holborn in 1760.

Location: Nos. 188-196 Regent Street, W1B 5BT. On the eastern side, to the south of the junction with Foubert's Place.

See Also: MUSEUMS The Museum of Childhood

Website: www.hamleys.com

The King's Road Shops

In the western section of the King's Road the shops and restaurants tend to be independent businesses or branches of small chains. In the eastern portion, national retailers are more evident.

Location: The King's Road, Chelsea, SW3 4(NX), SW3 5(EL), & SW10 0(TU).

Reading: Max Décharmé *King's Road: The Rise and Fall of The Hippest Street In The World* Weidenfeld & Nicholson (2005). A book that describes popular cultural activities on and off the road's Chelsea section during the 1960s and 1970s.

Richard Lester *Boutique London: A History: King's Road To Carnaby Street, 1960-2010* ACC Editions (2010).

Green & Stone: Green & Stone supplies artists' materials. The business was founded in 1927. It is an instance of how some people believe that shops should be.[1]

---

[1]   For those who like artists' materials to be sold on a supermarket scale there is Atlantis, Nos. 68-80 Hanbury Road, E1 5JL. On the southern side. (www.atlantisart.co.uk)

Location: No. 259 The King's Road, Chelsea, SW3 5EL. On the southern side, opposite Carlyle Square.

Website: www.greenandstone.com

Lillywhites

Lillywhites is a large sporting goods store. In the early and mid-19thC the Lillywhites were a renowned family of cricketers. In 1863 James Lillywhite opened a shop in Haymarket.

Location: Nos. 24-36 Lower Regent Street, Piccadilly Circus, SW1Y 4QF.

Milroy's of Soho

Milroy's of Soho is a whisky shop. The Milroy family withdrew from the business in the 1990s.

Location: No. 3 Greek Street W1D 4NX. At the northern end, on the eastern side.

Reading: Wallace Milroy *Malt Whisky Almanac: A Taster's Guide* Neil Wilson Publishing (1998). 7th edition.

Website: www.milroys.co.uk

New Bond Street

New Bond Street and Regent Street have rivalled one another over the years as to which of them is more upmarket than the other.

There are numerous jewellers along the southern section of New Bond Street.

Location: New Bond Street, W1Y 9(LA).

Website: www.bondstreet.co.uk

Paxton & Whitfield

The Paxton & Whitfield cheese shop can trace its antecedents back to a business that was established in the early 1700s in Clare Market, near the Aldwych. The firm's founder was one Sam Cullum, the son of a Suffolk swordmaker ('Cullum' disappeared from the enterprise's name in 1797). The shop has been in its present site since the late 1860s.

Location: No. 93 Jermyn Street, SW1Y 6JE. On the southern side.

Website: www.paxtonandwhitfield.co.uk

Pedestrianised Shopping Streets

See Also: CARNABY STREET; PERIOD PROPERTIES Woburn Walk

Gabriel's Wharf: Gabriel's Wharf is a small, temporary-looking cluster of shops and restaurants that is located on the South Bank to the west of the Oxo Tower.

Location: No. 56 Upper Ground, South Bank, SE1 9PH.

Websites: www.coinstreet.org/gabriels

Mayfair: There are a number pedestrianised streets and alleys to the west of the northern portion of New Bond Street. These include South Molton Street, Avery Row, and Lancashire Court.

Locations: Avery Row, W1K 4(AL); Lancashire Court, W1Y 9AD; and South Molton Street, W1Y 1(DE).

Website: www.mayfair-london.co.uk

St Christopher's Place: St Christopher's Place is a pedestrianised shopping street that runs northwards off Oxford Street. Its 19thC appearance has acquired an overlay of contemporary outdoor cafes and restaurants.

To the west of St Christopher's Place, James Street runs in parallel. The western pavement of the latter is also an example of how London has embraced *al fresco* eating.

Location: St Christopher's Place, W1U 1BF.

Website: www.stchristophersplace.com

Pollock's Toy Museum

There once existed a specialist trade of printing toy theatres. The final practitioner of this craft was Benjamin Pollock. His shop in Shoreditch was destroyed by an aerial bomb during the Second World War. Marguerite Fawdry purchased for her son's toy theatre an item that Pollock had printed. This led her to buying all of his stock and in 1956 setting up Pollock's Toy Museum.

In 1969 the Museum relocated to its present site, a building that was constructed in 1760.

Location: No. 1 Scala Street, W1T 2HL.

See Also: MUSEUM The Museum of Childhood

Website: www.pollockstoymuseum.com

Royal Warrants

Above the entrances of some shops can be seen royal warrants. A number of businesses hold more than one. They indicate that the retailer or service provider receives the commercial patronage of a senior member of the royal family. Those royals are: the sovereign, the sovereign's heir-apparent, and the consorts of past and present sovereigns. Warrants are

BY APPOINTMENT
TO HER MAJESTY THE QUEEN
LIVERY & MILITARY TAILORS
GIEVES & HAWKES, LONDON

BY APPOINTMENT
TO HIS ROYAL HIGHNESS
THE DUKE OF EDINBURGH
NAVAL TAILORS & OUTFITTERS
GIEVES & HAWKES, LONDON

BY APPOINTMENT
TO HIS ROYAL HIGHNESS
THE PRINCE OF WALES
TAILORS & OUTFITTERS
GIEVES & HAWKES, LONDON

GIEVES & HAWKES

No1 SAVILE ROW LONDON

issued for a number of years - ten years in the first instance. They end automatically with the death of the issuer. Periodically, they are reviewed and if the firm is no longer being used then the warrant will often be removed.

The warrant is attached to a specific individual within the business and if that person leaves - be it through death, retirement, or change of employer - then the warrant is reconsidered.

See Also: ROYALTY

Website: www.royalwarrant.org www.royal.gov.uk/ MonarchUK/ Symbols/Royalwarrants.apsx

Wedgwood

Josiah Wedgwood was born into a family of Staffordshire potters. As a child, he suffered an attack of smallpox. It left him with a weakened right knee. This meant that he was unable to work a potter's wheel. Therefore, he focused upon learning other aspects of the trade. He proved to be a talented designer. In 1765 Queen Charlotte commissioned him to make a gold and green creamware tea service for her. The following year he was appointed to be her official potter. This conferral gave his reputation a major boost. The Wedgwood creamware line was redubbed Queen's Ware.

Wedgwood spent most of his time at Etruria, a factory that he developed upon a small estate that he acquired in his native county. The development of the canal system in England meant that pottery could be transported long distances with only minimal rates of breakage. His business partner Thomas Bentley ran the business's London showroom and its Chelsea-based painting operation. The pair proved to be highly innovative retailers. They employed illustrated catalogues, direct mail, travelling salesmen, self-service, and money-back guarantees.

During the late 1760s the Soho showroom was very busy. The customers were drawn from society's wealthier *strata*. In 1772 Britain experienced an economic recession. The demand for consumer goods slackened. It soon became apparent that the business had a surplus of stock and that it was beginning to have a cash flow problem. The partners appreciated that there were several ways in which they could react to the situation. They were aware that if they took the wrong action they would probably ruin their firm.

Wedgwood sought to understand the business by scrutinising its accounts in fine detail. He compiled a set of data that costed every aspect of every product line's history from raw materials to the sales room. For the first time the potter appreciated that some items were far more profitable than others were. He realised that there was a distinction between fixed costs and variable ones; this insight was the birth of cost accounting. Thereby, he became the first person to analytically appreciate the commercial benefits of mass production. He and Bentley chose to respond to the market conditions by increasing production. That this involved fixed costs for the most part meant that unit costs were lowered. With this reduction in place, they availed themselves of the expanded profit margin to reduce their retail prices. Thereby, for the first time, many middle-class people were able to afford the partnership's products. As a result, its sales rose and soon matched the increased output. Overall profitability reached a new high.

Wedgwood made a series of technical breakthroughs. It took him over 5000 experiments to create a new, semi-vitreous form of stoneware that had a smooth, matte finish. He called it jasper. Cawk ($BaSO_4$) was its key secret ingredient. The powdered mineral gave the material a whiteness that enabled it to be dyed any colour. He introduced jasperware in 1774. His other innovations included inventing the pyrometer. The device enabled potters for the first time to know what the temperature was within fired kilns. It led to his being elected to be a Fellow of the Royal Society in 1783.

The 3rd Duke of Portland lent the Portland Vase to Wedgwood in 1787. The vessel was transported to the Etruria works. There, for a year, the potter and his principal technical associates studied it intensely. They engaged in a range of experiments with jasper in order to try to produce facsimiles of the item. A new dark blue variety of the substance was created, as well as an innovative technique by which chemically different varieties of the material were combined to make a single object.

By 1790 Wedgwood was satisfied with the quality of the Vase copies that his factory could produce. Less than a dozen of the highly-priced replicas were sold during his lifetime. As an immediate economic exercise, the project was a drain upon the partnership's resources. However, no other pottery had the expertise to be able to produce such an item, therefore, its pre-eminence within the industry was underscored. From this, commercial benefits flowed.

Locations: Wedgwood Mews, Soho. W1D 4BB. On the eastern side of Greek Street.

No. 8 St James's Square, SW1Y 4JU. Following the death of Bentley, Wedgwood's nephew Thomas Byerley started filling the fellow's role in London. In 1795 Josiah Wedgwood the younger bought No. 8 St James's Square. The cousins used the building as a showroom for their business's goods. Eventually, a downturn in trade prompted them to close the facility. The property was sold in 1830.

See Also: THE BRITISH MUSEUM The Portland Vase

Websites: www.wedgwood.co.uk www.wedgwoodmuseum.org.uk

Westfield

The Westfield London shopping centre opened in Shepherd's Bush in 2008. With just under 1.6m sq ft of floor space, it was then the UK's fourth-largest retail development. Westfield Stratford opened three years later. It had a vending footprint of over 1.6m sq ft. This made it the UK's fourth-largest shopping centre, demoting Westfield London to fifth position.

Locations: Westfield London, Nos. 1-3 Ariel Way, Shepherd's Bush, W12 7SL. To the north of the Shepherd's Bush Green.

Westfield Stratford, No. 2 Stratford Place, Montfitchet Road, Olympic Park, E20 1EJ.

Website: http://uk.westfield.com/london http://uk.westfield.com/stratfordcity

Whiteley's

William Whiteley served his apprenticeship as a draper in his native Wakefield. He visited the Great Exhibition of 1851 and was deeply impressed by the way in which an unprecedented array of goods were displayed in a single building. Four years later he moved to London and started to familiarise himself with the metropolis's wholesale and retail trades.

In 1863 Whiteley opened his first shop in Bayswater. He chose the district because it was a fashionable area and because it was then a terminus of the Metropolitan Line. The business proved to be a great success. It even attracted the custom of Queen Victoria.

The nascent department stores that outgrew their origins as drapery stores were deeply unpopular with those tradesmen in the neighbourhoods where they were located. This was because the small businessmen felt that their own livelihoods were being threatened. In 1876 an effigy of Whiteley was burned on Guy Fawkes night.

In the 1880s the retailer's private life made him a controversial figure. The way in which he conducted it prompted his wife to leave him.

From 1891 on, the business developed farms and food-processing factories at Hanworth to supply its store with produce.

Whiteley was murdered in 1907 by Horace Rayner, who was the son of one of his former mistresses. Mr Rayner believed himself to be the child of the retailer (and may well have been). The man was tried at the Old Bailey, where he was found guilty of the killing. However, there was a general call for clemency that saved him from being hanged. He was released from prison after having served twelve years' of his sentence.

Knightsbridge and Kensington became more fashionable districts than Bayswater. The business slipped into decline. In 1981 the store closed. Eight years later the building was reopened as a shopping mall.

Location: Queensway, W2 4YN. On the western side of the northern end.

See Also: DEPARTMENT STORES Selfridges
Website: www.whiteleys.com

SQUIRRELS

The red squirrel (*Sciurus vulgaris*) is native to the United Kingdom. The Eastern grey one (*Sciurus carolinensis*) is a recent arrival from North America.[1] Other than in a few portions of isolated woodland, it is now very rare for people in most of Britain to see a red squirrel.

Reds are more agile than greys are. This enables the former to thrive in pure coniferous forests since they can reach cones that the latter cannot. Reds do not fare as well as greys do in deciduous woodland, especially so when they are competing directly with one another; broadleaved woods are capable of supporting six times as many greys as reds. This is because the latter are fussier eaters than the former are. There are some berries and seeds - ash, hawthorn, rowan, and yew - that reds can eat but which greys cannot. Greys are able to eat acorns safely whereas reds, if they eat too many, are poisoned fatally by the tannin that the nuts contain.

It was reported in 2006 that grey squirrels might be a major factor in the inability of songbird populations to recover to their former levels in woodlands.

In 2008 there were estimated to be 120,000 red squirrels remaining in Britain.

Location: Kensington Gardens, W8 4PX.

See Also: PARKS; TRAFALGAR SQUARE Pigeons

Websites: www.red-squirrels.org.uk www.forestry.gov.uk/ forestry/ redsquirrel www.squirrels.info/uk/in_uk.htm www.theredsquirreltrust.co.uk http://rsst.org.uk (The Red Squirrel Survival Trust)

The Arrival of Grey Squirrels

During the late 19thC and early 20thC there were a number of separate releases of grey squirrels. The first recorded one occurred in 1876 in the grounds of Henbury Park, an estate in Cheshire that was owned by the banker Thomas Brocklehurst. The animals were regarded as being ornamental. It was thought that they would live in small, isolated

---

[1]   It should be born in mind that foxes and numerous species of bird have been transported from Britain to parts of the Anglophone world, where they have established breeding communities.

communities close to where they had been let loose. Ultimately, the case proved to be otherwise.

The greys carried with them the squirrel pox virus. The condition had minimal impact upon their health but was fatal to reds. Following the First World War, latter's population size crashed. People began to regard greys as being pests. In 1939 it became illegal to import them.

During the late 1940s and the early 1950s grey squirrel shooting clubs were issued with free cartridges. In 1953 a small bounty was introduced for each carcass that was presented. Over a million were submitted during the following half-decade.

Black Squirrels

Grey squirrels' coats are composed of a mixture of black, white, and yellow hairs. In 1912 black squirrels were observed for the first time. They were genetically variant grey squirrels. They do not have a section of DNA that the greys possess. Therefore, their fur is only black in colour. Their popular reputation for aggressiveness has not been substantiated in the scientific literature.

It was reported in 2008 that in some parts of East Anglia black squirrels were becoming the majority of the sciurines present. It was regarded as being a possibility that this development might presage an explosion of their population size.

Squirrel Meat

The taste of squirrel is akin to that of over-hung pheasant. The natives of Wisconsin regard the back legs as being the best bit of the critter.[1]

---

[1]   No squirrels were knowingly consumed during the creation of this book. The information is derived from Jonathan Raban's *Old Glory* (1986).

STATUES

See Also: COLUMNS; ROYAL STATUES; TRAFALGAR SQUARE
The Fourth Plinth

'Eros'

In 1893 the Sir Alfred Gilbert-sculpted *Angel of Charity* was erected as a memorial to the social reformer the 7th Earl of Shaftesbury. It is reputed that the statue faces the wrong way; there is said to have been a word/visual pun between the shaft of its arrow and the direction in which that arrow was meant to be pointing. *The Angel* swiftly acquired the pre-Christian nickname of *Eros*. In part, this derived from the fact that courting couples would arrange to meet by it.

Location: Piccadilly Circus, W1J 7BX.

The Belgian Years: Gilbert was a pupil of Sir Joseph Boehm.[1] He studied in Paris and Italy. While he was living in Perugia, he was visited by the painter Frederick Leighton, who commissioned him to create a sculpture. The resulting *Icarus* (1884) was held in high regard. When Gilbert returned to London, he was inundated with commissions. However, he proved to be a poor manager of his own financial affairs. He also had a tendency towards perfectionism that led him to destroy much of his own work.

In 1886 the government commissioned Gilbert to create *Eros*. In 1892 he was appointed to construct the tomb of the Duke of Clarence, the eldest son of the Prince of Wales. Gilbert found himself to be unable to finish the piece. His finances collapsed and debt collectors were called in. In 1901 he fled to Bruges.[2] He remained in 'exile' there until 1926 when he was cajoled back to finish the tomb. His final work was the memorial for Clarence's mother, Queen Alexandra, that was erected in Marlborough Gate opposite St James's Palace.

Location: Marlborough Road, SW1A 1(DD). Queen Alexandria's memorial.

See Also: MEMORIAL; ROYAL STATUES Queen Anne, St Paul's Cathedral

---

[1]   Boehm's other pupils included Princes Louise.

[2]   Sir Alfred Gilbert's grandson was the *avant-garde* artist Stephen Gilbert. There latter developed a European reputation while being little known in the UK.

Lord Napier

Field Marshal Lord Robert Napier spent most of his martial career in India, working as a military engineer; he laid out the hill station of Darjeeling. In 1842 he was the general who commanded the Indian Army force that defeated the Baluch army at the Battle of Meeanee. This was followed by British India's annexation of Sind (now in western Pakistan). After the encounter, Napier is reputed to have sent a telegram that consisted of just one word - '*Peccavi*' (the Latin for 'I have sinned').

The story was in fact the invention of a seventeen-year-old schoolgirl.

Location: Queen's Gate, SW7 5(EH).[1] At the northern end.

The National Gallery Statues

The statue that stands in front of the eastern wing of the National Gallery is of George Washington. He was a not altogether successful frontier commander[2] who engaged in some personal job creation by depriving Britain of some of her remoter colonies.

The figure in front of the institution's western portion is of King James II. His presence owes more to the artistry that the sculptor Grinling Gibbons exercised in executing his image rather than to any popular partiality for the monarch. The sovereign fled from his own realms during the Revolution of 1688.

How many other nations are there that have one of their foremost cultural establishments fronted not only by a rebel but also by a fugitive?

Location: Trafalgar Square, WC2N 5DS. The northern side.

See Also: GALLERIES The National Gallery; PARKS Green Park, Constitution Hill; WEATHER Wind, The Protestant Wind

Nudity

The Park Lane Achilles: The Richard Westmacott sculpted statue of Achilles (1822) was erected in the south-eastern corner of Hyde Park to honour the Duke of Wellington, the victor of the Battle of Waterloo. His grace lived in Apsley House to the south of the site. The figure was made from captured French guns that had been melted down. It was one of the first nude public statues to be erected in England. Upon its unveiling, the work rather dismayed the group that had commissioned it.

Location: Hyde Park, W2 2UH. The south-western corner.

---

[1]   In taxi slang Queen's Gate is known as 'Under The 'Orse's Tail.'

[2]   Washington's misadventures in the Ohio Valley had been one of the reasons why Britain had been drawn into the Seven Years' War of 1756-1763.

Zimbabwe House: Zimbabwe House (1907) was redesigned by Charles Holden for the British Medical Association. On its second storey *façade* there are *The Ages of Man*, a series of sculptures that were created by Jacob Epstein. It was the American's first high profile commission in Britain. There was an initial outcry about the nudity of the figures, however, the voiced concerns were soon placated.

The South Rhodesian High Commission acquired the building in 1937. The chaps then underwent some radical amendments. It was claimed that they had suffered frost damage which meant that there was a risk of passers-by being struck by a falling appendage, and that the changes had been made in order to try to avert such an eventuality.[1]

Location: No. 429 Strand, WC2R 0JR.

See Also: WEATHER

Two Too Many Beers

George Duke of Cambridge was a cousin of Queen Victoria. In 1856 he was appointed to be the Commander-in-Chief of the British Army. During his early years in the position he proved to be a reformer. However, with the passage of time, he developed a reputation for being opposed to change. As the consequence of piecemeal adjustments, administrative responsibilities became concentrated in his grace's hands. In 1890 a royal commission recommended that the position should be abolished and the duties reassigned to other officials. The duke felt himself to be physically well and held it to be his duty to continue to serve in place.

Rachel Beer and her husband Frederick owned both *The Observer* and *The Sunday Times* newspapers. Mrs Beer concluded that the duke's intellectual limitations meant that he was unable to execute his responsibilities properly. She waged a media campaign that sought to remove him from it. In 1895 Queen Victoria advised her cousin that he should resign. He did so. A bluff, kindly soul, he had been someone who had been genuinely popular within the Army.

The Beers were to have their own problems. Mr Beer underwent a mental deterioration that was probably a result of his having contracted syphilis. This caused him to engage in a number of eccentricities. He died in 1903. His widow then underwent her own collapse. As a result, her papers published a number of strange articles. These included one that argued that there were positive aspects to cannibalism. The following year she was diagnosed as being insane. Her trustees sold the

---

[1]   Epstein's portrayal of genitalia on London Transport's Broadway House also generated controversy, as did Eric Gill's work on Broadcasting House. (Rob Humphreys *The Rough Guide To London* Rough Guides (2008) 81 and 107)

newspapers. Subsequently, she regained her mental health. However, she chose not to return to public life.

Locations: No. 7 Chesterfield Gardens, Mayfair, W1J 5BQ. The Beers' marital home.

Whitehall, SW1A 2(EU). Between The Old War Office and Horse Guards. A statue of the duke.

Reading: Eilat Negev & Yehuda Koren *The First Lady of Fleet Street: The Life, Fortune and Tragedy of Rachel Beer* JR Books (2013).

See Also: MILITARY CUSTOMS A Week's Winter Fodder

STREET FURNITURE

See Also: BUSES Bus Shelters; THE CITY OF LONDON The Sentinel Dragons

A Gaseous Lily

The methane in the sewer system used to build up to dangerously high levels. Some tunnels became potentially fatal for people to work in. Therefore, it became a practice to lead off some of the gas. However, to have released large amounts of it into central London would have been unacceptable. Therefore, the Gas Light & Coke Company installed specially engineered lampposts. The hydrocarbon was fed up into these. They provided some streets with lighting 24 hours a day.

In Carting Lane there is a Webb Patent Sewer Gas Lamp. The structure is an Iron Lily that was made in the 1880s. It has Grade II heritage status.

Location: Carting Lane, WC2R 0(DW).

Gates

See Also: DOWNING STREET The Downing Street Gates

The Green Park Gates: The wrought iron Green Park Gates (*c.*1735) were made for what was to become the 1st Lord Heathfield's house at Turnham Green.[1] In 1837 they were re-erected a short distance away at Chiswick House, the Dukes of Devonshire's Middlesex country residence. In 1898 the gates were moved to stand in front of their graces' London townhouse - Devonshire House in Piccadilly. In 1921 they were re-re-erected where they now stand.

Looking southwards through the Gates it is possible to view a vista at the far southern end of which is the Queen Victoria Memorial (1911). The structure stands before Buckingham Palace.

Location: Opposite No. 92 Piccadilly, W1J 6(BD). At the northern end of Green Park's Broad Walk.

See Also: PARKS Green Park; ROYAL STATUES King Charles II Soho Square

---

[1]　Lord Heathfield was a general who was very fond of cats.

House Numbers

As part of a campaign to encourage householders to adopt house numbers, the Duke of Wellington (*d*.1852) agreed that Apsley House, his townhouse, could be given the address of No. 1 London, Hyde Park Corner. The thinking behind this allocation seems to have been that the property was the first building to the east of the Hyde Park Corner turnpike toll gate. (A sign to the left of the building's main door gives the address as being not No. 1 London but rather No. 149 Piccadilly.)

Location: No. 149 Piccadilly, W1J 7NT.

The London Stone

It is possible that the London Stone was a Roman milestone. For centuries, it stood in the middle of Cannon Street. A number legends and stories came to be associated with the object. The first written reference to it dates from the early 10thC. In the 12thC it was a notable enough feature to be referred to on maps. It became a place where people would make formal declarations. These they would solemnise by striking the Stone with something that they held in their hands.

In 1798 there was a proposal that the Stone should be removed because some people regarded it as being a hindrance to traffic. However, Thomas Maiden, a printer, led a successful campaign for it to be retained in the vicinity. As a result, it was set into the wall of St Swithin's Church.

The church was damaged by an aerial bomb in 1941. However, the Stone was relatively undamaged.

Location: No. 111 Cannon Street, EC4N 5AR. On the northern side, opposite Cannon Street Station.

Website: www.spectaclemakers.com/company/history.htm

Paving

Following the Great Fire of 1666 the streets of the City of London started to be paved with stone.

See Also: THE GREAT FIRE OF LONDON The Rebuilding of London

The Chewing Gum That Isn't: *Lecanora muralis* is a light grey-coloured lichen that looks like chewing gum that has been discarded onto a pavement and then trodden upon. At its edges the symbiont is much more frayed than the flattened confection is.

Website: www.thebls.org.uk

(The British Lichen Society)

The Paviors' Company: In 1479 the City Corporation endorsed the Paviors' Company's ordinances. This action bestowed upon the guild the right to control road maintenance in the City of London. In 1515 the Lord Mayor gave the Company the 56th place in the livery companies' order of precedence.

In 1672 the Paviors sought to be granted a royal charter. The City's Court of Aldermen vetoed the idea. During the 19thC there was a surge in construction. The Company had little to do with this. A royal charter was granted to the body finally in 2004.

Website: http://paviors.org.uk

The Westminster Paving Commission: Outside of the City of London, paving used to be the responsibility of individual householders. It was one that most people shirked.

The philanthropist Jonas Hanway was interested in a wide array of issues. In his pamphlet *A Letter To Mr John Spranger* (1754) he called for the streets of Westminster and Middlesex to be paved, cleaned and lit.

The Westminster Paving Commission was established under the provisions of the London Streets Act of 1762. The measure vested a range of statutory powers in the body. The first streets that it directed to be clad were Parliament Street, Charing Cross, Pall Mall, and Cockspur Street. Squared blocks of Aberdeen granite were used. From this start, the process spread out across the neighbouring districts.

The Westminster Streets Act of 1771 provided scope for some of the Commission's powers to be transferred to parish vestries. They were slow to assume these. The body was wound up in 1835.

Pillar Boxes

Sir Ron Dearing was an able, self-effacing person who had a successful career as a Whitehall mandarin. During the early and mid-1980s he served as the Chairman of the Post Office. It is reputed that, during the years that he led the body, he used to keep a tin of red paint in the boot of his car. While driving, whenever he saw a pillar box that had been defaced, he would stop the vehicle and personally repair the damage to his charge.

Locations: Nos. 276-280 Kensington High Street, W8 6ND. On the eastern corner of the junction with Melbury Road. One of the hexagonal, Victorian pillar boxes that survive in West London.

No. 12a Kensington Palace Gardens, W8 4QU. On the eastern side, towards the northern end Another.

No. 31 St Leonard's Terrace, SW3 4QG. At the western end. And another.

Railings

In 1941 most of London's squares were stripped of their railings to provide metal for the war effort. However, the action seems to have been done principally in order to try to boost people's morale. It is reputed that vast piles of the bars were left unused. Some of them have never been replaced.

Dr Roget's Perception: While looking out from his basement kitchen up through some vertical railings, the physician - and subsequently the creator of the *Thesaurus* - Peter Roget noticed that the illusion of the constant movement of a carriage wheel was not interfered with by the vertical bars. This prompted him to conclude that the retina briefly retains a memory of what it sees so that no space between the images is observed consciously. In 1825 he published his insight in a scientific paper. This triggered a craze for optical toys such as the zoetrope.

In the 20[th]C Hollywood chose to view Roget's publication as having furnished the theoretical foundation from which the movie industry had been able to develop.

Location: No. 39 Bernard Street, Bloomsbury, WC1N 1(LE). Gone.

Signage

Kensington High Street was the first road in Britain to have its signage stripped back to a minimum. The scheme was based upon the work of the Dutch traffic engineer Hans Monderman (*d*.2008). He believed that, by allowing motorists to use their intelligence, vehicles could be better integrated into the social fabric of communities. The late Mr Monderman had a test that enabled him to ascertain whether or not one of his implementations had created conditions that enabled drivers to respond to unusual events - he would walk out backwards into the oncoming traffic.

Exhibition Road is the London street that has been most remodelled to conform with the Dutchman's ideas.

Locations: Exhibition Road, SW7 2DD.
Kensington High Street, W8 6(SU).

Signs

In a society that had high rates of illiteracy, and in which glass, was very expensive, signs enabled businesses to make their trade known to passing members of the public. In 1762 a sign fell and killed four people. Subsequently, an Act of Parliament banned signs being hung over public thoroughfares in the City and Westminster.

Pub signs, barbers' red and white poles, and the three golden orbs of pawnbrokers are the only ones that are still widely recognised in Britain.

Location: Artillery Passage, E1 7LJ. (The passage is adorned with placard signs.)

See Also: PUBS

Lombard Street: Extending out over the pavements from both sides of Lombard Street are a series of street signs: a grasshopper; an anchor; a cat and fiddle (or cello, depending upon the relative size of the feline); a castle front; and a man with a large wig and a crown. These were hung in celebration of King Edward VII's 1902 coronation.[1]

Location: Lombard Street, EC3V 9(BQ).

Red Chinatown: In Chinatown the colour red is very evident. This is because people of Chinese culture traditionally associate it with good fortune and prosperity.

Street Signs

Chinatown: Chinatown's signs contain Chinese characters. Quite why there should be one for 'Macclesfield,' as in 'Macclesfield Street', is a mystery.

Location: Gerrard Street, W1D 6(JH).

Whitehall's End: Parliament Square seems to have a particular effect upon the roads that run into it - they suddenly assume new identities. Birdcage Walk becomes Great George Street, Victoria Street transforms into being Broad Sanctuary, and Whitehall metamorphoses into being Parliament Street. The last pair used to be physically separated from one another by

[1]   Rob Humphreys *The Rough Guide To London* Rough Guides (2008) 221

MACCLESFIELD STREET W1

麥 高 田 街

CITY OF WESTMINSTER 西敏市

Whitehall Palace's Holbein Gate (*c*.1532-1759).[1]

Street name changes often derived from the different sections of road running across land that belonged to different landlords.

Location: Parliament Street, SW1A 2(NH), and Whitehall, SW1A 2(NP).

See Also: PALACES DISAPPEARED & FORMER Whitehall Palace

Telephone Boxes

The General Post Office held a competition for the design of a telephone box. Sir Giles Gilbert Scott won it with his Kiosk No. 2.

In 1922 the architect had become the youngest person to have been elected a Royal Academician since Turner. The Academy is housed in Burlington House. The kiosks inside the complex's street entrance are Scott's original wooden models.

Scott used the shape of the ceiling of the dining room of the Sir John Soane Museum as the basis for the external shape of the roof of his telephone box. The architect wished that the kiosk should be silver-coloured. The GPO determined that it would be red. The K2 went into production in 1927. Eight years later he produced a simplified version of it, the K6. This became ubiquitous, furnishing an example of dignity in public spaces, whether they were affluent suburbs or squalid streets.

In 2007 there were about 14,000 K6s left.

Locations: Burlington House, No. 50 Piccadilly, W1J 0BD.

Bow Street, WC2E 7(AW). A cluster of telephone boxes that survives for reasons of tourism rather than of telephony.

St Pancras Church Graveyard, NW1 1UL. Soane's grave is topped by the shape.

[1]   King Street used to run parallel to Parliament Street to its west.

See Also: MUSEUMS The Sir John Soane Museum
Websites: www.posp.co.uk/old-st-pancras   www.avoncroft.org.uk[1]

Traffic Lights

J.P. Knight was a railway engineer by profession.   In 1868 he set up in
Parliament Square a device that had rotating red-and-green gas lanterns.
A few weeks after their installation, the lights exploded, injuring the
police officer who had been operating them.

William L. Potts built the first modern three-way traffic lights in
Detroit in 1920.   A dozen years later London's first permanent set started
operating.

In 1929 Scotland Yard convened a meeting with interested parties
about how the locomotion of motor vehicles should be regulated.   The
Royal Automobile Club asked that main road priority should be instituted
(the Automobile Association opposed the idea).   This was done.   The
development abandoned the Common Law principle of equal rights and
equal responsibilities.

<u>*Location*: Par</u>liament Square, SW1P 3AD.

[1]   The National Telephone Kiosk Collection is held by The Avoncroft Museum
of Buildings, Bromsgrove, Hereford & Worcester.   (Available for weddings.)

Chain Reaction: Leó Szilárd was a Hungarian *émigré* who was seeking to work out how a nuclear chain reaction might be triggered. In 1933, while he was walking along Southampton Row, the answer struck him. The thought was inspired by noticing the operation of a recently installed set of traffic lights.

In 1939 Szilárd and Eugene Wigner persuaded Albert Einstein to write to President Roosevelt to establish a nuclear weapons programme before the Nazis developed one. Six years later the Hungarian made a plea to James F. Byrnes, the American Secretary of State, that atomic bombs should not be dropped upon Japan.

Location: Southampton Row, WC1B 4(HH).

The Green Wave: A green wave is when a vehicle user experiences a continuous succession of traffic lights that are showing green during their cycle. This allows the person to travel for a much greater distance without having to stop at a junction than would normally be the case. It is reputed that many people who find themselves caught in one prefer to 'ride' it for as long as they can rather than turn off when they should. London's best known one involves City Road, Pentonville Road, Euston Road, Marylebone Road, Marylebone Flyover, the Westway, and beyond.

Pelican Crossings: The 'pelican' in pelican crossing is derived from the term 'pedestrian light-controlled' (pelicon) crossing.

In 1969 the metropolis's first pelican crossing was installed.

There are sets that enable the traffic island at Hyde Park Corner to be crossed to and from. These have buttons that are at a sufficient height so that they can be used by people who are on horseback.

Location: Hyde Park Corner, W1J 7NT. On the central island at roundabout.

STREET MARKETS

See Also: FOOD MARKETS, FORMER; SHOPPING
Websites: www.ilovemarkets.com www.londonmarkets.co.uk

Bermondsey Market

The Corporation of the City of London started to redevelop Smithfield Market in 1851. Four years later the mart's livestock section was moved to Copenhagen Fields in Islington. On the days when animals were not being sold, a general market operated on the site. This was called the Caledonian Market because of its proximity to the adjacent Caledonian Road. It became focused upon second-hand goods and antiques.

During the Second World War both marts were closed down. Following the return of peace, the market authorities permitted only the live cattle one to resume trading on the site. Many of the antiques dealers moved to Bermondsey Street in Bermondsey, where the New Caledonian Market took place. Others of their number migrated to Portobello Road.

Locations: Bermondsey Square, Southwark, SE1 4QB. The market takes place on Friday mornings.

Caledonian Market, Market Road, Islington, N7 9(PW).

See Also: PORTOBELLO ROAD

Berwick Street Market

Berwick Street Market is a street market that takes place in Soho six days a week. It is smaller than it used to be.

Location: Berwick Street, W1F 0(QA).

Costermongers

Pearly Kings & Queens: Pearly kings and queens are one of the archetypes of Cockney London. The monarchs wear black clothes that have thousands of pearl buttons sewn onto them. These are known as 'smother suits'. Ones that have fewer buttons and more patterns are known as 'skeleton suits'. The tradition of Pearly Kings & Queens was created in 1875 by Henry Croft. He had been raised in the Charlton Street Orphanage in Somers Town. At the age of thirteen he left it to work as a road sweeper in the local street market. He became friendly with the costermongers who had stalls there. Master Croft wished to help those who were in want. He appreciated that he needed a means of catching people's attention. He started to collect the pearl buttons that he frequently swept up in the street. These he sewed onto a cap. Eventually, he had enough to cover a suit. He wore this while collecting money for charitable purposes. Attired in it, he made visits to hospitals, orphanages, and workhouses.

Croft soon found that there were more calls upon his time than he could fulfil. Therefore, he turned to the costermongers. They responded to his appeal for help. In order to do so, they made their own appropriate attire. London was divided into kingdoms. As the city grew outwards so new domains were created.

Mr Croft's funeral was held in 1930. The occasion was attended by several hundred pearly royalty. His descendants still bear the title of 'Somers Town'.

Locations: Charlton Street, NW1 1(HS).

St Martins-in-the-Fields, St Martin's Place, WC2N 4JJ. The church contains a statue of Mr Croft.

See Also: BELLS Bow Bells, Windblown Cockneys

Websites: www.pearlykingsandqueens.com
www.pearlysociety.co.uk

East End Street Markets

The East End's street markets, being outside of the City wall, were not subject to either the Corporation or the guilds.

During the early years of the 21stC the area's Sunday markets became much more vibrant and youth-focused than they had been previously. In part, this was a side-effect of Shoreditch and the East End having become more fashionable and more affluent.

Reading: Paul Morris *A Toby In The Lane* The History Press (2014). A history of the East End street markets. (In rhyming slang a 'toby' is a mug. It is a term for a market inspector. Mr Morris is one.)

See Also: FOOD MARKETS, FORMER Spitalfields

Brick Lane Market: The original Brick Lane Market grew up during the 18thC. Its extramural location meant that it was not supervised by the City of London.

Location: Brick Lane, E1 6(QL). The southernmost portion of Brick Lane is known as Osborn Street.

See Also: CAMDEN TOWN Camden Market; PORTOBELLO ROAD

Website: www.visitbricklane.org

Broadway Market: Broadway Market is a small street market that by the end of the 20thC had long been in decline. It revived. The shops along the road are a mix of businesses that supply goods to the area's traditional inhabitants and to its incomers and visitors. In 2014 there were three bookshops located along it.

Location: Broadway Market, E8 4(PH).
Website: www.broadwaymarket.co.uk

Petticoat Lane Market: Petticoat Lane Market takes place in Middlesex Street (formerly Petticoat Lane) on Sunday mornings. During the 16thC the market started its association with cloth and clothing. There is a story that its name derived from its traders being able to steal a woman's petticoat from her as she entered the street and then sell the garment back to her in the centre without her even knowing that she had had it removed from her person.

The road's name was changed to Middlesex Street in 1870. This alteration is reputed to have been part of an attempt by the local authority to undermine the market. However, the name Petticoat Lane has continued to be used. The Shops Act of 1936 formally legalised the Sunday trading that was occurring along its length.

Many of the market traders pride themselves upon their spiel. The patter merchants refer to the silent stallholders as 'lurkers'.

Location: Middlesex Street, E1 7(EZ).
See Also: PARKS Hyde Park, Speakers' Corner

Farmers' Markets

London Farmers' Markets: Nina Plank, an American, came across farmers' markets while she was visiting California. She established London's first one in Islington. The district proved to be receptive to them. The phenomenon soon spread across the metropolis.

Website: www.lfm.org.uk

Whitecross Street Market

The first reference to Whitecross Street Market dates from the 17thC. It is held each weekday.

In the early 21stC a large proportion of the mart's stalls supplied lunchtime food for people who worked in the City of London, which is located to the south of the street.

Location: Whitecross Street, EC1Y 8(JL).

TAXIS

See Also: TEA Tea Bags, Tommy Cooper

London's first taxi rank was established in 1625. It was located by the Church of St Mary-le-Strand.

Location: Strand, WC2R 1BA. In the centre of the road, to the north of King's College.

Black Cabs

Until the 1940s motorised taxis were painted in a variety of colours. Subsequently, they became overwhelmingly black. This was because the cab manufacturers had taken to using pressed steel to create the vehicles' bodywork. They appreciated that black was the colour that dried most quickly. The practice that had been pioneered by the American car manufacturer Henry Ford.

The last horse-drawn cab came off the road in 1947. It had been pulled by a nag called Dolly.

Cabmen's Shelters

The Landed Gentry's Cabmen's Shelter Fund's shelters look like overgrown garden huts. Originally, they stood upon road surfaces rather than the neighbouring pavements. Therefore, their size had to be limited in terms of length and breadth. Individually, they did not take up more space than a horse and carriage would have.

The shelters' purpose was to provide somewhere, other than pubs, where cabmen could be that was neither cold nor wet. The green-coloured shelters came into being at the instigation of the social reformer the 7th Earl of Shaftesbury (*d*.1885). Thirteen of them are still in operation. They are run under the supervision of the Heritage of London Trust.

The individual shelters have nicknames. The one opposite Gloucester Road is called *The All Nations*, the one in Thurloe Place is known as *The Bell and 'Orns*, the one in Piccadilly opposite The Turf Club has been dubbed *The Junior Turf Club*, and the one by Albert Bridge is referred to as *The Kremlin*.

Location: Thurloe Place, SW7 2(SP). In the middle, to the north of The Rembrandt hotel, and almost opposite the eastern end of the Victoria & Albert Museum.

The Knowledge

Licensed taxi drivers are expected to be able to navigate London without needing to consult a book of maps; the ability to do this is The Knowledge. In order to acquire a license, candidates have to demonstrate that they know it. Usually, it takes nearly three years to memorise the information. This is done by walking or driving along 400 set routes. Knowledge Boys can be seen riding motor scooters that have clipboards fixed onto their handlebars. The secured sheet will have details of the 'run' that s/he is trying to learn.

Brain scans have revealed that learning The Knowledge leads to black cab drivers developing larger posterior hippocampi than members of the general population possess.

The Public Carriage Office

The Public Carriage Office regulates London licensed taxis. In 1850 the Metropolitan Police was charged with supervising the trade. It established the body.

In 2000 Transport for London was set up to oversee transport within London. Supervision of 'The Yard' was transferred from the Met to TfL.

Location: No. 197 Blackfriars Road, SE1 8NJ.

Website: www.tfl.gov.uk/tph

TEA

See Also: MUSEUMS The Horniman Museum & Gardens

Tony Benn

The Labour MP and minister Tony Benn was renowned for his copious intake of the brew. He expressed the view that food is 'an interruption between two mugs of tea'. In 1981 he gave the national newspapers copy when he was hospitalised with a nervous system condition. The tabloid press decided he had been driven mad by drinking too much of his favourite beverage, his previous political conduct being taken as the early signs of his supposed condition. In fact, he had Guillan-Barre syndrome. He recovered from it.

Locations: No. 12 Holland Park Avenue, W11 3QU. The late Mr Benn's home.

St Mary's Hospital, Praed Street, Paddington, W2 1NY.

Earl Grey

The reformist, Whig administration that was led by the 2nd Earl Grey ended the East India Company's monopoly of the tea trade in 1834. A citric-flavoured tea was named after the prime minister. There is a shroud of uncertainty as to who actually bestowed the designation. It may have been a backhanded compliment.

The bergamot oil that gave the beverage its distinctive flavour was employed as a substitute for orange and lemon leaves. These looked like tea when dried. Unscrupulous tea traders had been using them to adulterate their stocks with. Drinkers of the resulting brew had developed a taste for it. Therefore, a variety that had the flavour was created to meet this demand.

The Boscawen family have owned the Tregothnan estate in Cornwall since 1335. Evelyn Boscawen is a descendant of the Earls Grey. In 2013 it was reported both that he had been growing tea on the property and that he was planning to export some of it to Shanghai.

Reading: (Ernest) E.A. Smith (1924-1998) *Lord Grey, 1764-1845* Clarendon Press (1990).

Website: http://tregothnan.co.uk

An Essay Too Far

The prose style in which Jonas Hanway wrote his book *A Journal of Eight Days' Journey From Portsmouth To Kingston upon Thames* (1756) was very tedious. However, in the opinion of both Dr Samuel Johnson and Oliver Goldsmith, the work's principal flaw was the *An Essay On Tea* section that was appended to the principal text. In this, the man declared his opposition to the beverage. This was too much for the pair. They launched a joint assault upon Hanway's limited literary talents.

See Also: WEATHER Umbrellas, Jonas Hanway

Ig Nobel Prize Winners

Sir John Wolfe Barry's achievements included co-designing Tower Bridge (1894). The crossing is a metal structure that has a stone cladding. In 1901 the knight called upon the Council of the Institution of Civil Engineers to establish an entity that would oversee the standardisation of iron and steel sections. The Engineering Standards Committee was set up. Two years later the body registered the British Standard Mark to indicate that an item was 'up to standard'. This symbol became known as the Kitemark®. In 1931 the organisation changed its name to the British Standards Institution (BSI).

The 1999 Ig Nobel prize for literature was awarded to the BSI. This was done to acknowledge *Method For Preparation of A Liquor of Tea*, a six-page-long document (BS6008) that the Institution had issued upon the 'method for preparation of a liquor of tea'. The same year Len Fisher of the University of Bristol received the physics prize for working out the optimal manner in which to dunk a biscuit into a cup of the beverage.

Location: No. 389 Chiswick High Road, Chiswick, W4 4AL. The BSI's headquarters.

See Also: BRIDGES Tower Bridge

Websites: www.bsigroup.com www.improbable.com/ig

The Marquise Bethinks

In the 18thC part of the importance of taking tea socially lay in the fact that the sequence in which the people present were served indicated their social rank with respect to one another. The Marquise de Montendre (*d.*1772) was the widow of a Huguenot field marshal. She was of the view that her late husband's hereditary title gave her precedence over countesses. However, the fact that her departed spouse's French honour had been attainted by the French Crown meant that there was a degree of uncertainty about the issue. On the whole, she sought to carry the matter

While there's tea there's hope

by means of an air of haughtiness. However, upon occasion she preferred to avoid pressing it.

Horace Walpole knew of an incident when she and some other aristocratic women had been socialising with one another in the townhouse of one of the number. The tea items had been brought into the room where they were. Without referring to this development, the marquise had professed that the time had come for her to leave. The countesses present were served. The widow had then declared 'I have bethought myself, I think I will have one cup.'

See Also: CLASS

Tea Bags

In 1945 the Labour government lowered the price that it was prepared to pay for tea. The tea companies, in order to cut their own margins, started to pack leaves directly for the maturing bins. This led to drinkers of the beverage complaining about the amount of dust in the tea that they bought. However, the powder was important for ensuring that brews had a replete taste. Therefore, the firms sought to find a way of selling the public tea with the dust in a form that people would not mind it being in.

Sandy Fowler, an engineer then living in Ceylon (now Sri Lanka), with the assistance of his wife Ann, devised the modern tea bag. This proved to be the solution to the dust issue. Mr Fowler did not patent his invention.

Tommy Cooper: Tommy Cooper (*d*.1984) was a much loved comedian-magician. Whenever he had taken a ride in a taxi, he would pay his fare and declare that he was also going to give the cabbie 'something for a drink'. He would then reach into his wallet and hand over a tea bag.

Location: No. 51 Barrowgate Road, Chiswick, W4 4QT. Mr Cooper's home.

See Also: TAXIS

The Tea Trade

In the 1650s China teas became the first teas to be imported into Britain. 'The EIC began importing tea directly from Canton on a regular basis in 1717, and each succeeding decade until 1760 saw an accelerating growth in the volume of imports.'[1]

By the mid-19[th]C Mincing Lane was the centre of the wholesale tea trade. Indian teas that had been grown in Assam then began to arrive in London. Coming from a colony they had the considerable commercial advantage of not having a duty charged upon them. Chinese teas were relatively more expensive. This reinforced their cachet.

Location: Mincing Lane, EC3R 7(AA).

Twinings

Daniel Twining was a weaver in Gloucestershire. In the 1680s he concluded that the county's cloth industry was in decline. Therefore, he and his family moved to London. His son Thomas served an apprenticeship with an East India merchant. This left the youth with a knowledge of tea as a commodity.

In about 1706 the younger Twining became the owner of Tom's Coffee House in Devereux Court. This was one of London's leading coffeehouses. It drew much of its custom from the lawyers who worked in the nearby Inns of Court. The establishment was noted for the *savants* and wits who chose to congregate there. The proprietor drew upon his knowledge of tea to ensure that it developed a fine reputation for serving the beverage. He prospered and went on to set up a business that wholesaled tea and coffee.[2]

Richard Twining was a grandson of Thomas. The dynasty's growing wealth was testified to by the fact that he was schooled at Eton College. He entered the family business and soon became one of London's leading tea merchants. The action that he is remembered for was his persuading the government to reduce the rate of tax on the leaf. The American War of Independence - a conflict that had followed on from the Boston Tea Party of 1773 - had involved large military expenditure by the state. This had increased the size of the National Debt. The Treasury needed to find money with which it could service its enlarged financial obligations. Tea smuggling was occurring on a vast scale. Richard convinced the prime minister, William Pitt the younger, that if the duty on the commodity was reduced radically then the economic viability of the illicit trade would be removed and that the tea that was being handled within it would

---

[1]   Larry Neal *The Rise of Financial Capitalism: International Capital Markets In The Age of Reason* Cambridge University Press (1990) 135-6. Citing Chaudhuri *Trading World of Asia and The English East India Company, 1660-1760* (1978) 388
[2]   Thomas Twining honoured his father by becoming a member of the Weavers' Company.

TWININGS

enter its legal counterpart and thus become taxable. The premier used the Commutation Act of 1784 to lower the rate that was levied on the commodity from 100% to 25%. The merchant's evaluation of what would happen soon proved to have been correct. It was no longer worth the smugglers' while to handle tea. As a result, there was an increase in the revenue that the duty generated.

Location: Twinings, No. 216 Strand, WC2R 1AP.

Websites: http://twinings.co.uk www.twinings.com

White

During the 19thC various members of the Rothschild family had townhouses to the north of the western portion of Piccadilly. The water with which tea was brewed in the Seamore Place home of Alfred de Rothschild was delivered daily from his Buckinghamshire estate. This was because the financier regarded London water with suspicion. One visitor is reputed to have asked a servant if some milk could be added to his cup. The response came as to whether he would prefer it to be from a Hereford, a Jersey, or a Shorthorn.[1]

Location: Curzon Street, W1J 5(HQ). No 1 Seamore Place disappeared beneath a westward expansion of Curzon Street.

See Also: PARKS Green Park, Milkmaids' Passage

---

[1] Ed Glinert *West End Chronicles* (2008) 13

THE THAMES

See Also: BRIDGES; HERITAGE Richmond Hill; THE POLICE The River Police

The City of London and The Thames

King Richard I the Lionheart granted the Conservancy of the Thames to the City of London in 1197. In return, the settlement made a large contribution to his crusading funds. During the late Middle Ages the City used its economic strength to build up control over the watercourse from Staines[1] in Middlesex to the embouchure of the Medway, which flows into the Thames's estuary.

The exact nature of the Corporation's authority over the watercourse was unclear. Over time, other parties litigated against the City about the issue. The matter was only resolved after a direct confrontation occurred between the Corporation and the Crown. A proposal had been aired that the river should be embanked. Therefore, who had the right to do what to which part of the watercourse meant who was going to profit from any recovered land. The question of who the river belonged to became a hotly contested matter between the two parties. In 1857, the City caved in to the Crown's claim that the Corporation had only ever exercised stewardship and that the Crown had always been the owner.

See Also: THE CITY OF LONDON Good Numbers

The Embankment and Sir Joseph Bazalgette

Until the late 19[th]C the Thames was a broader, shallower river than it is now. The street name Strand has its origin in the Anglo-Saxon word for a beach or shore.

The Metropolitan Board of Works instructed Joseph Bazalgette to construct the Thames Embankment. This was to confine the river's flow. The watercourse became narrower and faster. One of the effects of speeding its current was to be to reduce any remaining proclivity that it had retained, in the wake of the early 1830s rebuilding of London Bridge, towards freezing.

The Embankment has a number of different sections. On the northern side, the Victoria Embankment (1864-1870) was built between

[1]   Staines in the now on the western edge of the conurbation.

Blackfriars Bridge and Westminster Bridge. The Chelsea Embankment (1871-1874) is its westward continuation. There is a gap between them that is filled by the Palace of Westminster, which nestles behind its own flood defences. On the southern bank of the river the Albert Embankment (1866-1870) was constructed between Lambeth Bridge and Vauxhall Bridge.

Bazalgette's commission had secondary features. He was required to construct a number of sewage drains and service tunnels. Along the Victoria Embankment he also integrated part of the District Line underground line. The engineer is commemorated by a bust that stands close to Hungerford Bridge. It presides over his creation.

Location: Victoria Embankment, WC2N 6PA.

See Also: BRIDGES The Freeing of The West; PARLIAMENT Liquid Refreshment, Taunting The Tourists

The Pool of London

The Pool of London was the heart of London's maritime life until the early 19thC when the walled docks began to develop rapidly. The Upper Pool extends from London Bridge to Cherry Garden Pier and the Lower one from the Pier to Limekiln Creek.

See Also: BRIDGES London Bridge; MILITARY CUSTOMS The Constable's Dues

The Port of London Authority

The Port of London Authority is a public body that manages the Thames from Teddington Lock to an abstract line that stretches over the river's estuary from the Crow Stone, Southend, to the London Stone at Yantlet Creek on the Isle of Grain, Kent. In 1909 the Authority took into public ownership the enclosed docks that lay between the Tower of London and Tilbury. The City of London transferred the Thames Conservancy to the body.

Locations: The Port of London Authority Building, No. 10 Trinity Square, EC3N 4AJ. The Authority's former home.

Teddington Lock, TW11 9(NR).

Website: www.pla.co.uk

Strand-on-the-Green

The process of embanking the Thames in central London swept away scores of riverside quays, houses, and workshops. A stretch of the riverside that retains an echo of the past is the portion at Strand-on-the-

Green. It is best appreciated from the watercourse's southern bank, to the east of the southern end of Kew Bridge.

Location: Strand-on-the-Green, W4 3(PD).

See Also: PERIOD PROPERTIES

The Tidal Thames

The Thames is tidal until it reaches Teddington Lock in the city's far western suburbs. To the east of the lock the river's mud-banks and beaches are exposed at low tide. (There is a small sandy beach close to Gabriel's Wharf.)

Website: www.thames-explorer.org.uk (The Thames Explorer Trust is an educational charity that is active along the tidal stretch of the Thames.)

Billies & Charleys: In the middle of the 19thC Billie and Charley were two people who eeked out a living by scouring the Thames's banks for artefacts that they could sell to dealers. In 1857 it struck the pair that it would be more efficient - and profitable for them - if they manufactured the 'antiquities' rather than searched for them. This they did, claiming that the sudden steady flow of items was being generated by the excavation of a new dock at Shadwell in East London. The following year their fraud was exposed by the archaeologist Henry Syer Cuming.

Billies & Charleys are still traded but openly so, being appreciated as curiosity items.

Locations: The Cuming Museum, Old Walworth Town Hall, No. 151 Walworth Road, SE17 1RY. The collection of items that was accumulated by Cuming and his father Richard Cuming formed the nucleus of the museum.

Shadwell Basin, E1W 3(TD).

Website: www.southwark.gov.uk/cuming museum

The Society of Mudlarks & Antiquarians: The Society of Mudlarks & Antiquarians is a group that carries on its activities within guidelines that are determined by the Port of London Authority. Between the Houses of Parliament and Thames Pier, the organisation's members search the river's foreshores. They look for artefacts that have been dropped there through the centuries. Any items that are discovered have to be offered to the Museum of London for a period of display before they can be sold.

Warehouses

Warehouses used to dominate the banks of the River Thames. Almost all of the ones in central London have been converted into being either offices or homes.

See Also: MUSEUMS The Design Museum

Wharves

In the Early Modern period goods were loaded and unloaded at wharves that had been constructed upon the banks of the Thames. By the mid-17thC it was clear that the City of London's landing stages were having difficulty coping with the volume of cargo that people were seeking to pass through them. Therefore, the City allowed items to be alighted at wharves on the southern bank. These were termed 'sufferance docks'. The area to the south of what is now Hay's Wharf became known as 'London's Larder'.[1]

See Also: FOOD MARKETS Billingsgate Market; WEATHER Fog, The Ponging Banks

---

[1] Rob Humphreys *The Rough Guide To London* Rough Guides (2008) 286

THEATRES

In the early 17thC theatres were established to the west of the River Fleet. During the English Republic, the Puritans closed them. Following the restoration of the monarchy in 1660 a number of playhouses were opened close to the Aldwych. In the early 18thC Her Majesty's Theatre (1705) and The Theatre Royal Haymarket (1720) were both built on Haymarket.

By the late 19thC the Strand had become London's principal theatrical district. Now the only theatres on the street are The Adelphi (1806), The Savoy (1881), and The Vaudeville (1870).

Theatres began to open along Shaftesbury Avenue in 1888. The road came to be regarded as the hub of London's theatreland, a position that it still retains.[1]

Locations: Shaftesbury Avenue: W1D 5(EA).

Strand, WC2R 1(DA).

See Also: PUBS Gin Palaces, The Salisbury; WILLIAM SHAKESPEARE The Shakespeare Globe

Website: www.theatrestrust.org.uk

The Apollo Victoria

The New Victoria Cinema (1930) was built in the art deco-style. It was closed in 1975. Six years later the building was reopened as a 2200-seat theatre.

Location: No. 17 Wilton Road, SW1V 1LG.

Website: www.atgtickets.com/venues/apollo-victoria-theatre

The Donmar Warehouse

The building that the 251-seat Donmar Warehouse theatre occupies had been a brewery's hop ripening facility and then a film studio before it became a banana warehouse. The playhouse owner Donald Albery bought it in 1960. He had it converted into being a rehearsal space. It was used by Margot Fonteyn's London Festival Ballet dance company; the name Donmar was derived from their forenames.

In 1976 the Royal Shakespeare Company moved into the building and used it to showcase new writing. In 1990 Roger Wingate of the

---

[1]   In taxi slang theatres are known as 'Gaffs' and Shaftesbury Avenue is called 'Gaff Street'.

Ambassador Theatre Group played the leading role in setting up the Donmar Trust, a not-for-profit charity.[1]

The Donmar's productions tend to differ from those that are mounted in the West End's other theatres. In part, this is because the venue has been able to draw a portion of its income from subscriptions that are paid to it by philanthropically-inclined members of its audience.

Location: The Donmar Warehouse, No. 41 Earlham Street, WC2H 9LD. On the northern side.

See Also: MUSEUMS The Design Museum

Website: www.donmarwarehouse.com

The Duchess Theatre

There is a story that when the construction of The Duchess Theatre (1929) was finished, the writer J.B. Priestley stood outside the building with its architect and asked him 'Where are the dressing rooms?' Subsequently, some were erected upon its roof.

Location: Nos. 3-5 Catherine Street, WC2B 5LA.

Website: www.nimaxtheatres.com/duchess-theatre

The Garrick Theatre

Location: The Garrick Theatre, No. 2 Charing Cross Road, WC2H 0HH.

Website: www.nimaxtheatres.com/garrick-theatre

The Gruesome Twosome: During the first half of the 20[th]C the satanist Aleister Crowley was one of the most controversial people in British public life. In 1944 The Garrick Theatre mounted a stage adaptation of Graham Greene's novel *Brighton Rock* (1938). In the production, the role of Rose was played by Dulcie Gray. The aging diabolist attended a performance and was favourably impressed by the actress. Subsequently, he sent her a fan letter that he had written in doggerel. The 'verse' conveyed his admiration of her. He ended the communication by declaring that he wished to sacrifice her at Stonehenge as Midsummer's dawn broke. She sent him a reply that declined his offer. The grounds that she gave were that she did not like rising early.

Mr Crowley's intuition may not have been altogether wrong. Ms Gray had a taste for the macabre. In later life she suffered a bout of serious illness. As a means of distracting herself she wrote a detective novel. This was published. It proved to be successful. She recovered her health

---

[1] Mr Wingate is also the principal figure behind the Curzon cinema chain. (www.curzoncinemas.com)

and resumed her acting career. However, in parallel, she continued to be an author. A constant strand in her crime books was that the murders were always perpetrated in a most unpleasant manner.

The Gielgud Theatre

The Gielgud Theatre (1906) was known formerly as The Globe Theatre. In 1995 the building's name was changed to honour the actor Sir John Gielgud. He had appeared there in numerous H.M. Tennent productions.

The thespian Sir Ian 'Gandalf' McKellen once asked Gielgud about how he should play King Lear. 'Get a light Cordelia!' came the reply. (The text requires that, during Act 5, Scene 3, the monarch should carry the corpse of his youngest daughter.)

Location: The Gielgud Theatre, No. 33 Shaftesbury Avenue, W1D 6AR.

Website: www.delfontmackintosh.co.uk/Theatres/gielgud_theatre. asp

H.M. Tennent: The theatrical agents 'Binkie' Beaumont and Harry Tennent came to know one another while they were both working for the production-managers Howard & Wyndham. In 1936 the pair set up their own agency H.M. Tennent Limited. 'The Firm', as it became known, was based at the Globe Theatre. The reclusive Mr Tennent died in 1941.

From the 1940s through to the 1960s 'The Firm' dominated British commercial theatre. H.M. Tennent did not exert its influence through contracts. Rather, its positive influence was expressed through the very considerable charm of Mr Beaumont and its negative one through its refusal to have anything to do with anyone who ran foul of him. His influence began to wane in the 1950s, however, he remained by far the most influential figure in British commercial theatre right up until his death in 1973.

'Binkie' disliked publicity. He believed his sway was the greater for being exercised discretely. He regarded money that was spent on advertising a hit as being wasted and money that was spent on publicising a failure as being counterproductive to its subsequent sweeping under the carpet.

Location: No. 14 Lord North Street, SW1P 3LD. 'Binkie''s home.

Her Majesty's Theatre

Her Majesty's Theatre (1705) was designed by Sir John Vanbrugh. The knight was an architect as well as a playwright. The building's name was resonant of the fact that theatres used to operate under the protection and the supervision of the royal court.

Location: Haymarket, SW1Y 4QL. On the western side, to the south of the junction with Charles II Street.

See Also: ARCADES The Royal Opera House

Website: www.hermajestystheatre.org

The London Palladium

The London Palladium hosts variety shows and musicals. For many British artistes, to appear at the theatre is regarded as being the pinnacle of their career. Since the late 1960s, the venue's management has hired the building out for one-off performances by individuals who are prepared to risk a wodge of money in order to fulfil their dreams of playing there.

Location: No. 7 Argyll Street, W1F 7TF. At the southern end.

Website: www.reallyuseful.com/theatres/London-palladium

The Donkey Run: The Palladium is renowned for its stage having a rotating section. It is reputed that originally this was made to turn by two harnessed donkeys being induced to walk on cue. As a result, the area below the centre of the platform became known as the Donkey Run.

The Lyceum

The Lyceum did not metamorphose into being a dramatic theatre until the late 19thC. Over the previous hundred years, the venue had hosted a variety of forms of entertainment. These had ranged from operas to waxworks.

Once the building had become a playhouse, it developed a close association with the actor Sir Henry Irving.

Location: No. 21 Wellington Street, WC2E 7RQ. The western side.

Website: www.atgtickets.com/venues/lyceum-theatre

Bram Stoker: Bram Stoker had been a civil servant in his native Ireland. All the while, he had had literary ambitions. He broke into the theatrical world by working as an unpaid drama critic. He came to know Irving. In 1878 the actor invited the pen-pusher to become his business manager. The latter accepted the offer and proved himself to be innovative in the position. He advertised theatrical seasons in advance rather than one play at a time; he was the first person to assign numbers to theatre seats; and he encouraged their advance reservation. In parallel, he established a moderately successful writing career, authoring a number of books in different genres.

See Also: HORROR FICTION Vampires, Dracula

The Lyric Hammersmith

The external structure of the Frank Matcham-designed Lyric Hammersmith (1895) was demolished in 1971 so that the King's Mall shopping centre could be built over the site. The venue's baroque interior had been taken apart and put into storage. The new complex included a new Lyceum theatre. The interior was re-assembled within this.

Location: Lyric Square, King Street, W6 0QL. On the square's eastern side, at its northern end.

Website: www.lyric.co.uk

Poor Chap: In 1958 Michael Codron mounted a production of Harold Pinter's play *The Birthday Party* at The Lyric Hammersmith. The dramatic piece opened to hostile reviews and ran for only a week. The small houses prompted the theatre's management to close off the circle. The playwright went to see his creation and chose to watch it from aloft. An usher tried to prevent him from doing so. Pinter identified himself. This prompted the response, 'Oh, you poor chap...in you go.' On the day after the play's closure, *The Sunday Times* newspaper published a strongly supportive appraisal by its influential drama critic Harold Hobson. This helped to establish the dramatist's reputation.

Website: www.haroldpinter.org

The Phoenix Theatre

The Phoenix Theatre (1930) was designed by the architect Sir Giles Gilbert Scott for Sydney Bernstein, the owner of the Granada cinema chain. The designer Theodore Komisarjevsky and the painter Vladimir Polunin fashioned the building's auditorium. The Russians created a fantastical pleasure dome. Subsequently, Bernstein commissioned the pair to create the interiors of a series of large, escapist-themed cinemas for him, notably the Tooting Granada (1931).

Locations: No. 112 Charing Cross Road, WC2H 0(JG). On the eastern side to the south of the junction with Flitcroft Street.

Nos. 50-60 Mitcham Road, Tooting, SW17 9NA. The Tooting Granada. A cinema that is now a bingo hall.

Website: www.atgtickets.com/venues/phoenix-theatre

The Playhouse Theatre

The Avenue Theatre (1882) was unusually sited away from both the Strand and Shaftsbury Avenue. It has been claimed that the true purpose of the impresario Sefton Parry, when he decided to develop it, was not to have another theatre. Rather, he seems to have been seeking to make a handsome profit on the project by charging the South Eastern Railway Company, the owners of the neighbouring Charing Cross Station, an extortionate amount to buy the property from him. This would be so that the concern could increase the number of tracks running into the terminus. However, it was disinclined to do so. Instead, it had its engineers create a platform above the theatre upon which additional lines were lain.

In 1905 an arch that spanned the station collapsed down onto the tracks, which in turn demolished the theatre. Six people were killed. Rather than buy the theatre, the railway proprietors commissioned a second, more robust platform. In the years that had passed since the theatre's original construction it had proven to be a commercial success. Therefore, its owners used their compensation payment to build the venue that now stands on the site. It was renamed The Playhouse Theatre.

Location: The Playhouse Theatre, Northumberland Avenue, WC2N 5DE.

Website: www.atgtickets.com/venues/playhouse-theatre

The Royal Court Theatre

In 1870 the New Theatre opened in Ranelagh Street on what had been the site of the Ranelagh Chapel, a former Nonconformist place of worship. The establishment moved to the eastern side of Sloane Square, where it became the Royal Court theatre.

The Royal Court closed as a playhouse in 1932. Three years later the building was reopened as a cinema. In 1952 it became a theatre club. This enabled it to mount productions of plays that had not been censored by the Lord Chamberlain's Office.

George Devine and Tony Richardson launched the English Stage Company in 1956. The former became the enterprise's artistic director. He was responsible for bringing to the London stage the works of dramatists such as John Arden and John Osborne. Each play was given only a short run at the Royal Court. This meant that the Company was able to present a large number of productions. Some of these transferred to the West End. The Company's founders included the cultural figure the 7th Earl of Harewood, who was a cousin of the queen. The Lord Chamberlain's Office was based in St James's Palace. From time to time, the peer was dispatched there in order to try to justify the nature of a particular piece.[1]

[1] Harewood went on to serve as the Chairman of the British Board of Film Classification. Under his leadership, the body became a tad less liberal than it

In 1958 the theatre presented the initial production of what was to prove to be a durable partnership - that of the playwright Arnold Wesker and the director John Dexter. The pair's working relationship contained an element of friction. Upon one occasion, Dexter became so overwrought by Wesker's suggestions that he was moved to exclaim, 'Shut up, Arnold, or I'll direct this play as you wrote it!'

Location: Sloane Square, Chelsea, SW1W 8(AN).

Website: www.royalcourttheatre.com

The Angry Young Men: George Fearon was the Company's publicist. During a meeting that he had with John Osborne, he termed the playwright an 'angry young man'. Soon afterwards Fearon realised that the phrase had potential. At his prompting, it was taken up by the media. The 'Angry Young Men' label became attached to a generation of writers who came to public prominence during the mid- and late 1950s - the likes of the novelist Sir Kingsley Amis and the author Colin Wilson.

The Rocky Horror Show: The actor Richard O'Brien conceived of what was to become the musical *The Rocky Horror Show* in 1965. It was largely the fruit of his having grown up watching old horror films on television in provincial New Zealand. In 1972 he was understudying the role of King Herod in the musical *Jesus Christ Superstar*. However, its producer Robert Stigwood - an Australian - decided that he was wrong for the part. The Kiwi's response to this setback was to turn his own idea into a script.

Early the following year the director Jim Sharman mounted a production of Sam Shephard's *The Unseen Hand* at The Royal Court. He cast O'Sullivan as Willie the Space Freak. The actor showed the director a copy of what he had written. It had the working title *They Came From Denton High*. Mr Sharman was taken by the material, which was retitled *The Rocky Horror Show*. He asked the thespian to write two more songs and add another ten pages of dialogue. He then persuaded the theatre's management to give the musical a three week run in its 60-seat Theatre Upstairs venue.

Tim Curry was cast as Frank-N-Furter. He decided how the character's accent would sound after he had sat on a bus and overheard two Knightsbridge ladies talking about 'a nice hyce'. His costume grew out of a corset that he had worn for a production of Jean Genet's play *The Maids* (1947). O'Brien played Riff Raff.

In summer 1973 the show opened in the Theatre Upstairs.

had been in its outlook when assessing movies that were essentially commercial exploitations of sex and violence.

PICTURE SHOW

Downstairs, the actress Coral Browne had been starring in a production of Edward Bond's *The Sea*. Her husband Vincent Price attended *The Show*'s opening night. Just before the curtain went up, O'Brien was looking out into the audience when there was a flash of lightning. The American horror actor was sitting below a skylight and so was spotlighted momentarily. The Kiwi took this elucidation to be a good omen. The night was a success. The musical developed a following. It transferred first to the Classic Cinema at No. 148 The King's Road and then to The Essoldo picture house at No. 279.

The movie version was filmed at Bray Studios, where the Hammer horrors had been shot. Upon its release, the flick failed to make much of an impact at the box-office. However, a year later in the United States a cinema started to run late night screenings of it. People took to dressing up as the characters when they went to watch it. The cult had been born.

Website: http://rockyhorror.co.uk

The Royal National Theatre

The idea of establishing a national theatre was mooted as early as 1848. The scheme was not pursued seriously until 1904 when H. Granville Barker prepared the document *A National Theatre Scheme & Estimate*. Appeals raised enough funds to enable a site in Cromwell Gardens to be purchased in 1937. However, the Second World War intervened.

The Festival of Britain was held on London's South Bank in 1951. It was decided that an arts complex should be developed as a legacy of the exhibition. The proposed national theatre was incorporated into the scheme. In 1963 the National Theatre Company was set up under the leadership of the actor Sir Laurence Olivier. The troupe's inaugural, temporary home was the Old Vic theatre.

The South Bank Theatre Board supervised the complex's design and erection. The body's chairman was Lord Cottesloe. He gave the architect Sir Denys Lasdun free rein. Construction began in 1969. The National Theatre has been described as being an instance of European Modernism reinterpreted through an English sensibility. Ever since the building's character became evident, it has been widely derided. This response is an instance of many Britons showing both their aesthetic limitedness and their capacity to act in a herd-like manner.[1]

The director Peter Hall succeeded Olivier as the head of the National in 1973. The theatre's South Bank building was opened three years later. Its three principal auditoria were: the Olivier (1150 seats), the Lyttleton (890),[2] and the Cottesloe (300). The last is now the Dorfman.

The Theatre developed a close relationship with the West End. A number of plays and musicals, such as *War Horse* (2007), that have started out as National Theatre productions, have transferred to the commercial stage.

Location: Upper Ground, SE1 9PX. To the east of the southern end of Waterloo Bridge.

Website: www.nationaltheatre.org.uk

St Martin's Theatre

Location: No. 20 West Street, WC2H 9NZ. On the north-eastern side. At the southern end.

Website: www.stmartinstheatre.co.uk

A Deathbed Undertaking: The barony of Willoughby de Broke is one of the oldest English titles of nobility. Since the late 17thC it has been held by members of the Verney family. In socio-economic terms, the dynasty were wealthy gentry rather than territorial magnates. None of their estates sat above a rich seam of coal or iron. As a result, they did not benefit financially from the Industrial Revolution in the way that some of their fellow peers did.

During the course of the 19thC many Britons came to appreciate that international free trade was to their material advantage. Support for the doctrine became the prevalent economic orthodoxy. As a result,

[1]   The London Studios complex (1972) to the east of the Theatre is a far less interesting building. Its only merit is that it helps to set off the National all the better.

[2]   The industrialist and politician Oliver Lyttleton served as the Chairman of the National Theatre. His parents had campaigned actively for the creation of such an institution. (*Reading*: Simon Ball *The Guardsmen: Harold Macmillan, Three Friends and The World They Made* HarperPerennial (2005). Lyttleton was one of the three.)

the United Kingdom took to importing much of her food from those overseas countries where edible commodities could be produced more cheaply than British farmers were able to supply them. As a result, in the early 1870s, the nation's agricultural sector entered a decades-long depression. Consequently, the incomes of most landowners declined. The Verneys experienced a decrease in the size of their rent receipts.

The Liberals had been careful to cultivate the urban middle classes. Through the Representation of The People Act of 1884, the party sought to expand the size of the franchise in rural constituencies. Many landowners regarded the reform as being an attack upon the traditional sway that they and their forebears had exercised over their tenants and neighbours. To them, the Liberals' Finance Act of 1894 must have appeared to have been a further assault. The measure imposed estate duties that were levied on the property that individuals owned at the time of their deaths.

The following year the Hon Richard Verney, the eldest son of the 18th Baron Willoughby de Broke, was elected to serve as a Conservative MP for Rugby. The town was in Warwickshire, which was where the family's principal acreage lay. 'Grev's' decision to sit in the Commons derived not from political ambition but rather from a belief that his aristocratic circumstances obligated him to perform certain roles in public life.

In the House, 'Grev' proved to be conscientious in his efforts to try to promote the agricultural interest. In the Chambers's deliberations, he proved to be a fluent speaker. In part, his articulacy may have derived from a childhood taste for amateur dramatics. In 1900 he stood down as an MP. Like his father and grandfather before him, his passion in life was for foxhunting. He was keenly aware of how railway lines and macadamed roads cut across the countryside in which he pursued his quarry. They had profoundly changed the land's character from how it would have been a century before.

'Grev's' father died in 1902. He became the 19th Baron Willoughby de Broke. The 1894 Act required him to pay large death duties upon the estates that he had inherited. The general election of 1906 saw the return of a Commons that was overwhelmingly composed of Liberals. The Conservatives responded to this development by using their majority in the Lords to oppose a series of measures that the new ministry introduced. Willoughby played a prominent role in this obstructive campaign.

The Liberal politician David Lloyd George was the Chancellor of the Exchequer. As such, he sought to use the Budget of 1909 both to introduce old-age pensions and to pay for the construction of a number of dreadnought battleships. The Upper House, in an action that flouted over two centuries of constitutional practice, rejected the measure. A crisis point had been reached. The impasse was broken by another election being called. The Liberals also won this. The Budget was passed. The ministry then sought to reform the senior Chamber by means of a Parliament Bill.

Willoughby opposed the item's passage, however, the government's underscored popular mandate meant that ultimately the measure became law. The peer's political outlook had always been imbued with a defensiveness that was informed by an awareness of the relative deterioration of his family's wealth and influence. The reactionary strand in his views became more apparent. He became an advocate of the eugenics movement. However, his broadly regressive outlook was not without its quirks. He proved to be a supporter of women's suffrage. This paradoxical stance stemmed from his concern for the 'nation's health'.

A factor that had benefitted some aristocratic families had been their ownership of properties that growing towns and cities had expanded onto during the course of the 18ᵗʰC and 19ᵗʰC. The urban-derived rental incomes of these dynasties had often outstripped their rural-derived ones. In London the Verneys owned a modest bloc of land that was located to the north-west of Covent Garden. Willoughby, given his taste for matters dramatic, allowed a small theatre to be constructed upon the plot. St Martin's Theatre opened in 1916.[1] The building's interior bears testimony to the Verneys' ownership of the property. Its proscenium arch is adorned by their coat of arms.

The money that the venue furnished made only a minor contribution to Willoughby's income. In financial matters, the baron was a realist. In 1921 he sold Compton Verney, his ancestral seat, and a large portion of the family's Warwickshire estates to a Yorkshireman whose initial fortune had come from manufacturing soap and who had subsequently become a railway company director.[2] The distastefulness of this development for the baron was almost certainly compounded by the fact that the following year Lloyd George bestowed a peerage upon the purchaser, who thereby joined him in the Lords.

In the post-First World War era Willoughby appreciated that he

---

[1]   Peers had been active investors in the construction of West End theatres for over two hundred years. The aristocratic members of the Kit-Cat Club had been the principal backers of Sir John Vanbrugh when he had erected Her Majesty's Theatre (1705) on Haymarket. (Willoughby had also been involved in the building of The Ambassadors Theatre (1913), which neighbours St Martin's.)
[2]   The Verneys continued to live and hunt in Warwickshire. Subsequent generations of the family contributed to the county's public life.

had little ability to influence the flow of events. He turned to writing as a means for expressing his worldview. His first book, *Hunting The Fox* (1920), was about his favourite sport. His second manuscript addressed other aspects of his life. It had not been completed at the time of his death. One of the planned but unwritten chapters was to have been about his interest in the theatrical world.

It is reputed that, to his very end, the baron remained true to himself. It has been claimed that upon his death-bed he made his son swear an oath that he would devote himself to ensuring that the motor car was not used for hunting foxes.

Location: No. 23 Gilbert Street, Mayfair, W1K 5HX. The town-house where Willoughby de Broke died. On the western side, towards the southern side.

See Also: PALACES Buckingham Palace, Death In The Gardens; PARLIAMENT The Lords; THEATRES Wyndham's Theatre

Website: www.comptonverney.org.uk (The Buckinghamshire property is now a centre for opera and the visual arts that welcomes the public.)

The Mousetrap: St Martin's Theatre houses the West End production of *The Mousetrap*. The play was written by the detective fiction author Dame Agatha Christie. It started its run at The Ambassadors Theatre in 1952. It transferred to St Martin's in 1974.

The text of *The Mousetrap* has not been printed in the UK. Christie was determined that it should not be issued until the run had ended. Part of the strategy that has enabled the show to continue for so long has been that only one production of it is allowed to be mounted outside of London each year.

Some people who are attending a performance of the play arrive by taxi. It is reputed that if unscrupulous cabbies are not tipped to a degree that they regard as being proper, they tell their former passengers which character is the murderer.

It was announced in 2012 that a statue of Dame Agatha was going to be erected at the junction of Great Newport Street and Cranbourn Street.

Websites: www.the-mousetrap.co.uk www.mousetrap.org.uk

The Savoy Theatre

The Savoy Theatre (1881) was developed by the *impresario* Richard d'Oyly Carte. It was the house that staged the initial productions of many of the operas of W.S. Gilbert and Arthur Sullivan. The theatre was the first public building in London to have electric lighting.

Location: Savoy Court, WC2R 0ET. On the western side.

Website: www.atgtickets.com/venues/savoy-theatre

Gilbert & Sullivan: W.S. Gilbert was one of the West End's leading play-wrights and Arthur Sullivan was a respected composer. They were intro-duced to one another by John Hollingshead, the owner of the Gaiety Theatre. Their first collaboration, *Thespis: or The Gods Grown Old* (1871), was staged at The Gaiety. It was not a success. They parted and went their own ways.

The pair were re-introduced to one another by Richard d'Oyly Carte. *Trial By Jury* (1875) was enough of a success to prompt the impresario to commission further work from them.

HMS Pinafore (1878) was an immense success in the United States, most of the productions there paid no royalties. The writers decided to respond to this reality by giving *The Pirates of Penzance* (1879) its premiere in New York.

Website: www.gilbertandsullivansociety.org.uk

Seating Arrangements

During the early 20[th]C Horace de Vere Cole was a renowned practical joker. Upon one occasion he hired a number of men and gave each of them a ticket for a performance that was due to take place at a West End's theatre. Their seats were located towards the front of the venue's stalls. All of the fellows turned up wearing hats. Unusually they did not hand in their headwear at the cloakroom. Instead, they assumed their places with their heads still covered. As soon as the auditorium's house lights had been dimmed they removed their hats in unison. Each of the chaps was bald. Their positions were such that collectively, when viewed from the balcony, their pates spelt out a particularly fruity Anglo-Saxon word.[1]

The Theatre Royal Drury Lane

In 1660 the monarchy was restored. The Crown granted Thomas Kil-ligrew a royal warrant to establish the King's Company of Players. He claimed that his troupe was the successor to the pre-Civil War King's Men and that therefore it should have the exclusive right to perform almost all of the English language plays then in existence, including those of Sir William Davenant, who ran the rival the Duke of York's Players company. In late 1660 the Lord Chamberlain made a distribution of the dramatic works. Davenant received his own compositions, John Web-ster's *Duchess of Malfi* (1623), and some of Shakespeare's plays. Killigrew

---

[1]   It wasn't either *aeppel* or *pere*.

was awarded a share of Beaumont & Fletcher's output,[1] Ben Jonson's plays, and the rest of the Bard's canon.

The Gordon Riots of 1780 saw London subjected to several days of anarchy. The Theatre Royal was attacked because 'papists and Frenchmen' had performed there. Subsequently, a military guard was posted outside the building each night. The practice was discontinued in 1796. By then the French Revolutionary War had turned numerous French Roman Catholics into being regarded as being stalwart allies of Britain.

In the 18thC and 19thC theatres burned down frequently. The actor and playwright Richard Brinsley Sheridan managed the Theatre Royal for many years. In 1809 the building caught fire. While it was aflame, he went to watch the spectacle. As he did so he drank some port that he had ordered from a nearby hostelry. When this *sang-froid* was commented upon, he remarked 'Surely a man may take a glass of wine by his own fireside.'

Location: The Theatre Royal, Catherine Street, WC2B 5JF. On the eastern side of the junction with Drury Lane.

See Also: THE BANK OF ENGLAND The Bank of England Picket

Website: www.reallyusefultheatres.co.uk/theatres/ theatre-royal-drury-lane

The Thunderous Heist: Until the early 18thC London theatre managers simulated the rumble of thunder by rolling metal balls within large wooden bowls. John Dennis was a well-respected critic of poetry and an indifferent playwright. For the - what proved to be very brief - run of his unremarkable play *Appius and Virginia* (1709) at Drury Lane Theatre, he devised a new technique for making the sound. This involved rolling balls down wooden troughs that had stops along their course. This replicated the sound in a manner that was far more impressive than the noise that the previous practice had been able to generate.

There is a story that subsequently, he went to a production of *Macbeth* at the theatre. During it, the rumbling of thunder was created by the use of his technique. He was moved to exclaim, 'They will not let my play run but they steal my thunder.'

The Theatre Royal Haymarket

The Theatre Royal Haymarket was established in 1720. Initially, the playhouse was known as The Little Theatre. In the mid-1730s Henry Fielding staged a number of controversial productions in the venue. The Licensing Act of 1737 ended his dramatic career. The success of Samuel

---

[1] Francis Beaumont and John Fletcher.

Richardson's novel *Pamela* (1740) pricked his interest. He parodied it with his book *Shamela Andrews* (1741). He went on to write *Joseph Andrews* (1742). Thereby, he became one of the fathers of the novel.

Location: No. 18 Suffolk Street, SW1Y 4HT. On the eastern side, to the south of the junction with Orange Street.

Website: www.trh.co.uk

Break A Leg!: The phrase that is used to wish an actor well for her/his performance is 'Break a leg!'

King George III was not minded to allow the Lord Chamberlain to grant Samuel Foote the licence that was required for The Little Theatre to be able to operate. Therefore, the actor-manager employed various ruses. They included furnishing free entry but recouping his outlay by charging high prices for refreshments. These tea parties circumvented the censorship system. (As a means for evading the authorities' proscriptions, they were to help to inspire the naming of the Boston Tea Party (1773).)

The king's younger brother Edward Duke of York was aware that Foote regarded himself as being an accomplished horseman. Therefore, the prince asked him to display his equine skills. This the latter agreed to do. However, the mount that the royal duke furnished him with had never been ridden before. Foote was thrown from it and broke one of his legs when he landed. The limb had to be amputated. His grace was full of remorse for what he had done. Therefore, he asked his older sib to grant the theatre the desired licence. This the monarch did. In 1766 The Little Theatre was renamed The Theatre Royal.

Wyndham's Theatre

The actor Sir Charles Wyndham played characters that re-enforced the social attitudes of his audience. He acquired a - not altogether deserved - reputation for respectability. When a property developer approached the 3rd Marquis of Salisbury with a request to be allowed to build on part of the peer's estate to the east of Charing Cross Road, the lord replied that if a theatre was to be constructed on the land it could only be raised for Wyndham.

Wyndham's opened in 1899.

Locations: No. 40 Charing Cross Road, WC2H ODA. On the eastern side. Bookended by St Martin's Court.

No. 21 Fitzroy Square, W1T 6EL. The marquis's townhouse.

See Also: THEATRES St Martin's Theatre, A Deathbed Undertaking

Website: www.delfontmackintosh.co.uk/Theatres/
wyndhams_theatre.asp

THE TOWER OF LONDON

See Also: THE CITY OF LONDON; CORONATIONS The Crown Jewels; PALACES, DISAPPEARED & FORMER; ZOOS The Royal Menagerie

The Tower of London has been a fortress since at least the time of the Normans. Lying downriver from the City of London, it both protected and menaced its charge.

Location: The Tower of London, EC3N 4AB.

Website: www.hrp.org.uk/toweroflondon

Captain Blood

In 1671 Captain Thomas Blood tried to steal the Crown Jewels from the Wardrobe Tower. He was apprehended. There is something of a mystery about the attempted theft and the officer's subsequent pardon by King Charles II. The monarch was nearly always short of money. He may have orchestrated the affair. If the jewels had been 'stolen' he would have been free to sell them surreptitiously, it being impolitic for him to do so publicly.

See Also: CORONATIONS The Regalia

CEREMONY OF THE KEYS

Ticket Holders Only

Please Wait Here

The Ceremony of The Keys

The Ceremony of the Keys takes place every night. Individuals who wish to attend it have to write in advance, giving the names and the addresses of those who will be attending. Once, during the Second World War, the ritual occurred ten minutes late. This was because the Luftwaffe had just bombed the Tower.

See Also: MILITARY CUSTOMS The Constable's Dues
Website: www.hrp.org.uk/TowerOfLondon/WhatsOn/
theceremonyofthekeys

The Chapel Royal of St Peter ad Vincula

In unmarked graves beneath the altar of the Chapel Royal of St Peter ad Vincula are buried the bones of numerous royal and noble individuals. Their remains were usually interred there because the state had regarded them as being contentious parties. Therefore, it was not politically expedient that their corpses should have public graves.

See Also: THE CHAPELS ROYAL
Website: www.hrp.org.uk/TowerOfLondon/Sightsand
stories/Prisoners/Towers/ChapelRoyalofStPeter

The Moat

When the Waterloo Barracks were constructed during the 1840s, the Tower's moat was drained.

Prisoners

The last time that the Tower was attacked from ground level was in 1554. The complex's principal function since Tudor times has been to act as a state prison rather than as a fortress or as a palace.

One of the most celebrated escapes from the Tower was that of the Jacobite rebel the 5th Earl of Nithsdale in 1716. The Scottish peer was incarcerated in the Queen's House. On the eve of his scheduled execution, his lordship engaged in the ruse of donning women's clothing and walking past his guards and out of the Tower. He died in exile in Rome nearly thirty years later.

Website: www.hrp.org.uk/TowerOfLondon/Sightsand
stories/Prisoners/Intro

Sir Walter Raleigh: The courtier and adventurer Sir Walter Ralegh's privateering activities in the Caribbean led to his running foul of the Spanish party at court. As a result, for many years he was imprisoned in the Tower. Within its walls, he led a leisured and congenial life. He wrote the book *The History of The World* (1614). Ultimately, the political current flowed against him more forcefully and he was executed.

The Ravens

After the Great Fire of 1666, ravens took to roosting in the Tower of

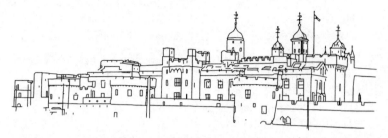

London. John Flamsteed the Astronomer Royal complained to King Charles II that the birds were interfering with the observations that he was seeking to make from the White Tower. The king ordered that they should be destroyed. However, he was informed of a prophecy that such an action would lead to the end of royalty in England. Therefore, he instructed that six of the corvids should be spared. An instance of science giving way - in part - to superstition. Ever since then a few of the birds have been kept in the Tower by a ravenmaster. They are let out every morning and called in every evening. It must be a pleasant life since some of them have lived to be several decades old.

At the end of the Second World War there was only one raven left at the fortress-prison. The others were believed to have been driven away by the aerial bombing.

In 1981 Grog escaped from the Tower. Subsequently, he was discovered outside *The Rose & Punchbowl*, an East End pub.

Despite their often brazen behaviour, ravens appear at heart to be bashful creatures. When the Tower wishes that the birds should mate it sends them to a zoo in Colwyn Bay, North Wales.

There is a graveyard for the corvids. It is located close to the principal entrance of the filled in moat.[1]

Location: *The Rose & Punchbowl*, No. 7 Redmans Road, E1 3AQ.

Reading: Boria Sax *City of Ravens* Gerald Duckworth (2011)

Websites: www.hrp.org.uk/TowerOfLondon stories/
theravens www.welshmountainzoo.org

Richard III

Thomas More's *The History of King Richard III* (*c*.1513) manuscript sought to blacken the monarch's reputation. The text attributed the dispatch of the young princes to the sovereign. Shakespeare perpetuated the view by crafting a vehicle for the actor Richard Burbage. The Bard's monarch was a sinister comic character.

[1]   Rob Humphreys *The Rough Guide To London* Rough Guides (2008) 234

See Also: WESTMINSTER ABBEY Royal Graves, Royal Graves Elsewhere

Website: www.richardiii.net (The Richard III Society)

A Butt of Malmsey: In 1478 the royal prince the Duke of Clarence is supposed to have been drowned in a butt of malmsey wine[1] in the Bowyer Tower. The murder may have been ordered by his grace's brother the Duke of Gloucester (later King Richard III).

Location: The Bowyer Tower

Website: www.hrp.org.uk/TowerOfLondon/Sightsand stories/Prisoners/Towers/BowyerTower

The Princes In The Tower: King Edward V and his brother Richard Duke of York were the young sons of King Edward IV. Their uncle King Richard III had them declared to be illegitimate by an Act of Parliament. There are records of their being alive up until the summer of 1483. Thereafter, nothing is known of them. It is assumed that their uncle had them murdered in order that they should never be able to challenge his possession of the throne. Two years later Richard's reign was ended when he was defeated by Henry Tudor (King Henry VII) at the Battle of Bosworth.

Renovation work was carried out on the fabric of the White Tower in 1674. During this, the skeletons of two children were discovered. King Charles II commanded that these remains should be buried in Westminster Abbey.

Location: The White Tower.

Website: www.hrp.org.uk/learninganddiscovery/Discover thehistoricpalaces/Prisoners/Theprinces

The Royal Armouries

The Royal Armouries is a collection of weapons and armour. It has been open to the public since the reign of King Charles II (*d*.1685).

See Also: MUSEUMS The Imperial War Museum

Website: www.royalarmouries.org/visit-us/tower-of-london

The Star Chamber

The Star Chamber Court acted without a jury. The body had the legal right to use torture. In a political concession that King Charles I (*d*.1649) made prior to the outbreak of the Civil Wars it was abolished.

'Star Chamber' has remained a term that is popularly applied to public bodies that are held to be behaving in an arbitrary way and that

---

[1]   Supposedly a rather good Malvasia from the east of Morea.

are regarded as being insufficiently accountable.

See Also: PUBS The Board of The Green Cloth

Website: www.hrp.org.uk/TowerOfLondon/stories/palace highlights/torture

The Tradition of Torture: The British are given to congratulating themselves upon the 'fact' that their armed services do not use torture. This has not always been the case. Within specialist sections of the Army there has existed a technical knowledge of how to utilise the practice in the conduct of interrogations.

In 1940, whilst the Second World War was being fought, the Army's Intelligence Corps established the Combined Services Detailed Interrogation Centre. The facility became known as the London Cage. Within it, torture was sometimes used on German officers. Following the return of peace the unit continued to operate. Its ostensible purpose was the investigation of war crimes. It functioned as part of a network that existed across Europe and North Africa. It was closed down in 1948.

Location: No. 8 Kensington Palace Gardens, W8 4QP. The site of the London Cage. The original building has been demolished.

Reading: Ian Cobain *Cruel Britannia: A Secret History of Torture* Portobello Books (2013).

Calder Walton *Empire of Secrets* Collins (2014). An account of how torture was used to extract intelligence in the immediate post-1945 era.

Tower Green

On Tower Green there is a board that has six names inscribed upon it. They are those of the people who were given the 'privilege' of being executed in this semi-private place rather than out on Tower Hill in front of a crowd. The sestet included two of King Henry VIII's (*d*.1547) six wives - Anne Boleyn and Catherine Howard.

Website: www.hrp.org.uk/TowerOfLondon/stories/tower green

The Western Gateway

In 1239 King Henry III commissioned the construction of a gateway on the Tower's western side. The monarch's intention was to impress the City of London. The structure collapsed the following year. It was rebuilt but fell down again in 1241. The collapses were attributed to the vengeful ghost of St Thomas à Becket (*d*. 1170). There was no further attempt to rebuild the section of wall as a portal. With the passage of time, its exact location was forgotten. That it had existed was known only through a reference to it in a 13thC chronicle.

In 1995 it was announced that members of the Oxford Archaeological Unit had unearthed the first physical evidence of the gateway.

Website: www.hrp.org.uk/TowerOfLondon/stories/ghosts

The White Tower

King William the Conqueror (*d*. 1087) commissioned the construction of the White Tower. It was the largest fortress to have been built in England since the time of the Romans. It had stone walls (the Anglo-Saxons had employed timber whenever they had erected fortified buildings).[1] The stronghold would have appeared particularly solid to Londoners because its wooden pitched roof was not visible from the ground. Therefore, it seemed to be much sturdier than it actually was.

Website: www.hrp.org.uk/TowerOfLondon/stories/White Tower

The Word

The password that is used within the Tower is issued by the Ministry of Defence. It is changed daily.

Yeoman Warders

The 35 Yeoman Warders are all former service personnel who have spent at least 22 years in the military and who have been awarded good conduct medals. They all live in the Tower. They are known as Beefeaters (which was a 17thC term for a well-fed domestic servant[2]).

In 2007 Moira Campbell became the first woman to be a Warder. She feminised her uniform by having pink braces. (These were not visible.)

(The ceremonial guards are serving soldiers. They are stationed in the Tower.)

Website: www.hrp.org.uk/TowerOfLondon/stories/yeoman warder

---

[1]   The Anglo-Saxons mostly used wood for religious buildings. However, upon occasion they did employ stone. The second St Paul's Cathedral, work on which started *c*.680, was probably built of stone.

[2]   Rob Humphreys *The Rough Guide To London* Rough Guides (2008) 232

°ENTRY TO THE TRAITORS GATE

THE TOWER OF LONDON   315

TRAFALGAR SQUARE

See Also: CHURCH OF ENGLAND CHURCHES St Martin-in-the-Fields; COLUMNS Nelson's Column; GALLERIES The National Gallery; ROYAL STATUES King Charles I, Charing Cross; ROYAL STATUES King George IV

Most of what is now Trafalgar Square was once occupied by the Royal Mews. This was a complex of buildings and yards that acted as the royal stables. The medieval structures had been created for keeping hunting birds in. Following a fire in 1534 the facility was expressly rebuilt to accommodate horses. A new main stable block (1732) was designed by William Kent.[1]

In the early 19[th]C the architect John Nash drew up the Charing Cross Improvement Scheme. This envisaged the square. It was part of his larger plan for beautifying the West End, which was centred upon the creation of Regent Street. In 1830 Kent's stable block and the rest of the Mews were demolished. Nash died before he could see his greater plan put into effect.

Location: Trafalgar Square, WC2N 5DS.

Website: www.london.gov.uk/priorities/arts-culture/trafalgar-square

The Centre of London

Were you to ask someone where the centre of London is, the person might well hesitate before giving you an answer. The response when it came would probably be 'Trafalgar Square'. The reason for the vacillation is that the City of London is decidedly older than the West End and that within the latter there are many sections that are older than Trafalgar Square, which is itself on the periphery of the area.

If the Square has a claim to being the centre of London it is one that it has purloined from its neighbour Charing Cross. This is the point from which mileage is measured from London to elsewhere in the country. Why this is so is uncertain. It has been claimed that the practice derived from the site being the mid-point between the royal court at Westminster and the western edge of the City.

See Also: ROMAN REMAINS The Leadenhall Basilica

---

[1]   On what was to become the site of the National Gallery.

The Fourth Plinth

The fourth plinth (1841) in the north-western corner of Trafalgar Square was intended to support an equestrian statue of King William IV. However, the effigy was not placed upon it and for over a century and a half the structure remained unburdened.

In 1996 the Royal Society for the Arts announced that over the following five years five sculptures would each spend twelve months upon the base. The Cass Sculpture Foundation supported the venture. In 1999 Mark Wallinger's *Ecce Homo* became the first work to be set upon the block. For the most part, the contemporary pieces that were mounted on it generated considerable comment. In 2003 the Greater London Council stated that Londoners would be allowed to select a new work of art for the plinth.

In 2005 responsibility for the square was transferred to the Mayor of London and the Greater London Authority.

See Also: STATUES

Websites: www.sculpture.org.uk (The Cass Sculpture Foundation) www.london.gov.uk/priorities/arts-culture/fourth-plinth

The National Gallery Passage

When William Wilkins designed the National Gallery (1838) he was required to incorporate a passage that would allow troops to be deployed in the Square at short notice from the barracks that were located behind the institution's west wing. During the 1840s Britain experienced a long economic depression. It is reputed that the space's fountains were added in 1845 in order to try to discourage mobs from assembling.

See Also: GALLERIES The National Gallery

Pigeons

Originally, pigeons were a species of coastal bird. With time, they extended their range inland. London's buildings provided them with a substitute for cliffs.

In 1996 it was reported that the police were investigating the mysterious disappearance of hundreds of pigeons from Trafalgar Square. A possible cause was a man whom passers-by had seen trapping the birds in baited boxes. It was speculated that he might have been selling their carcasses to chefs.

One theory forwarded at the time was that the warmth of the previous summer and autumn had led to a larger crop of berries and nuts than usual. This meant that wood pigeons were able to feed themselves in woodland. Therefore, they did not need to break cover to search for sustenance in fields. *Ergo*, they were less likely to be shot. This had created a rise in the price that restaurants were prepared to pay for pigeon meat, and thus an incentive for a spot of urban poaching.

A £50 fine for feeding pigeons in Trafalgar Square came into force in 2003. Subsequently, the number of the birds in the Square was estimated to have declined from 4000 to 200.

See Also: SQUIRRELS; WEATHER

Trafalgar Square Police Station

In the post-First World War era Britain was fraught by socio-political tensions. A temporary police box was erected by one of the entrances to Charing Cross Underground Station. When the Metropolitan Police proposed making the structure permanent there was a public outcry. Therefore, the force created a more discreet alternative facility on the Column-side of the road by having builders hollow out an ornamental lighting structure that had been built in the Square's south-eastern corner a century before.

The Trafalgar Square Police Station (1926) was the smallest police station in Britain. In an era before CCTV, the structure's principal purpose was to enable Scotland Yard to know what was going on within the Square. The facility had a direct telephone line to the Yard that enabled information to be reported there directly.

The Station is no longer used by the police.

See Also: THE POLICE

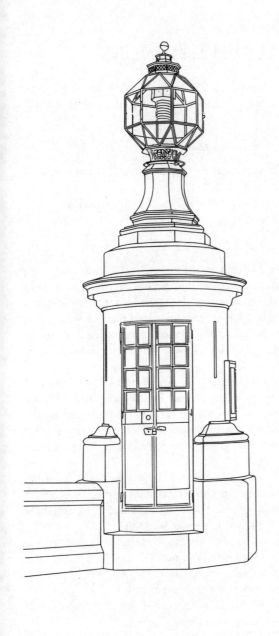

VISITOR ATTRACTIONS

See Also: THE OLYMPICS The 2012 London Olympics, The Orbit
Website: www.alva.org.uk (The Association of Leading Visitor Attractions)

The London Dungeon

The London Dungeon is a visitor attraction that appeals to some people's ghoulish natures.

Location: County Hall, Westminster Bridge Road, SE1 7PB.
Website: www.thedungeons.com/london/en

The London Eye

Julia Barfield and Davis Marks met one another while they both were students at the Architectural Association School of Architecture. In 1981 the pair married. By making models of possible buildings for practices such as that of Richard Rogers they advanced their understanding of the processes that are involved in large construction projects. In the late 1980s the couple started to submit their own entries to high-profile architectural competitions.

Barfield and Marks conceived of a giant Ferris wheel being part of the proposed Millennium celebrations. In 1994 they had a chance meeting with Bob Ayling, who was then the Chief Executive of British Airways. Six months later the airline provided £600,000 of finance that enabled the Millennium Wheel project to change from being an idea into existing as an undertaking.

In December 1999 it was reported that tickets for the London Eye were selling faster than those for the Millennium Dome. In February 2000 the Eye opened. In August that year Lambeth Council granted the structure a licence that allowed it to host weddings.

In June 2008 the London Eye had its 30,000,000th visitor. At the time, the attraction's lease was due to run until 2025.

Locations: The South Bank, Upper Ground, SE1 7PB. To the north of the eastern (southern) end of Westminster Bridge.

The Architectural Association School of Architecture, No. 36 Bedford Square, WC1B 3ES. On the western side.

See Also: COLUMNS The Monument

Websites: www.londoneye.com www.marksbarfield.com www.
aaschool.ac.uk

Madame Tussaud's

Anna Maria Grosholtz's mother became the housekeeper of Dr Curtius, a Swiss physician who was skilled at making wax models of body organs. The doctor identified in the girl a talent that was a nascent version of his own. He trained her in ceraceous modelling. In 1766 Curtius and his household moved to Paris. There, he established himself as a waxworks showman. For a time, Anna Maria lived at Versailles. During the French Revolution her head was shaved in preparation for her being guillotined. She was reprieved. In 1794 the physician died. He bequeathed his collection to Anna Maria. The following year she married a *Monsieur* Tussaud.

In 1806 *Madame* Tussaud started to tour England with her exhibits. 27 years later she settled her business in London. She identified and exploited the Early Victorian public's desire for 'rational recreation' rather than just mere entertainment. Charles Dickens found that he was unable to accept the cultural pretensions that she sought to claim for her attractions. In his novel *The Old Curiosity Shop* (1841), he used the character of Mrs Jarley to attack her flexible approach towards the truth. *Punch* magazine derided her Adjoining Room as 'The Chamber of Horrors'. The disparagement was first embraced by the business and then flaunted by it.

The Tussaud family owned the waxworks until 1967.

Location: Marylebone Road, NW1 5HT. On the eastern side of the junction with Allsop Place.

Website: www.madametussauds.com/London

THE WEATHER

See Also: TRAFALGAR SQUARE Pigeons

Barometers

Alexander Cumming was a maker of watches and scientific instruments. His business acquired premises on New Bond Street. In 1763 the Scot was invited to become a member of the Board of Longitude. The body adjudicated upon John Harrison's marine chronometer. It concluded that a second instrument should be made in order to prove that the carpenter had disclosed all of the techniques that he had used when he had made the first.

Cumming developed an interest in air pressure. He was aware of the ideas that the scientist Robert Hooke had had for a barometer. In 1765 the watchmaker presented King George III with what is believed to have been the first working recorder barograph. The following year, he built a refined version. He kept this in his own possession. After his death, it was bought by Luke Howard. The wholesale pharmacist used data derived from it as a basis for his book *The Climate of London* (1820).

Blue Skies

There is something deeply human about wondering why the unclouded portions of a daytime sky are blue. The tradition of trying to ascertain the reason for the phenomenon dates back to at least the Aristotelian treatise *On Colours*. The people who have examined the question have included: Roger Bacon, Leonardo da Vinci, Johannes Kepler, René Descartes, Sir Isaac Newton, Leonhard Euler, and Horace-Benedict de Saussure.

John Tyndall held the Professorship of Natural Philosophy at The Royal Institution. In 1859 he announced the Tyndall Effect. This describes how a light beam that is shone into a clear fluid is scattered by the particles of matter that it encounters in its path. A dozen years later the aristocrat and physicist John Strutt published two papers that were entitled *On The Light From The Sky, Its Polarisation and Colour* and *On The Scattering of Light By Small Particles*. These addressed the matter in greater detail and furnished a mathematical description for the atmospherical occurrence. The non-blue portions of the spectrum have longer wavelengths than the blue ones possess. Therefore, the former are able to pass through the gas molecules that are present in the ether. Whereas, the latter strike these and are reflected by them (in the Rayleigh Scattering) thereby creating the impression that the sky is blue.

Strutt's work utilised the accepted elastic solid theory of light. It did not draw upon the ideas that James Clerk Maxwell was propounding. However, the former's line of argument did not prevent the latter from regarding the man's ideas as being substantive. In 1873 Maxwell wrote to the now 3rd Baron Rayleigh, who by then had inherited his family title, to urge him to investigate the problem further. Intermittently, the peer spent time addressing it.

Rayleigh published a polished version of his theory in 1899 in an article that he entitled *On The Transmission of Light Through An Atmosphere Containing Small Particles In Suspension, and On The Origin of The Blue of The Sky*. In it, he maintained his erroneous opinion that the blue light was striking water vapour and dust in the atmosphere. The paper did not resolve every aspect of the subject. Albert Einstein became interested in the topic. He drew upon the work of the Polish physicist Marian Smoluchowski and in 1911 published a piece that explained those aspects of it that the baron had not settled. The Bavarian contended that the azure derived from the blue light's interaction with oxygen and nitrogen.

Locations: No. 4 Carlton Gardens, SW1Y 5AD. The Conservative politician Arthur Balfour was the leaseholder. He and Rayleigh had become close friends while they had both been students at the University of Cambridge. The scientist had married the future premier's younger sister Evelyn. Britain experienced a sustained agricultural depression at the end of the 19thC. This caused the baron's family finances to be (relatively) straitened. Therefore, he and his wife were the houseguests of her sib whenever they spent time in London during the period 1878 to 1897.

The Royal Institution, No. 21 Albemarle Street, W1S 4BS.

Websites: www.phy.cam.ac.uk (Rayleigh's financial circumstances caused him to hold the University of Cambridge's Cavendish chair of physics from 1879 to 1884. Maxwell had preceded him in the position) www.rigb.org www.ri.ac.uk (The Royal Institution)

Clouds

In the early summer of 1783 both the Asama volcano in Japan and the Laki volcanic fissure in Iceland erupted. As a result, the skies of the Northern Hemisphere became hazy and the sunsets had a coppery colour. The ten-year-old Luke Howard was struck by these phenomena.[1]

[1]   The painter Howard Hodgkin was a kinsman of Luke Howard and was

In 1796 he and his fellow Quaker William Allen became members of the Askesian Society, a philosophical group. Two years later the pair joined the Plough Court Pharmacy in Lombard Street.[1] In 1801 Howard started to maintain a systematic record of his meteorological observations. During the winter of 1802-3 he presented to the Society a paper on cloud formation. This almost certainly drew upon the Linnaean taxonomic system. In 1803 the material was published as *On The Modifications of Clouds*. This set out the three principal categories: *cirrus* (the Latin for 'a lock of hair'), *cumulus* ('a pile'), and *stratus* ('a layer'). In addition, there were also intermediate classifications and compound modifications.

Allen and Howard dissolved their business partnership in 1805. The latter moved to Stratford Mills in East London where he established a wholesale pharmaceuticals business as well as supplying chemicals to industry. His customers included the scientist John Dalton.

Howard's *The Climate of London* (1820) was the first study of the city's weather. He used the work to expound innovative ideas on subjects such as how rain is triggered and what the nature of atmospheric electricity is. The two-volume work changed the way in which clouds were represented in art. There is a high degree of probability that the painter John Constable's skyscapes soon came to be informed by *Climate*.

Locations: Chesterton House, Balaam Street, Plaistow, E13 8(AF). Howard's home. The building was demolished in 1960.

Plough Court, EC3V 9(BQ).

The Cloud Factory: London's clouds are made principally at Didcot Power Station in Oxfordshire. The fact became known to the general public after the poet Roger McGough overheard a small child refer to 'the cloud factory' during a railway journey.

The coal-powered facility is due to be closed in 2015. It is hoped that alternative arrangements for *cumulus* production will have been put in place by then.

Deadly and Anonymous

In early 1258 a volcano erupted on a scale that disrupted the world's weather patterns. The sulphurous gases that have been recovered from ice cores indicate that the explosion was eight times as large as that of named after him.

[1] The Plough Court Pharmacy had been founded in 1715 by Silvanus Bevan. Under the control of the Hanbury family, the firm evolved into Allen & Hanbury. This business was bought by Glaxo Laboratories in 1958. Glaxo became part of GSK. (*Reading*: Desmond Chapman & Ernest C. Cripps *Through A City Archway: The Story of Allen & Hanburys, 1715-1954* John Murray (1954).)

Krakatoa in 1883. 1258's harvests in Britain were minimal. A famine ensued. It has been calculated that about 15,000 Londoners died as a result. At the time, this represented almost a third of the city's population.

Geological science has as yet been unable to establish which volcano erupted. There are several candidates.

Location: Old Spitalfields Market, No. 105a Commercial Street, Spitalfields, E1 6BG. The market was built in part above the site of a mass burial pit of people who died in 1258.

See Also: HORROR FICTION Frankenstein

Fog

A Matter of Perspective: There is a story that upon one occasion a dense bank of fog settled across the English Channel. As a result, all of the ferry sailings to Europe were cancelled. One newspaper is reputed to have reported this development under the headline *Heavy Fog Strands Continent*.

The Ponging Banks: The banks of the Thames used to have numerous commercial wharves along them. Many of these specialised in particular varieties of goods. It has been claimed that when heavy fogs occurred in London, lightermen, who were out on the river and who could not see its sides, were able to ascertain their whereabouts by the smells that emanated from the landing stages.

See Also: THE THAMES Wharves

Lightning

The medieval Church of St Bride's Fleet Street was destroyed by the Great Fire of 1666. The present Sir Christopher Wren-designed building had the tallest steeple of any of his churches. In 1764 it was struck by lightning. Subsequently, it was generally agreed that a lightning conductor should be mounted upon the structure. However, what shape the rod's heavenward prong should be became a matter of public dispute. King George III favoured a blunt one, whereas Benjamin Franklin felt that a sharp one would be more apposite.

Location: St Bride's Passage, EC4Y 8AU. At the eastern end.

See Also: CHURCH OF ENGLAND CHURCHES St Bride's Church
Website: www.stbrides.com

Umbrellas

See Also: PARLIAMENT The Lords, Umbrellas

Jonas Hanway: Jonas Hanway worked as a Russia merchant. He spent much of the 1740s living in St Petersburg. During these years he made a journey to Persia in order to assess whether it might be worth developing an overland trade with the country. He concluded that one would not be economically viable. He noticed that the Persians used parasols to shield themselves from the Sun's rays. He appreciated that the accoutrement might be adapted to screen his person from falling rain. Thus, the umbrella came to be.

Hanway returned to London in 1750. His use of the device made him a singular figure. His eccentricity was compounded by the way in which he chose to walk about London with a sword dangling from his hip. The weapons were no longer sported in everyday life. His first book, *An Historical Account of The British Trade Over The Caspian Sea*, was published in 1753.

The returnee was interested in a wide range of issues. He wrote a variety of works that set out his beliefs and opinions. He was an advocate of the health-giving properties of wearing flannel underwear. Although he was widely regarded as being a bore, his actions proved to be able upon occasion to deliver practical solutions to contemporary problems. He was responsible for sauerkraut being issued to sailors during the American War of Independence as a means of trying to keep scurvy at bay.

Location: No. 23 Red Lion Square, WC1R 4SE. Kingsway Mansions stands on the site of Hanway's home.

See Also: TEA An *Essay* Too Far

Website: www.marine-society.org (Hanway founded The Marine Society in 1756.)

James Smith & Sons: James Smith & Sons is an umbrella and sticks retailing and repairing business. The firm was founded in 1830. It has had premises on New Oxford Street since 1857.

There is a story that upon one occasion a person was buying an umbrella in the shop. The sales assistant opened and closed it in order to ensure that it was in proper working condition. The customer commented, 'Isn't that unlucky?' 'Not with *our* umbrellas, sir', came the reply.

Location: Hazlewood House, No. 53 New Oxford Street, WC1A 1BL. On the south-eastern corner of the junction with Bloomsbury Street.

Website: www.james-smith.co.uk

Wind

See Also: BELLS Bow Bells; BELLS The Whitechapel Bell Foundry

The Protestant Wind: In 1685 King Charles II's younger brother James Duke of York acceded to the throne as James II. The new sovereign's elder daughter Princess Mary became his heir-apparent, she being his first-born daughter by his first wife Anne (*d*.1679). The political situation in Britain was tense because of the new monarch's wish to extend religious toleration so as to benefit his fellow Roman Catholics. Many Anglicans looked upon his actions with concern. They thought that they heralded the dawn of an era in which the Crown would try to compel the people of England to convert to Roman Catholicism, as had been the case during the reign of Queen Mary I.

James's second wife, Mary of Modena, became pregnant. This meant that Princess Mary, who was a devout Anglican, might not be her father's successor. This gave her husband Prince William of Orange an incentive to actively intervene in English politics. The monarch is reputed to have had a weathercock placed upon the northern end of the Banqueting House so that he could know when the wind was favourable for his son-in-law to set sail from The Netherlands.

In June 1688 Mary of Modena gave birth to a son. Five months later William invaded England - sailing with the 'Protestant Wind'. James put up a brief military resistance and then fled from the realm. The Dutchman became King William III and his wife Queen Mary II. There followed: the Bill of Rights, the passage of frequent short-term Mutiny Acts, the Triennial Act of 1694, and the birth of modern Parliamentary democracy.

Location: The Banqueting House, Whitehall, SW1A 2ER. On the southern side of the junction with Horse Guards Avenue. On the eastern side, to the south of the junction with Horseguards Avenue.

See Also: THE GUNPOWDER PLOT The Celebration of 5 November; HALLS The Banqueting House; PALACES Kensington Palace; PALACES, DISAPPEARED & FORMER Whitehall Palace; STATUES The National Gallery Statues

WESTMINSTER ABBEY

See Also: CHURCH OF ENGLAND CHURCHES; CHURCH OF ENGLAND CHURCHES St Margaret's Westminster; CORONATIONS; ST PAUL'S CATHEDRAL

Thorney Island was an isolated eyot that was bordered by the Thames, Tyburn Brook, and a marsh. Upon it, King Edward the Confessor founded Westminster Abbey as a Benedictine institution. The building was consecrated in 1065.

During the Reformation the monastery was dissolved. However, the complex's regal associations enabled it to metamorphose into being the Collegiate Church of St Peter, a royal peculiar.[1] As such, it operates under the jurisdiction of a dean and chapter and is subject only to the sovereign. Some of its revenues were transferred to St Paul's Cathedral (hence the phrase 'to rob Peter to pay Paul').

The towers at the building's western end were late additions (1739). They were designed by Nicholas Hawksmoor.

Location: The Sanctuary, SW1P 3PA.

Website: www.westminster-abbey.org

The Chapter House

During the reign of King Edward III (*d.*1377) the House of Commons and the House of Lords acquired distinct characters from one another. The Lower Chamber took to holding its meetings in the Abbey's Chapter House. In 1547 the body moved to St Stephen's Chapel in the Palace of Westminster.

From *c.*1550 until 1865 the Chapter House served as a state archive.

See Also: PARLIAMENT The Commons

Memorials and Graves

That a person is commemorated in Westminster Abbey by a memorial does not mean that her/his corpse has been interred there. The historic social standing of a number of professions can be gauged by when the Abbey started to honour their foremost members or t o receive their

---

[1] During the Reformation the materials from which numerous religious buildings had been constructed were cannibalised. The Abbey could easily have disappeared through this fate.

WESTMINSTER ABBEY

corporal remains.

See Also: MEMORIALS; ST PAUL'S CATHEDRAL Monuments

Doctors: Medicine was not held in any particular social regard until the mid-19[th]C. Originally, the corpse of the anatomist John Hunter (*d*.1793) was buried in the Church of St Martin-in-the-Fields.

Britain's cities were struck by a series of epidemics. These led to burial grounds and church crypts having corpses placed in them at a rate that was far higher than would have been the case otherwise. The General Board of Health sponsored the passage of the Public Health Bill of 1858 into law. The measure required either that public crypts should be sealed or that they should be emptied.

Hunter had been associated with St George's Hospital. Dr Frank Buckland had trained there. In 1859 the latter realised that the measure furnished an opportunity for the anatomist's corpse to be re-interred in Westminster Abbey, of which his own father, William Buckland, was then the dean. The process of identifying the man's coffin, among the many thousands that had been placed in St Martin's crypt, took almost a month.[1]

Locations: The Lanesborough, Hyde Park Corner, SW1X 7TA. (Formerly, the building housed St George's Hospital.)

The Church of St Martin-in-Fields, St Martin's Place, WC2N 4JJ.

See Also: CHURCH OF ENGLAND CHURCHES St Martin-in-the-Fields; CLASS

Engineers: In the northern aisle of the Abbey's nave is Engineers' Corner. Located there are memorials to the likes of John Smeaton (*d*.1792), James Watt, Thomas Telford, George Stephenson, his son Robert, and Isambard Kingdom Brunel (*d*.1859).

The Percies: The Percy Dukes of Northumberland are the only family who have the right of sepulture in the Abbey. Their vault is located below the Chapel of St Nicholas.

Poet's Corner: Geoffrey Chaucer (*d*.1400) spent his working life as a royal official. As a consequence, his corpse was buried by the eastern wall of the southern transept of the Abbey. In 1599 the poet Edmund Spenser's (*d*.1599) body was lain nearby. This helped to establish a tradition whereby writers were commemorated in that portion of the building or their remains were interred there. It became known as Poet's Corner. The literary figures who have been honoured there have included: John

---

[1]   Another sign of the social rise of medicine was the ennoblement in 1887 of Joseph Lister, the pioneer of antiseptic surgery.

Dryden (*d*.1700), John Gay (*d*.1732), Dr Samuel Johnson (*d*.1784), Richard Brinsley Sheridan (*d*.1816), Thomas Macaulay (*d*.1859), Charles Dickens (*d*.1870), Robert Browning (*d*.1889), Alfred Lord Tennyson (*d*.1892), Thomas Hardy (*d*.1928), and Rudyard Kipling (*d*.1936).

A prolonged delay between a writer's death and her/his receiving a memorial in the Corner was often the result of an unconventional private life casting, to the eye of the whoever might be the current Dean of Westminster, a shadow over the party's candidacy. With time, the author's work tended to be remembered more than her/his conduct and so the individual's literary reputation was commemorated if not necessarily her/his person. The monument to Shakespeare in Westminster Abbey was not erected until 1740, over 120 years after the dramatist-poet's death. (It might be that successive deans may have been privy to something about him that the rest of us have not. However, it may have derived from the fact that the Bard's reputation is something that has grown over time. Until well into the 18^{th}C Ben Jonson was regarded as being a more important playwright than Shakespeare was.)

A number of people who were not literary figures have also been buried in the Corner: Tom 'Old' Parr (*c*.1483-1635), the composer George Frederic Handel (*d*.1759), and the actors David Garrick (*d*.1779) and Laurence Olivier (*d*.1989).

Ben Jonson: The playwright Ben Jonson (*d*.1637) lived in the residential part of Westminster Abbey's precincts, and was buried in the building. He had declared that "Six feet by two feet wide is too much for me; two feet by two will do for all I want." Dean Williams obliged him by having his corpse interred standing upright.

Soldiers: Interred in the Abbey are the corpses of a number of soldiers who furnished royal dynasties with services. In 1660 George Monck overthrew the English Republic and restored the Stuart monarchy. A decade later the ennobled 1st Duke of Albemarle was the recipient of what can be deemed to have been the first modern state funeral. He has a grand tomb in the southern aisle of the Chapel of Henry VII. Underneath him are buried King Charles II (*d*.1685), Queen Mary II (*d*.1694), King William III (*d*.1702), Queen Anne (*d*.1714), and Prince George of Denmark (*d*.1708). They were all indebted to the duke for his actions. In contrast to the interment of the peer's body, the laying to rest of Charles II's corpse in 1685 was a low-key, night-time affair.

The presence of the corpse of Field Marshal George Wade (*d*.1748) is accounted for by the role that he played in suppressing the Jacobite Rebellion of 1745. Thereby, 'Grandmother' helped to preserve the

Hanoverian dynasty being overthrown by the Young Pretender.[1]

The Unknown Warrior: The Unknown Warrior was buried in Westminster Abbey on Armistice Day 1920.

> *See Also*: MEMORIALS The Cenotaph
> *Website*: www.kesr.org.uk (The Kent & East Sussex Railway)

A Known Warrior: Private John Thomson had been killed in 1917 during the Battle of Passchendale. The soldier's remains were unearthed at Molenaarelst in Belgium in 1998. Five years later it was reported that, at the start of the year, the Ministry of Defence's Casualty & Compassionate Unit had succeeded in identifying Agnes Spence, a resident of Kirkcudbrightshire, as being his niece. She and other relatives attended a reburial in Flanders that took place with full military honours.

The private's body was one of only two corpses to have been identified during the previous 25 years from the hundreds that had been recovered in the region. This was because the soil in which their remains were found was a wet clay, whereas in France it tended to be drier chalky ground, which meant that more collateral material survived. This could be utilised to identify associated human remains.

Royal Graves

King Edward the Confessor (*d*.1066) was the last of the Anglo-Saxon kings. In 1161 he was canonised.[2] King Henry III (*d*.1272) desired that his predecessor's remains should have a resting place that was commensurate with his predecessor's hagied status. Therefore, Westminster Abbey underwent extensive reshaping. From 1269 until 1760 royals were buried in the aggrandised building.

The Chapel of Henry VII was started by the Tudor king to commemorate his Lancastrian predecessor King Henry VI (*d*.1471).[3] This was a way of indicating the new dynasty's legitimate succession to both branches of the House of Plantagenet as the monarchs of England. When work on the Chapel was completed during the reign of King Henry VIII, the son chose to dedicate the structure to his father.

---

[1]   The Young Pretender was a member of Stuart dynasty. His grandfather, King James II, had opted to flee Britain during the Revolution of 1688.

[2]   On St Edward's Day (13th October), Roman Catholic pilgrims visit the shrine of St Edward the Confessor.

[3]   In large part, it was King Henry VI's political incompetence that had allowed the Wars of the Roses, an extremely bloody, 30-year-long succession of civil wars, to start in 1455. However, it was universally acknowledged that he had been very pious.

See Also: MEMORIALS Charing Cross; ROYALTY

Royal Graves Elsewhere: What was the London Post Office in King Edward Street in the City of London is built over the burial site of the corpses of both Queen Margaret (*d*.1312), the consort of King Edward I, and Queen Isabella (*d*.1358), the wife of King Edward II.

The kings who were buried in Old St Paul's Cathedral in London included King Aethelred the Unready (*d*.1016). The bodies of a number of monarchs lie below the Choir of Winchester Cathedral.

The remains of other royals are buried in France and St George's Chapel, Windsor Castle.

In 2014 King Richard III's skeleton was dug up. It had been lying beneath a car park in Leicester.

See Also: THE TOWER OF LONDON King Richard III

Websites: www.le.ac.uk/richardiii www.silverboar.org (The Society of Friends of King Richard III)

ZOOS

See Also: MUSEUMS The Natural History Museum

ZSL

LONDON ZOO

London Zoo

While serving as a colonial governor in Asia for the East India Company, Sir Stamford Raffles built up a menagerie. His favourite evening repast was champagne and mangoes. These he would share with his pet sun bear. Upon his return to London, he tried to bring over his animals. However, the vessel that was transporting them was shipwrecked.

The Zoological Society of London was founded in 1826 by Raffles and the scientist Sir Humphry Davy. In part, their action was prompted as a 'British' response to the recent establishment of the Museum of Natural History in Paris. The following year Decimus Burton laid out the Zoological Gardens in Regent's Park. The architect drew up a plan for the zoo as a whole but only portions of it were ever to be constructed. In 1829 the Society received its royal charter.

The zoo contains a number of structures that have been listed, *e.g.* Berthold Lubetkin's Penguin Pool (1935). Its distinctive Snowdon Aviary (1964) was designed by the architect Cedric Price, the structural engineer Frank Newby, and the royal spouse Lord Snowdon.

From 1955 until his 1984 resignation as President, Professor Solly

Zuckerman was the most influential figure within London Zoo. The South African was skilled at drumming up donations - the Clore Pavilion for Small Animals was paid for by the deal maker Sir Charles Clore, the Cotton Terraces (and the Snowdon Aviary) by the property developer Jack Cotton, and the Sobell Pavillions for Apes & Monkeys by the electrical goods manufacturer Sir Michael Sobell. In addition, Zuckerman, through his being an academic physiologist, was able to persuade charities that had interest in medical research - such as the Nuffield and the Wellcome - to fund less public but necessary support facilities.

Location: Regent's Park, NW1 4RY.

See Also: EXHIBITING GALLERIES The Hayward, Archigram

Website: www.zsl.org

The Royal Menagerie

Exotic animals were one of the standard coins of diplomatic exchange during the late medieval period. As a result, London has had displays of non-native species since at least the 13thC. The city's first zoo was the royal menagerie. This was housed within the walls of the Tower of London.

King James I (*d*.1625), during the early years of his reign, was given to staging fights between different animals in the menagerie. However, during one of these combats, a child was killed by one of the beasts. The monarch stopped holding the contests.[1]

In 1830 the Windsor Castle section of the Royal Menagerie was transferred to the care of the Zoological Society of London. The portion that was kept in the Tower followed it four years later.

Location: The Tower of London, EC3N 4AB.

See Also: THE TOWER OF LONDON

Website: www.hrp.org.uk/TowerOfLondon/Stories/ Palacehighlights/RoyalBeasts

---

[1]   Rob Humphreys *The Rough Guide To London* Rough Guides (2008) 234

GALLERIES, PALACES & TEA

MAPS

For a PDF of additional maps
e-mail **londonguidebook@gmail.com**

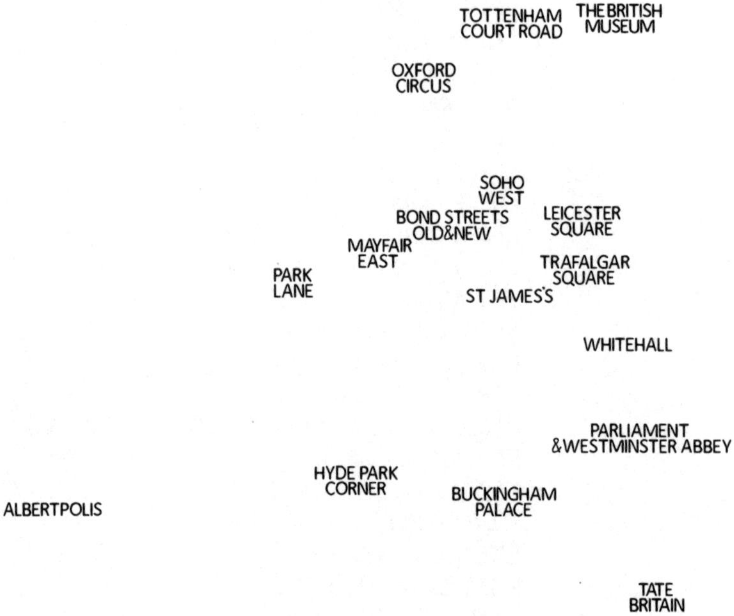

TOTTENHAM THE BRITISH
COURT ROAD MUSEUM

OXFORD
CIRCUS

SOHO
WEST
BOND STREETS LEICESTER
OLD&NEW SQUARE
MAYFAIR
EAST
TRAFALGAR
PARK SQUARE
LANE ST JAMES'S

WHITEHALL

PARLIAMENT
&WESTMINSTER ABBEY

HYDE PARK
CORNER BUCKINGHAM
PALACE

ALBERTPOLIS

TATE
BRITAIN

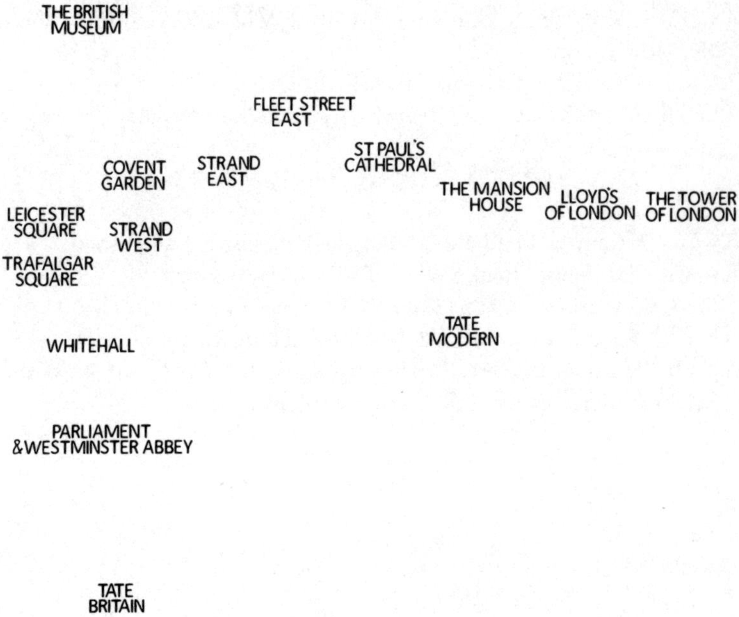

THE BRITISH
MUSEUM

FLEET STREET
EAST

ST PAUL'S
CATHEDRAL

COVENT   STRAND
GARDEN   EAST

THE MANSION   LLOYD'S   THE TOWER
HOUSE   OF LONDON   OF LONDON

LEICESTER
SQUARE   STRAND
WEST

TRAFALGAR
SQUARE

TATE
MODERN

WHITEHALL

PARLIAMENT
& WESTMINSTER ABBEY

TATE
BRITAIN

7.s, E.p - Cromwell Gardens, SW7 2RL: MUSEUMS The Victoria & Albert Museum

5.v, E.o - Cromwell Road, SW7 5BD: MUSEUMS The Natural History Museum

6.w, F.u - Exhibition Road, SW7 2DD: MUSEUMS The Science Museum

7.j, E.x - Exhibition Road, SW7 2(DD): MUSEUMS Umbrella Bodies, The Exhibition Road Cultural Group; STREET FURNITURE Signage

1.p, J.p - Gloucester Road, SW7 4(SS): TAXIS Cabmen's Shelters

2.r, I.l - Hyde Park Gate, (27&28) SW7 5DJ: WINSTON CHURCHILL

4.x, K.j - Kensington Gardens, W8 4PX: MEMORIALS The Albert Memorial

3.f, K.e - Kensington Gardens, W8 4(PX): SQUIRRELS

3.m, J.h - Queen's Gate, SW7 5(EH): STATUES Lord Napier

LONDON STORIES, LONDON LIVES

5.v, E.o - Cromwell Road, SW7 5BD: The Vanquisher Vanquished

6.w, F.u - Exhibition Road, SW7 2DD: Dollis Hill's Finest

7.m, A.m - Onslow Square, (38) SW7 3NS: Fitzroy

5.k, C.e - Reece Mews, (7) SW7 3HE: The Colony Room

5.e, J.b - Kensington Gore, The Royal Albert Hall, SW7 2AP: A Soufflé Celebrity of Substance; The Prussian Professor

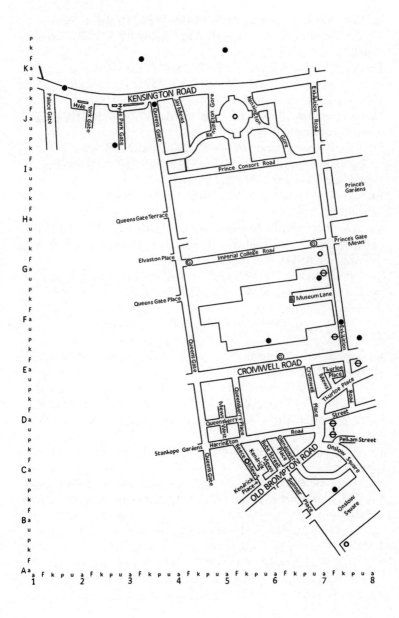

KENSINGTON ROAD

Palace Gate
Hyde Park Gate
Hyde Park Gate
Queens Gate
Jay Mews
Kensington Gore
Kensington Gore

Exhibition Road

Prince Consort Road

Prince's Gardens

Queens Gate Terrace

Prince's Gate Mews

Elvaston Place
Imperial College Road

Queens Gate Place

Queens Gate

Museum Lane

Exhibition Road

CROMWELL ROAD

Thurloe Place
Cromwell Mews
Thurloe Place
Thurloe Street
Thurloe Road

Queensberry Place
Queensberry Mews West
Cromwell Place

Road
Pelham Street

Stanhope Gardens
Harrington Road
Reece Mews
Kenrick Place
Bute Street
High
Glendower Place
Summer Place
Onslow Square

OLD BROMPTON ROAD

Onslow Square

Queens Gate

K
J
I
H
G
F
E
D
C
B
A
p k
f a u

1   2   3   4   5   6   7   8

3.x, D.h - Albemarle Street, (21) W1S 4BS: WEATHER Blue Skies

3.k, E.g - Bruton Street, (1) W1J 6TL: CARNABY STREET Swinging London

4.b, D.o - New Bond Street, W1S 2(JY): SHOPPING New Bond Street

3.j, E.w - New Bond Street, (26) W1S 2JY: PERIOD PROPERTIES New Bond Street, Lucie Campbell

3.h, F.a - New Bond Street, (34-35) W1A 2AA: WINSTON CHURCHILL French Trousers

1.t, G.r - New Bond Street, (103) W1Y 6LG: COLUMNS Nelson's Column

3.e, E.p - New Bond Street, (143) W1S 2TP: PERIOD PROPERTIES New Bond Street, No. 143 New Bond Street

4.x, C.q - Old Bond Street, (17) W1S 4PT: SHOPPING Charity Shops, The British Red Cross

6.a, C.d - Piccadilly, Burlington House, W1J 0BD: EXHIBITING GALLERIES The Royal Academy of Arts; MAPS William Smith's Map; STREET FURNITURE Telephone Boxes

5.o, C.b - Piccadilly, (51) W1J 0PW: ARCADES The Burlington Arcade

5.o, D.u - Savile Row, (3) W1S 3PB: THE BEATLES

LONDON STORIES, LONDON LIVES

4.l, C.h - Albemarle Street, W1S 4(BS): The Boxing Impresario and The Empress; The Barbecued Chevalier

3.x, D.h - Albemarle Street, (21) W1S 4BS: From Turnips To Telegrams

3.q, B.t - Berkeley Street, (13) W1J 5AD: A Bachelor's Final Distraction

4.f, F.s - Conduit Street, (14-15) W1S 2XJ: From The Shadows To The Skies

1.x, G.l - New Bond Street, (108) W1S 1EF: The New Bond Street Democrat

3.x, D.n - New Bond Street, (167) W1S 4AY: A Duke Becomes A King

4.d, D.h - New Bond Street, (171) W1S 4RD: The New Bond Street Democrat

5.e, B.t - Old Bond Street, (43) W1S 4QT: The Napoleon of Crime

5.t, B.u - Piccadilly, WIJ 0(BD): Horace de Vere Cole II

3.r, F.s - St George Street, W1S 1(FX): The Macaroni Parson

5.j, E.d - Savile Row, (8) W1S 3PE: An Honourable Honourable

4.p, E.t - Savile Row, (23) W1S 2ET: Flawed Reasoning and Commerce

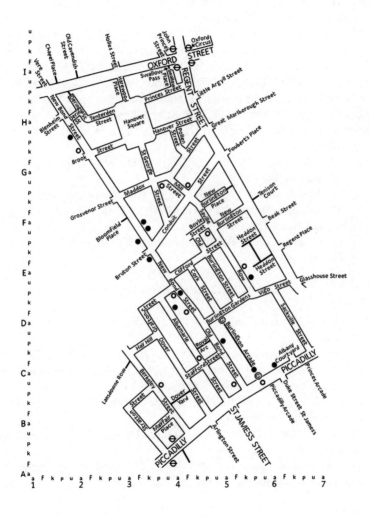

u p k u a
I a u p k f
H a u p k f
G a u p k f
F a u p k f
E a u p k f
D a u p k f
C a u p k f
B a u p k f
A a u p k f
A a a f k p u a f k p u a f k p u a f k p u a f k p u a f k p u a
1 2 3 4 5 6 7

Vere Street
Chapel Place
Old Cavendish Street
Holles Street

Oxford Circus

OXFORD STREET

John Prince's Street
Swallow Pass
Swallow Place
Princes Street
Little Argyll Street

New Bond Street
Blenheim Street
Dering Street
Tenterden Street
Haywood Place
Hanover Place
Hanover Square
Hanover Street
Pollen Street
St George Street
Great Marlborough Street
Foubert's Place

Brook Street
Maddox Street
Mill Street
St George Street
New Burlington Place
New Burlington Street
Tenison Court
Beak Street

Grosvenor Street
Bloomfield Place
Conduit Street
Boyle Street
Savile Row
Heddon Street
Regent Place

Bruton Street
New Bond Street
Clifford Street
Cork Street
Old Burlington Street
Heddon Street
Vigo Street
Glasshouse Street

Hay Hill
Dover Street
Albemarle Street
Grafton Street
Burlington Gardens
Old Bond Street
Burlington Arcade
Sackville Street
Albany Court Yard
PICCADILLY

Lansdowne Row
Berkeley Street
Dover Street
Dover Yard
Stafford Street
Bond Street
Royal Arcade
Piccadilly Arcade
Princes Arcade

St James Street
Mayfair Place
PICCADILLY
Arlington Street
ST JAMES'S STREET
Duke Street, St James's

REGENT STREET

BOND STREETS, OLD & NEW 345

2.h, C.e - Bedford Square, The Architectural Association School of Architecture (36) WC1B 3ES: VISITOR ATTRACTIONS The London Eye

6.h, H.c - Bernard Street, (39) WC1N 1(LE): STREET FURNITURE Railings, Dr Roget's Perception

5.v, B.o - Bloomsbury Way, WC1E 6DP: CHURCH OF ENGLAND CHURCHES St George, St George's Bloomsbury Way

4.q, D.e - Great Russell Street, WC1B 3DG: THE BRITISH MUSEUM; THE BRITISH LIBRARY The British Museum British Library; MUSEUMS Umbrella Bodies, Museum Mile

2.u, E.j - Keppel Street, WC1E 7HT: BUSES Steps To Health

5.a, J.e - Marchmont Street, (87) WC1N 1AL: HORROR FICTION Frankenstein

4.y, A.t - New Oxford Street, (53) WC1A 1BL: WEATHER Umbrellas, James Smith & Sons

4.h, F.l - Russell Square, WC1B 5(EA): TAXIS Cabmen's Shelters

3.y, F.d - Russell Square, (30) WC1B 4(JP): CEMETERIES Highgate Cemetery, Name Dropping

3.a, J.v - Woburn Walk, WC1H 0(JJ): PERIOD PROPERTIES Woburn Walk

LONDON STORIES, LONDON LIVES

7.c, C.q - Bloomsbury Square, WC1A 2(PJ): EXECUTIONS Bloomsbury Square

7.e, D.h - Bloomsbury Square, (40) WC1A 2(RA): The Countess's Travails

4.q, D.e - Great Russell Street, WC1B 3DG: The Boxing Impresario and The Empress, The Vanquisher Vanquished

2.f, F.w - Malet Street, WC1E 7HX: An 'Ole In 'Olborn & Maud; The Sand Man and The Zuckerman

4.e, A.o - New Oxford Street, (61) WC1A 1(DG): The Homicidal Homeopath

6.c, E.w - Russell Square, (57-58) WC1B 4HS: Tested To Destruction

3.v, I.l - Tavistock Square, (6) WC1H 9NA: Big Tich

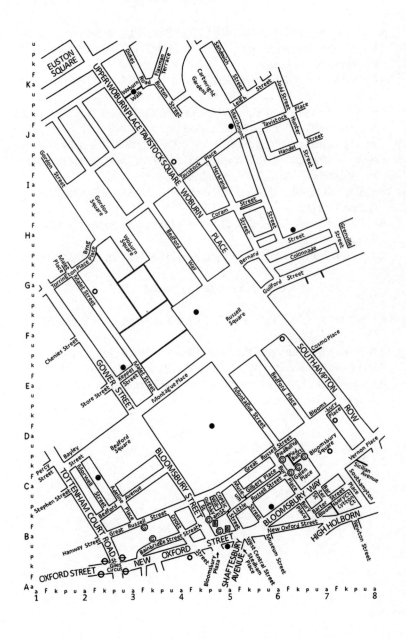

4.l, J.x - Buckingham Palace, SW1A 1AA: PALACES Buckingham Palace

4.t, K.c - Buckingham Palace, SW1A 1AA: MILITARY CUSTOMS The Changing of The Guard

4.h, I.x - Buckingham Palace Road, SW1A 1AA: GALLERIES The Royal Collection, The Queen's Gallery

3.h, K.w - Constitution Hill, SW1A 2BJ: PARKS Green Park, Constitution Hill; ROYALTY The Constitution

1.m, G.p - Grosvenor Gardens, SW1H 0(DH): TAXIS Cabmen's Shelters

6.w, F.q - Howick Place, SW1E 6(QX): DEPARTMENT STORES The House of Fraser, Army & Navy Stores

5.g, K.n - The Queen Victoria Memorial, SW1A 1AA: MEMORIALS The Queen Victoria Memorial

6.x, G.b - Victoria Street, (101) SW1E 6QX: DEPARTMENT STORES The House of Fraser

4.c, F.c - Wilton Road, (17) SW1V 1LG: THEATRES The Apollo Victoria

LONDON STORIES, LONDON LIVES

4.l, J.x - Buckingham Palace, SW1A 1AA: The Whitby Trade; How Much One Is Loved

3.h, K.w - Constitution Hill, SW1A 2BJ: How Much One Is Loved

4.j, H.r - Palace Street, SW1E 5(BD): The Macaroni Parson

3.j, E.p - Victoria Railway Station, SW1V 1JT: The Great Railway Crash of 1866

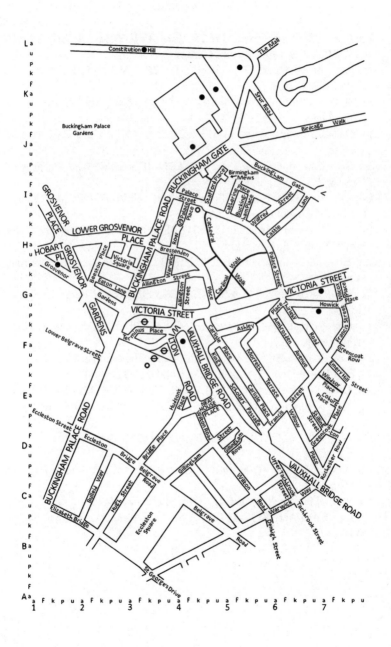

BUCKINGHAM PALACE 349

3.p, C.t - Bedford Street, WC2E 9ED: CHURCH OF ENGLAND CHURCHES St Paul's Covent Garden

4.j, E.u - Broad Court (Bow Street), WC2E 7(AW): STREET FURNI-TURE Telephone Boxes

5.m, E.b - Catherine Street, WC2B 5JF: THEATRES The Theatre Royal Drury Lane

5.y, D.k - Catherine Street, (3-5) WC2B 5LA: THEATRES The Duchess Theatre

2.t, B.k - Chandos Place, (51-52) WC2N 4HS: PUBS The Marquis of Granby

4.d, D.e - Covent Garden Piazza, WC2E 8HB: FOOD MARKETS, FORMER Covent Garden

4.a, D.b - Covent Garden Piazza, WC2E 8HB: PUBS Gin Palaces, The Punch Tavern, Punch & Judy

2.h, F.b - Earlham Street, (41) WC2H 9LD: THEATRES The Donmar Warehouse

2.q, F.t - Endell Street, (45-47) WC2H 9AJ: FISH & CHIPS, *ETC.* Fish & Chips

5.i, G.p - Great Queen Street, (61-65) WC2B 5DA: MAPS William Smith's Map

2.l, C.x - Rose Street, (33) WC2E 9EB: PUBS The Lamb & Flag

1.r, E.v - Seven Dials, WC2H 9(DD): COLUMNS Seven Dials

5.w, C.w - Wellington Street, (21) WC2E 7RQ: THEATRES The Lyceum

5.q, D.j - Wellington Street, (26) WC2E 7DD: CHARLES DICKENS

LONDON STORIES, LONDON LIVES

3.h, D.w - Floral Street, (40) WC2E 9DG: Flawed Reasoning and Commerce

3.x, E.n - Hanover Place, WC2E 9(JP): The Water Poet

2.j, D.r - Long Acre, (127-130) WC2E 9AA: From The Shadows To The Skies

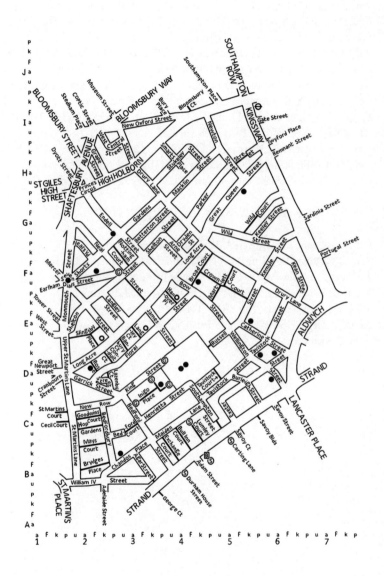

2.w, C.v - Fleet Street, (17) EC4Y 1AA: HERITAGE Prince Henry's Room

6.h, D.g - Fleet Street, (99) EC4Y 1DE: PUBS Gin Palaces, The Punch Tavern

3.i, D.h - Fleet Street, (186a) EC4A 2HD: ROYAL STATUES Queen Elizabeth I St Dunstan-in-the-West

3.d, C.k - Inner Temple Lane, EC4Y 7BB: CHURCH OF ENGLAND CHURCHES The Temple Church

6.m, C.i - New Bridge Street, (14) EC4V 6AG: PALACES, DISAP-PEARED & FORMER Bridewell Palace

5.w, D.a - St Bride's Passage, EC4Y 8AU: CHURCH OF ENGLAND CHURCHES St Bride's Church, WEATHER Lightning

4.x, D.n - Wine Office Court, EC4A 2BU: PUBS Ye Olde Cheshire Cheese

LONDON STORIES, LONDON LIVES

3.s, D.s - Crane Court, EC4A 2EJ: The Master President

3.f, G.k - Dyers' Buildings, (2) EC1N 2JT: The Countess's Travails

4.x, H.n - Ely Place, EC1N 6RY: Prelatic Immunity; Bess's Boys

3.u, E.x - Fetter Lane, (84) EC4A 1EQ: Liberty's Libertine

5.f, D.n - Fleet Street, (135-141) EC4A 2(BP): Breakfasts Past

2.l, G.t - High Holborn, Staple Inn Hall WC1V 7QJ: Flawed Reasoning and Commerce

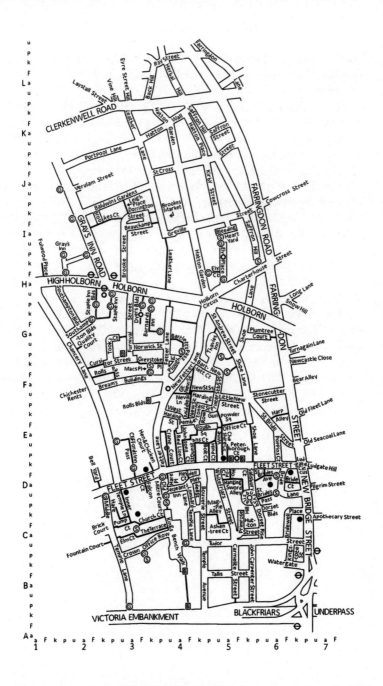

FLEET STREET EAST

353

1.t, G.x - Belgrave Mews West, (6) SW1X 8HT: PUBS The Star Tavern

6.m, J.a - Buckingham Palace Gardens, SW1A 1AA: ROYALTY Royal Garden Parties

4.q, K.y - Hyde Park Corner, W1J 7NT: ARCHES Constitution Arch

5.k, L.a - Hyde Park Corner, W1J 7NT: STREET FURNITURE Traffic Lights, Pelican Crossings

3.q, K.t - Hyde Park Corner, The Lanesborough, SW1X 7TA: WEST-MINSTER ABBEY Memorials and Graves, Doctors

4.b, L.p - Piccadilly, (149) W1J 7NT: GALLERIES The Royal Spanish Art Collection; STREET FURNITURE House Numbers

1.r, J.r - Wilton Place, (32a) SW1X 8SH: CHURCH OF ENGLAND CHURCHES St Paul's Knightsbridge

LONDON STORIES, LONDON LIVES

1.v, E.l - Chesham Street, (30) SW1X 8(NQ): Big Tich

2.q, E.o - Eaton Place, (84) SW1X 8LN: Saturday Night -Phenia

4.i, E.n - Eaton Square, SW1W 9(BE): The Timely Chancellor

4.o, E.h - Eaton Square, (37) SW1H 9DH: The Appeasers and Their Fates

3.l, E.q - Eaton Square, (86) SW1W 9AG: The Appeasers and Their Fates

6.q, E.x - Ebury Street, (22a) SW1W 0LU: A Bachelor's Final Distraction

6.j, C.n - Eccleston Place, SW1W 9(NE): How Much One Is Loved

3.q, K.t - Hyde Park Corner, The Lanesborough, SW1X 7TA: Cough Tarts

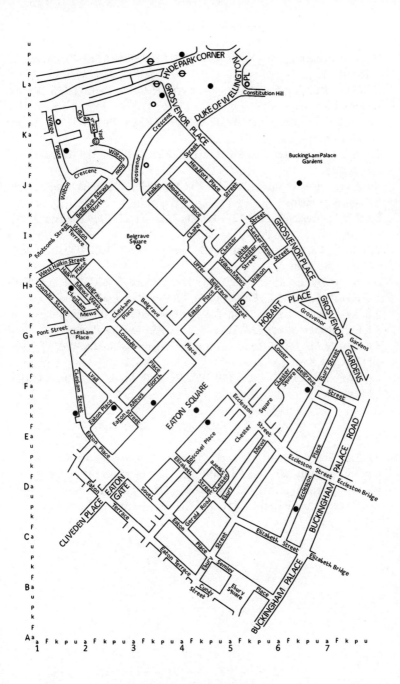

5.x, C.h - Charing Cross Road, (2) WC2H 0HH: THEATRES The Garrick Theatre

5.u, D.f - Charing Cross Road, (40) WC2H ODA: THEATRES Wyndham's Theatre

3.n, D.l - Gerrard Street, W1D 6(JH): STREET FURNITURE Street Signs, Chinatown

3.c, C.b - Haymarket, (34) SW1Y 4HA: PERIOD PROPERTIES Fribourg & Treyer

4.p, C.k - Leicester Square, WC2H 7(LE): ROYAL STATUES King George I Leicester Fields

5.c, C.j - Leicester Square, (28) WC2H 7LE: MUSEUMS The Hunterian Collection

3.u, D.w - Macclesfield Street, W1D 5(BP): STREET FURNITURE Street Signs, Chinatown

5.r, B.u - Orange Street, WC2H 7(HH): CHARLES DICKENS The Old Curiosity Shop; VISITOR ATTRACTIONS Madame Tussaud's

2.f, B.v - Regent Street, (24-36) SW1Y 4QF: SHOPPING Lillywhites

3.f, D.f - Rupert Street, (28) W1D 6DJ: PUBS The Blue Posts

4.v, B.v - St Martin's Street, Westminster Reference Library, WC2H 7HP: SHERLOCK HOLMES

6.g, D.a - St Martin's Lane, (90) WC2N 4AP: PUBS Gin Palaces, The Salisbury

LONDON STORIES, LONDON LIVES

4.l, E.e - Gerrard Street, (4) W1D 5QD: The Queen of Curves

4.v, B.v - St Martin's Street, (35) WC2H 7EL: The Master President

3.j, D.j - Wardour Street, (33) W1D 6PU: Saturday Night -Phenia

3.m, D.m - Wardour Street, (41-3) W1D 6PY: Horace de Vere Cole

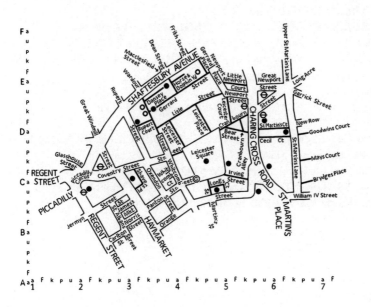

LONDON STORIES, LONDON LIVES

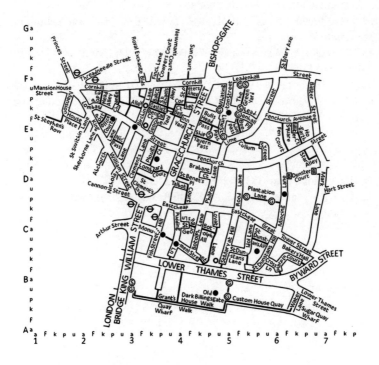

3.q, E.t - Bow Churchyard, EC4M 9DQ: CHURCH OF ENGLAND CHURCHES St Mary-le-Bow; BELLS Bow Bells

5.y, C.t - Cannon Street, (111) EC4N 5AR: STREET FURNITURE The London Stone

6.a, E.f - The Mansion House, EC4N 8BH: THE LORD MAYOR OF LONDON

6.w, B.w - Martin Lane, (6) EC4R 0DP: PERIOD PROPERTIES City of London Hostelries, The Old Shades

4.f, D.l - Queen Street, EC4N 1(SR): THE GREAT FIRE The Rebuilding of London

4.v, D.t - Queen Victoria Street, EC4V 4(BJ): ROMAN REMAINS The Temple of Mithras

7.a, E.y - Threadneedle Street, EC2R 8AR: THE BANK OF ENGLAND

5.t, D.s - Walbrook, (39) EC4N 8BN: CHURCH OF ENGLAND CHURCHES St Stephen Walbrook

LONDON STORIES, LONDON LIVES

4.u, E.p - Cloak Lane, EC4R 2(RU): The Elephant & Castle

6.a, E.f - The Mansion House, EC4N 8BH: A Rose Ceremony

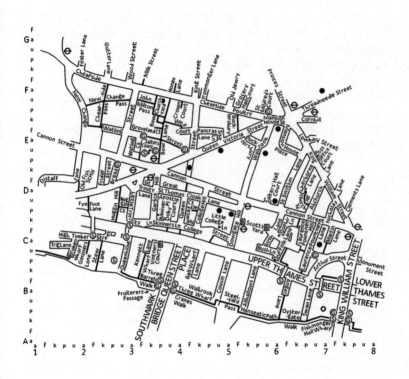

THE MANSION HOUSE   361

5.i, F.j - Charles Street, (5) W1J 5DE: PUBS The Only Running Footman In London

3.n, D.y - Chesterfield Gardens, (7) W1J 5BQ: STATUES Two Many Beers

5.v, F.c - Fitzmaurice Place, W1J 5JD: DEPARTMENT STORES Selfridges

3.e, J.c - Gilbert Street, (23) W1K 5HX: THEATRES St Martin's Theatre, A Deathbed Undertaking

6.m, B.q - Green Park, W1J 9BR: PARKS Green Park

5.l, J.d - Lancashire Court, W1Y 9AD: SHOPPING Pedestrianised Shopping Streets, Mayfair

6.i, C.r - Piccadilly, (opposite 92) W1J 6(BD): STREET FURNITURE Gates, The Green Park Gates

6.q, D.l - Piccadilly, (82) W1J 7(BP): MUSEUMS The Ranger's House Greenwich Park

4.a, K.e - South Molton Street, W1Y 1(DE): SHOPPING Pedestrianised Shopping Streets, Mayfair

LONDON STORIES, LONDON LIVES

5.i, F.r - Berkeley Square, (50): W1J 5BA: Premature Redunacy

4.e, D.y - Chesterfield Street, (4) W1J 5JF: The Appeasers and Their Fates

2.l, K.b - Duke Street, (69) W1M 5(DG): Groovy Bob & The Butterflies

2.h, H.h - Grosvenor Square, (40) W1K 2(HN): The Countess's Travails

2.p, H.j - Grosvenor Square, Millennium Hotel (44) W1K 2HP: Premature Redundancy; Polished Off With Polonium

2.y, H.m - Grosvenor Square, (48) W1X 9AB: The Countess's Travails

6.a, C.y - Half Moon Street, (46) W1J 7(BN): O'Kelly's Wonder

3.f, C.c - Hertford Street, (26) W1J 7SA: The Remains of A Vanished Giant

2.r, G.n - Mount Street, (23) W1K 2RP: Groovy Bob & The Butterflies

2.w, G.i - Mount Street, (95) W1K 2TA: The Buddha of Mount Street

3.w, G.q - Mount Street, (120) W1K 3NN: Groovy Bob & The Butterflies

2.y, C.k - Park Lane, W1K 1BE: The Sort of Grandee Who Makes You Wonder

5.w, C.u - Piccadilly, (94) W1J 7BP: How Much One Is Loved

4.h, B.c - Piccadilly, (127) W1J 7PX: Horace de Vere Cole II

3.p, K.j - South Molton Street, (28) W1K 5RE: How Much One Is Loved

5.r, C.s - White Horse Street, W1Y 7(LB): The Indentured Earl

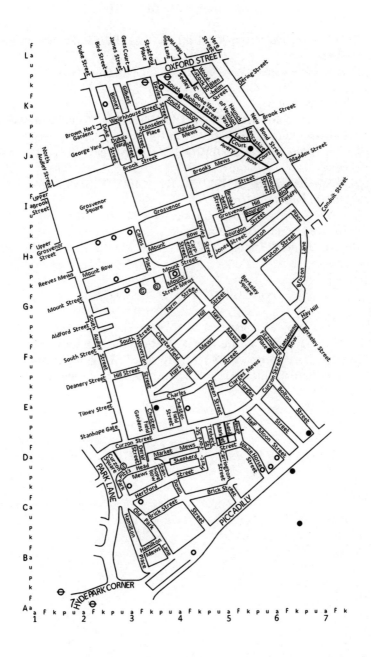

MAYFAIR EAST

4.b, F.h - Hallam Street, W1N 5(LH): GALLERIES Dulwich Picture Gallery

3.j, A.x - Holles Street, W1G 0(BN): HERITAGE Blue Plaques

2.j, E.x - New Cavendish Street, (61) W1G 7LP: MUSEUMS The Natural History Museum

3.j, A.o - Oxford Street, W1A: DEPARTMENT STORES; ROMAN REMAINS Roman Roads, Oxford Street

3.c, B.b - Oxford Street, (300) W1A 1EX: DEPARTMENT STORES John Lewis

2.l, A.w - Oxford Street, (318) W1C 1HF: DEPARTMENT STORES The House of Fraser

3.y, D.r - Portland Place, Broadcasting House (2-22) W1A 1AA: STATUES Nudity, Zimbabwe House

3.w, D.h - Portland Place, (1c) W1B 1JA: SHERLOCK HOLMES Mycroft Holmes

LONDON STORIES, LONDON LIVES

2.o, C.c - Cavendish Square, (17) W1M 9AA: The Lady of Langham Place

2.q, B.u - Cavendish Square, (19) W1M 9AD: The Unresurrected Mole

1.w, E.p - Harley Street, W1N 1(AE): An 'Ole In 'Olborn & Maud

3.k, D.t - Portland Place, (11) W1N 3AA: The Lady of Langham Place

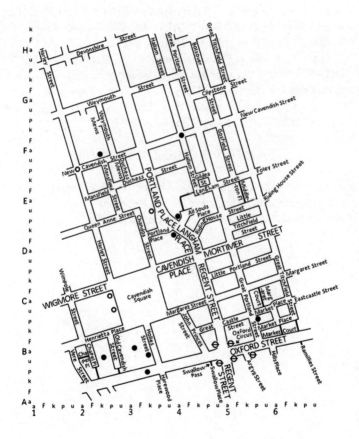

7.m, D.s - Curzon Street, W1J 7(HQ): TEA White

6.n, C.d - Hyde Park, W2 2(UH): STATUES Nudity, The Park Lane Achilles

3.s, D.y - Hyde Park, W2 2(UH): PARKS Hyde Park; MILITARY CUSTOMS Royal Salutes

2.n, J.a - Hyde Park, W2 2(UH): PARKS Hyde Park, Speaker's Corner;

2.s, J.x - Marble Arch, W1H 7AP: ARCHES Marble Arch; ROYAL STATUES King George IV Trafalgar Square

5.b, G.r - Park Street, The Grosvenor House Hotel (35) W1K 7(TN): ESTATES The Grosvenor Estates, Mayfair; Park Lane; PARKS Hyde Park, Speaker's Corner; HOTELS The Grosvenor House Hotel

7.h, G.g - South Audley Street, W1K 2PA: CHURCH OF ENGLAND CHURCHES The Grosvenor Chapel

LONDON STORIES, LONDON LIVES

6.e, I.g - Grosvenor Square, The United States Embassy, W1A 1AE: Liberty's Libertine; Soft Power Sounds Rebound

6.v, I.i - Grosvenor Square, W1A 1(AE): The Hairies

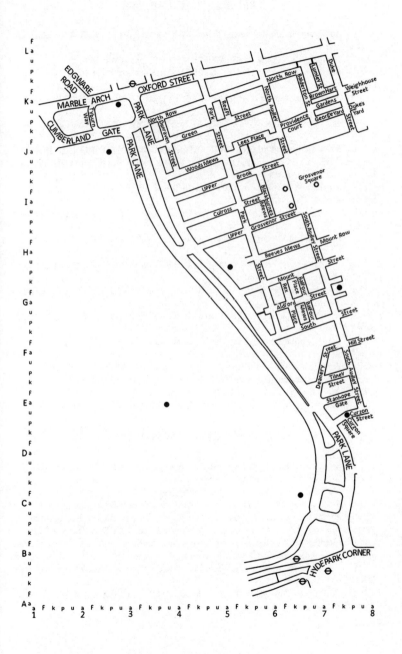

4.d, C.i - Abingdon Street, The Jewel Tower, SW1P 3JY: PARLIAMENT The Palace of Westminster

2.f, F.u - Birdcage Walk, (1) SW1H 9JJ: MUSEUMS The Imperial War Museum

2.i, D.g - Broad Sanctuary, SW1P 3(JS): STREET FURNITURE Street Signs, Whitehall's End

2.f, E.y - Great George Street, SW1P 3(SA): STREET FURNITURE Street Signs, Whitehall's End

2.i, F.t - King Charles Street, SW1A 3AQ: WINSTON CHURCHILL The Cabinet War Rooms

5.i, D.s - The Palace of Westminster, SW1P 3AD: THE CITY OF LONDON The Remembrancer; THE GUNPOWDER PLOT; INNS & TAVERNS The Star & Garter, The Wicked Lord Byron; PARLIAMENT

5.f, E.l - The Palace of Westminster, The Elizabeth Tower, SW1P 3AD: BELLS Big Ben, The Speed of Light

5.p, D.j - The Palace of Westminster, The River Terrace, SW1P 3AD: PARLIAMENT Liquid Refreshment, Taunting The Tourists

4.u, D.p - The Palace of Westminster, Westminster Hall, SW1P 3AD: HALLS Westminster Hall

4.h, G.g - Parliament Street, SW1A 2(NH): MEMORIALS The Cenotaph; MILITARY CUSTOMS Remembrance Sunday

4.a, D.u - St Margaret Street, SW1P 3JX: CHURCH OF ENGLAND CHURCHES St Margaret's Westminster

5.k, G.k - Victoria Embankment, The Curtis Green Building, SW1A 2JL: THE POLICE New Scotland Yard

5.j, F.y - Victoria Embankment, The Norman Shaw Building, SW1A 2HZ: THE POLICE New Scotland Yard

3.r, D.h - Westminster Abbey, SW1P 3PA: WESTMINSTER ABBEY; CORONATIONS

6.y, E.r - Westminster Bridge, SE1 7EH: BRIDGES Westminster Bridge

4.a, F.i - Whitehall, SW1A 2AH: MAPS The Radcliffe Line

4.c, G.g - Whitehall, SW1A 2(NP): STREET FURNITURE Street Signs, Whitehall's End

LONDON STORIES, LONDON LIVES

3.g, G.a - King Charles Street, SW1A 2AH: The Appeasers and Their Fates; Repeated Inspiration; Dollis Hill's Finest; Germany's Midwife

4.q, C.u - Old Palace Yard, SW1P 3JY: The Whitby Trade

5.i, D.s - The Palace of Westminster, SW1P 3AD: The Ruthless Reverend; Lawyers!; The Whitby Trade; The Countess's Travails; His Majesty's Pleasure; The Unresurrected Mole; Premature Redundancy; The Remains of A Vanished Giant; Big Tich; The Not So Honourable Member for Burnley; Horace de Vere Cole; The Fascist Baronet; The Appeasers and Their Fates; Germany's Midwife; An Honourable Honourable

4.u, D.p - The Palace of Westminster, Westminster Hall, SW1P 3AD: Bess's Boys; Lawyers!; His Majesty's Pleasure

3.r, D.h - Westminster Abbey, SW1P 3PA: An Old, Old, Very Old Man; The Master President; The Cannibal Dean

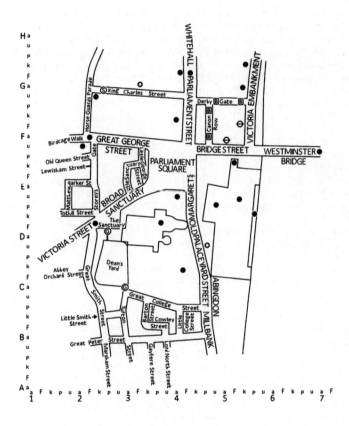

2.e, E.e - Arlington Street, (5) SW1A 1RA: DOWNING STREET No. 10 Downing Street

2.j, D.v - Bennet Street, (6) SW1A 1RP: PUBS The Blue Posts

3.l, D.w - Bury Street, SW1Y 6(AL): PARLIAMENT The Commons, Parliamentary Privilege

6.i, C.t - Carlton Gardens, (4) SW1Y 5AD: WINSTON CHURCHILL French Trousers; WEATHER Blue Skies

6.k, C.v - Carlton House Terrace, (1) SW1Y 5AF: ROYALTY The Constitution, The Sovereign and The Prime Minister, The Marquis Curzon

3.y, C.b - Cleveland Row, SW1A 1NP: PALACES St James's Palace

4.s, E.y - Duke of York Street, The Red Lion (2) SW1Y 6JP: PUBS Gin Palaces

4.e, F.a - Jermyn Street, (89) SW1Y 6JH: SHOPPING Floris

4.k, F.d - Jermyn Street, (93) SW1Y 6JE: SHOPPING Paxton & Whitfield

4.u, C.b - Marlborough Road, SW1A 1DD: ROYAL RESIDENCES Marlborough House

4.o, C.b - Marlborough Road, SW1A 1BS: CHAPELS ROYAL The Queen's Chapel

4.p, B.v - Marlborough Road, SW1A 1(DD): STATUES Eros, The Belgian Years

2.w, B.e - Milkmaids' Passage, SW1A 1(BB): PARKS Green Park, Milkmaids' Passage

5.l, D.e - Pall Mall, (89) SW1Y 5HS: STREET FURNITURE Traffic Lights

5.u, D.j - Pall Mall, (99) SW1Y 5(ES): GALLERIES The National Gallery, John Julius Angerstein

5.y, D.l - Pall Mall, (100) SW1Y 5HP: INNS & TAVERNS The Star & Garter

4.k, F.p - Piccadilly, (197) W1J 9LL: CHURCH OF ENGLAND CHURCHES St James's Piccadilly

3.m, F.f - Piccadilly, (181) W1A 1ER: DEPARTMENT STORES Fortnum & Mason

2.t, C.o - St James's Place, (29) SW1A 1NR: WINSTON CHURCHILL

5.j, E.f - St James's Square, SW1Y 4(LB): ROYAL STATUES King William III, St James's Square

5.d, E.v - St James's Square, (8) SW1Y 4JU: SHOPPING Wedgwood

6.b, E.i - St James's Square, (31) SW1Y 4JR: HERITAGE Period Groups, The Georgian Group

3.v, C.p - St James's Street, (3) SW1A 1EG: PERIOD PROPERTIES Berry Brothers & Rudd

3.p, B.i - Stable Yard Road, SW1A 1AA: ROYAL RESIDENCES Clarence House

LONDON STORIES, LONDON LIVES

3.l, D.w - Bury Street, SW1Y 6(AL): The Indentured Earl

3.m, F.f - Duke Street St James's, (27) W1A 1ER: How Much One Is Loved

3.r, F.b - Jermyn Street, (40) SW1Y 6DN: Rock'n'Premiums

3.x, E.v - Jermyn Street, (85-6) SW1Y 6JD: Big Tich

4.b, E.x - Jermyn Street, (87) SW1Y 6JD: The Master President

4.y, B.a - The Mall, SW1A 2BN: How Much One Is Loved

4.u, C.b - Marlborough Road, SW1A 1DD: A Lateral Retribution

4.t, C.s - Pall Mall, (79) SW1Y 5ES: Poor Nelly

6.i, D.r - Pall Mall, (104) SW1Y 5EW: A Soufflé Celebrity of Substance

2.t, D.i - Park Place, (12) SW1A 1LP: Fishmonger Hall

4.o, E.g - St James's Square, (15) SW1Y 4LB: La Belle

4.x, D.p - St James's Square, (20-1) SW1Y 4JY: Flawed Reasoning and Commerce

5.a, D.m - St James's Square, (21) SW1Y 4JP: The Whitby Trade

3.o, D.a - St James's Street, (10) SW1A 1EF: Fishmonger Hall

2.v, E.d - St James's Street, (32a) SW1A 1HD: The Prussian Professor

2.h, E.i - St James's Street, (50-3) SW1A 1JT: Fishmonger Hall

3.q, C.g - St James's Street, (87) SW1A 1PL: The Countess's Travails

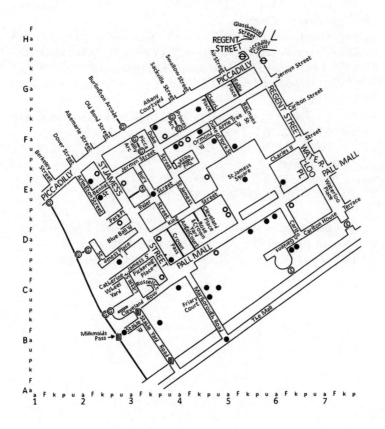

ST JAMES'S 371

2.s, A.f - Blackfriars Bridge, EC4P 4(BQ): BRIDGES Blackfriars Bridge, The City Bridge Trust; THAMES The Embankment and Sir Joseph Bazalgette

5.k, C.t - Carter Lane, The Billingsgate Porter (22) EC4V 5AD: FISH & CHIPS, *ETC*. Fish & Chips

3.v, D.l - Ludgate Hill, EC4A 2HR: ROYAL STATUES Queen Elizabeth I St Dunstan-in -the-West

5.y, B.u - Queen Victoria Street, EC4V 4BT: CLASS The College of Arms

3.d, B.v - Queen Victoria Street, (174) EC4V 4EG: PUBS The Blackfriar

6.d, D.j - St Paul's Cathedral, EC4M 8AD: BELLS Saved By The Bell; THE OLYMPICS The 1908 London Olympics, Not The Winning; ST PAUL'S CATHEDRAL

5.h, D.g - St Paul's Churchyard, EC4M 8AD: ROYAL STATUES Queen Anne, St Paul's Cathedral

4.f, D.r - Stationers' Hall Court, EC4M 7(DR): THE BRITISH LIBRARY The King's Library

LONDON STORIES, LONDON LIVES

2.s, A.f - Blackfriars Bridge, EC4P 4(BQ): The Suspended Banker

2.t, E.l - Old Seacoal Lane, EC4A 4(AB): O'Kelly's Wonder

6.d, D.j - St Paul's Cathedral, EC4M 8AD: An Unwarranted Creation

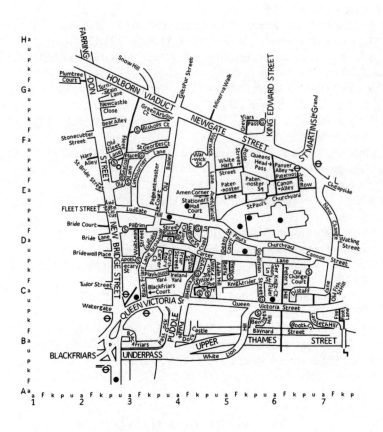

ST PAUL'S CATHEDRAL 373

2.k, F.k - Argyll Street, (7) W1F 7TF: THEATRES The London Palladium

1.w, F.y - Argyll Street, (18) W1F 7TP: PUBS Gin Palaces

5.t, E.j - Berwick Street, W1F 0(QA): STREET MARKETS Berwick Street Market

5.p, E.t - Berwick Street, (20) WIF 0PY: FISH & CHIPS, *ETC.* Fish & Chips, The Dining Plaice

5.n, E.w - Berwick Street, (22) W1F 0QA: PUBS The Blue Posts

3.l, E.a - Carnaby Street, W1F 7(DE): CARNABY STREET

3.x, D.q - Carnaby Street, (41) W1F 7DX: CARNABY STREET John Stephen

5.q, F.b - Duck Lane, W1F 0(HT): PUBS The Blue Posts, The Dog & Duck

3.u, C.v - Golden Square, (30) W1F 9LD: THE BEATLES

2.n, E.x - Great Marlborough Street, W1B 5AH: DEPARTMENT STORES Liberty & Co.

5.b, D.b - Great Pulteney Street, (38) W1F 9NU: HORROR FICTION Vampires, Dracula

2.y, E.d - Kingly Street, (18) W1B 5PX: PUBS The Blue Posts

3.h, E.o - Newburgh Street, (15) W1F 7RX: CARNABY STREET John Stephen

5.w, B.i - Piccadilly Circus, W1J 7BX: STATUES Eros

4.f, G.f - Poland Street, (23) W1F 8QL: PUBS The King's Arms

3.w, G.e - Poland Street, (38) W1F 7LY: FISH & CHIPS, *ETC.* Fish & Chips

3.c, F.v - Ramillies Street, (16-18) W1F 7LW: EXHIBITING GALLERIES The Photographers' Gallery

3.f, C.o - Regent Street, W1R 5(DF): DEPARTMENT STORES

2.o, E.a - Regent Street, (188-196) W1B 5BT: SHOPPING Hamleys

6.j, C.l - Shaftesbury Avenue, W1D 5(EA): THEATRES

6.r, D.b - Shaftesbury Avenue, (33) W1D 6AR: THEATRES The Gielgud Theatre

LONDON STORIES, LONDON LIVES

5.n, E.m - Berwick Street, (91) W1F 0BP: The King of Corsica

5.j, D.d - Brewer Street, (38) W1F 9(TA): The Chevalier d'Éon

3.s, G.l - Oxford Street, (165) W1R 1TA: Soft Power Sounds Rebound

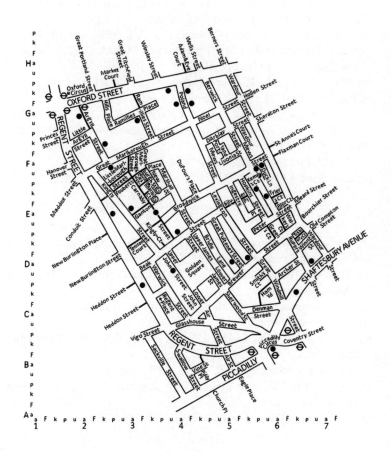

2.r, E.u - Portsmouth Street, (13-14) WC2A 2ES: PERIOD PROPERTIES The Old Curiosity Shop

2.u, E.h - Portugal Street, WC2A 2(HJ): ROYAL RESIDENCES Somerset House

2.o, B.e - Somerset House, WC2R 1LA: ROYAL RESIDENCES Somerset House; GALLERIES The Courtauld Gallery

2.y, C.f - Strand, St Mary-le-Strand, WC2B 1ES: CHURCH OF ENGLAND CHURCHES St Mary-le-Strand; ROYAL STATUES Queen Anne Queen Anne's Gate; TAXIS

4.p, D.b - Strand, St Clement Danes, WC2R 1DH: CHURCH OF ENGLAND CHURCHES St Clement Danes

5.f, D.q - Strand, The Royal Courts of Justice, WC2A 2LL: THE LORD MAYOR OF LONDON The Lord Mayor's Procession; THE CITY OF LONDON Good Numbers

5.g, D.e - Strand, (216) WC2R 1AP: TEA Twinings

4.h, B.c - Temple Place, WC2N 6(NS): TAXIS Cabmen's Shelters

LONDON STORIES, LONDON LIVES

2.q, C.w - Aldwych, Bush House, WC2B 4PH: Repeated Inspiration

5.i, C.n - Essex Street, WC2R 3(AA): Bess's Boys

3.h, D.v - Houghton Street, WC2A 2AE: From Crocodile Hunter To Financephalographist

2.g, D.f - Kingsway, (1) WC2B 6AN: Boffin *vs*. Boffin; From Thunderstorms To Firestorms

3.j, F.f - Lincoln's Inn Fields, (35-43) WC2A 3PE: The Vanquisher Vanquished

4.f, B.x - Norfolk Street (Gone), WC2R 2(PR): Lawyers!

5.f, D.q - Strand, The Royal Courts of Justice, WC2A 2LL: The Custom of The Sea; The Hairies

6.f, B.c - Victoria Embankment, WC2N 6(PB): Steadlast

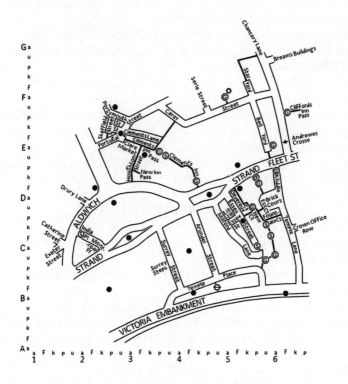

5.i, D.h - Carting Lane, WC2R 0(DW): STREET FURNITURE A Lamppost

2.s, B.v - Charing Cross Railway Station, WC2A 2LL: MEMORIALS Charing Cross, The Charing Cross Monument

3.u, A.o - Northumberland Avenue, WC2N 5DE: THEATRES The Playhouse Theatre

2.v, A.x - Northumberland Street, The Northumberland Arms (11) WC2N 5DA: SHERLOCK HOLMES

5.d, D.s - Savoy Court, WC2R 0EU: THEATRES The Savoy Theatre

5.w, D.s - Savoy Hill, WC2R 0DA: PALACES, DISAPPEARED & FORMER The Savoy Palace

5.y, D.x - Savoy Street, WC2R 0DA: CHURCH OF ENGLAND CHURCHES The Savoy Chapel

3.n, D.a - Strand, (429) WC2R 0JR: STATUES Nudity, Zimbabwe House

3.x, B.n - Villiers Street, Gordon's Wine Bar (47) WC2N 6NE. PUBS The Board of Green Cloth

7.e, D.a - Waterloo Bridge WC2E 7(EB): BRIDGES Waterloo Bridge; BRIDGES The Freeing of The West

LONDON STORIES, LONDON LIVES

5.m, G.b - Catherine Street, The Theatre Royal WC2B 5JF: Poor Nelly; His Majesty's Pleasure

3.e, B.g - Craven Passage, The Ship & Shovell (1-3) WC2N 5PH: The Sea Clock

3.v, C.o - Durham House Street, WC2N 6HG: Bess's Boys

4.m, A.v - Embankment Place, WC2N 6NS: A Minded Mind The Gap

4.o, C.t - John Adam Street, (1-4) WC2N 6EY: The Countess's Travails

6.q, D.m - Lancaster Place, (1) WC2E 7ED: Germany's Midwife

5.l, D.s - Savoy Court, WC2R 0EU: The Autowidow

4.v, D.o - Strand, (80) WC2R 0RL: Bess's Boys; The Not So Honourable Member for Burnley

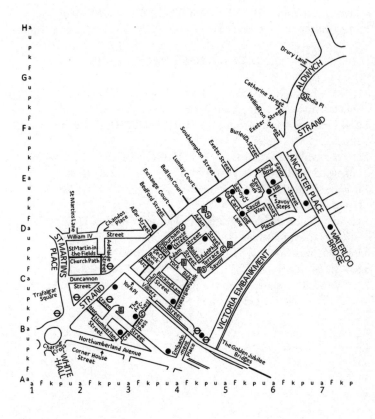

6.v, I.j - Albert Embankment, SE1 7(JU): THAMES The Embankment and Sir Joseph Bazalgette

7.g, J.m - Lambeth Palace Road, SE1 7JU: HALLS The Great Hall, Lambeth Palace

4.g, J.h - Millbank, Imperial Chemical House, SW1P 3GE: MUSEUMS The Imperial War Museum

3.i, F.n - Millbank, (52) SW1P 4RG: GALLERIES Tate Britain

3.i, J.k - Romney Street, (41) SW1P 3RF: PUBS The Marquis of Granby

LONDON STORIES, LONDON LIVES

3.k, K.x - Lord North Street, (2) SW1P 3LB: CARNABY STREET The Official Monster Raving Loony Party

3.e, K.s - Lord North Street, (14) SW1P 3LD: THEATRES The Gielgud Theatre, H.M. Tennent

4.e, I.o - Millbank, (21-41) SW1P 4QP: The Timely Chancellor; The Longest Suicide Note In History

3.i, F.n - Millbank, Tate Britain (52) SW1P 4RG: How Much One Is Loved; The Kiss

3.o, J.u - Smith Square, Transport House, SW1P 3HZ: The Longest Suicide Note In History

3.f, K.o - Smith Square, (5) SW1P 3HS: Steadlast

3.p, K.p - Smith Square, (8-9) SW1P 3HT: The Fascist Baronet

2.y, J.w - Smith Square, Conservative Central Office (former) (32) SW1P 3EU: The Longest Suicide Note In History

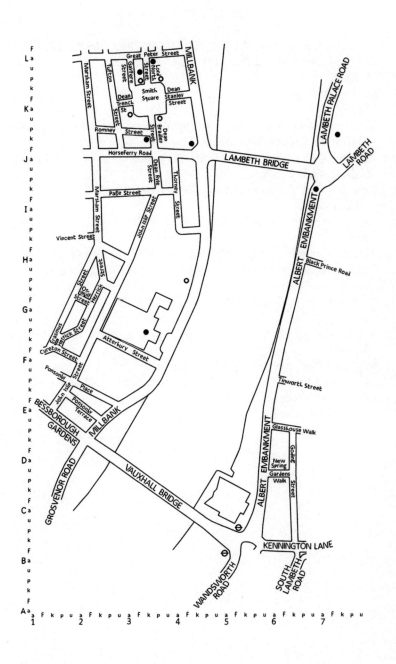

2.u, G.r - Bankside, (49) SE1 9JE: PERIOD PROPERTIES Bankside

7.d, D.x - Borough Market, SE1 9AH: FOOD MARKETS Borough Market

2.f, I.a - Millennium Bridge, EC4V 4EN: BRIDGES The Millennium Bridge

7.m, E.y - Montague Close, SE1 9DA: CHURCH OF ENGLAND CHURCHES Southwark Cathedral

3.g, G.r - New Globe Walk, (21) SE1 9DT: WILLIAM SHAKESPEARE Shakespeare's Globe

4.o, F.n - Park Street, SE1 9(AS): WILLIAM SHAKESPEARE Shakespeare's Globe

4.c, F.v - Park Street, (56) SE1 9AS: WILLIAM SHAKESPEARE The Rose Theatre

5.b, I.d - Southwark Bridge, SE1 9HL: BRIDGES The City Bridge Trust

1.u, G.i - Sumner Street, (25) SE1 9TG: GALLERIES Tate Modern

LONDON STORIES, LONDON LIVES

6.p, A.t - Angel Place, SE1 1(JA): The King of Corsica; The Countess's Travails

6.p, F.n - Clink Street, SE1 9DG: Prelatic Immunity

5.j, F.i - Park Street, (34) SE1 9EF: The Hyena Hunters of Southwark

6.s, D.u - Southwark Street, The Southwark Tavern (22) SE1 1(TU): The Horse Shoe Wave

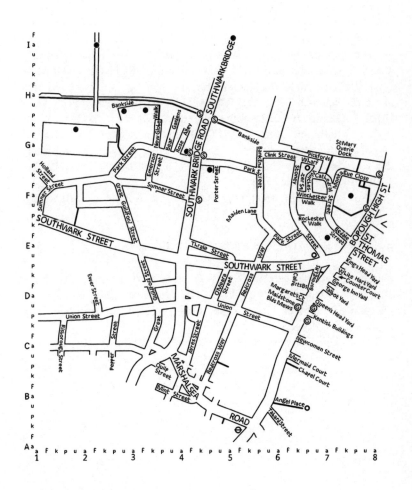

3.o, D.y - Cleveland Street, (22) W1T 4(HZ): CHARLES DICKENS Please, Sir!

2.y, E.v - Cleveland Street, (44) W1T 4JT: CHARLES DICKENS Please, Sir!

2.f, H.m - Fitzroy Square, (6) W1T 5DX: HERITAGE Period Groups, The Georgian Group

1.j, H.c - Fitzroy Square, (21) W1T 6EL: THEATRES Wyndham's Theatre

2.s, B.v - Margaret Street, (7) W1W 8JG: CHURCH OF ENGLAND CHURCHES All Saints Margaret Street

4.r, B.p - Newman Street, (81) W1T 3EU: PUBS The Blue Posts

7.h, B.i - Oxford Street, The Tottenham (6) W1D 1AN: PUBS Gin Palaces

5.e, C.q - Rathbone Street, (2) W1T 1NT PUBS: The Marquis of Granby

4.q, E.s - Scala Street, (1) W1T 2HL: SHOPPING Pollock's Toy Museum

5.i, E.p - Tottenham Court Road, (64-67) W1P 9(PA): THE GUNPOWDER PLOT The Catesbys

4.s, F.d - Tottenham Street, Gigs (12) W1T 4RE: FISH & CHIPS *ETC.* Fish & Chips

LONDON STORIES, LONDON LIVES

6.g, H.s - Gower Street, WC1E 6BT: Practical Altruisism

1.n, G.v - Fitzroy Square, (29) W1P 5HH: Horace de Vere Cole

7.s, B.n - Tottenham Court Road, The Dominion Theatre (269) W1P 9(AA): The Horse Shoe Wave

5.f, H.w - University Street, (21) WC1E 6DE: The Conservative Radical

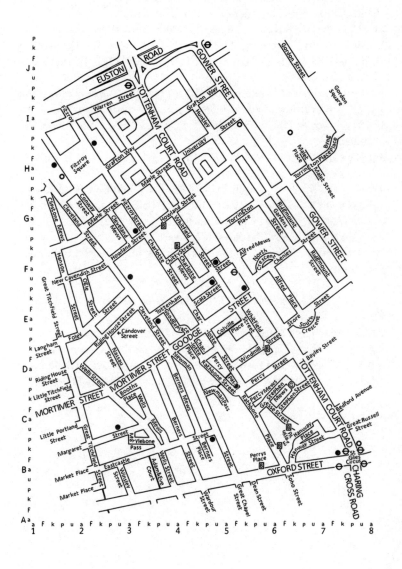

5.l, H.p - Aldgate High Street, The Hoop & Grapes (47) EC3N 1AL: PERIOD PROPERTIES City of London Hostelries

2.m, D.c - Byward Street, EC3R 5BJ: ROMAN REMAINS Boudicca

2.n, E.l - Hart Street, (8) EC3R 7NB: CHURCH OF ENGLAND CHURCHES St Olave's Hart Street; THE GREAT FIRE The Fire, Surviving Churches

3.r, A.h - The Pool of London, SE1 2(UP): THAMES The Pool of London

5.j, A.l - Tower Bridge, SE1 2UP: BRIDGES Tower Bridge

4.h, D.g - Tower Hill, EC3N 4(DU): ROMAN REMAINS Tower Hill Cathedral

3.y, B.w - The Tower of London, EC3N 4AB: THE TOWER OF LONDON Tower Green

4.o, C.c - The Tower of London, EC3N 4AB: THE TOWER OF LONDON; CORONATIONS The Regalia; CORONATIONS The Tower of London; MILITARY CUSTOMS The Constable's Dues; PALACES Historic Royal Palaces; ZOOS The Royal Menagerie

3.j, D.v - Trinity Square, (10) EC3N 4AJ: THAMES The Port of London Authority

LONDON STORIES, LONDON LIVES

2.t, F.f - Fenchurch Place, EC3M 4AJ: The Müller Cut-Down

2.r, D.v - Seething Lane, (33-36) EC3N 4(AH): A Rose Ceremony

4.o, C.c - The Tower of London (The Royal Mint), EC3N 4AB: The Real Falstaff; An Oppressive Conscience; La Belle, The Master President

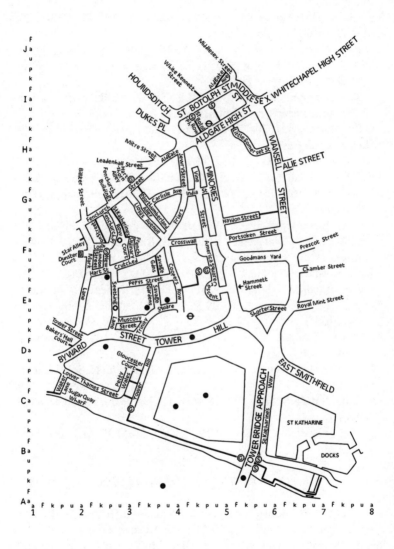

THE TOWER OF LONDON

3.t, A.s - Carlton House Terrace, SW1Y 5AF: COLUMNS The Duke of York's Column

3.r, A.u - Carlton House Terrace, SW1Y 5(AH): ROYAL RESIDENCES, DISAPPEARED Carlton House

6.c, B.q - Charing Cross, WC2N 5DS: MEMORIALS Charing Cross; ROYAL STATUES King Charles I Charing Cross; TRAFALGAR SQUARE The Centre of London

5.e, B.v - Cockspur Street, SW1Y 5(BL): STREET FURNITURE Paving, The Westminster Paving Commission

3.v, C.v - Haymarket, The Theatre Royal, SW1Y 4HT: THEATRES The Theatre Royal Haymarket

3.t, C.h - Haymarket, SW1Y 4QL: THEATRES Her Majesty's Theatre

3.n, C.b - Pall Mall, SW1Y 4UY: ARCADES The Royal Opera Arcade

6.b, D.o - St Martin's Place, WC2N 4JH: GALLERIES The National Portrait Gallery

6.n, D.c - St Martin's Place, WC2N 4JJ: CHURCH OF ENGLAND CHURCHES St Martin-in-the-Fields; STREET MARKETS Costermongers, Pearly Kings & Queens

5.w, C.i - Trafalgar Square, WC2N 5DS: TRAFALGAR SQUARE

5.y, C.c - Trafalgar Square, WC2N 5DS: COLUMNS Nelson's Column

5.m, C.r - Trafalgar Square, WC2N 5DS: ROYAL STATUES King George IV Trafalgar Square

5.q, C.y - Trafalgar Square, WC2N 5DS: GALLERIES The National Gallery

5.l, C.x - Trafalgar Square, WC2N 5DS: STATUES The National Gallery Statues

5.w, D.b - Trafalgar Square, WC2N 5DS: STATUES The National Gallery Statues

3.g, B.q - Waterloo Place, SW1Y 4(AU): MEMORIALS The Scott Memorial

LONDON STORIES, LONDON LIVES

3.x, A.u - Carlton House Terrace, (11) SW1Y 5AH: Fishmonger Hall

4.f, C.g - Pall Mall East, (1&2) SW1Y 5AU: A Dandy Fellow

5.i, B.j - Spring Gardens, (8) SW1A 2(BN): The Lady of Langham Place

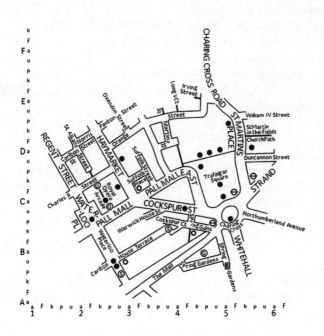

TRAFALGAR SQUARE

3.o, C.u - Downing Street, SW1A 2AA: DOWNING STREET

3.a, E.c - Horse Guards Parade, SW1A 2AX: MILITARY CUSTOMS Trooping The Colour

2.r, G.a - The Mall, SW1A 2BN: ARCHES Admiralty Arch

6.e, G.a - Northumberland Avenue, WC2N 5(AQ): TAXIS Cabmen's Shelters

1.v, D.v - St James's Park, SW1A 2BJ: PARKS St James's Park

6.k, F.t - Victoria Embankment, WC2N 6PA: THAMES The Embankment and Sir Joseph Bazalgette

3.x, E.q - Whitehall, SW1A 2EU: STATUES Two Many Beers

4.h, E.e - Whitehall, The Banqueting House, SW1A 2ER: HALLS The Banqueting House; THE WEATHER Wind, The Protestant Wind

4.g, F.j - Whitehall Place, (4) SW1A 2(DY): THE POLICE Peelers

5.o, E.b - Whitehall, SW1A 2ER: PALACES, DISAPPEARED & FORMER Whitehall Palace

LONDON STORIES, LONDON LIVES

3.o, C.u - Downing Street, SW1A 2AA: The Ruthless Reverend

3.q, C.x - Downing Street, (10) SW1A 2AA: Horace de Vere Cole II; An Untimely Report; The Timely Chancellor

4.x, C.p - Richmond Terrace, SW1A 2NJ: The Boxing Impresario and The Empress

2.u, E.w - Whitehall, The Old Admiralty Building, SW1A 2PA: The Dead Deceive

3.n, F.d - Whitehall, (32) SW1A 2DY: Germany's Midwife

5.r, F.r - Whitehall Place, (1) SW1A 2HE: The Not So Honourable Member for Burnley

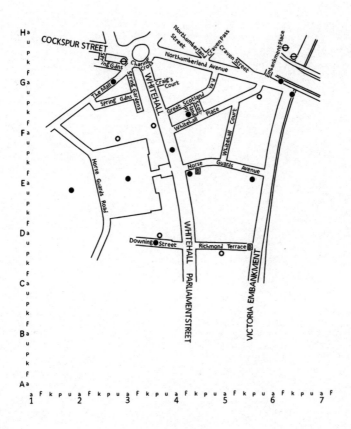

GALLERIES, PALACES & TEA

INDEX

Aalto, Alvar (1898-1976) *26*
Abdication Crisis *44*
<u>Abingdon Street</u>: The Jewel Tower, SW1P 3JY *199, 368-9*
abstract art, European *91*
academics; university lecturers; don *162, 166*
accent *164, 230, 300*
Achilles *268*
Acropolis *29*
<u>Acton Lane</u>: NW10 7NS *36*
actors; actresses; stage *23, 57, 137-8, 226, 231, 231n, 254, 295-7, 300-1, 307-8, 311, 333*
Adam, Robert (1728-1792) *208*
Adam Room *208*
<u>Adam Street</u>: (4) WC2N 6AA *48, 378-9*
Adastral House *52*
Adelphi, The (development) *132*
Adelphi, The (theatre) *294*
Admiralty, The *44, 54*
Admiralty, First Lord of the *44-5*
Admiralty, Lords of *54*
Admiralty Arch *2*
advertising; publicity *167, 296-7*
advertising industry; ~ mogul *112, 115*
Aestheticism; Aesthetic *71, 84*
Aethelred II the Unready, King (*c.*969-1016) *55, 335*
<u>Albemarle Street</u>: (21) W1S 4BS *163, 324,* 344-5
Albert, Prince (1819-1861) *2, 111, 151, 175, 183,*
Albert Bridge: SW11 4PL *15*; SW11 4(PL) *282*
<u>Albert Embankment</u>: *291. See Also:* embankment
Albert Memorial, SW7 2AP *151*
Albery, Donald (1914-1988) *294*
alcove *18*
Alderman (City of London) *144*
Aldermen, Court of *63, 144, 215, 273*
<u>Aldersgate Street</u>: EC1A 4(DD) *122*
Aldershot *2*
<u>Aldgate High Street</u>: (47) EC3N 1AL *211*
Aldini, Giovanni (1762-1834)

136
<u>Aldwych</u>: Bush House WC2B 4PH *294, 376-7*
Alexandra, Queen (1844-1925) *235, 267*
al Fayed *79-80*
Allen & Hanbury *325*
All England Tennis & Croquet Club *181*
Alleyn, Edward (1566-1626) *254*
All Hallows by the Tower *122, 232*
Allied; allies (Napoleonic Wars) *71*
Allied; Allies (WW1) *45*
All Saints Margaret Street *48*
altar *58, 76, 205, 310*
Ambassadors Theatre, The *295, 304n*
America; America, North (place) *251, 265*
America (state) *177n*
American (non-people) *114*
American (people) *19, 78, 96, 178, 179n, 251-2, 254, 281-2, 301*
American War of Independence *218, 258, 288, 327*
Amis, Sir Kingsley (1922-1995) *300*
Ancient Monuments Protection Acts of 1900 and 1910 *133*
Andrews, Bernie (1933-2010) *83*
Angel, The (district) *139, 230*
Angel, The (pub, Islington) *230*
Angel, The (pub, Rotherhithe) *188*
Angel of Charity *267*
<u>Angel Place</u>: SE1 1(JA) *382-3*
Angels Fancy Dress *256*
Angerstein, John Julius (1735-1823) *107, 110*
Anglican *49, 56, 73, 125, 194, 328-9*
Anglo-American *47, 177 243*
Anglophile *252*
Anglophone *265n*
Anglo-Saxon *314*
Anglo-Saxon (language) *290*
Anglo-Saxon (words) *306*
Anglo-Saxon kings *199, 314,*

334
Angry Young Men *300*
Anne, Queen (1665-1714) *24, 185, 241, 333*
Anne of Denmark, Queen (1574-1619) *187*
Anselm, Archbishop of Canterbury (*c.*1033-1109) *206*
Antarctic *155*
Anthony & Cleopatra *253*
Antipodeans *80*
antiques; ~ dealers *220, 245, 279*
Apollo Victoria *294*
Apostles *141*
Apple Corp *8*
apprentices; apprenticeship *263, 288*
Apsley House *2, 112, 268, 272*
Aquatic Centre *180*
Arab Hall (1877) *212*
Arbroath Abbey *76*

ARCADES 1

ARCHES 2

archaeology *50, 164, 171, 234, 254*
Archigram *91, 181, 254*
architects; architectural profession *21, 26, 56, 58, 116, 151n, 153, 173, 181, 183, 196-7, 202, 208, 225, 325, 237n, 237, 254, 275-6, 295-6, 298, 302, 316, 320, 336*
Architectural Association School of Architecture *181, 320*
architecture *130-2, 235*
Arden, John *299*
Arden, Paul (1940-2008) *112n*
<u>Argyll Street</u>: (5&6) W1F 7TE *8*; (7) W1F 7TF *297, 374-5*; The Argyll Arms (18) W1F 7TP *224, 374-5*
Ariel Way: W12 7SL *179, 263*
aristocracy; aristocratic *27, 77, 132, 139, 191, 194, 196, 303-4, 304n, 323*
<u>Arlington Street</u>: (5) SW1A 1RA *89, 370-1*
Army *2, 44, 68, 71, 157-8, 269, 313*
Army & Navy Stores *81-2*

Arsenal (soccer) *181*
art *113*, *147*, *325*
art collectors; art collection *91*, *94*, *107*, *111n*
art critics *96*, *115*, *170*
art dealing *8*, *31*, *106*, *115*
art history; art historians *105*, *115*, *166*
<u>Artillery Lane</u>: (56) E1 7LS *94*
<u>Artillery Passage</u>: E1 7(LJ) *275*
artists; painters *54*, *71*, *91-2*, *96*, *114-6*, *133*, *147*, *212*, *250*, *267n*, *298*, *324-5*
art nouveau *222*
Arts Council, The *95*
Arup *21*
Ashburnham House *24*
Ashkenazim *99*
assassinations; assassinated *124*, *226-7*, *246*
assembly, right of public *194-5*
asthma *185*, *244*
astrology *27*
Athens *28*, *30*, *177*
athletes, Olympic *177n*, *179-80*
Atlantis *258n*
Attainder of 1605, Act of *124*
auction *63*, *74*, *96*
Auerbach, Frank *91*
Augusta, Princess (1719-1772) *142*, *237*
Augustus (*né* Gaius Octavius) (63 BC-14 AD) *30*
Austerity Games *179*
Australia *177*
Austria *177*
Austria-Hungary *107*, *177*
Austrian (people) *252*
Austro-Hungary *106*, *177*
Automobile Association *277*
avant-garde art *267n*
<u>Avenue Road</u>: NW8 7(PU) *15*, *17*
Avenue Theatre *298*
<u>Avery Row</u>: W1K 4(AL) *260*
Axis *153*
Aylesbury *180*
Aztec *27*
Bacon, Delia (1811-1859) *251*
Bacon, Sir Francis; 1st Viscount St Albans (1561-1626) *251-2*
Bacon, Francis (1909-1992) *114*
Bacon, John (1740-1799) *250*
Bacon the younger, John (1777-1859) *244*
Bacon, Roger (*c.*1214-1294) *323*
Bairstow, Leslie *172*
baiting pit, animal *253*
Baker, Sir Herbert (1862-1946) *6*
<u>Baker Street</u>: *321*; (221b) NW1 6XE *134-5*
<u>Balaam Street</u>: E13 8(AF) *325*

Baldwin, Stanley (1867-1947) *245*
Balfour, Arthur; 1st Earl of Balfour (1848-1930) *324*
Balmond, Cecil *181*
Baltic Exchange *117*
Baluch *268*
banana warehouse, former *160*, *294*
Bangladesh *148*

THE BANK OF ENGLAND *5*

Bank of England Building *6*
bankrupt *63*, *147*
banks, bankers, banking *135*, *266*
Banks, Sir Joseph (1st Bt.) (1743-1820) *142*, *169*
<u>Bankside</u>: SE1 9TG *20*, *115*, *253-4*; (49) SE1 9JE *208*, *382-3*
banquets *62*, *128*, *144-5*, *194*
Banqueting House (Lord Mayor's) *65*
barbers' polls *118*, *275*
Barbon, Dr Nicholas (*c.*1640-1698) *123*
Barfield, Julia *320*
Barker, H. Granville (1877-1946) *301*
Barking Abbey *17*
Barlow, William (1812-1902) *15*,
Barnett (*née* Weston), Henrietta (1851-1936) *95*
Barnett, Canon Samuel Augustus (1844-1913) *95*
barns *57*
barograph *323*
barons, the; nobles *188*, *206*
baroque; Baroque *298*
Barrier Block; Southwyck *39*, *39n*
barrister; counsel *148*, *164*, *252*, *257*
<u>Barrowgate Road</u>: (51) W4 4QT *287*
Barry, Sir Charles (1795-1860) *200-1*
Barry, Edward (1830-1880) *154*
Barry, John Wolfe (1836-1918) *21*, *286*
<u>Bartholomew Lane</u>: *6*
<u>Bateman Street</u>: (18) W1D 3AJ *222*
Bath *18n*
Battersea *192*
Battersea Bridge SW22 3(BZ) & SW3 5(LT) *17*
Battersea Fields *192*
Battersea Park, SW11 4NJ *192*
Battersea Park Act of 1846 *192*
battlefield *158*

Bavarian (people) *29-30*, *324*
Bayswater *65*, *263*
<u>Bayswater Road</u>: W2 2(LJ) *234*; (123) W2 3JH *230*
Bazalgette, Sir Joseph (1819-1891) *17*, *290*
BBC *11*, *256*
BBC Radio *83*
beaches *290*, *292*
Beating Retreat *156*

THE BEATLES *8*

Beatles, The *8*, *23*
Beauclerk, Osborne; St Albans, 12th Duke of (1874-1964) *74*
Beaumont, (Hugh) 'Binkie' (1908-1973) *296*
Beaumont, Sir George (1753-1827) *107*
Beaumont & Fletcher; Francis Beaumont (1584-1616); John Fletcher (1579-1625) *307*
Beck, Harry (1903-1974) *150*
Beck, Jeff *40*
Becket, Thomas à (1118-1170) *313*
Bedford, Dukes of; ~, Earls of. *See* Russell
Bedford, Eric (1909-2001) *197*
Bedford House *103*
Bedford Park *133*
<u>Bedford Square</u>: (36) WC1B 3ES *320*, *346-7*
<u>Bedford Street</u>: WC2E 9ED *57*, *350-1*
Bedlam; Bethleham Royal Hospital *166*
Beefeaters *314*
beer *5*, *224*
Beer, Frederick (*d.*1903) *269*
Beer (*née* Sassoon), Rachel (1858-1927) *269*
Belfast, H.M.S. *166-7*
Beit, Alfred *172*
Belgian *99n*, *163*, *224*
Belgium *157*, *334*
<u>Belgrave Mews West</u>: (6) SW1X 8HT *231*, *354-5*
Belgravia *79*, *231*
belief system belief; pagans *55*
belief system practice *311*
Bell, Joseph (1837-1911) *134*
Bell, Tim *115*

BELLS *11*

Belt, Richard Claude (*c.*1854-1920) *238*
<u>Belvedere Road</u>: SE1 7(GF) *91*; SE1 8XX *91*
Benedictine *330*
Benn, Tony; Anthony Wedgwood Benn; 2nd Viscount Stansgate (1925-2014) *285*
<u>Bennet Street</u>: (6) SW1A 1RP

GALLERIES, PALACES & TEA

GALLERIES, PALACES & TEA

162-3, *165*
Mond, Sir Robert (1867-1938) *163*, *165*
Monderman, Hans (1945-2008) *275*
money *5*, *31*, *60-1*, *63*, *223*, *297*
moneylending; moneylender *104*, *251*
Monster Raving Loony Party *see* Official Monster Raving Loony Party *40*
Montagu, George; 4th Duke of Manchester (1737-1788) *176*
Montagu House *27*
Montague Close: SE1 9DA *58*, *382-3*
Montendre, 4th Marquis de; François de la Rochefoucauld (1672-1739) *286*
Montendre, Marquise de; Mary Anne de la Rochefoucauld (*née* Marie-Anne von Spanheim) (*d*.1772) *286*
Montfitchet Road: E20 1EJ *263*
Monument, The, EC3R 8AH *68-9*, *122*, *358-9*
monuments *154*, *249*, *333*
Monument Street: EC3R 8AH *69*, *122*, *358-9*
Moon, Keith (1946-1978) *40*
Moore, Henry (1898-1986) *58*
Moorgate (gate) *18*
Moorgate: EC2M 6(SA) *18*
More, Sir Thomas (1478-1535) *48*, *311*
Morley, 11th Baron *see* Parker, William
Morris, (Jeremiah) 'Jerry' (1910-2009) *35-6*
Morris, William 'Topsy' (1834-1896) *133*
Morris Minor Traveller *255*
Moulton, John; 1st Baron Moulton (1844-1921) *164-5*, *167*
Mount Street: (23) W1K 2RP *362-3*; (95) W1K 2TA *362-3*; (120) WIK 3NN *362-3*
Mount Terrace: E1 2BB *123*
Mousetrap, The *305*
MPL Music Publishing *8*
MPs *133*, *164*, *166*, *176n*, *202-3*, *205*, *247*, *303*
Mudlarks & Antiquarians, Society of *292*
Mulcahy, William; William Lloyd *31-2*
Mulgrave, 3rd Earl of *see* Sheffield, John
Munch, Edvard (1863-1944) *216*
Municipal Corporations Act of 1835 *60*

Municipal Corporations Commission *63*
murder *149*, *264*, *296*, *312*, *320*
Museum of Brands, Packaging & Advertising *167*
Museum of London *145*, *168*, *191*, *234*, *292*

MUSEUMS *160*

musicals *294*, *297*, *300*, *302*
music hall *214*
Muslim League *148*
Muslims *148*, *180*
Mutiny Act *191*
Mycenae Road: (90) SE3 7SE *109*
nails *62*
Napier, Field Marshal Lord Robert (1810-1890) *268*
Napoleon Bonaparte (*né* Buonaparte) (1769-1821) *54*, *71*, *112*, *244*
Napoleonic Wars; French Revolutionary War *5*, *307*
Nash, John (1752-1835) *3*, *183*, *196-7*, *316*
National Gallery *107*, *109*, *113*, *163*, *268*, *316n*, *317*
National Lottery *116*
National Maritime Museum *188*
National Portrait Gallery *110*
National Tennis Centre *181*
National Theatre Company *301*
National Trust, The *131*
Natural History, Museum of (Oxford) *170*
Natural History Museum, The *27*, *169-71*
Natural Philosophy, Professor of *323*
Nature *161*
NatWest Tower; Tower 42 *117n*
Navy Office *55*, *122*
Nazi; Nazism *45-6*, *95*, *278*
Neale, Thomas (1641-1699) *72*
Nelson, Horatio; Lord Nelson (1758-1805) *71*, *249*
Nelson's Column *71*, *318*
Netherlands, The *162*, *329*
New Age *37*
New Bond Street: *260*; W1Y 9(LA) *259*, *323*, 344-5 (21) W1S 2(JY) 344-5; (26) W1S 2JY *212*; (34-35) W1A 2AA *47*, 344-5; (103) W1Y 6LG *71*; (143) W1S 2TP *212*
New Bridge Street: *187*
Newburgh Street: (15) W1F 7RX *42*, *374-5*
Newby, Eric (1919-2006) *79*
Newby, Frank *336*
New Caledonian Market *279*
New Covent Garden Market,

SW8 5NQ *103*
New Cross *139*, *230*
New Cross Inn *139*, *230*
Newgate Gaol; Newgate Prison *63*, *130*, *136*
New Generation exhibition *96*
New Globe Walk: SE1 9DT *255*, *382-3*
Newington Causeway: SE1 6BN *233*
Newman Street: (81) W1T 3EU *222*, *384-5*
New Musical Express, The; The NME *40*
New Oxford Street: *52n*; (53) WC1A 1BL *327*, *346-7*
New Palace Yard *199*
New River House *214*
New Scotland Yard *11*, *215-6*
newspapers *36*, *50*, *95n*, *166*, *203-4*, *206*, *269-70*, *285*, *326*
New Street Railway Station *110*
Newton, Sir Isaac (1642-1727) *323*
Nicholas II, Tsar; Mr Romanov (1868-1918) *173*
Nicholas Nickleby (1839) *85*
night; night-time *7*, *12*, *46*, *224*, *307*, *333*
Nine Elms *103*
Nobel Industries *166*
Norfolk, Dukes of *66*, *73*
Norfolk House *132*
Norfolk Street: WC2R 2(PR) (Gone) *376-7*
Normans *128*, *248*, *309*
North-East England *172*, *205*, *251*
Northumberland, Dukes of; Percies, the *330*
Northumberland Arms, The (pub) *134n*
Northumberland Avenue: WC2N 5(AP) *134n*, *378-9*; WC2N 5(AQ) *282*, *390-1*; WC2N 5DE *299*, *378-9*
Northumberland House *134n*
Northumberland Street: *The Northumberland Arms* (11) WC2N 5DA *134*, *378-9*
North Woolwich Road: E16 2(BG) *167*
notorious *49*, *52*, *54*, *83*
Nottinghamshire Club *140*
Notting Dale *38*
Notting Hill *220*
Notting Hill Hippodrome *220*
novels *28*, *209*, *308*
November 5th *124*
nuclear weapons; atomic bomb *278*
Nuffield Foundation *337*
nursery rhyme *68*

(1906-1996) *147*
Pearsall, Richard *147*
peculiar, royal *53, 58, 330*
pedestrianised *41, 214, 259-60*
Peel, Sir Robert (1788-1850)
63, 217
Peelers *217*
Pelican crossing *278*
pelicans *198*
Penguin Pool *336*
Penny Lane 23
Penrose, Roland (1900-1984) *96*
Pentonville Road: N1 9(JL) *278*
Pepys, Samuel (1633-1703)
55, 122
Percy family *134n, 332*

PERIOD
PROPERTIES *208*
Petrarch, Francesco (1304-
1374) *253*
Pevsner, Sir Nikolaus (1902-
1983) *133*
pew *55, 122*
philanthropy *110, 273, 295*
Phoenix Theatre, The *298*
Photographers' Gallery, The
92-3
photography *95n, 135*
phrase; saying; saw *227, 300,
308, 330*
physicians *27, 31, 75, 111,
134, 136, 138, 141, 241, 251,
274, 321*
physics *286, 323-4*
Picasso, Pablo (1881-1973)
95, 95n
Piccadilly: W1J 0(BD) *192, 205,
282, 289*, 344-5, *362-3*; (50)
W1J 0(DX) *150, 276*; (51)
W1J 0PW *1*, 344-5, *362-3*;
(82) W1J 7(BP) *173*, 344-5,
362-3; (92) W1J 6(BD) *271*;
(94) W1J 7BP *362-3*; (127)
W1J 7PX *362-3*; (149) W1J
7NT *112, 272, 354-5*; (181)
W1A 1ER *78, 370-1*; (197)
W1J 9LL *53, 370-1*
Piccadilly Circus: W1J 7BX
267, 374-5
pigeons *317-8*
pillar boxes *274*
Piltdown Man *172*
Pinafore, H.M.S. (1878) *306*
Pinter, Harold (1930-2008) *298*
Pirates of Penzance, The (1879)
306
Pitshangar Manor, Ealing *174*
Pitt the Younger, William
(1779-1806) *6, 288*
Playhouse Theatre *299*
plays *212, 251, 253, 307*
playwright *227, 296, 298, 300,
307, 333*

Please Sir! *87*
plinths *64, 239, 317*
Plomer, William (1903-1973) *74*
Plough Court: EC3V 9(BQ)
325, 358-9
Plough Court Pharmacy *325*
Plumber's Row: E1 1EQ (7-9)
258n
Poe, Edgar Allen (1809-1849)
134
poetry *31, 179n, 198, 227, 249,
251-2, 307, 333*
poets *250, 325*
Poet's Corner *332*
Pogues *38*
Poland *105*
Poland, Stanislaus Augustus
King of (1732-1798) *105*
Poland Street: W1F 8QL (38)
W1F 7LY *99, 374-5*
Polari *190*

POLICE *215*
police, Metropolitan *21, 38, 44,
63, 85, 141, 205, 215-7, 215n,
246, 277, 284, 317-8*
Police Commissioner *141, 217*
Polidori, John (1795-1821) *136,
138, 138n*
Polish; Poles *324*
politics *144, 159, 164, 166, 193,
203, 245, 285, 303-4, 310,
328-9*
Pollock's Toy Museum *260*
Ponting, Clive *47*
Pool of London, The: SE1 2(UP)
18, 156, 291, 386-7
Pop Art *96*
Pope, Alexander (1688-1744)
252
poppy *157*
popular protest *125, 130, 194-5*
population *326*
Populous (architects) *181*
Porgès, Jules (*né* Yehuda Porges)
(1839-1921) *172*
porphyria *241*
porters, market *102*
Portland, Duchess of; Margaret
Cavendish Bentinck (*née*
Cavendish Harley) (1715-
1785) *24, 31*
Portland, Dukes of. *See*:
Cavendish-Bentinck;
Cavendish-Scott-Bentinck,
William Henry
Portland Place: (1c) W1B 1JA
135, 364-5; (11) W1N 3AA
364-5
Portland Vase *30-2, 262*

PORTOBELLO ROAD
220
Portobello Road: W10 5(SY)
and W11 2(DY) *40*

Port of London *122*
Port of London Authority *291-2*
Portsmouth, Duchess of; Louise
de Kéroualle (1649-1734)
226-7
Portsmouth Street: (13-14)
WC2A 2ES *213, 376-7*
Portugal Street: WC2A 2(HJ)
236n, 376-7
Post-Modernism; PoMo
(architectural style) *121*
Post Office; postal; penny post
274, 276, 335
Post Office Tower *197*
potatoes *33, 99, 99n*
Potter, Beatrix (1866-1943) *131*
Potts, William L. *277*
power stations *19, 115, 325*
Practical Art, Central School
of *175*
practical joker *205, 306*
Praed Street: W2 1HQ *285*
Pre-Raphaelites *71, 84, 133*
Prescott, John *246-7*
Price, Cedric (1934-2003)
226, 336
Price, Vincent (1911-1993) *301*
priest *18*
Priestley, J.B. (1894-1984) *295*
Prime Minister; Premier *2, 15,
39n, 89, 144, 184, 195, 245,
285, 288-9, 324*
Prince Henry's Room *129*
Princes In The Tower, The
311-2
Princess Louise, The (pub) *224*
Princes Street: EC2R 8AD *6*
printing *50, 95n, 136, 260,
272, 305*
Priory Gardens: (4) W4 1TT
133
prison reformer *249*
prisons *187, 239, 310*
Profumo, John (1915-2006) *40*
progressive views *53, 96, 114,
125, 158, 169, 194, 226*
Proof House *14*
Prospect of Whitby, The (pub)
229
Protestant Wind *191*
Prussia *106*
Public Carriage Office *284*
Public Health Act of 1858 *332*
Public Monuments &
Sculptures Association, The
151
publishing; publisher *31, 134,
136, 147, 320, 327*

PUBS *222*
pubs *99, 227*
pub signs *275*
Pudding Lane: EC3R 8AH *122,
358-9*

GALLERIES, PALACES & TEA

You may also enjoy:

LONDON STORIES, LONDON LIVES:
135 TALES OF THE METROPOLIS
AND ITS INHABITANTS

ISBN: 978-1-909542-01-3